Bell Curve City

Paul Kersey

Bell Curve City
St. Louis, Ferguson, and the Unmentionable Racial Realities that Shape Them
Paul Kersey

Copyright © 2015

All rights reserved.

ISBN-13: 978-1511752978

ISBN-10: 1511752971

Dedicated to Officer Darren Wilson and to those who will dedicate their lives to restoring Freedom of Association to the United States of America, thereby ensuring another Ferguson never, ever happens again.[1]

---

[1] http://www.vdare.com/articles/feds-lynching-ferguson-but-first-they-fouled-it-up-with-section-8-housing

[2] http://www.stltoday.com/news/local/crime-and-courts/police-ferguson-teen-struggled-over-officer-s-gun-before-being/article_f9d627dc-e3c8-5bde-b2ab-

Table of Contents

August 2014... p. 8

September 2014... p. 104

October 2014... p. 166

November 2014 ... p. 270

December 2014... p. 372

January 2015... p. 432

February 2015... p. 469

March 2015... p. 526

April 2015... p. 580

May 2015... p. 601

Not so long ago, in a suburb like any other in America...

On August 9, 2014, an altercation between a white police officer and a black male in a suburb of St. Louis set in motion a course of events capturing international attention and creating a revolutionary zeal amongst blacks exacerbated by the black President of the United States and the black Attorney General of the Department of Justice.

Time magazine ran a cover story on the situation, dubbing the aftermath Officer Darren Wilson's encounter with Michael Brown "The Tragedy of Ferguson."

But the true tragedy of what happened to Ferguson and metropolitan St. Louis has yet to be told: until now.

This is the Ferguson War Journal, a day-by-day account of what happened in the media-created maelstrom ultimately culminating in Darren Wilson's complete exoneration of any wrongdoing.

Paul Kersey, the author of *Escape from Detroit*, focuses his attention on the racial history of not only Ferguson, but the entire St. Louis region in Bell Curve City, where a combination of white flight from black crime and the federal government mandated Section 8 Housing created the conditions enabling the scenario of what happened on August 9 between Wilson and Brown.

Bell Curve City proves the cry of "Black Lives Matter" is not only a hypocritical one, but a mantra devoid of any historical evidence to support the assertion of the sanctity of black life: especially when one looks at the unmentionable racial realities shaping St. Louis and Ferguson.

Written as a series of journal entries, Bell Curve City will explore exactly how Ferguson became Ferguson... and what it means for not just St. Louis, but all of America.

August 10, 2010

The Police Need to Stop Policing Majority Black Cities

Civilization is not a right, any more than water is a right.

Police, an extension of the state, must exercise the monopoly on violence if decent people are to be expected to call a city "home."

In once all-white suburbs of cities like Atlanta, Birmingham, Charlotte, St. Louis, Baltimore, Chicago, Memphis, Nashville, Orlando, Detroit, and Milwaukee, police are basically full-time babysitters; they exist to keep high schoolers from driving too fast, throwing a kegger when their parents aren't home, or rolling an ex-girlfriend's house.

But in cities where white people are primarily only visiting for 40-hours/a week (commuting to for - and from - work) or wearing a badge as an officer of the law, the police are the last vestiges of a civilization quickly regressing to the black mean.

Cue the Michael Brown intro... [Police: Ferguson teen struggled over officer's gun before being shot to death, St. Louis Post-Dispatch, 8-10-14]:

> An unarmed teenager killed Saturday by Ferguson police, spawning continuing community unrest, had struggled for an officer's gun in a patrol car first, authorities announced this morning.
>
> St. Louis County Police Chief Jon Belmar said one shot was

fired by the officer's gun inside the car during the struggle, hitting no one, and that the officer then fired multiple times at Michael Brown, 18, as he ran away.

Belmar did not indicate whether police think the shooting was justified.

He said the shots that hit Brown were "more than just a couple but I don't think it was many more than that." He said an autopsy was pending and that a toxicology test would take as long as six weeks to determine whether Brown had alcohol or drugs in his system.

Belmar promised a full investigation that might also include the FBI. He said the results would be forwarded to St. Louis County Prosecuting Attorney Robert P. McCulloch, whose office would decide whether criminal charges were justified.

The chief noted that as Ferguson Police Chief Thomas Jackson arrived at the scene Saturday, he called Belmar personally to ask for a county investigation. "I would not think anybody would do that if they had anything to hide," Belmar said.

Belmar said he had not consulted the FBI but would call today. The FBI can investigate a police use-of-force incident as a possible violation of constitutional rights. Belmar emphasized that these are "standard protocols."

In Washington, a Justice Department spokesperson said that Attorney General Eric Holder has asked attorneys from the civil rights division to monitor the case.

The officer who fired, whose name has not been disclosed, is now on administrative leave. Belmar said that officer has been on the Ferguson force for six years and appears to have "no other issues" in his past.

Belmar said the officer had an encounter about noon Saturday with two "individuals" and was pushed back into his car and "assaulted" by Brown. The chief did not again mention the second person, nor did he describe the reason for the initial contact.

Belmar and Jackson left the press conference as reporters continued to call out questions.

Officials said later there was no truth to a rumor sweeping social media that the second person, a young man, had been found dead. Some protesters who continued a vigil this morning outside the Ferguson police station said Jackson told them that man planned to bring his lawyer to meet with police.

State Sen. Jamilah Nasheed, D-St. Louis, and the St. Louis NAACP also have said they would seek a federal investigation.

Angry residents took to the streets after Brown was killed in the 2900 block of Canfield Drive. Some shots were heard in the crowd that gathered, but nobody was injured. Some people chanted obscenities and "kill the police" as about 60 officers from multiple jurisdictions gathered.

Today, a large group of protesters remained outside the police station at 222 South Florissant Road — some of them screaming at officers standing watch and calling for the name and resignation of the officer who killed Brown.

One of those present, Shontell Walters, of Berkeley, said many took exception to the presence of police dogs. "They are trying to instill more fear in us," she complained.[2]

Eric "My People" Holder and Barack "If I had a Son" Obama won't let this injustice stand. One of them will address this shooting in the next two days, if not sooner.

One of the 10 simple ways to restore balance to the universe would be the cessation of policing majority black cities in America.

Police, trying to uphold the white man's law in these majority black areas, are damned if they do and damned if they don't: if they set up

---

[2] http://www.stltoday.com/news/local/crime-and-courts/police-ferguson-teen-struggled-over-officer-s-gun-before-being/article_f9d627dc-e3c8-5bde-b2ab-7f0a3d36a083.html

stings trying to get dangerous criminals off the streets (thereby making the black community safer), they are deemed as 'profiling'; if they don't do anything to stop the carnage of black on black crime, professional black agitators and black clergy will march, protest, and hold news conferences where a fawning local - and national media - will immediately side with anyone but the police.

Granting police extra powers (in the name of defending civilization) means they are prepared to act on behalf of civilization, thwarting the spread of barbarism and working to keep property owners investments in the community safe from the ravages of the Visible Black Hand of Economics.

Black communities, where the only white person seen is a member of law enforcement, lack amenities white people take for granted (restaurants, quality schools, retail, non-Plexiglas convenient stores, non-potholed streets, and manicured lawns) for simple, undeniable reason: they lack black people who, in large numbers, work to drive away restaurants - since they have no purchasing power, outside the EBT/Food Stamp card - and convince those few businessman still operating in the area to invest heavily in Plexiglas to keep their employees and property safe.

Civilization is not a right, any more than water is a right.

If every act - by the police - against an individual black person is interpreted as an act against the black community at large, then it's time to remove this burden once and for all... pull the police from black communities, areas now virtually indistinguishable from Port-au-Prince, Haiti, or Monrovia, Liberia.

August 11, 2014
Michael Brown's hometown: The Truth of 67% Black Ferguson, Missouri

Suburbs exist for one reason: the opportunity for white people to keep alive some flame of the civilization their white ancestors built over centuries on a landmass previously occupied by illiterate, nomadic tribes.

St. Louis long ago quit being a city capable of preserving the civilization white people created, with the regression to the black mean a mere formality at this point.
In 1950, St. Louis was 82 percent white and 17.9 percent black (coincidentally, the same year it reached its peak population of 856,000.]

Today, St. Louis is 49 percent black and 43 percent white.

One guess as to what happened.

Crime.

Black crime.

More importantly, the legitimate fear of white people that they may become victims of black crime (or seeing their property values suffer the economic fact or racial differences and depreciate to the black mean).

But wherever whites go and build a civilization out of the wilderness, the same forces that ensure the wilderness returns follows[3]... just ask the few remaining white people in Spanish Lake (North St. Louis County).[4]

Talk about 'mapping decline" all you want; the only statistic that matters to a city's viability is its percentage of black people. More than 10 percent, and your city is inevitably doomed.

Here's what white people correctly flee from in St. Louis (remember, the city is 49 percent black and 43 percent white). According to 2012 Metropolitan Police Department, City of St. Louis: Annual

---

[3] http://mappingdecline.lib.uiowa.edu/map/

[4] http://news.stlpublicradio.org/post/new-documentary-explores-white-flight-spanish-lake

Report to the Community:

> • 84.7% of those arrested for aggravated assault in St. Louis in 2012 were black.
> • 91.8% of those arrested for robbery in St. Louis in 2012 were black.
> • 97.6% of those arrested for murder in St. Louis in 2012 were black. [5]

Crime, in St. Louis, has a color.

It's black.

Which brings us to Michael Brown's hometown of Ferguson, a once lily-white suburb of St. Louis.

Out of population of 21,000 (roughly), the city is 28 percent white and 67 percent black.

Back in 2000, the city was 44 percent white and 52.7 percent black (out of roughly 22,000).

Here's the main point about what life is like in this city where the civilization whites created is quickly being replaced by a fast regression to the black mean (and the abandonment of business, tax-base, and hope that comes with white flight):

> WHITE FLIGHT: Ferguson and other parts of north St. Louis County were predominantly white communities before school desegregation. The community's racial makeup changed as many white suburban families moved to outlying areas such as St. Charles County, parts of which are more than 40 miles from St. Louis.
>
> DEMOGRAPHICS: About two-thirds of residents are now black. Fewer than half of the approximately 9,100 homes are owner-occupied, and about a quarter of residents live below the federal poverty level.

---

[5] http://www.slmpd.org/images/2012AnnualReport_D.pdf

> SCHOOLS: Several North County school districts – including the Normandy system from which Brown recently graduated – have lost state accreditation because of declining test scores and other academic shortcomings. Some students from the failing districts were bused to better-performing schools in other districts.
>
> RACIAL PROFILING: Some Ferguson protesters say members of the city's predominantly white police force disproportionately target black motorists during traffic stops. A 2013 report by the Missouri attorney general's office found that Ferguson police stopped and arrested black drivers nearly twice as frequently as white motorists but were also less likely to find contraband among the black drivers.[6]

Interesting, but that doesn't tell us enough about the city 18-year-old Michael Brown was reared in… but this does. [Blame poverty, age for weak North County home market, St. Louis Post-Dispatch, 8-18-2013]:

> Barbara Bandy has been trying to sell her house for nearly a year, with no luck. Could the problem be that it's in north St. Louis County?
>
> She was optimistic when she started. It's a nice Cape Cod with four bedrooms and two baths, built in the 1950s. In 2011, the St. Louis County assessor put its value at $117,500. She says she spent $20,000 fixing it up for sale.
>
> "I'm up to here on credit," she says, holding her hand up to her nose.
>
> But when Bandy put it on the market, it sat. It wouldn't sell at $98,000.
>
> She cut the price to $94,000. She switched real estate agents, cut the price to $84,500 and still it sits.

---

[6] http://www.sunherald.com/2014/08/11/5740443/a-look-at-town-where-police-shot.html

"Now they want me to strike the price down again. Do you think that's fair?" asks the elderly widow, who lived in the house for 40 years.

Her real estate agent also wants her to offer to finance part of the buyer's mortgage. "What do they think I am? A bank?"

Her problem may be location. Her house is in Ferguson.

Ferguson is a picture of pleasant suburbia, a town of tree-lined streets and well-kept homes, much of them built for the middle class at mid-century.

But Ferguson is in north St. Louis County, and the area is suffering from one of the region's weakest real estate markets. That's worrying county officials, who fear it may reflect deeper economic problems in parts of North County.

In North County, however, prices remain weak and may be sinking still.

"We see a continuing decline in home prices in North County, and it's been steeper than in the rest of the county," said County Assessor Jake Zimmerman.

County officials and real estate pros give these reasons:

• The spread of poverty into a wider area of North County.

• The hangover from the subprime lending spree of the last decade. That, combined with a loss of jobs, left North County with an abundance of foreclosed houses selling cheap, usually to landlords who turn them into rentals.

• An older stock of housing, much of it small and out of fashion.

North County is a big place, and it can't be painted with one brush. Much of Hazelwood, Florissant, Overland, Ferguson and other towns are solidly middle class. Some neighborhoods are monuments to stability.

But poverty is expanding out from long-suffering inner-ring suburbs toward areas north and west. Two of the area's school districts — Normandy and Riverview Gardens — lost their accreditation, making families with children look elsewhere.

The result of all that is a weak real estate market, even in many middle-class neighborhoods in untroubled school districts.

According to the assessor, the median value of residential property in the county dropped 7 percent in the two years ending January of this year. But the losses were highest in the north.

St. Louis County saw a 21 percent increase in black population during the last decade, census figures show, while the white population dropped 10 percent. Much of that demographic shift was reflected in North County. Ferguson, for example, went from 52 percent black in 2000 to 67 percent in 2010.

That increase may play into perceptions of real estate values. Walking streets in Ferguson, and speaking randomly to residents of both races, a reporter found two white residents who volunteered that they felt the large black population meant lower real estate prices.[7]

Suburbs exist for one reason: the opportunity for white people to keep alive some flame of the civilization their white ancestors built over centuries on a landmass previously occupied by illiterate, nomadic tribes.

St. Louis long ago quit being a city capable of preserving the civilization white people created, with the regression to the black mean a mere formality at this point.

Because Freedom of Association (Restrictive Covenants) has been outlawed in the United States of America, every suburb of St. Louis will share the fate of the Ferguson and Spanish Lake.

---

[7] http://www.stltoday.com/news/local/metro/blame-poverty-age-for-weak-north-county-home-market/article_95c998e5-bb87-5bc0-9054-83e801b357ac.html

Wherever whites go, the black undertow will follow: no matter what conservatives do at this point, it's merely rearranging the deck chairs on the Titanic (with the band on the doomed boat replaced by recitations of the Pledge of Allegiance to a country that hates you and dooms your posterity to a fate worse than modern Detroit)....

There are some people who just want to watch the world burn; count me among them.

Funny thing though: we don't even have to light the match.

Nature will.

And inevitably Ferguson will soon be nothing more than 98 percent black East St. Louis.

August 12, 2014
"And the sign said, The words of the prophets are written on the subway walls And tenement halls"

Remember when the French government issued travel warnings for several American cities?

Immediately denounced by the American press as 'bigoted' and 'racial' (because the warnings for French citizens traveling to America warned of the dangerous conditions of primarily black cities), one of those area the French were warned about visiting was North St. Louis. [*French Government Issued Travel Warning For North St. Louis, CBS St. Louis, 11-24-13*]:

> It was 250 years ago that Frenchmen Pierre Laclede and Auguste Chouteau founded the fur trading post that would become St. Louis. Now the French government has some

warnings for travelers coming here.

On a French government website, readers can find a list of American cities the government of France has issued travel warnings about, organized by region.

Listed in the "Sud" – or South – region is St. Louis. The warning reads "éviter le quartier nord entre l'aéroport et le centre-ville, mais la navette reliant l'aéroport est sûre."

Translation: Avoid the northern area between the airport and the city center, but the airport shuttle is safe.

"The French government can do what it wants but in the end, you know, we're still going to have people come in and enjoy our city," Mayor Francis Slay said.[8]

The French government care far more for the people they are tasked with protecting than does the American government, where the Attorney General, Eric "My People" Holder, actively works to promote the interests of blacks and create a legal buffer protecting them from any form of criticism, justice, or standards (be that academic, creditworthiness, behaving in K-12 public schools, or being forced to sit in jail for a criminal offense).

Though scores of buildings have been looted by blacks in the St. Louis area,[9] Mr. "My People" has his sights set on being 'color brave' in Ferguson, Missouri. [Holder opens federal probe of slain teen, The Hill, 8-12-14]

Yet, going back to the warnings of the French government for their citizens to avoid North St. Louis, it's important to consider what Chuck Ross of the Daily Caller just reported. [FAA Issues Flight Restriction After Rioters Fired 'Multiple Times' At Police Helicopter, 8-12-14]:

---

[8] http://stlouis.cbslocal.com/2013/11/14/french-government-issued-travel-warning-for-north-st-louis/

[9] http://www.thegatewaypundit.com/2014/08/looting-spreads-shoe-carnival-in-south-st-louis-city-hit-overnight/

> The Federal Aviation Administration issued a temporary flight restriction on Tuesday for an area surrounding Ferguson, MO., the town where a police officer fatally shot an unarmed 18-year-old black man, after a St. Louis County police helicopter was fired upon Sunday night.
>
> The flight restriction was issued Tuesday at 1:15 p.m. local time. The reason for the notice is "TO PROVIDE A SAFE ENVIRONMENT FOR LAW ENFORCEMENT ACTIVITIES."[10]

Read the CBS St. Louis story one more time:

> *On a French government website, readers can find a list of American cities the government of France has issued travel warnings about, organized by region.*
>
> *Listed in the "Sud" – or South – region is St. Louis. The warning reads "éviter le quartier nord entre l'aéroport et le centre-ville, mais la navette reliant l'aéroport est sûre."*
>
> *Translation: Avoid the northern area between the airport and the city center, but the airport shuttle is safe.*

Where is Ferguson located again? Where is the FAA No-Fly Zone?

Oh...

And for those still convinced *white people commit just as more much crime as black people,* may we present the reality of why the French government advised French citizens to "*Avoid the northern area between the airport and the city center, but the airport shuttle is safe."*

Remember, the city of St. Louis is 49 percent black and 43 percent white.

Each year, the City of St. Louis Metropolitan Police Department, releases an Annual Report to the Community. This report breaks

---

[10] http://dailycaller.com/2014/08/12/faa-issues-flight-restriction-after-rioters-fired-multiple-times-at-police-helicopter/#ixzz3ADW6UvBQ

down violent crime and the overall percentage of the racial group arrested for each offense (note because of lack of trust with police, many violent crimes/homicides lack suspects. The black community would rather have criminals among them than in jail).[11]

Here's the breakdown 1999:

> • 84.94% of those arrested for aggravated assault in St. Louis in 1999 were black.
>
> • 91.74% of those arrested for robbery in St. Louis in 1999 were black.
>
> • 90.2% of those arrested for murder in St. Louis in 1999 were black.
>
> • 88.89% of those arrested for forcible rape in St. Louis in 1999 were black.[12]

Here's the breakdown for 2000:

> • 85.18% of those arrested for aggravated assault in St. Louis in 2000 were black.
>
> • 90.33% of those arrested for robbery in St. Louis in 2000 were black.
>
> • 91.67% of those arrested for murder in St. Louis in 2000 were black.
>
> • 85.19% of those arrested for forcible rape in St. Louis in 2000 were black.[13]

---

[11] http://fox2now.com/2013/07/19/st-louis-murders-remain-unsolved-because-lack-of-trust-and-fear/

[12] http://www.slmpd.org/pi/SLMPDARText20002001.pdf

[13] http://www.slmpd.org/pi/SLMPDARText20002001.pdf

Here's the breakdown for 2002:

> • 86.26% of those arrested for aggravated assault in St. Louis in 2002 were black.
>
> • 91.02% of those arrested for robbery in St. Louis in 2002 were black.
>
> • 94.78% of those arrested for murder in St. Louis in 2002 were black.
>
> • 91.06% of those arrested for forcible rape in St. Louis in 2002 were black.[14]

Here's the breakdown for 2003:

> • 85.51% of those arrested for aggravated assault in St. Louis in 2003 were black.
>
> • 89.21% of those arrested for robbery in St. Louis in 2003 were black.
>
> • 96.77% of those arrested for murder in St. Louis in 2003 were black.
>
> • 94.19% of those arrested for forcible rape in St. Louis in 2003 were black.[15]

Here's the breakdown for 2004:

> • 86.26% of those arrested for aggravated assault in St. Louis in 2004 were black.
>
> • 91.02% of those arrested for robbery in St. Louis in 2004were black.

---

[14] http://www.slmpd.org/pi/20022003-STLMPD.pdf

[15] http://www.slmpd.org/pi/30722-STLMPD.pdf

- 94.78% of those arrested for murder in St. Louis in 2004were black.
- 91.06% of those arrested for forcible rape in St. Louis in 2004were black.[16]

Here's' the breakdown for 2005:

- 86.97% of those arrested for aggravated assault in St. Louis in 2005 were black.

- 90.59% of those arrested for robbery in St. Louis in 2005 were black

- 91.55% of those arrested for murder in St. Louis in 2005were black.

- 87.37% of those arrested for forcible rape in St. Louis in 2005 were black.[17]

Here's the breakdown for 2006:
- 85.7% of those arrested for aggravated assault in St. Louis in 2006 were black.
- 89.9% of those arrested for robbery in St. Louis in 2006 were black.
- 91.8% of those arrested for murder in St. Louis in 2006 were black.
- 90.02% of those arrested for forcible rape in St. Louis in 2006 were black.[18]

Here's the breakdown for 2007:
- 85.7% of those arrested for aggravated assault in St. Louis in 2007 were black.

---

[16] http://www.slmpd.org/pi/20022003-STLMPD.pdf

[17] http://www.slmpd.org/pi/30722-STLMPD.pdf

[18] http://www.slmpd.org/images/SLMPD AR Final 20062007.pdf

- 80.1% of those arrested for robbery in St. Louis in 2007 were black.
- 92% of those arrested for murder in St. Louis in 2007 were black.
- 91.2% of those arrested for forcible rape in St. Louis in 2007 were black.[19]

Anything different in 2008? No:

- 87.2% of those arrested for aggravated assault in St. Louis in 2008 were black.
- 85.6% of those arrested for robbery in St. Louis in 2008 were black.
- 97.7% of those arrested for murder in St. Louis in 2008 were black.
- 88.8% of those arrested for forcible rape in St. Louis in 2008 were black.[20]

2009? Is it still almost all-black? Yes:

- 87.3% of those arrested for aggravated assault in St. Louis in 2009 were black.
- 92.7% of those arrested for robbery in St. Louis in 2009 were black.
- 97.1% of those arrested for murder in St. Louis in 2009 were black.
- 88.2% of those arrested for forcible rape in St. Louis in 2009 were black.[21]

Please, tell me 2010 is different...:
- 86.9% of those arrested for aggravated assault in St. Louis in 2010 were black.

---

[19] http://www.slmpd.org/images/SLMPD AR Final 20062007.pdf

[20] http://www.slmpd.org/images/SLMPD ARG%C3%87%C3%B68-31-10.pdf

[21] http://www.slmpd.org/images/SLMPD AR 2009-FINAL.pdf

- 92.7% of those arrested for robbery in St. Louis in 2010 were black.
- 92.4% of those arrested for murder in St. Louis in 2010 were black.
- 78.1% of those arrested for forcible rape in St. Louis in 2010 were black.[22]

2011? Same old song:

- 86.7% of those arrested for aggravated assault in St. Louis in 2011 were black.
- 90.3% of those arrested for robbery in St. Louis in 2011 were black.
- 92% of those arrested for murder in St. Louis in 2011 were black.
- 86.2% of those arrested for forcible rape in St. Louis in 2011 were black.[23]

According to 2012 Metropolitan Police Department, City of St. Louis: Annual Report to the Community:

- 84.7% of those arrested for aggravated assault in St. Louis in 2012 were black.
- 91.8% of those arrested for robbery in St. Louis in 2012 were black.
- 97.6% of those arrested for murder in St. Louis in 2012 were black.
- 78.6% of those arrested for forcible rape in St. Louis in 2012 were black.[24]

Remember when the French government issued travel warnings for several American cites?

It's because black people make St. Louis a dangerous place.

---

[22] http://www.slmpd.org/images/2010 Annual Report to the Community -2.pdf

[23] http://www.slmpd.org/images/2011_ANNUAL_REPORT_F.pdf

[24] http://www.slmpd.org/images/2012AnnualReport_D.pdf

It's because black people, shooting guns in the air, force the FAA to impose a flight restriction over the 67 percent black city of Ferguson. [FAA Issues Flight Restriction After Rioters Fired 'Multiple Times' At Police Helicopter, Daily Caller, 8-12-14]

The lies of our world are so transparent we become conditioned to believe some form of evidence exists to prove them correct.

Either you stand for civilization or you support barbarism.

The latter will always produce Detroit; the former is something along the lines of what we saw take off from Cape Canaveral on July 16, 1969.

August 13, 2014
This Fact is "Heartbreaking," Mr. President: Ferguson, Missouri went from 73.1 percent white in 1990 to 28 percent white today...

"If I had a world of my own, everything would be nonsense. Nothing would be what it is, because everything would be what it isn't. And contrary wise, what is, it wouldn't be. And what it wouldn't be, it would. You see?" -- *Alice in Wonderland*

Mike Brown, the 18-year-old black male who refused to cooperate with the police in 67 percent black Ferguson, was an "aspiring rapper" and a "good boy." [Who was Mike Brown? Profile of black teenager shot in Missouri, Christian Science Monitor, 8-13-14]

Mike Brown, the 18-year-old black male who assaulted a police officer in 67 percent black Ferguson, was - once - the living embodiment as to why Barack Obama's hundred+ million "My Brother's Keeper" program was started.

His death is not "heartbreaking," unlike how the President of the

United States described the events leading to his life being extinguished.[25]

What is "heartbreaking is the deleterious effects an almost entirely black population had upon the quality of life in Ferguson, specifically Normandy High School.

Out of 1190 students, the school is 97 percent black.[26]

And, thanks to the individual contributions of black people like the late Michael Brown, it's one of the most dangerous high schools in all of St. Louis. [Normandy High: The most dangerous school in the area, St. Louis Post Dispatch, 5-5-13]:

> Daija'h Jackson is among the hundreds of Normandy High School students who arrive each morning ready to learn.
>
> But this requires strategy in a place where fights can erupt multiple times a day, where students target one another for living on the wrong street.
>
> On March 5, Daija'h, 15, was worried.
>
> A girl from her block had threatened to attack her in the cafeteria. Facebook taunts were escalating. Daija'h took refuge during lunch in the classroom of an English teacher in East Hall at Normandy High School.
>
> When the lunch period was over, she walked into the hallway and found herself face to face with several girls, including the one making threats. One tore off Daija'h's backpack and pushed her against the wall. Daija'h panicked and grabbed her pepper spray. She inadvertently sprayed the English teacher.
>
> "She was trying to break it up," Daija'h said later. "It's not a safe environment."

---

[25] http://www.whitehouse.gov/blog/2014/08/12/president-obama-issues-statement-death-michael-brown

[26] http://www.movoto.com/schools/saint-louis-mo/normandy-high-school-292265001248/

At Normandy High, hallways have become places where neighborhood problems come to a head, where threats made on Facebook and Twitter are carried out.

As the Normandy School District struggles to improve its academics, it's also struggling with a culture of violence that erupts almost daily at the high school.

Normandy stands apart not only for its sheer number of fights, but for a dramatic spike in serious discipline incidents — which have nearly doubled since 2009, according to district figures reported to the state.

The increase coincides with a period of crisis in which the

When asked about the violence at his school, Principal Calvin Nicholas chose his words carefully.

"We don't have a problem with the kids," Nicholas said, sitting behind his desk. He pointed out that after two years leading the school, he would not be returning this fall. He declined to answer questions about what needed to be done to improve safety, and whether he had adequate central office support to crack down on behavior. The problems at the high school are "adult problems," he said.

In 2012, the school reported 285 discipline incidents — such as assaults, drugs and weapons — that resulted in out-of-school suspension, a rate of more than one for every four students, the highest among high schools in the region.

In March, two sociology professors at the University of Missouri-St. Louis notified Normandy High parents of their study exploring the causes and consequences of violence at the school "in hopes of lessening its negative effects," the letter to parents states.

Wellston Police Chief G. Thomas Walker said violence at the high school had been a problem for years. Students at Normandy come from 24 municipalities, some with longstanding rivalries. Social networking websites and the prevalence of cellphones have made the problem more difficult to control, he said.

"We respond to more fights on campus than off campus," Walker said. "It takes very little to irritate these kids and cause them to take physical action."

Teachers describe an environment that is equally challenging.

"Teaching is very difficult," said Dawn Baldesi, the English teacher who was pepper-sprayed. "Teachers get cussed out, yelled out. There are so many write-ups you can't keep up."

Other teachers, who asked that their names not be used, say group fights at the school have left students with broken noses and asthma attacks. But a few cases have been more serious. [27]

What's "heartbreaking" is not the death of a black male, who assaulted a police officer believing this action wouldn't be considered a threat to what little semblance of law exists in the 67 percent black city; no, what's "heartbreaking" is that the 1990 U.S. Census reports Ferguson was 73.8 percent white merely 24 years ago versus roughly 28 percent white today.[28]

The city was 25.1 percent black in 1990, versus 67 percent black today. Conversely, Normandy High School (perhaps named for when the all-white US Army stormed Normandy Beach in France on June 6, 1944...) is now one of the most dangerous high schools in all of Missouri... and it's 97 percent black.

Ferguson, the same city burning now thanks to black riots, had 22,286 residents according to the 1990 U.S. Census (p. 37): of those, 16,454 were white and 5,589 were black...[29]

From 73.1 percent white in 1990 to 28 percent white in 2010...

---

[27] http://www.stltoday.com/news/local/education/normandy-high-the-most-dangerous-school-in-the-area/article_49a1b882-cd74-5cc4-8096-fcb1405d8380.html

[28] https://www.census.gov/prod/cen1990/cp1/cp-1-27.pdf

[29] https://www.census.gov/prod/cen1990/cp1/cp-1-27.pdf

That's "heartbreaking" President Obama.

Civilization recedes with the oncoming of the black undertow.

It regresses to the black mean.

Yes. That's truly "heartbreaking."

More "heartbreaking?"

White people will never dare publicly admit why the city went from 73 percent white in 1990 to 28 percent white today: the backwards rationale for Obama's "My Brother's Keeper" program is the obvious one, with white families deciding black dysfunction isn't something they want to raise their children around.

Funny: as a city's black population rises, the level of dysfunction increases (contra Robert Putnam, who thought a homogeneous population would breed social capital; black people breed social dysfunction and ruin... we call this the Detroit Corollary).

White people will go to their grave singing the "Star Spangled Banner," never knowing it was the federal government's policy of black (minority) advancement that put them there...

August 14, 2014
"You've got rights, lots of rights. Sometimes I count them just to make me feel crazy...": Explaining How Ferguson Went from 25% black in 1990 to 67% black today

Years ago, I was reading Frank Miller's excellent *Dark Returns* graphic novel.

If you laugh at comics and find them juvenile, sit down and read this: it's the ultimate Batman story and, ultimately, the only "superhero" story that matters.

It tells the story a retired caped crusader, coerced into returning to stalk the roofs of Gotham City after a crime wave has overwhelmed his beloved city: after all, he made a promise to his parents to avenge their murders.

But there's one line I've never been able to quite shake; it's always, always stuck with me.

And watching the reaction by police in 67 percent black Ferguson, Missouri try and restore law and order after multiple days of black riots/looting/burning/protests (and the disgusting howling of civil rights violations by the media), the line came back to me like a bolt of lightening:

> Thug: No! Stay back, I got RIGHTS!!!
>
> Batman: You've got rights, lots of rights. Sometimes I count them just to make me feel crazy...

The city of Ferguson is lost.

Not to the lawlessness masquerading as a protest for justice in the wake of Michael Brown's death; no, because the city of Ferguson went from 73 percent white in 1990 to 28 percent white today.

With a majority black population (Ferguson was 25 percent black in 1990 versus 67 black today), the city was forced to assimilate to the type of character and culture black people could only create -- and one white people migrated away from.

This black population growth had to come from somewhere, right? If you guessed St. Louis, you'd be correct.

You see, long ago the city of St. Louis was built to be, in the words of famed city planner Harland Bartholomew, a place where:

> "the objective of a city plan is the improvement of living

> *conditions, the stimulation of prosperity, and the creation of intangible values in added health, comfort, convenience, and community well-being."*

Does Batholomew's breakdown of what a proper city plan should do describe any contemporary American city, be it large municipality or suburb?

No.

Ferguson was 73 percent white in 1990 and is 28 percent white today because the rise in the black population (immigrants from St. Louis in search of apartments with Section 8 vouchers in hand) meant the decline of living conditions, the retardation of prosperity, and the annihilation of intangible values via reduced health, comfort, convenience, and community well-being.

Ferguson is the personification of the concept of the black undertow, with the complete depletion of social capital complete via the displacement of whites (fleeing black crime and lowered property values) and growth of the black population.

And in Black-Run America (BRA), it is the right and duty of individual black people to collectively ruin the social capital of a once prosperous white city like Ferguson, reducing it into a micro-version of the urban environment from which whites fled in the first place.

So who are the black people that make up the 67 percent black population (remember: since 1990, they had to displace more than 13,000 white people to take demographic control of the city).

This article from the *St. Louis Post-Dispatch* should shine some light into the content of character of not just blacks in St. Louis, but blacks who once called the city home but now live in suburbs like Ferguson. [Girl's burial spotlights a culture of violence, *St. Louis Post-Dispatch*, 3-20-2011]:

> Follow Martin Luther King Drive west from the Mississippi River, through the heart of the city, until the street name changes after a set of railroad tracks just inside the county.

On the right is a classic stone entrance to a cemetery, where, on a recent day, gravediggers were busy on a hill.

They worked amid a landscape of tombstones, from tall granite blocks to groupings of flat stones lying flush with the soggy ground. In the spirit of a high school yearbook, some of the stones have color photographs of the deceased.

The collage of faces - a teen here, a 20-something there - offers a snapshot of young people caught in a culture of violence.

The new grave on the hill was for Jade Hamilton, a 16-year-old girl who was shot in the neck Feb. 20. Three men approached the car she was in at Mount Pleasant Park in south St. Louis. At least one of the men opened fire, an incident that turned out to be a meager offering for the day's news in a city that had 144 homicides in 2010.

"It doesn't make sense," grumbled Adam Osborne, 24, one of the gravediggers at Lake Charles Park Cemetery. "Someone gets shot, then someone gets shot for that, then someone gets shot for that."

He added: "Do they think it's going to end by killing somebody?"

Guns, drugs and poverty have plagued St. Louis for generations, but officials say age-old ways of settling disputes are now eclipsed by violence that can escalate in an instant. African-Americans fall prey at striking rates, with nine out of 10 homicides in the city involving blacks. And of those killed, half are males under the age of 30.

Gun violence has become so common that it's no longer jarring. But one daring shooting three months ago was impossible to ignore. It put the spotlight on gangs in particular because of where it took place: outside a funeral home near the city's cultural center.

The unsolved case served as a reminder of a world in which gangs offer a support system for youths and for adults who have racked up felony offenses. It's a world in which someone who reaches the age of 35 is considered a survivor. And it's a world that city aldermen don't want to associate with their wards.

Bystanders are often quick to suspect gangs are involved in brazen crimes. An FBI report indicates that gang membership is on the rise and is to blame for as much as 80 percent of the crime in certain areas.

The city of St. Louis has 92 known gangs, from the Compton Street Crips to Village Mob to the Krazie Vietnamese Boys, according to police records, in addition to many outside the city.

Officials hesitate to mention any of the gangs because they don't want to validate them, though others argue that residents need to know who's running their neighborhoods. Gang killings are typically targeted, but crimes such as vehicle thefts and robberies are often random.

It's hard to tell who is responsible. A rigid no-snitch code on the street - "Snitchers and talkers get stitches and walkers" - often gives police no suspects, while leaving victims to settle their own beefs, either out of honor or fear of attack. And beefs can last for years.

Police Chief Dan Isom said gangs can be useful in identifying certain individuals, but he downplayed the issue, saying the criminal landscape was much broader.

"Oftentimes when you say gangs, it just stops at that: 'We need to just get rid of gangs,' " he said. "Well, it's not that easy. It's about a culture within certain communities where violence is an option for too many people."

That could involve a gang, or two or three people who don't like each other or a domestic dispute, he said.

That could involve killings of young people such as Jade, whose death remains a mystery, illustrating how difficult it can be to place a neat label such as "gang-related," on a killing.

Jade was buried March 1 in an area of the cemetery called the "garden of memory." The hillside is planted with many more sad stories.[30]

Remember what famed city planner Harland Bartholmew said a city plan should do:

> *"the objective of a city plan is the improvement of living conditions, the stimulation of prosperity, and the creation of intangible values in added health, comfort, convenience, and community well-being."*

How can you ensure a city can improve living conditions when the blueprint for such an act requires a homogeneous population (though, East St. Louis at 98 percent black, represents a powerful reminder the blacker the city the less stimulation of prosperity and social capital exists)?

In a multiracial society, you can't (unless you have built in legal measures such as restrictive covenants, which the Supreme Court declared unconstitutional in 1948); in a city that goes from 73 percent white to 28 percent white in the span of 20 years, you have a situation like the one in Ferguson, Missouri.

Freedom of association is the only right that matters: boiled down, it means you have the right to discriminate.

It means you have the right to implement a city plan encouraging the *"improvement of living conditions, the stimulation of prosperity, and the creation of intangible values in added health, comfort, convenience, and community well-being,"* as opposed to what we have in Black-Run America: where the federal government mandates via threat of legal action and military intervention *the decline of living conditions, the retardation of prosperity, and the annihilation of intangible values via reduced health, comfort, convenience, and community well-being.*

---

[30] http://www.stltoday.com/news/local/metro/girl-s-burial-spotlights-a-culture-of-violence/article_26bd5032-f188-514a-ba93-1e9ac727e745.html

Jesse Jackson said, when speaking to black agitators/insurrectionists in Ferguson, said "there's a Ferguson near you," as if to warn black people police nationwide were prepared to open fire on blacks (never mind Michael Brown was attacking an officer in his car and going for the cops gun when he was shot).[31]

Oh, but Jackson is right: There is a Ferguson near you, whitey.

A city that once boasted an all-white population, good schools, a thriving business district and an opportunity to raise a family in the peace and tranquility of whiteness; but Ferguson is now a city with one of the worst schools in Missouri, a crumbling business district, depreciating property values, and the instability and violence of blackness.

This is why white people in Ferguson abandoned the city: because the very people they tried to escape from followed them to the place they escaped too.

August 15, 2015
After the boys of summer have gone... The hilarious turn in the Michael Brown/Ferguson saga has me on the floor, laughing to the point of tears.

Then the tears turn to something else.

---

[31] http://www.usatoday.com/story/opinion/2014/08/12/jesse-jackson-ferguson-riots-column/13957197/

In a normal world, not one person would care about the trials and tribulations of a Swisher Sweet robbing, middle of the straight walking, aspiring rapper, good boy thug... but we do not live in a normal world.

So to break up the steady flow of largely inaccurate information on what's happening in 67% black Ferguson, Missouri, a quick trip down memory lane is order to restore the balance.

Recall, St. Louis (49 percent black and 43 percent white) is a city where the black population works overtime to keep homicide detectives busy. Well, also officers tasked with tracking down rape and robbery suspects, as well as following leads on aggravated assaults.[32]

Don't forget the Knockout Game task force found only in St. Louis... courtesy of black suspects.[33]

So where can a white person go in St. Louis to be... white? To be free of a massive police presence and enjoy a moment of levity from the fear of being the victim of a knockout game attack?

Try Busch Stadium, home of the St. Louis Cardinals. [No African-Americans on Cardinals roster, few in the stands, St. Louis Post-Dispatch, 4-12-12]:

> When the Los Angeles Dodgers were in town recently to play the Cardinals, family and friends of Nashonda Porter plopped the 2-year-old girl onto the base of the statues in front of Busch Stadium. The 10 statues near the main gate reflect the legacy of St. Louis baseball.
>
> Porter, going to her first ball game, struck a pose by Lou Brock, who is frozen in time running, looking for his hit to drop somewhere beyond the corner of South Eighth Street

---

[32] http://www.stltoday.com/news/local/crime-and-courts/st-louis-homicides-up-in-but-overall-crime-dipped-percent/article_eef26c6e-8857-5c03-bff9-0f0d7134e6be.html

[33] http://latino.foxnews.com/latino/opinion/2013/11/27/rick-sanchez-hell-yes-knockout-game-is-hate-crime/

and Clark Avenue. She reached up and held the hand of James "Cool Papa" Bell, one of the fastest ever to play the game. And she stood in her small sandals next to Ozzie Smith diving for a ball.

The three statues were particularly special for Porter's entourage.

"They are history," said Lucretia Hall, the girl's godmother, "because of the fact they are African-American and Ozzie Smith was one of the best players in his era."

When asked who was her favorite African-American playing for the Cardinals today, Hall paused, struggling to name one. Then her friend, Cornelius Washington, leaned in to help.

"There ain't none," he said.

Washington, 67, of Jennings, came to see the Dodgers play, not the Cardinals. His soul has been with that team since he grew up in Mississippi and Jackie Robinson made history in 1947 as the first black player in big league baseball's modern era.

Still, he often studies the Cardinals' 40-man roster looking for African-Americans to watch. That's become a harder task over the years. For a spell in 2006, the Cardinals had no African-Americans, but there was a hitting coach who was black.

For his part, Cardinals manager Mike Matheny said his focus is on performance, not race — a sentiment echoed by a few of his players.

On not having any African-Americans on the roster, he said, "It's the first I've thought about it. It's just whoever is the best player."

The trend is evident in the stands at Busch Stadium, which is filled primarily with white fans, as was the case last month when the Cardinals played the Dodgers.

As the stadium filled for one game, Joe Trice, 39, who is black, fed a parking meter a few blocks away, indifferent about the game. Yet he wore a black and gray St. Louis Cardinals cap. He likes the St. Louis connection, but he's not a fan. The cap just matched his high tops.

"I was never into that sport, really, just basketball," he said. "And I like golf, pool and boxing."

Lower down in the stadium, right behind home plate, Derrick Williams, 40, sat with his wife and two sons. They were among seven African-Americans seated in the Cardinals Club section. Williams, a warehouse employee from north St. Louis County, coaches little league, goes to as many games as he can and says baseball is "just part of me."

He said he didn't like having any African-Americans on the team to root for, "but it's the state of baseball."

"I can tell them" about baseball, he said of his two boys. "But kids are very visual. When I was growing up, I had Ozzie. I had (Willie) McGee. That was a big deal to see them play."[34]

For three hours, roughly 81 nights a year, white people can venture into Busch Stadium and be generally unmolested by a black presence.

What were those words from the Don Henley song? *"Those days are gone forever, I should just let them go..."*

Funny: white people in St. Louis, particularly business owners whose investment caters to Cardinals fans (read: white people), don't want to let go of those days of old when St. Louis boasted a safe downtown. [Ballpark Village dress code: No riffraff, St. Louis Post Dispatch, 3-26-14]:

> Gents, don't come to Busch Stadium in a tank top this summer with plans to grab a postgame beer at Ballpark Village. Sleeveless shirts, for men, are one of the many items banned from bars and restaurants in the new complex after 9

---

[34] http://www.stltoday.com/news/local/metro/no-african-americans-on-cardinals-roster-few-in-the-stands/article_011a2213-e60d-5f85-bf48-de32c2d05e82.html

p.m.

Athletic shorts are barred after dark. As are sweat suits, team jerseys (unless it's game day, of course) — and children.

Minors must always be accompanied by a legal guardian, according to policies listed on the Ballpark Village website. And no one under 21 can enter after 9 p.m.

Ballpark Village, the long-awaited joint venture between the Cardinals and co-developer Cordish Cos. of Baltimore, opened to media Tuesday, revealing the complex in all its sports-bar glory: A 35-foot television (measured on the diagonal), a retractable glass roof and red leather bench seats worthy of a cigar bar or late-night lounge.

The complex officially opens Thursday, with a ribbon-cutting and a free concert by Third Eye Blind.

But if Cordish's other developments are any indicator, it's the dress code that could cause the most controversy.

Cordish's rules on proper attire have stirred outrage in Louisville, Ky., where the company developed Fourth Street Live, and Kansas City, where it runs the Power & Light entertainment district.

In both cities, civic and civil rights leaders charged that the dress codes targeted African-Americans, and, worse, were selectively enforced. Just this month, attorneys filed a class action suit alleging a pattern of discrimination at Power & Light.

The dress codes at several Ballpark Village bars, according to the website, are similar to those at Power & Light.

Ballpark Village, itself, doesn't have a dress code, noted Ron Watermon, vice president of communications for the Cardinals. Nor does the team's restaurant, Cardinals Nation. Team executives, he said, are expecting fans to adhere to the same rules they follow in the ballpark: no obscene or indecent clothing.

"Our focus is on creating a family environment," Watermon

said of the restaurant.[35]

Any business trying to create a "family environment" is one attempting to cater to white people.

Any business attempting to cater to black people is one that proudly accepts EBT/Food Stamps.

Busch Stadium is an oasis of white civility in St. Louis, but this is merely a mirage.

Just a mirage.

Three or four hours of seeing the country as it existed in prior to 1963, before our borders were flung open and elected officials of both political party's decided it was time to elect a new people.

"Those days are gone forever, I should just let them go..."

But we can't let them go. The past must be our guide to a better a future.

August 16, 2014
The Black Insurrection in 67% Black Ferguson Continues (What They Want Is What Victor Hill Did in Clayton County in 2005)

The US Constitution is a document scoundrel politicians cite only when it is advantageous for them to do so, callously ignoring it at every opportunity when such an action advances their prospects at reelection.

---

[35] http://www.stltoday.com/news/local/metro/ballpark-village-dress-code-no-riffraff/article_6146ca68-f57c-578c-af2c-1e837bd1ae86.html

Or, it's a document Conservative Inc. peddle in front of gullible white people who still believe Ronald Reagan's Ghost will arrive - as Hamlet's father did - and demand revenge on those who killed the American Dream.

The Police State measures enacted by the Ferguson Police Department on Wednesday were done to restore the monopoly on violence; neutered after images of "brutality" were widely disseminated and criticized by libertarians, conservatives, liberals, and civil rights leaders, the monopoly on violence was handed over to the black mob/looters/rioters/arsonists on Thursday night.

Peace for one night was more accurately a victory celebration.

On Friday night, the violence returned. The looting returned. The exclusively black carnage returned to the 67% black city experiencing a Negro Insurrection.

The police, impotent to do anything: such an action would embolden Eric "My People" Holder to call for more than just black police officers in Ferguson, but unleash federal officers to protect black insurrectionists right to riot/mob/loot/burn/and blame white people for their actions.[36]

All the while, the United States of America flag presumably flies over Ferguson, while black protestors proudly wave the black, green, and red flag of black nationalism on the ground.

Power is all that matters, even if it's an illusion.

And the power is firmly in the hands of the negro (call them black if you want) insurrectionists, with President Barack Obama failing to condemn the rioters in the same language he used to throw the - proper - police state response by the police on Wednesday under the bus.

---

[36] http://www.businessinsider.com/eric-holder-ferguson-police-should-consider-becoming-more-racially-diverse-2014-8

Do the black rioters (insurrectionists) want justice for Michael Brown, an 18-year-old "aspiring rapper" who, for $43 dollars worth of Swisher Sweets lost his life? Apologies Hank Williams Jr. ...

No, the extreme racial demographic changes in Ferguson (the city was 73 percent white in 1990, but the oncoming of Michael Brown clones convinced individual white families to seek safer real estate, meaning Ferguson is 28 percent white today) have yet to lead to black political control of City Hall, the police department, the fire department, and all the joys of public offices...

Never, ever forget what happened in Clayton County (Georgia) in 2005: long a white working-class county located close to Atlanta, extreme demographic changes in a short period of time changed the all-white county into just another colony of downtown Atlanta.

In 1980, Clayton County was 91 percent white; in 2010, the county is less than 30 percent white.

The character of the city changed: where businesses once flourished, boarded up buildings remained where white people did not.

And once blacks took power by the ballot box, white people were screwed. So screwed, in fact, most of the white officers were fired by the new black sheriff and marched out like prisoners of war. With black officers brandishing sniper rifles on the roof of the police headquarters. [Sheriff Deploys Snipers After Firing Dozens, Fox News, 1-4-2005]:

> A newly elected sheriff who deployed snipers to the roof of his jail on his first day in office, then fired more than two dozen people, has been ordered to rehire them.
>
> Victor Hill (search), who started as sheriff in suburban Clayton County Monday, called 27 department employees to the jail, stripped them of their guns and badges, and had his new chief deputy hand them photocopied dismissal papers.
>
> Sheriff's department snipers stood guard on the roof of the jail as the fired workers were escorted out. Because they were no longer allowed to use their county cars, some former deputies were driven home in vans normally used to

transport prisoners. On Tuesday, a judge ordered the new sheriff to immediately rehire them.

"It appears ... that employees of the Sheriff were terminated without cause and in violation of the provisions of the Clayton County Civil Service system," Clayton Superior Court Judge Stephen Boswell (search) wrote in his order.

Hill, 39, told The Atlanta Journal-Constitution that he fired the employees to "maintain the integrity of the department."

The firings had a racial overtone. Hill was among a spate of black candidates elected last year in the county once dominated by rural whites. The county seat, Jonesboro (search), was the setting for the fictional plantation Tara in "Gone With The Wind."

The fired sheriff's employees included four of the highest-ranking officers, all of them white. Hill told the newspaper their replacements would be black.

Hill's firings sparked outrage by another of the newly elected black officials. Eldrin Bell (search), new county commission chairman and former Atlanta police chief, called Hill's firings unlawful and filed for a 30-day restraining order, which Boswell granted Tuesday.

Hill, who also is keeping armed guards to protect him and his home, defended the tactics to the newspaper for a Monday story.[37]

What happened in Clayton County is only a few years away from happening in Ferguson, where the 67% black population will soon exert complete political control of the city.

Ronald Reagan's Ghost is not coming back; hell, an apparition of Calvin Coolidge isn't going to reappear either.

Control is all that matters.

---

[37] http://www.foxnews.com/story/2005/01/04/sheriff-deploys-snipers-after-firing-dozens/

The black mob, no... the black insurrectionists have it in 67% black Ferguson, where a white liberal "quislings" cheer them on in a hilarious "Justice For Mike Brown" alcohol-free kegger type environment.

It's about who controls government and the levers of power -- the shooting of the Swisher Sweet stealing Mike Brown was just an excuse by the black community to vent frustrations against the perceived white oppressors (the police and remaining vestiges of the white power structure in the local government); judging by the continued looting/violence/riots, all promoted by black agitators and their white enablers, Ferguson will be less than 10 percent white in one year.

And blacks will have control of a city completely denuded of a tax-base... then they'll decamp for the next all-white suburb to overwhelm demographically (black crime is tactic of this form of colonization).

Or, if you live in California, it will be Mexican oppressors.

If you, one day, find yourself being lead out of a building with high-powered .308 rifles pointed at you from on high, just remember this: Ronald Reagan's Ghost isn't going to save you.

Reverence for the Founding Fathers won't save you.

Dr. Ben Carson isn't going to save you.

The riots in Ferguson aren't about Justice for Michael Brown; the riots in Ferguson represent a black insurrection, a pubic display of blackness.

August 17, 2014
The Ultimate Ferguson Question: Pentagon 1033 Program vs. HUD's

Affirmatively Furthering Fair Housing (Weaponizing Equality)

In all of talking, editorializing, and tweeting about the black insurrection in Ferguson, Missouri, one politician's Drudge-linked piece stands out as the silliest and most juvenile.

Then again, this same elected official did consider Republican outreach to the 83 percent black city of Detroit a winning strategy...[38]

Sen. Rand Paul, beloved leader of the nebulous liberty movement (meaning: liberty means whatever the current zeitgeist demands it conform to mean), took to Time.com to write an article denouncing the police state measures enacted by the besieged white police force trying to maintain order after multiple days of black rioting in the 67 percent black city of Ferguson.[39]

After denouncing the militarization of our police departments (courtesy of the Pentagon's 1033 program, which distributed military surplus equipment)[40], Sen. Paul writes a paragraph seemingly plagiarized from the speeches of Attorney General Eric "My People" Holder when he addresses he an adorning black crowd:

> When you couple this militarization of law enforcement with an erosion of civil liberties and due process that allows the police to become judge and jury—national security letters, no-knock searches, broad general
>
> warrants, pre-conviction forfeiture—we begin to have a very serious problem on our hands.

---

[38]http://stuffblackpeopledontlike.blogspot.com/2013/12/senator-rand-paul-believes-earth-is.html

[39] http://fox2now.com/2014/08/12/mugshots-of-ferguson-looters-released-to-the-public/

[40] http://www.newsweek.com/how-americas-police-became-army-1033-program-264537

Given these developments, it is almost impossible for many Americans not to feel like their government is targeting them. Given the racial disparities in our criminal justice system, it is impossible for African-Americans not to feel like their government is particularly targeting them.[41]

With all due respect to Sen. Paul, but couldn't those racial disparities exist in our criminal justice system because individual black people break the law at an extraordinary rate when compared to other racial groups?

The obvious answer to this question is "yes," but it's one Sen. Paul and every card-carrying member of Conservative Inc. knows (or never considers) is completely off-limits if they desire maintaining solid standing in the Beltway and with the gatekeepers at Fox News.

And why is Sen. Paul thinking "collectively" when aggregating black individuals in a manner Ayn Rand would declare the worst form of racism? Isn't this a repudiation of his "libertarian" cred?
So here are the main points to make about Ferguson, Missouri and the black riots that broke out after a police officer shot 18-year-old "aspiring rapper" Michael Brown.[42]

- The city of Ferguson was 73 percent white in 1990 and is now 28 percent white

- St. Louis, of which Ferguson is a suburb of, is 49 percent black and 43 percent. Violent, the same racial group Sen. Paul believes is the victim of racial profiling and correctly has grievances with the judicial system

Why are these the main points, you're probably asking yourself?

Because Ferguson has seen its black population from 25 percent of the overall population in 1990 to 67 percent black today; the distrust between the police department in Ferguson (50 of the 53 police are

---

[41] Rand Paul: We Must Demilitarize the Police, Time. 8-14-14

[42] Who was Mike Brown? Profile of black teenager shot in Missouri, Christian Science Monitor, 8-13-14

white, precisely because the dramatic shifts in the racial demographics didn't allow the relocation of public employees as easily as private sector employees)[43] and the increasingly black community exists because the former group are arresting suspected members of the latter group frequently.

The racial changes have happened so quickly in Ferguson that the nearly 3/4ths black city still has a white mayor, and five of the six city council members are white.

Thus, why the riots/looting/pillaging/burning of buildings and private property is correctly labeled a black insurrection. The anger at the shooting death of Michael Brown was the catalyst for finally demanding real change in a city where the now-white minority must placate the black majority before surrendering actual power.

Thus, one of the primary reasons the Ferguson Police Department reacted with such a dramatic – and, sadly, maligned by both conservatives and liberals – use of force on Wednesday to subdue the black rioters (enabled by a sympathetic mainstream media looking for another Trayvon Martin-figure to canonize).

The actions of the almost entirely white Ferguson Police Department conjured up images of Bull Conner and his attempts to maintain order in 1963 Birmingham, providing ample fodder for a media to paint sympathetic images of black protestors in the face of a violent reaction by the state.

How did Birmingham turn out again... oh, that's right.[44]

Replaced where images of black looters and burnt-out buildings; in their place, where blacks running from armored-clad white officers brandishing AR-15 and black agitators scampering through clouds of tear gas.

---

[43] http://stlouis.cbslocal.com/2014/08/13/ferguson-mayor-the-african-american-community-has-something-against-law-enforcement-in-many-ways/

[44] http://stuffblackpeopledontlike.blogspot.com/2013/01/fifty-years-forward-birmingham.html

The monopoly on violence by the police in Ferguson was supplanted by an outpouring of vitriol against their actions, which handed over power to the black mob in the city.

The monopoly of violence is the black mob, with the fear of looting, rioting, arson and even shootings by this rebel force keeping the police from action (of course, any action will be seen as *casus belli* for black people nationwide to riot as well).

This fact was crystallized by the governor of the state of Missouri putting Captain Ron Johnson, a black police officer, in charge of the police in Ferguson. He became a man of the people, as he grew up in Ferguson:

> Captain Ronald Johnson will lead police response for the highway patrol.
>
> "I grew up here," Johnson told reporters. "This is currently my community and my home...I understand the anger and fear of the citizens of Ferguson, and our officers will respect both of those."[45]

Images of Captain Johnson leading the black protestors around Ferguson on August 15th, marching around with them and even "fist bumping" them, represented the surrender of the city to anarchy and inevitable black political rule.

This changed, of course, when blacks to rioting again on Friday and Saturday nights (even after a curfew was imposed by the feckless governor of the state of Missouri).

But there's a silver-lining lost in the story of the fall of Ferguson, Missouri: the political architects of a new, post-white America fail to realize what the Pentagon 1033 program means, especially when viewing what the Ferguson Police Department did on Wednesday night when trying to reclaim the city from black rioters.

---

[45] Missouri Highway Patrol Will Take Command in Ferguson Operations, Riverfront Times, 8-14-14

White Americans, courtesy of HUD's Affirmatively Furthering Fair Housing program, increasingly have nowhere to run; they have nowhere to hide:

> In a move some claim is tantamount to social engineering, the Department of Housing and Urban Development is imposing a new rule that would allow the feds to track diversity in America's neighborhoods and then push policies to change those it deems discriminatory.
>
> The policy is called, "Affirmatively Furthering Fair Housing." It will require HUD to gather data on segregation and discrimination in every single neighborhood and try to remedy it.
>
> HUD Secretary Shaun Donovan unveiled the federal rule at the NAACP convention in July.
>
> "Unfortunately, in too many of our hardest hit communities, no matter how hard a child or her parents work, the life chances of that child, even her lifespan, is determined by the zip code she grows up in. This is simply wrong," he said.[46]

The sinister sounding Affirmatively Furthering Fair Housing program means the federal government is dedicated to eradicating social capital around America, replaced with the promotion of social justice.

And they did just that with Ferguson:

> Long before the nation rested its collective conscience on the protests along West Florissant Avenue, there was a different mobilization going on.
>
> Hundreds of people were moving out of their urban neighborhoods to this north St. Louis County suburb seeking a safe and affordable place to live.
>
> They found it in an isolated corner of Ferguson that was flush

---

[46] Obama administration using housing department in effort to diversify neighborhoods, Fox News, 8-8-13

with sprawling apartment complexes. Far from Ferguson's leafy residential streets and quaint downtown, many people didn't even know the apartments were part of the city until young Michael Brown was shot and killed there Aug. 9.

But not the police. They knew.

After decades of relative calm and stability, the apartments have become a tinderbox for crime. Canfield Green Apartments and the nearby Oakmont and Northwinds complexes are a study of the slow encroachment of poverty and social distress into what had been suburban escapes.

Angela Shaver has witnessed that sea change since she moved into Canfield Green Apartments 20 years ago. The state employee said she raised a prom queen there and sent her off to college.

There used to be a swimming pool. Now, there's a bullet hole in the door below her. That shooting, and many others, happened long before all the vigil candles melted in the middle of the street for Brown.

Even as Shaver explained the frequency of gunfire, she was cut off by a sudden blast coming from Northwinds Apartments, a hulking spread with more than 400 low-income units.

Boom!

Shaver paused to listen. No screams. No more shots. She picked up the interview where she'd left off.

"I hate to say I got used to them," she said of the gunshots.

Ferguson's crime and poverty rate is lower than some of the other North County municipalities. But the small southeast corner of the city where the apartments are glows bright red on crime maps.

That area along West Florissant Avenue and just east of it accounted for 18 percent of all serious crimes reported between 2010 and August 2012, according to a Post-Dispatch analysis of crime data provided by St. Louis County.

> The area accounted for 28 percent of all burglaries, 28 percent of all aggravated assaults, 30 percent of all motor vehicle thefts and 40 percent of all robberies reported in the city of 21,000 people.
>
> It's a cluster of densely populated complexes that stand apart from the predominantly single-family streets of Ferguson.
>
> On a map, the area sticks out like an appendage, one that was added to Ferguson by annexation. Many of the children who live there aren't even part of the Ferguson-Florissant school system.
>
> Adding to that isolation, police have blocked off nearly all access roads to the apartments with concrete barriers, fences and gates.[47]

You have nowhere to run, white people. The black undertow will follow, and with HUD's Affirmatively Furthering Fair Housing program, the federal government has found a way to weaponize equality...

But the Pentagon's 1033 program means more small towns across America are being armed with military-grade weapons straight from warzones around the world... and as crime rates rise in city across city (thanks to the mandated dispersing of blacks via HUD's Affirmatively Furthering Fair Housing program), a similar situation to the one the St. Louis Post-Dispatch described above will occur: an almost entirely white police force will encounter a growing black community hostile with the police for daring to arrest perennially "good boys"...

Strange that, like Ferguson, America's future seems to be a warzone, courtesy of a federal government mandating the legislation of equality and arming local municipalities with military-grade weapons.

As we see in Ferguson, this is all going to end in tears...

---

[47] Why did the Michael Brown shooting happen here?, St. Louis Post-Dispatch, 8-16-14

Police State America or Detroit 2014: this is what those in charge of Black-Run America (BRA) have in mind for your future.

August 18, 2014
Support Officer Darren Wilson: The Police Guard the "Thin Blue Line" Between Civilization and the Black Barbarism of "Detroit"

It wasn't but a month ago the black cop killer Lawrence Campbell's wife ranted he should have killed more cops before he was killed. [Cop killer's widow rages: He should've killed more cops, NY Post, 7-14-14]:

> The widow of the thug who executed a Jersey City cop over the weekend said Monday that her husband should have killed even more officers — as her neighbors set up a sickening memorial to her fame-seeking spouse.
>
> "He should've taken more [officers] with him," Angelique Campbell said of husband Lawrence, who killed rookie Officer Melvin Santiago in an ambush early Sunday, before being killed by police.[48]

Vigils went up in the memory of Lawrence Campbell, a black cop killer instantly celebrated by the black community in Jersey City as some sort of hero.[49]

---

[48] http://nypost.com/2014/07/14/cop-killers-widow-rages-he-shouldve-taken-more/

[49] http://www.nydailynews.com/news/crime/person-interest-arrest-jersey-city-killing-article-1.1866138

Almost at the same time Campbell was being celebrated in Jersey City, in Indianapolis - a city undergoing rapid white flight - a white officer was gunned down by a black career criminal (whose father was also a career criminal).

Officer Perry Renn got "out of his car" to confront Major Davis Jr., who had brought an AK-47 to a family picnic. He'd be dead soon after, when Davis' rifle tragically found its mark.[50]

And the black family was quick to point out Officer Renn would still be alive if he'd "stayed in his car."[Family Of Cop-Killer: If Officer Had Stayed In His Car, He Wouldn't Have Been Shot, IJReview.com, 7-15-14]:

> The family said it "felt sorry" for Officer Renn's family, but that the shooting may have been avoided if he had stayed in his car since he could see Davis had a gun. Incidentally, the alleged killer has an extensive criminal background that dates back to 2006.[51]

Had Officer Renn survived the gun battle with Davis, and the AK-47 toting Davis fallen, you can bet the incident in 67 percent black Ferguson (and the black lynch mob demanding Justice for Mike Brown) would have gotten started a month early in Indianapolis.

For in the words of the family of Major Davis Jr. in Indianapolis we see a mentality that unites blacks nationwide: from Ferguson to Jersey; from Indianapolis to the Oval Office and the Attorney General's of the Department of Justice... [Murder suspect's family speaks out about shooting, WISHTV.com, 7-6-14]:

> The family of Major Davis Jr., the man accused of killing Officer Perry Renn, is speaking out about the shooting. His aunt, cousins and his children's grandmother all talked to 24-Hour News 8 on Sunday afternoon.

---

[50] http://www.indystar.com/story/news/2014/08/08/impd-get-car-campaign-going-viral/13816595/

[51] http://www.ijreview.com/2014/07/154582-family-cop-killer-officer-stayed-car-wouldnt-shot/

The family is still struggling to accept that Davis Jr. could be a part of something like this. He is a father with four children, ages 10 and under. His family has had a long, tense history with Indianapolis police officers.

"You don't know what he been through with IMPD. We do. He's scarred for life," said his children's grandmother, Pam Moornan.

The Davis family's history with police began with Major Davis Sr. He served at least three years on a drug conviction and was arrested again in 2003 for public intoxication.

He died of a heart attack in police custody when Davis Jr. was a young teen. Though the coroner's report said the officers weren't at fault for any fatal injuries, the family still holds officers responsible.

"He wasn't a bad person. His father was killed by IMPD. That is enough to hurt a person and scar him for life," said Moornan.

One of the officers listed in that 2003 police report is Officer Perry Renn.

"I imagine he figured they were going to try and kill him. I mean cause look what they did to his father," said Moornan.

On Saturday night, the family says they were having a cookout.

"Next thing, I just heard shots and everybody running in the house and everybody hit the floor," said Yvonne Moornan, Davis Jr.'s aunt.

By the time they got outside, they realized those shots were Davis Jr. and Officer Renn shooting at each other. Davis had an assault rifle.

"Major is not a bad person in spite of what happened. Things happen," said Pam Moornan.

Now, the Davis family is worried about their son's reputation and again, questioning police tactics.

> "It's horrible about what took place, but, I mean, I don't think it's fair though for them to keep dragging him through the mud," said Moornan.
>
> And again, questioning police tactics.
>
> "I don't know how the police was shooting. I don't know if they took concern of any kids running around," said Yvonne Moornan.
>
> The family did say it is sorry for Officer Renn's family, but they said the tragedy may have been avoided if Officer Renn would've stayed at his car since he could see Davis had a gun.[52]

We grant police the ability to protect civilization, knowing they must administer the monopoly on violence: a thin veneer separating stability and progress from chaos and anarchy.

Which is why Officer Darren Wilson must be supported.

He's already been thrown under the bus by the mainstream media, the Obama Administration, the Department of Justice, black agitators, and a growing sense in the black community the only justice for Mike Brown will be the public lynching of Wilson... damn the evidence Brown wasn't a "good boy."

Highway Patrol Capt. Ron Johnson, the black avatar in charge of acting as the agent in charge of the capitulation to black power in Ferguson, even tossed Officer Wilson under the bus when speaking to a black church yesterday. He said this:

> Earlier in the day, Johnson said he had met members of Brown's family and the experience "brought tears to my eyes and shame to my heart."
>
> "When this is over," he told the crowd, "I'm going to go in my son's room. My black son, who wears his pants sagging, who wears his hat cocked to the side, got tattoos on his arms, but

---

[52] http://wishtv.com/2014/07/06/murder-suspects-family-speaks-out-about-shooting/

that's my baby." Johnson added: "We all need to thank the Browns for Michael.

Because Michael's going to make it better for our sons to be better black men."[53]

We've been trying to make America a better place for "black men" for decades; and no matter how much money we spend, how many quotas we set on jobs in both the private the public sector, and how many handouts (affirmative action) we give, we still require President Obama's "My Brother's Keeper" program to try and help blacks - and browns - reach levels of accomplishment your average white boy easily attains on his own.

The tears we at SBPDL shed aren't for Mike Brown or the black agitators/protestors/rioters/looters/arsonists currently ensuring that 67% black Ferguson drives away all white residents by 2015, but for the memory of Officer Renn who in Indianapolis was gunned down by a black career criminal and was told by the black family he "should have stayed in the car"; for those cops who must patrol Jersey City, knowing Angelique Campbell wishes her late husband had killed more of them; and for Officer Darren Wilson, who was only doing when he stopped Mike Brown in Ferguson as the "Gentle Giant" gallantly gaily down the middle of the road, flouting the rules governing proper behavior in the process.

There's one act of defiance you can do in Black-Run America (BRA), an implicit move immediately indicating you stand by those protecting civilization: Make a donation to Officer Darren Wilson.

The Department of Justice, the Obama Administration, and every black agitator in the contiguous United States of America will be gunning for Officer Wilson.

Being explicitly on the side of white civilization is tantamount to being a child molester in America; making an anonymous donation to Officer Wilson's eventual legal fund is a move akin to giving the finger to a people who desire his immediate lynching (damn the

---

[53] http://abc7chicago.com/news/national-guard-sent-to-ferguson-by-missouri-governor/267881/

evidence of innocence).

August 18, 2014
"All we do crumbles to the ground, though we refuse to see": 38% of Blacks in St. Louis County & 60% of Blacks in City of St. Louis County are on EBT/Food Stamps

"Now, don't hang on, nothing lasts forever but the earth and sky

It slips away, and all your money won't another minute buy." - Kansas

"Don't these people have jobs?"

It's the question eluding all journalists embedded in the war zone of 67% black Ferguson, where a never-ending supply of black protestors seem to mill around the streets of a town increasingly devoid of white people.

Who employs these black people, perpetually upset over the shooting death of Mike Brown (though each day provides more and more information seemingly sufficient enough to defuse the situation to a rational mind -- but the Disingenuous White Liberal and collective black mind is far from rational...) and capable of meandering down the streets of Ferguson without fear of lost wages?

So we'll ask again: do the black protestors in Ferguson have jobs?

If not, who in the world is paying for their mortgage/rent, phone, food, and 401k/retirement plan?

Nothing lasts forever, not even Black-Run America (BRA). [Ferguson,

Mo. Emblematic of Growing Suburban Poverty, Brookings, 8-15-14][54]

And in the gnashing of teeth by the left, right, liberal, conservative, libertarian, prepper, conspiracy theorists, biblical end of timer, and constitutionalists, one fundamental truth escapes them all: the races are different, and the failure of blacks (in not just Ferguson, but nationwide) to create a community where commerce, peace, and social capital is not the fault of white racists or the lack of white people living amongst the blacks. [Deep Tensions Rise to Surface After Ferguson Shooting, New York Times, 8-16-14][55]

It's simply the inability of black people to replicate the civilization whites instinctively create on their own, and, when blacks inherit a city from whites due to white flight from black criminality (Ferguson was 73 percent white in 1990 vs. 28 percent white today), even sustain/maintain the standard of living the former majority race enjoyed. [White St. Louis Has Some Awful Things to Say About Ferguson, New Republic, 8-15-14][56]

Race.

Four letters, when combined, proclaim a fundamental truth behind the collapse of Ferguson: the black rebellion/insurrection in the majority black city isn't about Michael Brown; it's about black people demanding power being surrendered into their hands via the shrinking white minority.

But power means nothing when those in control lack the ability to sustain the living conditions of those who once called the city home (white people).

And with this in mind, we come back to the original question: "Don't these black people protesting in Ferguson have jobs?"

The answer rests in the frightening finality found in The Day The

---

[54] http://www.brookings.edu/blogs/the-avenue/posts/2014/08/15-ferguson-suburban-poverty

[55] http://www.nytimes.com/2014/08/17/us/ferguson-mo-complex-racial-history-runs-deep-most-tensions-have-to-do-police-force.html

[56] http://www.newrepublic.com/article/119102/what-white-st-louis-thinks-about-ferguson

EBT Card Runs Out.

The unrests built into the Black-Run America (BRA) is the key to surviving what's coming: our ability to bribe the black population from rioting (via transfer of wealth schemes including Section 8 vouchers/ welfare/ WIC and EBT, Food Stamps) is collapsing as the pressure of the inherent dysfunction in the emerging black underclass builds up.

Literally, we have millions of unemployable black people bred via white tax dollars to... do... nothing but breed (and ultimately lock away into the prison system for crimes largely committed against their fellow blacks).

And no city illustrates the instability of the American Experiment better than St. Louis and St. Louis County (home to Ferguson).

Consulting the 2009 New York Times Food Stamp Usage Across the Country interactive map, we learn this about the city of St. Louis (49 percent black and 43 percent white):

> • As of 2009, 60 percent of blacks were on EBT/Food Stamps in the city of St. Louis
> • As of 2009, 10 percent of whites were on EBT/Food Stamps in the city of St. Louis[57]

St. Louis County (different from the city of St. Louis) is just over one million people in population. It's home to Ferguson, that lovely post-white suburb boasting a growing, self-insufficient black population. [Ferguson: Gentrification and its discontents, Al-Jazeera, 8-16-14][58]

Of those one million people, 68 percent of the county's population is white and 23.7 percent is black. Consulting the 2009 New York Times Food Stamp Usage Across the Country interactive map, we learn this about the county:

---

[57] http://www.nytimes.com/interactive/2009/11/28/us/20091128-foodstamps.html?_r=0

[58] http://america.aljazeera.com/articles/2014/8/16/ferguson-and-thepoliticsofzipcodeapartheid.html

- As of 2009, 38 percent of blacks were on EBT/Food Stamps in the city of St. Louis
- As of 2009, 4 percent of whites were on EBT/Food Stamps in the city of St. Louis[59]

Ferguson is now a third-world city (85 percent white in 1970 vs. 67 percent black today) because it has a third-world population. [Why Ferguson Looks Like the Inner City, Business Week, 8-15-14][60]

It has a third-world population, because the majority black population there is incapable of sustaining, maintaining, or replicating the type of civilization/community white people of varying social classes/intelligence can create (a fact the increasingly irrelevant wimps at *American Conservative* blame on racism).[61]

The Day The EBT Card Runs Out.

It will come.

It won't be pretty.

Conservatives and liberals; libertarian or socialist; nor Republican or Democrat can articulate what's coming.

Preppers try, but stop short of utilizing the one word/one syllable that would liberate from the tyranny of the times: RACE.

---

[59] http://www.nytimes.com/interactive/2009/11/28/us/20091128-foodstamps.html?_r=0

[60] http://www.businessweek.com/articles/2014-08-15/why-ferguson-missouri-looks-like-the-inner-city

[61] http://www.theamericanconservative.com/ferguson-and-the-troubled-spirit-of-st-louis/

August 20, 2014
The Spirit of Bell Curve City: Eric "My People" Holder and the Birth of New Nation

> *"The junior hoodlums who roamed their streets were symptoms of a greater sickness; their citizens (all of them counted as such) glorified their mythology of 'rights'... and lost track of their duties. No nation, so constituted, can endure."* -- Starship Troopers

The Spirit of ~~St. Louis~~ Bell Curve City.

Where once a nation was motivated to greatness, though momentarily silenced by the awe-inspiring courage of Charles Lindbergh and his feats piloting the *Spirit of St. Louis,* the proud revolutionaries of an entirely new nation are joining Attorney General Eric "My People" Holder in wearing their *color brave* ribbon. [Holder: 'Change is Coming' After Police Shooting in Mo., Boston Globe, 8-20-14][62]

Proudly wearing their *Color Brave* ribbon, knowing Mr. "My People" is guaranteeing "justice" (he's a self-proclaimed "activist"[63]) for the blacks and the family of Mike Brown, the black community across is America is poised to be liberated from the long white arm of the law. [Top Obama advisers tell African American leaders that justice will prevail in Ferguson, Washington Post, 8-20-14]:

> The administration has been working behind the scenes to assure leading civil rights groups that it is determined to see justice achieved as Obama — who has been criticized by some African American leaders for not visiting Ferguson

---

[62] http://www.boston.com/news/nation/2014/08/20/latest-ferguson-protests-are-smaller-more-subdued/6Zjz2MPw5WD2f10F3nzoWN/story.html

[63] http://washingtonexaminer.com/eric-holder-im-an-activist-its-my-responsibility-to-change-things/article/2551624

himself — seeks to preserve his support in the black community with his handling of the racially charged case.

Holder and senior Obama adviser Valerie Jarrett briefed 1,000 African American leaders, community organizers and civil rights groups in private conference calls this week, White House aides said. The strategy was aimed at enlisting the groups to "help keep the situation calm and focused," said a senior administration official, speaking on the condition of anonymity to describe the conversations.

In an open letter published on the St. Louis Post-Dispatch's Web site Tuesday, Holder said his goal was to "ensure that this tragedy can give rise to new understanding — and robust action — aimed at bridging persistent gaps between law enforcement officials and the communities we serve."[64]

Oh, Holder's Color Brave letter to the black community, published in the *St. Louis Post-Dispatch,* echoes a truth so few are willing to take to heart: we have the power now, white man, and your fate is exactly that of your race in Rhodesia and South Africa. [From Eric Holder: A message to the people of Ferguson, *St. Louis Post-Dispatch, 8-19-2014*][65]

Remember: any opposition to Barack Obama (and, by extension, Eric Holder) means you have racial animus against their agenda. You aren't being color blind (whites must be blinded to race, while non-whites are brave about advocating on behalf of their race...). [Holder sees 'racial animus' in opposition, The Hill, 7-13-14][66]

Holder has dispatched 40 FBI agents[67] and members of the Criminal

---

[64] http://www.washingtonpost.com/politics/top-obama-advisors-tell-african-american-leaders-that-justice-will-prevail-in-ferguson/2014/08/19/67983100-27d5-11e4-958c-268a320a60ce_story.html

[65] http://www.stltoday.com/news/opinion/from-eric-holder-a-message-to-the-people-of-ferguson/article_ea8b7358-67a3-5187-af8c-169567f27a0d.html

[66] http://thehill.com/blogs/blog-briefing-room/news/212082-holder-sees-racial-animus-in-opposition

[67] http://www.justice.gov/opa/pr/2014/August/14-ag-873.html

Section of the Civil Rights Division of the Department of Justice[68] (sic) to 67% black Ferguson to unearth clues on the shooting of Mike Brown; in reality - and after a third autopsy of (in the spirit of John) Brown's body - it is this army of investigators that are tasked with framing the innocent Officer Darren Wilson, whose only crime was being a white police officer protecting his life from a rampaging black man.

Recall: the FBI launched a civil rights investigation into the shooting on Monday, August 11 (though Ferguson Police were well aware Officer Wilson sustained a heavy beating at the hands of Brown, which required the former be hospitalized). [FBI will investigate death of black teenager in Missouri, Los Angeles Times, 8-11-14][69]

Amid the violent protests and looting/arson committed by black insurrectionists in Ferguson, Holder was troubled - not by their actions - by the force utilized by the police in trying to restore order to a town regressing to the black mean. [Federal Authorities Wade Deeper Into Teen's Death: Justice Department Orders Autopsy of Shooting Victim Michael Brown, Wall Street Journal, 8-17-2014]

"Tell them to remove the damn tanks," Mr. Holder told his deputies on Thursday [August 14th], according to a law-enforcement official, referring to heavily armored vehicles the local police had used. That day there were discussions among local officials about how to scale back the armed presence, officials said.

Though the white police in Ferguson needed to "remove the damn tanks," Holder was also quick to point out the much-maligned police department need to remove white people from its ranks... in favor of blacks. [ERIC HOLDER: Ferguson Police Should 'Consider' Becoming More Racially Diverse, Business Insider, 8-14-14]:

U.S. Attorney General Eric Holder is suggested the police authorities in Ferguson, Missouri should diversify in order to sooth racial tensions with the community.

---

[68] http://www.justice.gov/opa/pr/2014/August/14-ag-873.html

[69] http://www.washingtonpost.com/politics/fbi-will-investigate-death-of-black-teenager-in-missouri/2014/08/11/991b3dce-2165-11e4-8593-da634b334390_story.html

"Over time, ... [the police] should consider the role that increased diversity in law enforcement can play in helping to build trust within communities," Holder said in a statement released Thursday afternoon.

Tanks to restore order and regain the monopoly from the black insurrectionists? No good.

More black officers, taking jobs away from white people? Oh so sweet to Mr. Color Brave Holder...

With black people in Ferguson, St. Louis, and across the nation rejecting the rule of law in favor of a lynch mob mentality (due process is somehow racist), it's important to consult the words of Mr. My People, when he addressed the 2013 NAACP Conference. On the heels of the George Zimmerman acquittal, Holder denounced Stand Your Ground laws, an obvious forerunner to denouncing white cops ability to use force against black people threatening their life or engaging in criminal activity (the soon to come Michael Brown Act).[Attorney General Eric Holder Addresses the NAACP Annual Convention, Justice.Gov, Tuesday, July 16, 2013]:

> In the days leading up to this weekend's verdict, some predicted – and prepared for – riots and waves of civil unrest across the country. Some feared that the anger of those who disagreed with the jury might overshadow and obscure the issues at the heart of this case. But the people of Sanford, and, for the most part, thousands of others across America, rejected this destructive path. They proved wrong those who doubted their commitment to the rule of law. And across America, diverse groups of citizens, from all races, backgrounds, and walks of life, are instead overwhelmingly making their voices heard – as American citizens have the right to do – through peaceful protests, rallies, and vigils designed to inspire responsible debate – not incite violence and division; and those who conduct themselves in a contrary manner do not honor the memory of Trayvon Martin.[70]

Interesting to compare and contrast the words of Holder in 2013, to

---

[70] http://www.justice.gov/iso/opa/ag/speeches/2013/ag-speech-130716.html

the actions of blacks nationwide today; the justification for blacks anger in 67% black Ferguson is somehow centered with the obvious lie of Mike Brown having his "hands up and saying don't shoot" prior to Officer Wilson executing him in cold blood...

Do those black people looting/rioting/vandalizing/burning/graffiti-ing in Ferguson disgrace the memory of Mike Brown, Mr. Holder? ['Time To Kill A Cop': Ferguson Protesters Throw Urine, Bottles At Police, CBS St. Louis, 8-20-14][71]

That's the story black people in Ferguson, St. Louis and the nation over believe, though it's a legend even Liberty Valance would find incredulous.

Despite the mountain of evidence available, which the DOJ actively tried to suppress and keep out of the public eye, Holder probably believes Mike Brown was executed... knowing his roots to severing racial injustice go back decades. [DOJ asked Ferguson police not to release Michael Brown video, Washington Times, 8-16-14][72]

Where once it was the policy of the federal government to protect the property values of white homeowners and business owners (who were actually invested into the long-term stability of a city, which would generate not only profits, but appreciate over time), the new policy of the federal government is beautifully articulated in the words of Holder when he demanded black rioters/looters/arsonists/insurrections be allowed to sack Ferguson unmolested by the white police:

> "Tell them to remove the damn tanks..."

The spirit of the times in Bell Curve City, personified by the presence of Eric "My People" Holder: let the blacks riot and loot, as long as the white man removes those damn tanks impeding their ability to remake the city of Ferguson in their image.

---

[71] http://stlouis.cbslocal.com/2014/08/20/time-to-kill-a-cop-ferguson-protesters-throw-urine-bottles-at-police/

[72] http://www.washingtontimes.com/news/2014/aug/16/doj-asked-ferguson-police-not-release-michael-brow/

AUGUST 21, 2014

The Black Undertow on Ferguson: a "... growing danger which is more menacing than fire or the elements"

Mapping Decline: St. Louis and the Fate of the American City by Colin Gordon is a book any citizen of St. Louis or an expat living in the suburbs surrounding the dystopia needs to read.

It's in chapter 2 ("The Steel Ring: Race and Reality in Greater St. Louis") that you get to read about a time in American history when the official policy of the federal government was to actually protect wealth, instead of the policy of today when HUD seeks to destroy it and the Attorney General of the Department of Justice (sic) sides with the black insurrection in 67 percent black Ferguson saying, [Holder says he understands mistrust of police as Ferguson protests dwindle, Fox News, 8-21-14]:

> "I understand that mistrust," Holder said. "I am the attorney general of the United States. But I am also a black man."[73]

Remember: Ferguson was 73 percent white in 1990 and is only 28 percent white today (the white population decreased 44 percent courtesy of the arrival of the black undertow).[74]

---

[73] http://www.foxnews.com/politics/2014/08/21/holder-says-understands-mistrust-police-as-ferguson-protests-dwindle/

[74] http://www.forbes.com/sites/niallmccarthy/2014/08/19/chart-ferguson-white-flight/

Gordon's subhead for this chapter is *Zoning and the "Negro Invasion," 1914-1917*:

> The first such effort was quite blunt. At a time when cities were first exploring the politics and legality of local zoning, St. Louis was one of a handful of cities to propose - as a matter of municipal law and policy - formalizing racial segregation.
>
> And, in St. Louis and elsewhere, the push to clean up the City by regulating the location of tanneries or stockyards or tenements extended logically to the "nuisance" of black occupancy as well.
>
> The fear of "negro invasion" in St. Louis was best expressed, and carefully orchestrated, by local realtors. In 1915, the St. Louis Real Estate Exchange (SLREE) created a new organization - the oddly named "United Welfare Association" - to drum up support for a racial zoning ordinance and to use new initiative and referendum procedures to place a zoning ordinance on the 1916 ballot. In its campaign, the Exchange hammered away at the fundamental threat to property values. "Before buying a home in an unrestricted locality, a man usually ascertains very nearly just what his interest, taxes, repairs, etc. are going to cost him," one pamphlet put it, "but there is no present method by which he may determine how much the property will depreciate because of the NEGRO invasion." Protection from such an invasion, by this logic, was as reasonable and responsible as fire insurance:
>
> Do YOU REALIZE that at any time you are liable to suffer an irreparable loss, due to the coming of NEGROES into the block in which you live or in which you own property?... Perhaps you do not think your neighborhood will be invaded. Neither do you believe you are going to have a fire when you pay your fire insurance. While perhaps you have not yet been affected by this class of people coming into your neighborhood, you surely want protection against this growing danger which is more menacing than fire or the elements. At present you have no remedy in a matter of this

kind.[75]

Those white realtors knew of the problems caused by blacks, which no one is allowed to admit is behind the decay in the quality of schools, business district, housing stock (blight is black-in-origin), and property values: basically every metric measuring quality of life drops significantly once a city goes from majority white to majority black. [Blame poverty, age for weak North County home market, St. Louis Post-Dispatch, 8-18-2013][76]

So, while the *New York Times* whines about "apartheid" in 67 percent black Ferguson (the "white power structure"[77]), let's look at a late 2013 article published in the same paper, detailing the quality of life black people create in North St. Louis... home to Ferguson. [In Places Like North St. Louis, Gunfire Still Rules the Night, New York Times, 11-19-2013]:

> The unmistakable pop of a gunshot ricocheted through the park in the humid air, and Montez Wayne could only hope that the bullet did not have his name on it. He sprang from his seat beneath a sprawling bald cypress, ready to make his move.
>
> Was today the day?
>
> He had seen it play out too many times before: the blast of gunfire, the blood, the body. In Mr. Wayne's neighborhood and others on the North Side of St. Louis, drugs, poverty and struggle go hand in hand with gun violence. He barely knows his father. His mother died when he was 14, around the time he started selling drugs. His list of dead friends grows each year.

---

[75] Gordon, C. (2008). Mapping decline: St. Louis and the fate of the American city. Philadelphia: University of Pennsylvania Press, p. 69-70

[76] http://www.stltoday.com/news/local/metro/blame-poverty-age-for-weak-north-county-home-market/article_95c998e5-bb87-5bc0-9054-83e801b357ac.html

[77] http://www.nytimes.com/2014/08/18/opinion/in-ferguson-black-town-white-power.html?src=recg

Mr. Wayne lives in a poor, mostly black community, where, as in similar neighborhoods across America, residents are fed up with persistent gun violence. Victims die one by one, or in clusters. In Chicago, 23 people were shot in a matter of hours in September, 13 of them in a park in a gang-related attack. Three died.

Some communities have begun their own initiatives. The 21st Ward was the first to install street surveillance cameras, spending $600,000 out of the ward's capital improvement budget on 25 of them. A 46-inch flat-screen television in a community center shows footage from every camera, but no one currently monitors them full time. Shortly after they went up two years ago, one camera caught a drive-by shooting. The police caught the assailants a short time later, said Antonio French, the ward's alderman.[78]

Remember what we learned from *Mapping Decline: St. Louis and the Fate of the American City,* and realize it's the Federal Government's mandate to ensure the blossoming of 1,000 Ferguson nationwide:

Do YOU REALIZE that at any time you are liable to suffer an irreparable loss, due to the coming of NEGROES into the block in which you live or in which you own property?... Perhaps you do not think your neighborhood will be invaded. Neither do you believe you are going to have a fire when you pay your fire insurance. While perhaps you have not yet been affected by this class of people coming into your neighborhood, you surely want protection against this growing danger which is more menacing than fire or the elements. At present you have no remedy in a matter of this kind.[79]

100 years later, every city that goes from majority white to majority black collapses, a problem far more menacing to the overall health of

---

[78] http://www.nytimes.com/2013/11/20/us/in-neighborhoods-like-north-st-louis-gunfire-still-rules-the-night.html

[79] Gordon, C. (2008). Mapping decline: St. Louis and the fate of the American city. Philadelphia: University of Pennsylvania Press, p. 69-70

the community - and value of both private and residential property - than a fire or the elements.

A city can rebuild after a fire, an earthquake, a hurricane (in the case of Hiroshima and Nagasaki: an atom bomb attack), but it cannot rebuild once it goes majority black.

Where civilization once flourished, a food desert is now lamented...

AUGUST 22, 2014
St. Louis and the Racial Tipping Point: "Once a municipality passes 30% African American, it accelerates toward becoming overwhelmingly black"

So here's what we know:

> In 1970, Ferguson was 99 percent white[80]; In 1980, Ferguson was 85 percent white and 14 black[81]; In 1990, Ferguson was 73.8 percent white and 25.1 percent black; In 2000, Ferguson was 44.8 percent white and 52.4 percent black; In 2010 Ferguson was 29.3 percent white and 67.4 percent black[82]

More to the point, the racial transformation of Ferguson isn't unique to the city of St. Louis and its surrounding suburbs. Once restrictive covenants (freedom of association) was declared unconstitutional in 1948 by the Supreme Court, the last line of defense for maintaining the integrity of white communities was

---

[80] http://www2.census.gov/prod2/decennial/documents/39204513p18ch09.pdf

[81] http://www.nytimes.com/2014/08/13/opinion/racial-history-behind-the-ferguson-protests.html?_r=0

[82] http://www.forbes.com/sites/niallmccarthy/2014/08/19/chart-ferguson-white-flight/

gone.

St. Louis Metromorphosis: Past Trends and Future Directions (edited by Brady Baybeck and F. Terrence Jones), published in 2004 by the Missouri Historical Society Press, offers illuminating reading into the vast history of the black undertow overwhelmingly formerly all-white communities in the St. Louis metro-area, and gives us this information on the "racial tipping point" *(once a municipality passes 30 percent African American, it accelerates toward becoming overwhelmingly black)*:

> In 1960, the St. Louis region had yet to begin dismantling much of the legal segregation affecting housing patterns. Although restrictive covenants had been declared unconstitutional in 1948, the legacy of past segregation continued, and more affirmative fair housing legislation banning private discrimination would not be passed until later in the 1960s. It is not surprising that 84 percent of the municipalities were predominantly white (i.e., less than five percent black) and only 6 percent were more than one-fifth African America, with one-third of these being two historically all-black communities: Brooklyn and Kinloch.
>
> From 1970 forward, however, many municipalities have experienced substantial racial transition... at least since 1980, whites are unlikely to avoid areas or flee them when the African American share exceeds 5 percent but remains under one-fifth. They do, however, become increasingly nervous as the proportion goes past one-fifth and toward one-half. Shifting to political power, both because they are on average young and because their political participation rates are lower, blacks have some but less than proportional control when their share exceeds a majority but is less than about two-thirds. African American then typically achieve political control above 65 percent and, once the community exceeds 95 percent, it is essentially as single race as the 95 percent+ white cities.
>
> Between 1960 and 2000, over half the cities developed at least a visible (i.e., 5 percent or higher) black population and only a minority - although a substantial one at 42 percent - remain predominantly white. For some municipalities, the

transition from white to black was rapid. Each decade witnessed cities having their African American share increase 30 percentage point or more, indicating that racial tipping - a dramatic shift from white to black - has not gone out of style. Here are some example: for 1960 to 1970, Alorton (18 percent to 80 percent black) and Wellston (8 percent to 69 percent black); for 1970 to 1980, Berkeley (9 percent to 49 percent), Pagedale (23 percent to 79 percent), Pine Lawn (29 percent to 81 percent), and Washington Park (0 percent to 49 percent); for 1980 to 1990, Bel Ridge (25 percent to 61 percent) and Moline Acres (32 percent to 64 percent); for 1990 to 2000, Dellwood (9 percent to 58 percent), Jennings (48 percent to 78 percent), and Cahokia (5 percent to 38 percent). Over forty years, eighteen cities went from less than 1 percent black to more than 65 percent African American: Bel Ridge, Berkely, Cool Valley, Country Club Hills, Flordell Hills, Greendale, Hanley Hills, Hillsdale, Jennings, Moline Acres, Normandy, Northwoods, Pagedale, Pasadena Hills, Pine Lawn, Velda City, Velda Village Hills, and Washington Park.

Is racial tipping inevitable? Once the black share began to increase, has any city been able to stabilize at some equilibrium short of two-thirds or more black? Yes, but the numbers are few. Only two have gone past 30 percent black and not passed 60 percent black within two decades: the City of St. Louis, which went from 29 percent black in 1060 to 41 percent in 1970 but now is just ten points higher (51 percent) in 2000, and University City, which leapt from 0 percent black to 43 percent between 1960 and 1980 but has stayed much the same (45 percent in 2000) since then.

Even during the past two decades when there has been heightened awareness about the social costs of residential segregation and the negative consequences of rapid racial transition and awareness of recent examples such as University City about what policies might achieve a stable racial mix, the prevailing pattern has been: once a municipality passes 30 percent African American, it accelerates toward becoming overwhelmingly black.[83]

Which brings us back to 1948, when Shelley vs. Kraemer was decided in the Supreme Court and restrictive covenants were declared unconstitutional.

Just who is the Shelley? Hilariously, the surname Shelley belongs to a black man who wanted to live in a white community in St. Louis... [Shelley House: Historic Places of the Civil Rights Movement, National Park Services (NPS.gov)]:

> This modest, two-story masonry residence built in St. Louis, Missouri in 1906 is associated with an African American family's struggle for justice that had a profound effect on American society. Because the J. D. Shelley family decided to fight for the right to live in the home of their choosing, the United States Supreme Court addressed the issue of restrictive racial covenants in housing in the landmark 1948 case of Shelley v. Kraemer.
>
> In 1930, J. D. Shelley, his wife, and their six children migrated to St. Louis from Mississippi to escape the pervasive racial oppression of the South. For a number of years they lived with relatives and then in rental properties. In looking to buy a home, they found that many buildings in St. Louis were covered by racially restrictive covenants by which the building owners agreed not to sell to anyone other than a Caucasian. The Shelleys directly challenged this discriminatory practice by purchasing such a building at 4600 Labadie Avenue from an owner who agreed not to enforce the racial covenant. Louis D. Kraemer, owner of another property on Labadie covered by restrictive covenants, sued in the St. Louis Circuit (State) Court to enforce the restrictive covenant and prevent the Shelleys from acquiring title to the building. The trial court ruled in the Shelleys' favor in November of 1945, but when Kraemer

---

[83] Baybeck, B. (2004). St. Louis Metromorphosis: Past trends and future directions. St. Louis: University of Missouri Press, p. 287-289

appealed, the Missouri Supreme Court, on December 9, 1946, reversed the trial court's decision and ordered that the racial covenant be enforced. The Shelleys then appealed to the United States Supreme Court.

On May 3, 1948, the United States Supreme Court rendered its landmark decision in Shelley v. Kraemer, holding, by a vote of 6 to 0 (with three judges not sitting), that racially restrictive covenants cannot be enforced by courts since this would constitute state action denying due process of law in violation of the 14th Amendment to the Constitution. Although the case did not outlaw covenants (only a state's enforcement of the practice), in Shelley v. Kraemer the Supreme Court reinforced strongly the 14th Amendment's guarantee of equal protection of the laws, which includes rights to acquire, enjoy, own, and dispose of property. The Shelley case was a heartening signal for African Americans that positive social change could be achieved through law and the courts.

The Shelley House, a National Historic Landmark, is located at 4600 Labadie Avenue in St. Louis, Missouri. The house is a private residence and is not open to the public.[84]

The ruin of an entire metro region (St. Louis) has occurred: not by asteroid, nuclear strike, famine, earthquake, or an invading foreign army, but by the unleashing of blacks via declaring restrictive covenants unconstitutional.

Just look at how quickly communities have collapsed to the emergence of the black undertow (the racial tipping point is 30 percent, then the community goes black fast)...

But what of the Shelley House, a National Historic Landmark, in 2014?

Oh, it's a fitting tribute to the Civil Rights movement.

You can consult Google StreetView for a taste of racial realities only a

---

[84] http://www.nps.gov/nr/travel/civilrights/mo1.htm

God who doesn't play dice would see fit to ensure exists via the Visible Black Hand of Economics.[85]

As late as 2011, a house (which had been there since the 1920s) was located to the left of the National Historic Landmark "Shelley House," but it has since been razed.[86]

So here's what we know:

- Ferguson went from 99 percent white in 1970 to 27 percent white today
- Not just Ferguson, but scores of St. Louis metro-communities went from almost entirely white to majority black, with the ability for the white residents to practice freedom of association (restrictive covenants) declared unconstitutional
- The National Historic Landmark "Shelley House" is a silent witness to the black undertow effect, a reminder the Visible Black Hand of Economics is far more devastating long term weapon than any weapon currently in the United States Military arsenal

Remember: God might not play dice, but he has a great sense of humor... just look at the state of the Shelley House in 2014.

August 22, 2014
Chuck and Dawn of St. Louis: "What daring! What outrageousness! What insolence! What arrogance! ... I salute you."

Lost in the madness of the Ferguson black insurrection is the story of

---

[85] https://www.google.com/maps/@38.667263,-90.244794,3a,75y,217.59h,96.2t/data=!3m4!1e1!3m2!1s-Nq6-RZ6RrnmtRONuYdp1A!2e0?hl=en

[86] http://www.urbanreviewstl.com/tag/shelley-v-kraemer/

two people, who dared stand against the tide of lies, expose true hatred, and then require police protection to survive potential black mob violence/lynching.

The right to peaceful assembly and the right to freedom of speech collapse into a pile of lies when the right of a black mob to assemble (burn/loot/throw piss at police) is impeded by two white civilians.

A white man and a white woman, daring to walk amongst a bloodthirsty crowd of black people salivating for the sacrifice of Officer Darren Wilson, boldly holding signs in support of a white police officer.

As King Osric told Conan the Barbarian: "What daring! What outrageousness! What insolence! What arrogance! ... I salute you."

The same can't said for Breitbart.com, which edited the comments of Fox News Correspondent Mike Tobin, who was reporting live from Ferguson when a black mob gathered to confront the white supporters of Officer Wilson (He incorrectly identified Officer Wilson as "Officer Williams").

Appearing on "The Kelly File," Tobin told host Megyn Kelly:

> "If you can see the small crowd right here – a little agitated right now – what happened is you had a couple of white people, a couple of supporters for Officer Williams (sic) showed up here on West Florissant Avenue. Not a very good idea if you're concerned with your safety. And that drew a big crowd in. The bottles were coming over the crowd," he reported. And "they were walking along, they had a sign in front of them, said something in support of the officer, and as they were walking there was a huge crowd that formed around them, bottles coming over the top of the crowd, the whole nine yards."

Without mentioning "white people" were being attacked by the black crowd in Ferguson, what kind of story do you have?
Answer: you have no story.

Notice how the great and powerful Breitbart reported the story (hint: they omit Tobin's candid admission it was "white people" who were attacked). [Report: Pro-Darren Wilson Protesters Attacked in Ferguson, Breitbart, 8-21-14]:

> Fox News Correspondent Mike Tobin said that supporters of Officer Darren Wilson had bottles thrown at them during protests in Ferguson on Wednesday night.
>
> "A couple of supporters of Officer Williams show[ed] up here, here on West Florissant Avenue. Not a very good idea if you're concerned with your safety. And that drew a big crowd in. The bottles were coming over the crowd," he reported.
>
> And "they were walking along, they had a sign in front of them, said something in support of the officer, and as they were walking there was a huge crowd that formed around them, bottles coming over the top of the crowd, the whole nine yards."
>
> He added, "that's the second time this happened today. Some supporters of the officer showed up at the Justice Center earlier today, same thing. For their own protection, the officers put them in the car and got them out of there."

Real bold of you Breitbart to leave out the most important point. Real bold.

Here's how the *Daily Mail* Reported the incident.[Darren Wilson defender 'attacked' in clash with Michael Brown supporters on streets of Ferguson amid claims cop was beaten by teen and had his eye socket broken before firing, Daily Mail, 8-21-14]:

> Unrest in Ferguson, Missouri was exacerbated on Wednesday night when Darren Wilson supporters showed up to a Michael Brown rally, sparking tensions.
>
> The small group of pro-Wilson supporters arrived after dark in the rally area, with one woman in a rainbow-striped shirt holding up a sign criticizing the governor's reaction to the police-shooting death: 'Vigorous prosecution Jay Nixon? Justice is for everybody even P.O. Wilson'.

A video post to YouTube shows the woman and another man getting into a verbal argument with Brown protesters, before they were escorted from the scene by police. They are identified as Chuck and Dawn of St Louis, in the video's caption.

It appears another woman came to the protest in defense of Wilson, according to the Washington Post which reported she was hit over the head while waving a 'I support Darren Wilson' sign and shouting, 'Y'all need to get your facts straight'.

Police to rush to her side after she was hit, put her in a truck and drove her away.
'That sign was meant to provoke us. I asked the police why are you letting her protest causing problems over here?' said 30-year-old Tenisha Wheeler said: 'I wouldn't dare go to a rally supporting Wilson with my own self.'[87]

Chuck and Dawn of St. Louis have more heart, more balls, more drive, and more tenacity then the entirety of Conservatism Inc. put together.[88]

This one video, of two white people definitely walking through a throng of blood-thirsty black "peace" protestors is more powerful than the most finely crafted piece of unsolicited snail mail addressed from a Beltway non-profit or email blast promoted by a "Save School Prayer" conservative group.

It's real.

It's dirty.

And it exposes the reality of the United States Constitution so many white people maintain deep reverence for is dead, except when it

---

[87] http://www.dailymail.co.uk/news/article-2730229/Ferguson-cop-shot-dead-Michael-Brown-severely-beaten-teenager.html#ixzz3B9IT6Im5

[88] http://www.washingtonpost.com/news/morning-mix/wp/2014/08/20/amid-mostly-peaceful-ferguson-protests-a-darren-wilson-supporter-is-attacked/

comes to protect black people's rights to assemble in a peaceful or bellicose manner.

Never mind the stores that blacks looted and burned down in Ferguson, the *New York* magazine was quick to poke fun at Chuck and Dawn.

Taking a break from noticing only white people are supporting Officer Wilson (as if this is a sin, considering 57 percent of blacks want him charged with murder, damn the evidence) New York magazine couldn't contain their glee at the white "proles" who dared defy the air of black arrogance/supremacy permeating Ferguson. [Is This White Woman at the Ferguson Protests With a Misspelled Sign a Performance Artist?, New York, 8-21-14]:

> Supporters of Ferguson police officer Darren Wilson, the one who shot and killed unarmed 18-year-old Michael Brown, have mostly been wise enough to stay behind their computers. Not this lady, who was so hyped up on inserting herself, idiotically, into last night's largely peaceful protest that she spelled Missouri Governor Jay Nixon's name wrong. "??" indeed.
>
> She didn't go over so well in town, obviously — "fuck that sign" seems like an appropriate reaction considering the penmanship and lack of copyediting:
>
> Is that Sacha Baron Cohen in a wig and top from Talbots? Was she sent by Jimmy Kimmel to make white people look bad? At which downtown gallery will this poster board be presented against a plain white wall?
>
> Unfortunately, she appears to be the real deal. Protesters intent on not letting her win reportedly locked arms and formed a ring around her to prevent any additional ugliness. Then the cops got rid of her, without rubber bullets and tear gas, somehow.
>
> Her name is Dawn. His name is Chuck. Of course. Chuck and Dawn.[89]

---

[89] http://nymag.com/daily/intelligencer/2014/08/white-lady-misspelled-sign-

So Chuck and Dawn misspelled a word: they haven't caused any property damage in Ferguson or engaged in looting/violence/arson requiring thousands of overtime hours for police to be logged, as black people have done.

So they didn't show up in Ferguson and immediately use their whiteness as a shield against the black masses; Department of Justice Attorney General Eric Holder flew into Ferguson and couldn't contain his glee of having a hint of blackness, telling much darker citizens of the city:

> "I am the Attorney General of the United States, but I am also a black man," Holder told Ferguson residents at a community meeting. "I can remember being stopped on the New Jersey turnpike on two occasions and accused of speeding. Pulled over. ... 'Let me search your car' ... Go through the trunk of my car, look under the seats and all this kind of stuff. I remember how humiliating that was and how angry I was and the impact it had on me."[90]

He'd even go farther in siding with the blackness of Michael Brown supporters, all but indicating Officer Darren Wilson's guilt is guaranteed:

> U.S. Attorney General Eric Holder spoke Thursday about his visit to Ferguson to check in on the federal civil rights investigation into Brown's shooting.
>
> "This attorney general and this Department of Justice stand with the people of Ferguson," he told reporters in Washington.
>
> Holder has assigned scores of FBI agents and Justice Department investigators to look into Brown's August 9 death in the suburban St. Louis city.[91]

---

visits-ferguson.html

[90] http://www.usatoday.com/story/news/nation/2014/08/20/holder-ferguson-investigation/14356869/

[91] http://www.cnn.com/2014/08/21/us/missouri-teen-shooting/index.html

Chuck and Dawn don't stand with Ferguson.

They stand by Officer Darren Wilson.

Two white people faced down a bloodthirsty black crowd (who cared little for facts other than a black criminal being gunned down by a white cop -- race is all that matters, evidence of Brown's guilt is extraneous to this racial truth), "agitating" them in the words of a Fox News reporter: "What daring! What outrageousness! What insolence! What arrogance! ... I salute you."

August 24, 2014

"Against the assault of laughter nothing can stand."

Repeat after me: you are not obligated to participate in the Obama Administration's "My Brother's Keeper" initiative.

You have the right to laugh at this program, realizing it's an implicit admission by the state on the enormity of racial differences that no tenured whiteness studies professor can explain away anymore.

No matter the dollar amount pumped into the "My Brother's Keeper" program, the Obama Administration (and successive administrations) will be unable to nurture cognitive development/self-control nature never intended.

Go ahead and add another zero to the programs budget (you know what? add two or three), and you'll still have a situation reminiscent of Lucy pulling the football from an onrushing Charlie Brown.

Failure.

Hilarious failure.

When President Obama dispatches the chairman of the My Brother's Keeper Task Force to Ferguson to attend the funeral of 18-year-old Michael Brown, if you aren't laughing then you'll never get the joke. [White House aides to attend Michael Brown funeral, St. Louis Post-Dispatch, 8-24-14]:

> President Barack Obama is sending three White House aides to the funeral of Michael Brown, the young black man whose fatal shooting by a white police officer sparked days of racial unrest in Ferguson, Missouri.
>
> The announcement came Sunday as Rep. Lacy Clay, the Democratic congressman representing Ferguson, credited a visit by U.S. Attorney General Eric Holder for defusing some of the tension in the North St. Louis County suburb.
>
> Leading the White House group for Monday's service will be the chairman of the My Brother's Keeper Task Force, Broderick Johnson. My Brother's Keeper is an Obama initiative that aims to empower young minorities.
>
> Also attending will be the deputy director of the White House Office of Public Engagement, Marlon Marshall, and an adviser for the office, Heather Foster.[92]

There's no reason to be upset with Obama's racial loyalty in this situation; the only thing to find offensive is, by this point, images of Officer Darren Wilson immediately following his encounter with Brown should have been viewed by the Obama and the Department of Justice (sic).

They have sided with a black criminal, who severely beat a white officer before his life was (correctly) extinguished; the facts exonerating Officer Wilson should have been hurriedly sent around 1600 Pennsylvania Avenue and the offices of the Department of Justice, immediately causing an immense amount of embarrassment for those black government officials who leaned on Al Sharpton's on-the-ground reports for guidance. [Revved Up: How Al Sharpton

---

[92] http://www.stltoday.com/news/local/crime-and-courts/white-house-aides-to-attend-michael-brown-funeral/article_8179cb06-98fe-5698-a9f7-de5ce84945e8.html

became Obama's go-to man on race., Politico, 8-21-14]:

> And the White House, as the crisis following Brown's death seemed to flare out of control, worked extensively behind the scenes to maximize The Rev's doing what he does, using him as both a source of information and a go-between. After huddling with Brown's family and local community leaders, Sharpton connected directly with White House adviser and First Friend Valerie Jarrett, vacationing in her condo in the exclusive Oak Bluffs section of Martha's Vineyard, not far from where President Obama and his family were staying. Obama was "horrified" by the images he was seeing on TV, Jarrett told Sharpton, and proceeded to pepper him with questions as she collected information for the president: *How bad was the violence? Was it being fueled by outside groups— and could Sharpton do anything to talk them down? What did the Brown family want the White House to do?*
>
> It was a heady consultation for Sharpton, who spent years on the outside dreaming of a place in the pantheon of the civil rights leaders he revered as a teenage street preacher in Brooklyn, and it's an irony lost on no one that his rise to White House adviser has come thanks to Barack Obama...[93]

An advisor to the President of the United States.

Don't be mad about this development, but instead laugh.

Let it out.

Take your time with this one.

Step back from the computer, go outside and laugh.

Do it.

You'll feel better.

Immensely.

---

[93] http://www.politico.com/magazine/story/2014/08/al-sharpton-obama-race-110249.html#ixzz3BM0Y7ICq

Anger is the wrong emotional response at this point.

Just laugh.

Put another couple of "zero's" at the end of the number for the "My Brother's Keeper" program, just so Broderick Johnson, chairman of the My Brother's Keeper Task Force, can be flown to attend every funeral of a non-white male gunned down before he could fulfill his potential and provide the cure to cancer, the chemical equation for ending all pollution, and patenting the most efficient dietary supplement for eradicating obesity.

America stopped being a serious country long ago, so don't take stories such as these two seriously.

Just laugh.

Hard and long.

It's much, much healthier to laugh.

Anger can come when the photos of Officer Wilson are released, showcasing the injuries he sustained while fighting for his life with a belligerent Brown; anger can come when black politicians and leaders such as Attorney General Eric Holder (who obviously knew every detail of Officer Wilson's encounter with Michael Brown before he went to Ferguson on Wednesday, August 20th) refuse to castigate or condemn the "Hands Up, Don't Shoot" movement, instead clinging to a fictional narrative of an evil, white racist cop executing a black choir boy.

On second thought, even when the photos are released and Slate, Huffington Post, Gawker, and Twitter explode into an orgy of stories and Tweets explaining how Officer Wilson's injuries - sustained when he merely confronted Brown walking down the middle of a street, imploring to walk on the sidewalk - don't matter (caved in face, to be more accurate), laughter will be a far greater response than anger.

"Against the assault of laughter nothing can stand."

August 25, 2014
Officer Darren Wilson Supporters: "Oh, don't get all P.C. on me. It's tribal, not racist."

The *Washington Post* unleashed nine reporters[94] to unlock the key to Officer Darren Wilson's 'racist' past so the Department of Justice could unleash a federal civil rights suit against the man who executed Michael "No Angel" Brown.[95]

Wait, he didn't execute Mr. Brown?

Then why does the media always introduce the "Gentle Giant" by proclaiming he was "unarmed" at the time of his death?

Panning for racial gold in Officer Wilson's past (you know, the same kind of off-color remark about blacks the FBI was supposed to find when they interviewed 30 people familiar with George Zimmerman in 2012...[96]), the *Washington Post* was unable to locate the nugget of bigotry immediately showcasing as to why he so callously gunned-down Brown.

Wait... he didn't gun-down Brown in cold blood?

Then why are blacks rioting/looting/burning/stealing/and threatening more violence if they don't get 'justice' (and if you don't rebuild the business blacks looted/burned/stole from/and

---

[94] http://www.washingtonpost.com/national/darren-wilsons-first-job-was-on-a-troubled-police-force-disbanded-by-authorities/2014/08/23/1ac796f0-2a45-11e4-8593-da634b334390_story.html

[95] http://www.nytimes.com/2014/08/25/us/michael-brown-spent-last-weeks-grappling-with-lifes-mysteries.html

[96] http://www.csmonitor.com/USA/Justice/2012/0712/FBI-report-No-evidence-George-Zimmerman-is-racist

intimidated store employees of, well, "it's gonna be hell to pay")?[97]

Why indeed.

If you're paying attention to the intense display of racial loyalty broadcasting out of 67% black Ferguson, you'll know lines have been drawn and, to paraphrase the most important scene from *Orange is the New Black*, blacks understand it's vital that "they look out for our own."[Nearly 6 in 10 African Americans say Michael Brown shooting was 'unjustified', Washington Post, 8-25-14][98]

Most white people will recoil with horror and incredulity at the thought of "we look out for our own," just as the white female anti-hero did in the first episode of *Orange is the New Black*.

But it's the reality of life that too few white people want to accept.

Candid.

Unabashed.

And a truism that, if neglected, will simply result in the complete dispossession of whites in America.

To directly quote *Orange is the New Black* this time, "Oh, don't get all PC on me. It's tribal, not racist."

Which is why the report by *Mother Jones* highlighting the words of racial encouragement left by anonymous white donors to Officer Wilson GoFundMe page should bring a smile to the face of any white person beginning to realize the truths of prison should never be forgotten when the prison bars are invisible. [Fundraising Effort for Ferguson Cop Who Shot Michael Brown Gets Ugly: *Donors praise the officer for shooting "a common street thug" and removing an "unnecessary thing from the public!"*, Mother Jones, 8-21-14]:

---

[97] http://www.thegatewaypundit.com/2014/08/ferguson-protesters-rebuild-our-quiktrip-or-there-will-be-hell-to-pay-video/

[98] http://www.washingtonpost.com/blogs/the-fix/wp/2014/08/25/most-arent-sure-what-happened-in-ferguson-but-blacks-have-largely-made-up-their-mind/?tid=pm_politics_pop

Among the comments left by donors:

"Ofc. Wilson did his duty. Michael Brown was just a common street thug."

"Waste of good ammo. It's my privilege to buy you a replacement box."

"Black people can be their own enemy and I am not white...He was shot 6 times cause the giant wouldn't stop or die. Evil people don't die quick"

"All self-respecting whites have a moral responsibility to support our growing number of martyrs to the failed experiment called diversity."

"I am so sick of the blacks using every excuse in the book to loot and riot."

"I support officer Wilson and he did a great job removing an unnecessary thing from the public!"

The collection of comments above was compiled by Jon Hendren, a comedy writer in San Jose, California. Hendren told *Mother Jones* that he took screenshots of the comments on the page that seemed especially offensive and compiled them into one image using Photoshop. "There were maaaany more that were borderline or ambiguous or a small dollar amount that I would've also captured, but I got so annoyed that I began to get a headache, so I stopped when I did," he explains.[99]

A "headache?"

Anonymous white donors give money to Officer Wilson's GoFundMe page, while blacks loot/burn/pillage/steal/and threaten more violence if they don't get their way, and a few messages on the Internet give you a "headache?"

My message is far more blunt than any you've read, Jon Hendren:

---

[99] http://www.motherjones.com/politics/2014/08/darren-wilson-donors-racist-ferguson

'The Gentle Giant', the man the New York Times noted was "No Angel," Michael Brown got justice.

As the St. Louis Post-Dispatch makes clear, in an article highlighting a (all-white) rally for Darren Wilson, those rallying for the Ferguson Police Officer still don't understand the truth espoused in the first episode of *Orange is the New Black*...[Darren Wilson supporters rally in south St. Louis, St. Louis Post-Dispatch, 8-24-14]:

> Supporters of Ferguson police Officer Darren Wilson, who fatally shot Michael Brown, gathered Saturday at a rally in south St. Louis, with many asking the public to withhold judgment on the case until the investigation is finished.
>
> "Everybody needs to pull together and find the truth," said Jeff Swiney, who said he has friends who are police officers and wanted to show support for Wilson and the judicial process.
>
> "They put on their badge every morning and might not come home," he said. "I appreciate that."
>
> People came and went during the day, with more than 100 in attendance about 1:30 p.m. As many as 20 people stood along Chippewa Street holding signs with messages such as "Justice Comes In All Colors," "I don't support a race, I support the truth" and "Innocent until proven guilty." Some motorists driving by honked in apparent solidarity throughout the late morning and early afternoon.
>
> Many in the largely white crowd wore T-shirts with a badge insignia that reads: "Officer Darren Wilson, I stand by you." The shirts were for sale at a tablenear the entrance of the bar. A woman selling the shirts, who declined to give her name, said they had sold about 500 for $20 each over the course of the day. The shirts are also for sale at teespring.com.
>
> She said media coverage of Brown's death and the ensuing protests has been biased, and that supporters of Wilson have received death threats. "Can justice ever be attained if one

> side's supporters live in fear of speaking out?"
>
> She would not identify herself. "You want my name?" she said, concluding the brief statement she read to a throng of media and supporters in the parking lot. "My name is Darren Wilson. We are Darren Wilson."
>
> Many of the people at the rally also did not want to give their names or speak to the media, saying they worried they would be targeted for their support of Wilson.
>
> Several participants said organizers were asking participants to not give their names to reporters. "They want to protect themselves," said the woman selling T-shirts.[100]

If it wasn't about race, then why would the almost entirely white supporters of Darren Wilson be fearful of identifying themselves as public supporters of Darren Wilson?

What do they want to protect themselves from?

Oh, those same black people who almost universally believe Darren Wilson should be immediately charged with the murder of Michael "No Angel" Brown...

But it gets better. [Supporters of Ferguson officer Darren Wilson met by counter-protesters, Washington Post, 8-23-14]:

> "They are saying it's murder because a white officer killed a black man," said Karen Kennedy, who attended the rally with her daughter Katie. "I don't know where that comes from. This is about two men and the events that unfolded between them. We don't have the facts yet."
>
> The crowd was almost entirely white, and had organized through a Facebook group called "Support Darren Wilson." Though the group has been active online since shortly after the Aug. 9 shooting, raising several hundred thousand dollars

---

[100] http://www.stltoday.com/news/local/crime-and-courts/darren-wilson-supporters-rally-in-south-st-louis/article_26e925cb-cecd-59bb-ba31-9e59b742c62a.html

on Wilson's behalf, this was the first significant public event. Some held signs outside the pub saying "Innocent Until Proven Guilty" or "Law Enforcement Officer Wife."

Passers-by were asked to honk in a show of support. Many did.

"I don't know him. The people here don't know him, but law enforcement is family," pub owner Rhea Rodebaugh said. "The poor guy is in hiding. He was doing his job. People who become police officers, they do it because they love it."

The rally was organized in part by a woman who stood before reporters wearing aviators and a ballcap, reading a statement of support. She refused to give her name. She also criticized media coverage of the case, calling it "unethical." Since the shooting, Wilson, 28, has not appeared or spoken publicly, nor have any of his family members.

At one point, a motorist raced up in a bright yellow car, braked abruptly in the middle of the street, danced, and flipped off the pro-Wilson people. She threw a juice can at them before pulling away.

"You are disgusting!" screamed one protester at the Wilson supporters.

The person who started the counter-protest, Nakarla Rimson, said they began with two people, and that as people drove by, they parked their cars and joined them. It was hard to keep things peaceful, but she tried to tell people to "allow everyone to have their opinion."

Tempers flared on the other side of the street, too, with some people screaming and making rude gestures of their own. By 8 p.m., the pro-Wilson organizers had moved their tables and chairs inside.

"We are trying to get everyone inside to calm things down," said one of the organizers, who declined to give her name.[101]

---

[101] http://www.washingtonpost.com/news/post-nation/wp/2014/08/23/supporters-rally-for-ferguson-officer-darren-wilson/

Just as the heroic Chuck and Dawn of St. Louis found out when they dared show up amid the black "peaceful" protestors in Ferguson, showcasing signs supporting Darren Wilson, the story is one completely about race; were it not, the police wouldn't have immediately stepped in to keep the "peaceful" black protestors in Ferguson from tearing Chuck and Dawn limb from limb like some missionaries attempting to bring civilization to an eternally barbaric tribe...

Daring to stand by Officer Wilson, who by all accounts was merely protecting his life from being taken by an 'unarmed' Michael "No Angel" Brown (though his fist, which is anatomically at the end of the arm, did fracture Wilson's orbital bone...), is somehow "disgusting."

Remember: America is nothing more than an open-air prison for white people; you might not be able to see the bars, but they exist right in front of you.

If not, why would a white female supporter of Officer Wilson be afraid to show her face or give her name to the *Washington Post* reporter...

Just recall these words from *Orange is the New Black* about the racial reality of life in prison:

> When Piper arrives, black women glare and white women smile; a new friend clarifies what's happening. "We look out for our own," she says—then, after Piper's glance, adds,
>
> "Oh, don't get all P.C. on me. It's tribal, not racist."[102]

Conservatism Inc. would have you believe it's about tax breaks, family values, traditional morality, school vouchers, education, or keeping the American flag free of being the victim of pernicious flames (you know, a flag burning amendment...), but it's simply about "looking out for our own."

Oh, and don't get all Ben Carson on me. It's tribal, and it's about race: were it not, Chuck and Dawn wouldn't have been immediately

---

[102] http://www.newyorker.com/magazine/2013/07/08/vice-versa-2

whisked away by police from the "peaceful" black crowds/protestors in Ferguson...

August 26, 2014
This Week's Sign the Black People Are Among Us: Ferguson, Missouri has been an "Enterprise Zone" since 2003...

The Visible Black Hand of Economics waits for no invitation to strike, immediately swinging into action once the demographic tidal wave has capsized a formerly robust economic community.

Ferguson, Missouri is one of those communities where the Visible Black Hand of Economics has seen fit to push Adam Smith's views on commerce and free enterprise to the side.

Ferguson/year	White (% of population)	Black (% of population)
1970	99%	1%
1980	85%	14%
1990	73.8%	25.1%
2000	44.8%	52.4%
2010	29.3%	67.4%

The key to understanding the black insurrection in currently 67 percent black Ferguson, Missouri over the shooting death of Michael "No Angel" Brown by a white police officer can be found in this simple chronological exposé of the demographics of the city.

In 1970, Ferguson was 99 percent white; In 1980, Ferguson was 85 percent white and 14 black; In 1990, Ferguson was 73.8 percent white and 25.1 percent black; In 2000, Ferguson was 44.8 percent white and 52.4 percent black; And in 2010 Ferguson was 29.3 percent white and 67.4 percent black

What does a demographic change of such magnitude (from 99 percent white in 1970 to 29.3 percent white in 2010) do to the economic well being of the city of Ferguson?

With the erosion of social capital, comes the need for incentives to encourage new economic development in a quickly de-whitening city. Enter the "enterprise zone"... [FERGUSON OKS ENTERPRISE ZONE, St. Louis Post-Dispatch, 9-1-2003]:

> With Mayor T.R. Carr of Hazelwood looking on, the Ferguson City Council has agreed to join the proposed enterprise zone that would include the Hazelwood Ford plant and the commercial-industrial area being developed in Kinloch, Ferguson and Berkeley.
>
> Cool Valley aldermen also approved the zone at a separate meeting last week. The zone will provide income-tax credits to companies making new investments and creating jobs, plus credits for training employees and for hiring residents and people with disabilities.
>
> The zone would stretch over a long and irregularly shaped section of north St. Louis County along the north and east sides of Lambert Field from the Robertson area and the Ford plant to an industrial area around the intersection of Paul Drive, South Elizabeth Road and Bermuda Road in Ferguson.
>
> The zone also would include parts of Berkeley, Kinloch and Bel-Ridge and was plotted to include the proportions of low-income residents, unemployed residents and underused industrial land needed to meet state requirements.
>
> One significant part of the area is the nearly 500-acre tract east of Lambert Field including parts of Berkeley, Kinloch and Ferguson that some experts consider the best site for an industrial park in the St. Louis area. The three cities and the county have been negotiating a tax-increment-financing plan and special zoning to spur development of the tract but have

yet to reach a final agreement. That TIF project and the enterprise zonedo not conflict with each other and could complement each other, says Patrick McKeehan, project director of the Ford-Hazelwood Task Force, the group that hatched the idea of the enterprise zone.

Businesses that move to enterprise zones get state income-tax credits and are eligible for property-tax benefits from local governments for improvements to their buildings, McKeehan says.

For the zone to become a reality, all six municipalities plus St. Louis County and the Missouri Department of Economic Development must approve. Hazelwood, Bel-Ridge and Cool Valley have approved the enterprise zone.

Berkeley City Council members expect to approve the enterprise zone at their next meeting, says Mike Heimericks of the Missouri Department of Economic Development, who attended the Ferguson, Berkeley and Cool Valley meetings with McKeehan.

When the municipal approvals are complete, the Department of Economic Development will need approval from the joint committee on economic-development policy and planning of the Legislature.

Since McKeehan made the proposal to Ferguson in July, Ferguson officials asked him to expand the zone to include the industrial area near Bermuda, Elizabeth and Paul. McKeehan crunched the numbers and agreed.

Mayor Hughes of Hazelwood thanked the Ferguson City Council for approvin g the enterprise zone.

"This is a prime example of North County communities using cooperation for a viable economic tool," he said.

Members of the Ford Hazelwood Task Force drew up the plan. Gov. Bob Holden appointed the task force last year after Ford Motor Co. said it would shut down its assembly plant in Hazelwood by mid-decade to cut costs. McKeehan's team hopes the enterprise zone and other incentives will convince

Ford to keep the plant open.[103]

An "enterprise zone" is a tacit admission of racial differences and the dramatic measures needed to encourage economic development and capital investment in an area quickly seeing the displacement of whites by the growth in the black population.

The prior paragraph perfectly describes the situation in Ferguson, Missouri, a city where the future is so dim no light - no matter how bright - could offer a momentary flicker of hope. Just look at the state of the high school (sic -- publicly funded day center) Brown just graduated from, where the American flag flew at half-mast in honor of his memory on the first day of the 2014 year [At Brown's impoverished high school, students try to make gains against odds, Washington Post, 8-25-14]:

> The specter of Michael Brown is inescapable inside his high school.
>
> Hundreds of students, most of them African American, walk the same halls and sit in the same lunchroom as Brown did — before his hard-won graduation and, days later, his death in the middle of Canfield Drive not far away.
>
> The American flag at the entrance of Normandy High School flies at half-staff. Students write and draw in their journals and read essays about police brutality, Brown's fatal shooting by a white police officer on Aug. 9 considered the most vivid case study at hand.
>
> Teachers rush from class to weep, behind closed doors, in faculty restrooms. They say they are crying not only for Brown, but also for Normandy and the students who remain in their classrooms.
>
> If education is the gateway to a better future, the door here was shut long ago, fueling a mix of resignation and rage.
>
> The school system's entrenched dysfunction helps explain the street anger that has unfolded in neighboring Ferguson

---

[103] FERGUSON OKS ENTERPRISE ZONE, St. Louis Post-Dispatch, 9-1-2003

since Brown was killed by officer Darren Wilson in what Wilson's supporters have called an act of self-defense.

For years, Normandy High was considered the most dangerous school in the city, with abysmal test scores, underperforming teachers, a student body in which nine in 10 students qualify for subsidized or free lunches, and graduation rate that's less than 50 percent.[104]

Ninety percent of students (out of an almost entirely black student body) enjoy lunch for free or at a significant discount; and you wonder why "enterprise zones" exist...

These students will graduate and go on to ensure the declining economic fortunes of Ferguson continue unabated, regardless of whatever measures are taken to prolong a full-fledged collapse.

This week's sign the black people are among us is the realization a large section of Ferguson became an enterprise zone 11 years ago, though the move failed to generate an economic revitalization in the city because the racial tipping point had already been passed.

Three things are certain in life:

Death.

Taxes.

And the reality no city can escape the vise the Visible Black Hand of Economics has on a community's commercial viability (or lack thereof).

---

[104] http://www.washingtonpost.com/politics/at-browns-impoverished-high-school-students-try-to-make-gains-against-odds/2014/08/25/d8a33842-2b98-11e4-994d-202962a9150c_story.html

August 27, 2014
The "Shelley House" at 4600 Labadie Avenue in North St. Louis: For $45,000, You Can Own America's Future

$45,000.

That's it.

In what appears to be a bombed-out neighborhood, the famed Shelley House (a National Historic Landmark) is found to have a value of $45,000 in 2014.[105]

No war was fought in North St. Louis, where the Shelley House is found on 4600 Labadie Avenue; no, instead the community went from almost 100 percent white in 1945 to nearly 100 percent black in 2014.

That's it.

Not even the condition of 83 percent black Detroit in 2014 - a bankrupt, black-run metropolis - is a more powerful symbol for the complete failure of America's post-World War II race policies than what 4600 Labadie Avenue represents.

Not even close.

Here's Clarissa Rile Hayward and Todd Swanstrom's words on 4600 Labadie Avenue, as they wrote in the introduction to *Justice and the American Metropolis*:

> A modest two-story brick home sits at 4600 Labadie Avenue in the heart of St. Louis's North Side. Nothing sets this house

---

[105] http://www.zillow.com/homedetails/4600-Labadie-Ave-Saint-Louis-MO-63115/2963569_zpid/

apart from its neighbors but a small metal plaque, which commemorates its role in the landmark Supreme Court decision *Shelley v. Kraemer* [1948].

In October 1945, J.D. and Ethel Shelley, an African-American couple, purchased 4600 Labadie Avenue. At that time, the house was cored by a deed restriction that prohibited occupancy by "any person not of the Caucasian race" and specifically by "people of the Negro or Mongolian Race." A white couple, Fern and Louis Kraemer, were the plaintiffs, chose to represent the Marcus Avenue Improvement Association (whose covenants covered a total of fifty-seven parcels in the vicinity of 4600 Labadie Avenue) because Fern's mother had been a party to the 1911 agreement that originated the covenant. In is Shelley v. Kraemer decision, the U.S. Supreme Court rule that, although as private contracts racial deed restrictions were legal, state enforcement of such contracts violated the equal protection clause of the Fourteenth Amendment.

Following Shelley v. Kraemer, major civil rights triumphs in the second half of the twentieth century opened up important new opportunities for African-Americans, especially for middle-class blacks. But segregation persisted. Although after 1950 the black population expanded into the previously all-white neighborhood around 4600 Labadie Avenue, for most African-Americans in North St. Louis this change represented not the achievement of equality or equal opportunity so much as a move from the compacted Jim Crow ghetto to the lower-density ghetto of the post-civil rights movement years.

In the second half of the last century, the neighborhood in which the house at 4600 Labadie Avenue sits experienced significant population loss. By the year 2000, the census tract in which the house is sited was 98.6 percent black. At that time, a full 21.3 percent of the neighborhood's residents lived below the poverty level, and the median value of single-family homes in the area was less than half that for the St.

Louis metropolitan area as a whole.[106]

Nature has a well-know racial bias.

No matter the efforts to keep nature at bay via social engineer, the best intentions of those who would manipulate nature always are exposed in the end.

The celebrated Shelley House at 4600 Labadie Avenue is a testament to this truth.

As I wrote at VDare days ago [Restrictive Covenants To Maintain Property Values Were Banned In 1948–How's That Working Out?, August 22, 2014]:

> In the past, land titles many white neighborhoods had "restrictive covenants" stating that the land could only be sold to another white person. This was meant to maintain property values, a reason the Supreme Court said was not good enough. [Eric Holder, Freedom Of Association, And The Forgotten Case For Restrictive Covenants, August 27, 2013]
>
> The most destructive SCOTUS case (*Shelley v. Kraemer,* 1948) was based around three cases on restrictive covenants: one came from St. Louis.
>
> The "Shelley House" is a National Historic Landmark.
>
> Here's a black-and-white historical photograph.
>
> I looked on Google Maps/street view.... look at the house today (below).
>
> This is... unbelievable.[107]

---

[106] Hayward, C. (2011). Justice and the American metropolis. University of Minnesota Press, p. 1-2

[107] http://www.vdare.com/posts/restrictive-covenants-to-maintain-propert-values-were-banned-in-1948-hows-that-working-out

No.

This is just the reality of race and why restrictive covenants were so important in protecting the integrity and property values of neighborhoods (homes).

The fate of the Shelley House at 4600 Labadie Avenue in North St. Louis is a representation of what happens when a civilization/community goes from 100 percent white (1945) to 100 percent black by 2000.

It would be invaluable to find out what the property went for back in 1945, when the first black family (Shelley) purchased the house, so as to quantify the cost of trying to fool nature and engineer equality.

August 28, 2014
Quantifying the Whole Three/Fifths Compromise...

Call this a continuation of what was written yesterday: The "Shelley House" at 4600 Labadie Avenue in North St. Louis: For $45,000, You Can Own America's Future.

It turns out the first black couple to move onto Labadie Avenue, J.D. and Ethel Shelley, purchased the long-celebrated (it's a National Historical Landmark after all...) "Shelley House" for $5,700 in 1945.[108]

The neighborhood was 100 percent white until this transaction, which of course was illegal due to the restrictive covenant placed on the property.

But that was 69 years ago.

---
[108] http://ehocstl.org/jd-ethel-shelley/

Located in zip code 63115, 4600 Labadie Avenue is in an area that is now nearly 100 percent black.[109]

It wasn't but 69 years ago two atomic bombs were dropped on Hiroshima and Nagasaki to end World World II; but the end of World War II saw the birthing of a new nation...

Today, the "Shelley House" has an appraised value of $15,000.[110]

Consulting an inflation calculator (God Bless the Internet), we learn that a house valued at $5,700 in 1945 would be worth $75,445.83 in today's money; and yet the Labadie Avenue property at 4600 is appraised by the city of St. Louis for $15,000 in 2004.

What's that? Five times less today than what it was worth in 1945, when the community was all-white?

Now that's how you quantify the whole three/fifths compromise...

Remember this simple fact when appraising property value (commercial or private property) in America in 2014: the greater the percentage of the black population, the lesser the value; the lesser the percentage of the whole is the black population, the greater the value.

August 31, 2014
Oh, I wish I was in the land of cotton...

What are these people protesting?

---

[109] http://www.city-data.com/zips/63115.html

[110] https://www.stlouis-mo.gov/data/address-search/index.cfm?addr=4600 LABADIE AV&stname=LABADIE&stnum=4600&parcelId=37110201100&CategoryBy=form.start,form.RealEstatePropertyInfor&firstview=true

To ensure black people's right to attack and maim police officers remains unmolested, eventually to be protected via a constitutional amendment? [Ferguson protesters plan to halt highway traffic on Labor Day, Fox2Now.com, 8-31-14]:

> There's a call from Ferguson protestors that could have an impact on-your- holiday weekend. During the massive, but peaceful "National March on Ferguson" Saturday, demonstrators revealed a new plan for civil disobedience: halt highway traffic across the St. Louis area on Labor Day.
>
> More than a thousand people took to the streets Saturday for the march. They shut down West Florissant Avenue, marching to the spot where Michael Brown was shot and killed three weeks ago, then to a park in Ferguson. It was there, in the rain, that the plan was thrown out by organizers. They're asking everyone involved to drive onto highways around St. Louis at 4:30pm on Monday, Labor Day and stop their cars for four and a half minutes. The time frame is intended to symbolize the four and a half hours Michael Brown's body was in the street after he was shot.
>
> Organizers say this will just be the beginning of such disturbances.
>
> Zaki Baruti said, "If some of our demands are not dealt with, you'll see more civil disobedience in the spirit of Dr. King, because we're not just going to sit by and just let injustice be constantly impacting us."
>
> Most notable of their demands, the firing and arrest of Ferguson police officer Darren Wilson, who shot Michael Brown. That is currently in the hands of a grand jury.
>
> It is unclear at this point how many people might participate in the seemingly dangerous practice of stopping cars on an interstate highway. No word at this point how police might respond.[111]

---

[111] http://fox2now.com/2014/08/31/ferguson-protesters-plan-to-halt-highway-traffic-on-labor-day/

America is held hostage by its black population, which always rallies behind the lowest of its members whenever such a show of force can secure more rights, more money, and more tribute...

September 1, 2014
The Farce of Ferguson

The editors of *Time* dedicated a cover to the events in Ferguson for the September 1, 2014 edition; showing a picture of a black individual with their "hands up" (you know, the whole "Hands Up, Don't Shoot" meme[112]) facing down the police as they tried to restore order in the 67 percent black city, the caption reads "The Tragedy of Ferguson."

Call it the Tiananmen Square photo of the black insurrection in America's heartland.

But let's go back to the day the now infamous event between Michael Brown and Officer Darren Wilson occurred, and realize this entire event may have represented the initial tremor before a major tectonic shift. [Officer-Involved Fatal Shooting in Ferguson, CBS St. Louis, 8-9-14]:

> Few details have been released but police are confirming a male subject was shot and killed by a Ferguson police officer.
>
> St Louis County Police Officer Brian Schellman says the situation was tense for a while. A large group gathered and confronted police with obscenities and chants of "kill the police". Several times-gunshots could be heard. Police remain on the scene.
>
> St. Louis County Police have taken over the investigation and say details will be released later.
>
> Ferguson, MO (KMOX) Officers from several agencies responded to the Canfield Green apartment complex in the 2900 block of Canfield Drive in Ferguson this (Saturday) afternoon following reports of a disturbance in the street there.

---

[112] http://www.fastcompany.com/3034486/hands-up-dont-shoot-and-growing-power-of-protest-memes

> St. Louis County Police Officer Brian Schellman tells KMOX when County Police arrived at the scene, officers were confronted by a large crowd, some of them armed.[113]

Wait... the black crowd gathering immediately following the shooting of Michael Brown not only chanted "kill the police" but gunshots were heard?

Was this ever investigated?

Was anyone arrested?

What are the odds those guns were even purchased through legal channels?

This was on August 9, days before the looting began and the subsequent (much-maligned) attempt by the almost all-white police force in Ferguson to restore order to a city quickly descending into the anarchy and chaos of amplified spontaneous blackness.

Once the looting, rioting, and arson had stopped, an interview with a white St. Louis police officer shed light onto the truly hostile conditions those representatives of the legitimate "state" encountered when trying to subdue the black insurrection. [FERGUSON COPS: HERE'S HOW IT WENT DOWN: 'Our tactical units have been shot at a number of times', WND, 8-22-14]:

> While many different voices have drawn attention amid the unrest in Ferguson, Missouri, after the shooting of a black teen by a police officer, little has been heard from the police officers on the ground.
>
> So when St. Louis Police Lt. Jeff Fuesting had the opportunity to speak to the Associated Press, he didn't pull any punches.
>
> Fuesting said the two weeks of unrest, which has included rioting, looting, burned buildings and gunshots, have been just as tough on the cops as on residents. "Our tactical units have been shot at a number of times, officers have been shot at a number of times. We have not responded back with

---

[113] http://stlouis.cbslocal.com/2014/08/09/police-confronted-by-angry-crowd-in-ferguson/

lethal force. Yes, we have deployed less lethal force and tear gas. That is to disperse the crowd," he said.[114]

Officers shot at by participants in the black insurrection (what some still incorrectly label a peaceful protest for justice), and you wonder who has the monopoly on violence in America?

It's not the police, whose members know one wrong encounter with a black male suspect and they could be the next Officer Darren Wilson; it's the black population, whose showed in Ferguson they can gather near a crime-scene and shout "kill the police" and then fire volley after volley of gunfire in the direction of police and never expecting any reprisal save the lobbing over of tear gas...

And what did the "Tragedy of Ferguson" cost the taxpayer (the people who supply the revenue to pay for a police force that has lost the monopoly on violence to black insurrectionaries) in Ferguson and St. Louis County? Try $100,000 a day from August 10 - 18. [Bills for extra law enforcement for Ferguson coming due, *St. Louis Post-Dispatch*, 8-28-14]:

> St. Louis County so far has spent about $1 million in police overtime responding to Ferguson, Chief Operating Officer Garry Earls said. That amount includes about $100,000 a day for the first nine days after the shooting.
>
> He said the county incurred many other expenses, most of which were still being tallied, for food, equipment, streets work, fuel costs and other emergency services. "All this workforce out there had to be fed," he said. "We used up all of our tear gas and pepper spray."
>
> He said county police experienced equipment losses, and he expects workers' compensation claims from officers injured during the rioting.
>
> Earls said the county and other municipalities hope the state will defray at least some of their costs.
>
> "If this was a storm, the FEMA folks would have shown up

---

[114] http://www.wnd.com/2014/08/ferguson-cops-heres-how-it-went-down/

already," he said, referring to the Federal Emergency Management Agency. "We are searching for the FEMA equivalent (regarding) civil unrest. We're certainly going to ask the state for that."

In addition, the county plans to spend up to $1 million to provide support to residents who need help because of the unrest, looting and vandalism in Ferguson and neighboring communities.[115]

But it wasn't a storm that hit Ferguson; it was a black insurrection, whose excuse for forming wasn't a change in temperature or atmospheric pressure, but merely a white police officer daring to protect himself from being maimed or even murdered by Michael Brown.

Ferguson will never, ever recover.

But the lesson of Ferguson is one few have dared even try to comprehend: the fault-lines within the already failed American experiment are far more volatile than the San Andreas Fault; the racial divisions are irreparable (just spend a few minutes reading the hysterical essays being published at Newsone.com), forces of nature as immutable as the huge continental plates slowly shifting under our feet.

Just as an earthquake can't be prevented from occurring, conversely, one can prepare for it's occurrence.

The tragedy of Ferguson is, in the end, a farce: just as the bulk of blacks voted for Barack Obama because he's a (nominally) black man, the bulk of blacks support the "Hands Up, Don't Shoot" movement and will only believe justice for Michael Brown happens when Darren Wilson is arrested and thrown into jail.

Or executed.

---

[115] http://www.stltoday.com/news/local/crime-and-courts/bills-for-extra-law-enforcement-for-ferguson-coming-due/article_8ada1a79-fc18-509b-884e-4932b8d9a613.html

One wrong encounter by a white police officer with a member of the perpetually aggrieved black community in a city such as Baltimore, Chicago, Milwaukee, or Indianapolis would instantly trigger another Ferguson.

A political system where these types of events are programmed into the proverbial software is one that can't be fixed with a patch; it's flawed and beyond salvation.

That the Ferguson black insurrection was geographically situated in America's heartland is a reminder of just how terminal the whole situation is, and why, no matter what concessions are made to the rioters/protestors/looters, it won't prevent the next black seismic event.

September 2, 2014
We Now Return You To Your Regularly Scheduled Program

The belief a racist, ~~right~~ white-wing leaning police officer executed a "Hands Up, Don't Shoot" proclaiming, Bible-thumping, good black boy in cold blood (not to mention in broad daylight, in the middle of an almost entirely black ghetto) lacks credibility, unless you live in a world where *Mississippi Burning, A Time to Kill, 12 Years a Slave* and *Django Unchained* are the only movies playing.

Though sites like Conservative Treehouse and Gateway Pundit will continue to do excellent work exposing the already unraveling media/state-crafted narrative in Ferguson, it's important to consider the facts as to why the 67 percent black city looks like an "inner-city." [Why Ferguson Looks Like the Inner City, Business Insider, 8-15-14].

Simply put, Ferguson went from being 99 percent white in 1970 to roughly 27 percent white today; from less than 1 percent black in 1970 to more than 67 percent black today.

Race tells not just part of the story behind Ferguson's demise, but the entire story.

And it's this story, published today at Fox2Now.com, which should help describe just why the city of Ferguson saw such massive white flight when the first trickle of blacks starting to dribble into the city: the legitimate fear by white people of individual blacks (as the numbers increase, so does the percentage of blacks for whites to be correctly fearful of).... [Mother of murder victim calls for focus on black on black crime, Fox2Now.com, 9-2-14]:

> Rochelle Cook has watched the riots in Ferguson unravel while mourning the death of her daughter Aniya. The 18-year-old was murdered in 2012 while sitting in a car in St. Louis. Cook says while there's a big focus on Ferguson and police brutality these days, black on black crime should not get lost in the shuffle. Cook is also frustrated because she recently reached out to community leaders to participate in her annual march against crime and got no response.
>
> 'What angers me the most is the community leaders, religions leaders where were you when I sent you an email to march with us it hurts. We are all hurting since we don't have our children anymore.' Said Cook
>
> FOX 2 asked James Clark of Better Family Life about why more people were compelled to embrace the Ferguson protests. Clark also says the solution to black on black crime is to connect with young people on the street.
>
> 'They have felt for years that they had no power, now they see they can make the whole world listen. Now we have to move and stop the black on black violence and disrespect. There's a certain type of leadership that comes from the neighborhood.
>
> There is a tier of neighborhood leadership that we have to embrace. It's was not traditional leaders that kicked this off it was people from the streets that kicked this off.' Said Clark
>
> As the events in Ferguson evolve, unfold and gain momentum. Rochelle cook is hoping a movement in honor of

her daughter called 'The Team Naiya Movement' will do the same.

'We cannot lose this opportunity and deal with the issue of black on black crime.

We need the Michael Browns to step up right now and say I will work in my neighborhood to stop crime and violence that`s who we need right now.' Clark said.[116]

No white person fears being the victim of "white on white" crime, because crime committed by white people is overwhelmingly personal, whereas black on black crime is impersonal, arbitrary, and utterly savage in nature.

No one in their right mind has ever even uttered the words "white on white" crime, because such concentrated criminality by white people (jeopardizing the health and vitality of communities, as well as the strength/value of commercial and private property) is found nowhere in America.

But black on black crime is found wherever black people in America are found, meaning those living near America's permanent underclass must be mindful of the negative effects of such concentrated criminality (depreciating property value and collapse of once healthy, vibrant business/commercial districts).

When you see a food desert, immediately know the threat of black on black crime is near (which convinced smart grocery store owners not to invest in the area).

When you see boarded up buildings, where formerly business was conducted and a community flourished, know the threat of black on black crime is near (which drove away the sense of community and convinced a smart business owner to divest from the area). [McClellan: Black-on-black crime is fact we can't deny, St. Louis Post-Dispatch, 10-9-2010]:

Murders are such a common occurrence in the gangster

---

[116] http://fox2now.com/2014/09/01/mother-of-murder-victim-calls-for-focus-on-black-on-black-crime/

culture that they are no longer considered very newsworthy.

In St. Louis, the gangster culture is largely a black phenomenon.

You can blame it on anything you want. Unwed mothers, hip-hop music, bad schools, vestiges of slavery, poverty, drugs, the welfare state. Liberals can blame it on one thing, conservatives can blame it on another.

But nobody can get away from the fact that it exists.[117]

Why not just blame it on black people?

The collapse of property value in (not just... but all of America) metro St. Louis is entirely a black phenomenon... just consult the history of that vaunted National Historical Landmark, the Shelley House... white people flee the biological detritus of unwed black mothers, the bad schools their progeny inherently create and the poverty that proliferates courtesy of the crime committed by individual blacks that inhibits any outside capital investment due to the high risk/no reward scenario (remember: Ferguson has been an enterprise zone since 2003).

Just as race tells not just part of the story behind Ferguson's demise, but the entire story, so does this four letter word accurately summarize America's decline.

---

[117] http://www.stltoday.com/news/local/columns/bill-mcclellan/mcclellan-black-on-black-crime-is-fact-we-can-t/article_f8cb6307-7040-5b21-a184-b86601e43526.html

September 3, 2014

Hypothetically Speaking, Of Course...

Why do police stop so many black people in St. Louis?

We've already established, via analyzing the City of St. Louis Metropolitan Police Department Annual Report to the Community (from 1999-2013), that the black population of the city is responsible for virtually all the homicides.

Mind you, the city of St. Louis is 49 percent black and 43 percent white.

So when the black newspaper in the city of St. Louis, the *St. Louis American*, reports about some sort of "gun crisis" please automatically understand it has nothing to do with white people.[118] ['Gun Violence is a Crisis', *St. Louis American*, 6-20-13]:

> Children and adults gathered on the steps of St. Louis City Hall last Friday to remember Sandy Hook Elementary victims and to ask legislators to push for more rigorous gun-control laws.
>
> The candlelight vigil was part of a national movement, yet it couldn't have been more timely for St. Louis. On June 10, 17 people were injured in gun violence during seven different incidents all in one night. Four days later, four people were shot and killed in a murder-suicide at a Cherokee Street business.
>
> "The amount of gun violence is a crisis," said 21st Ward Alderman Antonio French, who spoke at the candlelight vigil. "It needs to be a treated as crisis. It's an emergency situation."
>
> Every year, the majority of murder victims in the St. Louis

---

[118] https://www.ncjrs.gov/pdffiles1/nij/191332.pdf

region are young African-American men.

"Gun violence is a leading cause of death among some groups in our community," French said.

James Clark, vice president of community outreach for the nonprofit Better Family Life, was not surprised to hear about 17 people being shot in one night.

"What disappoints me is our apathetic response as a community," he said.[119]

When a white cop shoots an 'unarmed' black "gentle giant," the apathy and indifference of the black community in metropolitan St. Louis is replaced with righteous indignation.

Remember though: hypothetically speaking, without a black population, the metropolitan St. Louis region would be virtually free of gun crime and have a homicide rate approaching... well, it would so small as to represent a statistical anomaly.[120]

Gun violence will always be a problem in the black community, because these communities are full of black people. No matter if the National Association for the Advancement of Colored People (NAACP), the St. Louis Clergy Coalition's law and order committee, the St. Louis Initiative to Reduce Violent Crime, the Put Down Your Pistol campaign, Better Family Life, the St. Louis County chapter of the National Urban League, or churches of various disciplines intervene, the gun violence will persist. [Groups want end to St. Louis gun violence, St. Louis Post-Dispatch, 8-6-12][121]

Remember, the formula for Baltimore's condition in 2014, Low

---

[119] http://www.stlamerican.com/news/local_news/article_fa9dcade-d937-11e2-a460-0019bb2963f4.html

[120] http://www.unewsonline.com/2013/05/02/documentary-looks-at-stl-gun-violence/

[121] http://www.stltoday.com/news/local/crime-and-courts/groups-want-end-to-st-louis-gun-violence/article_bf75e3dc-8047-11e1-b941-001a4bcf6878.html

Impulse Control + Poor Future Time-Orientation + Low IQ(x)Jury Nullification (black political control)², also helps explain the city of St. Louis' state.

Even when you factor in all the time and effort from scores of private organizations/foundations (funded with grants from both private and private organizations/institutions), black-in-origin gun crime/violence doesn't subside.

Which brings us to the point of this whole exercise in considering this hypothetical: if there were no black people in the St. Louis metropolitan region, would there be any fatal police shootings? Consulting research by University of Missouri-St. Louis Criminologist David Klinger, the answer is 'no'. [Diverse police forces are not a panacea for fatal police shootings, *St. Louis Post-Dispatch*, 9-3-14]:

> Amid the firestorm of protests following the shooting of Michael Brown — an unarmed black teen who was killed by a white police officer — have come repeated calls for hiring a more diverse police force.
>
> But a growing body of research suggests that intractable circumstances of economics, culture and geography have more to do with shootings by police than the race of the officers.
>
> According to the research, neglected minority neighborhoods that are poor and prone to violence are a hotbed for such shootings — regardless of the complexion of the police.
>
> David Klinger, and other criminologists at the University of Missouri-St. Louis, including Isom, wrote an academic paper about 230 shooting incidents involving 315 St. Louis police officers between 2003 and 2012. Of those, about two-thirds of the shooters were white and one-third were African-American. According to the paper, the distribution was reflective of the police department during that period.
>
> Of the known suspects police were shooting at in those cases, 92 percent of them were African-American.
>
> St. Louis is 49 percent black.

According to St. Louis police data for 2012 and 2013, 94 homicide suspects were African-American; two were white; one was Hispanic; and one was Asian.

Of 4,713 inmates sentenced in St. Louis who are in state prison, 598 are white and 4,083 are black.[122]

And to think: St. Louis is situated near to the very heart of the contiguous United States of America.

More to the point: the violence found almost exclusively courtesy of black individuals (byproducts of the black community) in St. Louis, is routinely over something as trivial as "an outstanding drug debt worth about $20 to $40."[Residents on Thrush Avenue look for safety from shootings, St. Louis Post-Dispatch, 7-26-14]:

> In the wake of back-to-back shootings that killed one person and injured three others recently, residents in the 700 block of Thrush Avenue are understandably on edge.
>
> There is a sense that retaliation is coming.
>
> "It's like something spiritual, something I can feel," said Venus Houston, 38, from her front porch. "It's heavy."
>
> During the day, she and others on the block seem to watch every vehicle that turns onto the dead-end street in the Baden neighborhood in St. Louis, hoping to catch a glimpse of a familiar face behind the wheel, not another shooter.
>
> Thursday evening, after darkness fell, Houston searched for friendly headlights.
>
> She hoped it was her ride out of there for the night.
>
> Too many in the family to stick together, three of her children, a sister and young nieces who live with her had already departed for havens, a recent regular routine to

---

[122] http://www.stltoday.com/news/local/crime-and-courts/diverse-police-forces-are-not-a-panacea-for-fatal-police/article_0718a4ea-9b6e-5ec0-95e6-afa5a1041ad8.html

escape the threat of violence. Houston and her 7-year-old son, Elijah, were going to be the last to go.

Their ride was running behind.

"It has been inconvenient because for the most part we haven't been sleeping here," Houston said of the shootings.

Drug Infested

A worn sign on North Broadway speaks to the days when this was a German neighborhood: "Danke schoen for visiting Baden."

"The majority of people are good, hard-working," said the Rev. Don Buhr, of nearby Our Lady of the Holy Cross Catholic Church. "Many are unemployed. Not because they are unwilling. It's just there are no jobs."

Where one street is calm, another is rough.

"It's definitely infested," Buhr said. "Anybody who is on drugs, keep away from them."

Crime in Baden has been declining over the years, according to city police statistics.

The rate is above that of the city as a whole, but ranks below a couple dozen other neighborhoods.

A vast majority of the area's crime, like in many parts of the city, is related to burglary, larceny, robbery and vehicle thefts. Between 2000 and 2010, the area lost 14 percent of its residents, according to U.S. Census statistics.

When Dana Stiebel started buying property around Baden Avenue about 10 years ago, she said it was like a McDonald's drive-in for drugs and prostitution. She said she is known as a no-nonsense landlord.

"None of these people, if you look at them, are angels," she said. "That's not who lives here."[123]

There are no jobs in this area, because the risk/reward for an investor (owner of capital) to open a business in this formerly German community is 100 percent considered a "risk" of unimaginable proportions.

Once where Germans built a community in this landmass located in metropolitan St. Louis, now the black inhabitants create conditions where no business can flourish.

It's simply a hypothetical, but if this area was still inhabited by German's, would the *St. Louis Post-Dispatch* write melancholy stories of the woeful state of all-black areas of St. Louis in an attempt to induce white guilt?

No.

Because this community is drug-infested and filled with criminality (with shootings and homicides over drug debts of $20 to $40 dollars) courtesy of its black inhabitants.

Just as St. Louis and the suburbs surrounding the city would have virtually no homicides or gun violence without (hypothetically speaking, of course) its black population.

Just as police would be nothing more than glorified babysitters (occasionally putting out an A.B.P. for white teenagers who dared to toilet paper a neighbors house) were the city and metropolitan - hypothetically - without a black population.

Instead, nearly all police shootings involve a black suspect...

And because the black population of St. Louis and the city's suburbs are unable to produce the same quality of life as their white counterparts, organizations such as the National Association for

---

[123] http://www.stltoday.com/news/local/crime-and-courts/residents-on-thrush-avenue-look-for-safety-from-shootings/article_7a2e1138-9e3a-5c96-9dbd-f8ba11d06ed3.html

the Advancement of Colored People (NAACP), the St. Louis Clergy Coalition's law and order committee, the St. Louis Initiative to Reduce Violent Crime, the Put Down Your Pistol campaign, Better Family Life, and the St. Louis County chapter of the National Urban League must exist to lobby exclusively on their behalf.

Hypothetically speaking, of course, but do you begin to understand what St. Louis would be like if there were only white people? :

- The swift execution of criminals convicted of murder or rape, with no organizations existing on their behalf to label such judicial actions as "racist" or whine over "social justice"
- Police allowed to do their job, instead of being fearful over every encounter with a black male suspect (believing their job, pension, or life might be at stake if the interaction leads to a "civil rights" inquiry), knowing an "Officer Darren Wilson Scenario" could occur on any given shift...
- The end of "white flight" because white people would have no reason to abandon a city like Ferguson, that went from 99 percent white in 1970 to 27 percent white today (less than.1 percent black in 1970 to 67 percent black today)
- The establishment of communities (where roots could be established, multiple generations of families could live, work and build), free of drugs and petty violence over a $20 dollar drug debt that leaves cars and houses riddled with bullets...

But it's all a hypothetical, of course.

September 4, 2014
Ride with the Devil: If Ferguson is America's Future, is the Omega East St. Louis?

News that Attorney General Eric "My People" Holder is opening a Justice Department civil rights investigation to see if the Ferguson Police Department practiced discrimination broke today. [Attorney General Holder Delivers Remarks at Press Conference Announcing

Pattern or Practice Investigation into Ferguson Police Department, Justice.gov, 9-4-14][124]

The Washington Post uses the adjective "probe" to describe the impending DOJ investigation of potential discrimination by members of the overwhelmingly white Ferguson Police Department, a city that was once also overwhelmingly white but now is nearly 3/4th's black (99 percent white in 1970; 86 percent white in 1980; 75 percent white in 1990; 44 percent white in 2000; 27 percent white today).

Sadly few people will dare "probe" into just why white people abandoned the city of Ferguson once the black population began to move, though it would be wise to do so if Ferguson is America's future.

If, as the following articles asserts, America was built on "white male supremacy" could we surmise the country is being torn apart by the belief in equality and lowering the standards "white male supremacy" once set (and maintained) to something even blacks can achieve? [How Ferguson could be America's future, Fox2Now.com, 8-23-14]:

> The protests in Ferguson, Missouri, have been described as a mirror into contemporary America, but they are also something else: A crystal ball.
>
> Look past the headlines — the debates over race and police militarization that have surfaced after the killing of an unarmed black youth by a white police officer — and one can glimpse America's future, some historians and political scientists say.
>
> No one is talking about an impending race war or a police state, but something more subtle. Unless Americans re-examine some assumptions they've made about themselves, they argue, Ferguson could be the future.
>
> Robert Putnam, author of "Bowling Alone," says his studies of multiracial neighborhoods in America show that more

---

[124] http://www.justice.gov/iso/opa/ag/speeches/2014/ag-speech-140904.html

diversity initially erodes community.

In his 2007 paper, "E Pluribus Unum: Diversity and Community in the Twenty-first Century," Putnam says members of multiracial communities initially tend to expect the worst, distrust neighbors and withdraw.

"Residents of all races tend to 'hunker down,' " Putnam writes. "Trust (even of one's own race) is lower, altruism and community cooperation rarer, friends fewer."

If Americans want to live in a tranquil country that's free of racial conflict they would have to change their character and history, another scholar says.

They would have to become like Iceland.

There are no Fergusons there. The United Nations commissioned a report last year that concluded its citizens are among the most contented in the world.

Iceland is so free of conflict that the nation was shocked last year when a police officer shot a man to death. It was the first time police had killed anyone in Iceland in 70 years. Most police in Iceland don't carry guns.

But that happiness comes at a price, says Lisa Corrigan, director of the Gender Studies Program at the University of Arkansas, who cites the Iceland comparison.

Iceland has one of the most homogeneous populations in the world — everyone looks the same. And they deliberately keep it that way.

"Iceland is one of the happiest places in the world," Corrigan says.

Corrigan doesn't accept the notion that most white people will welcome the browning of a country that she says was built on white male supremacy.

"It's going to get worse before it gets better," she says, "because power is shifting and white people think that their whiteness is property to be defended."[125]

Iceland is free of violent crime because it is free of black people; conversely, New Orleans is overwhelmed by violent crime because the city is overwhelmingly (60 percent of the population) black.

But what we already know a homogeneous black population doesn't enjoy the same peace, prosperity, and crime-free atmosphere as Iceland. In fact, 98 percent black East St. Louis is one of the most violent places in all of America.

	2000 White Population %	2000 Black Population %	2010 White Pop. %	2010 Black Pop.	% of Black cops/2010
Bel-Nor	57.20%	39.60%	48.70%	46%	20%
Bell. Neighbors	53.70%	44.40%	25.70%	73%	3%
Berkeley	20.60%	76.70%	14.30%	81%	55%
Beverly Hills	4.60%	94.50%	4%	96%	64%
Breckenridge Hills	65.90%	28%	61.00%	32%	8%
Calverton Park	75.00%	22.20%	53.40%	41%	0%
Charlack	61.50%	32.60%	58.90%	35%	20%
Edmundson	73.80%	18.80%	61.00%	26%	9%
Ferguson	44.70%	52.40%	29.30%	67%	7%
Flordell Hills	16.90%	82.10%	5.00%	91%	25%
Florissant	85.70%	11.50%	69.30%	27%	8%
Hazelwood	80.20%	16.00%	64.10%	30%	3%
Maplewood	76.20%	15.90%	74.10%	17%	10%
Maryland Heights	85.40%	5.60%	73.20%	12%	1%
Moline Acres	12.20%	85.50%	6.30%	92%	79%
Normandy	26.80%	66.70%	21.30%	71%	14%
Northwoods	6.20%	92.70%	4.00%	94%	59%
Olivette	70.40%	21.90%	60.90%	24%	9%
Overland	83.60%	11.20%	73.30%	16%	0%
Pagedale	5.70%	92.10%	4.60%	93%	60%
Pine Lawn	2.40%	96.00%	1.50%	96%	45%
Richmond Heigh	81.50%	13.30%	81.70%	12%	7%
Riverview	58.00%	39.70%	27.00%	70%	0%
Rock Hill	68.10%	27.40%	70.60%	23%	10%
St. Ann	82.70%	11.40%	69.50%	22%	5%
St. John	81.80%	14.00%	67.40%	23%	5%
St. Louis	43.80%	51.00%	43%	48%	34%
St. Louis County	76.80%	19.00%	70.30%	25%	10%
University City	49.30%	45.40%	50.80%	41%	42%
Velda City	3.10%	96.00%	3.00%	95%	20%
Vinita Park	33.00%	61.70%	30.10%	65%	55%
Wellston	6.30%	92.10%	2.40%	95%	63%
Woodson Terrace	84.40%	11.60%	71.50%	21%	6%

Breaking down those metropolitan St. Louis cities featured in the St. Louis Post-Dispatch "Out of Balance" cover-story by demographics - white/black - from 2000 to 2010. Notice how the white population decreases substantially in many cities. The last column is the % of blacks on the police force as of 2014. [Source: 2000 and 2010 U.S. Census]

---

[125] http://fox2now.com/2014/08/23/how-ferguson-could-be-americas-future/

If America's future is Ferguson, then - inevitably - the future will be nothing more than that of East St. Louis, because white people have no tolerance for living around blacks (the incredible decline of the white population in Ferguson over the past 40 years punctuates this fact).

It should be remembered the East St. Louis "Stop the Violence[126]" march on the Friday before Memorial Day 2012 (which featured Trayvon Martin's parents!!) was followed by a weekend of two homicides and three shootings. [East St. Louis Cops Outgunned as Cuts Let Killers Thrive, Bloomberg, 1-4-2013]:

> Dodging open manholes where thieves had swiped cast-iron covers, Stephen Wigginton drives the crumbling streets of his hometown, East St. Louis, Illinois, pointing out new landmarks in America's most violent city.
>
> There's the shopping mall where a police officer was shot in the face, a youth center that saw a triple homicide in September, and scattered about the city of 27,000 are brightly lit gas stations that serve as magnets for carjackers, hit-and- run robbers and killers.
>
> "It's the Wild West," said Wigginton, the U.S. attorney for the Southern District of Illinois. With a murder rate 17 times the U.S. average, the nation's highest according to the FBI, East St. Louis offers a glimpse at the future for budget- strapped cities like Detroit and Camden, New Jersey, that have made deep cuts to their police forces.
>
> The Illinois city's reputation for crime has scared away economic development from a place that sits just across the Mississippi River from its better-known urban namesake in Missouri and at the nexus of several interstate highways. It also has drawn the attention of federal law enforcement, with Attorney General Eric Holder vowing during a Nov. 30 visit to provide help.

---

[126] http://www.kmov.com/news/local/East-St-Louis-erupt-154880015.html

> "We've got to put the clamp on the crime," said Mayor Alvin Parks, recalling a recent conversation with a business operator considering locating in East St. Louis. The chief obstacle: the city's killings, which hit 25 in 2011, the most recent year for which FBI statistics are available, or 9.23 per 10,000 people compared with the national rate of 0.55.
>
> Police Cuts
>
> The city reduced its police force by 33 percent from 2008 to 2011, the 12th-largest reduction among cities with more than 25,000 people, according to Federal Bureau of Investigation data. Among the 20 biggest U.S. police jurisdictions during that period, the number of officers fell 2.7 percent to 99,312.[127]

So as a city gets blacker, the ability for the citizens to provide tax revenue to pay for a police force declines; and as a city gets blacker, the rate of violent crime increases.

If Ferguson is America's future, I'm not so sure this future America will be a place for white people. Certainly, East St. Louis is no longer hospitable to white people or one boasting a civilization of their design.

Which brings us to a question the St. Louis Post-Dispatch asked: Why do so few metropolitan St. Louis municipalities have black police officers?

The answer: many of these cities, now sporting a majority black population, where but one decade ago majority white.

Why white people flee a city going majority black is the question no one dares ask. [St. Louis County police forces often don't reflect communities, St. Louis Post-Dispatch, 8-24-14]:

> About 67 percent of Ferguson's residents are African-American, but only 7 percent of the city's commissioned police officers are black.

---

[127] http://www.bloomberg.com/news/2013-01-04/east-st-louis-cops-outgunned-as-cuts-let-killers-thrive.html

> That lopsided representation, brought to light after a black teen was killed by a white police officer two weeks ago, has city leaders pledging to try harder to improve race relations.
>
> The disparity is common among communities in St. Louis County with significant black populations. Many police departments do not reflect the communities they serve.
>
> Many reasons for the disparity are given, including difficulty in recruiting black police officers; the lack of interest in policing by minorities; and the changing demographics in North County over the past two decades.
>
> From 1990 to 2010, Ferguson's African-American population rose by more than 150 percent.
>
> And of the 230,000 African-Americans who live in St. Louis County, more than 90 percent of them reside in communities along and north of Olive Boulevard, based on census data. That's where 29 of the 31 police departments patrol.
>
> Police chiefs cite various reasons for their departments not keeping up with this change, including a lack of minority applicants and black officers frequently leaving for jobs at bigger, better-paying departments.[128]

Or, the simple answer: many of these cities were once overwhelmingly white, but the influx of black people drove away those white people who were employed in the private sector; those white people still employed in the public sector (police officers) couldn't be fired for being white...

Yet, at least.

Those descendants of modern-day Liberians still living in America have a strange migratory pattern, easily discernible when looking at history of modern metropolitan St. Louis: wherever whites go and build, blacks follow and ultimately debase.

---

[128] http://www.stltoday.com/news/local/metro/st-louis-county-police-forces-often-don-t-reflect-communities/article_a29dc3e4-91bb-5cf5-9b30-9ebb95c5e1c6.html

The "Shelley House," a National Historical Landmark, is testament to this indisputable fact.

Understanding Ferguson is America's future is understanding the Department of Justice will be quite busy investigating police departments nationwide that fail to reflect the demographic of which they are sworn to protect and serve.

White flight is daring to believe a tiny spark of the Old America can be ignited, while the Federal Government works overtime to douse whatever remains of the Historical American Majority by consent decree, HUD's Affirmatively Furthering Fair Housing, and by outlawing Freedom of Association.

America's future is East St. Louis, with the federal government declaring war on not only whites, but white police officers as well.

Fitting that the city of East St. Louis, at 98 percent black, looks an awful lot like Monrovia, Liberia...

September 7, 2014
The Forgotten "Public Caning" Controversy from 1994 in St. Louis

Back in 1990, Philadelphia experimented with Norplant to reduce the black underclass.

Back in 1993, Baltimore experimented with Norplant to reduce the black underclass.

And in 1994, with rising black-in-origin (the violence originating not from poverty or racism, but the growing courtesy of the growing black underclass) crime in St. Louis, the father of the first black mayor of the city proposed "public canings" as a means to corral growing black property crime. [Canings for Vandals Proposed in St. Louis, New York Times, 5-21-1994]:

> An alderman today proposed public caning as a punishment for graffiti vandals, saying a whipping or two had never hurt his own son, who is now the Mayor of St Louis.
>
> "Fining them doesn't seem to be the answer," the alderman, Freeman Bosley Sr. told the city's Board of Aldermen. "Maybe whopping them on their behind a few times might be a better message."
>
> The board voted 17 to 10 to hold a hearing on the idea, effectively burying it.
>
> Graffiti vandals in St. Louis face $500 fines and jail terms of up to 90 days.
>
> Apparently inspired by the recent caning in Singapore of an American teen-ager, Michael Fay, for vandalism, Mr. Bosley said youngsters did not get enough discipline at home.
>
> "I think you need to spank them while you talk to them," he said. "My mother whipped my tail plenty, and my dad did, too, and I've put the strap to the Mayor."
>
> Mayor Freeman Bosley Jr. had no comment on his father's remarks.[129]

The first black mayor of the city might not have commented on his father's sensible policy, but Bosley Sr. would elaborate on his idea. [St. Louis alderman seeks caning for graffiti writers, Nevada Daily Mail, 5-13-1-1994]

> Bosley said much of the graffiti is spray-painted by gang members. The graffiti spoils the city landscape, costs thousands of dollars to clean up and discourages people from moving into a neighborhood because it signals that gang activity takes place there, he said.

---

[129] http://www.nytimes.com/1994/05/21/us/canings-for-vandals-proposed-in-st-louis.html

> Bosley said the canings should be held in public. "That's the only way it would work. That humiliation in itself would also be a deterrent," he said.
>
> Criminals would received "three or four" lashes for their crimes, Bosley said. "I don't want to maim them, but I most certainly think they should be lit up a little bit," he said.[130]

Whereas Norplant (or Depo-Provera) is a logical, sane proposal to prevent the continued degradation of a community, public canings as a deterrent to future criminality is also a logical, sane proposition.

Especially for a city like St. Louis, teetering on the edge of going the route of Detroit (i.e., massive abandonment from the city by white people due to high rates of black crime, which in turn cedes control of said city to the emerging black population).

Mayor Freeman Bosley Jr. never addressed the public caning idea his dad proposed, but he did appeal directly to the emerging black majority of St. Louis in hopes of getting re-elected. [Racial Split In a Primary Disturbs Core Of St. Louis, New York Times, 3-10-1997]:

> A mayoral Democratic primary between two black candidates has ended in defeat for the incumbent and provoked some racial soul-searching here.
>
> The primary became a bitter fight in which blacks supporting the Mayor, Freeman Bosley Jr., accused the challenger, Clarence Harmon Jr., of selling himself to the white establishment. Mr. Harmon, the city's first black Police Chief, won on Tuesday with 56 percent of the vote, to Mr. Bosley's 43 percent. Mr. Harmon drew 94 percent of the white vote.
>
> Mr. Bosley, who was elected the city's first black Mayor four years ago, won 83 percent of the black vote this time, to 17 percent for Mr. Harmon. St. Louis is roughly 50 percent white and 50 percent black, but the white voting-age population is larger.

---

[130] St. Louis alderman seeks caning for graffiti writers, Nevada Daily Mail, 5-13-1-1994

The defeat left some Bosley supporters thinking that the city's blacks had lost an opportunity.

"For the first time, we had a Mayor sensitive to North St. Louis and its problems: schools, crime, the infrastructure of the inner city," said James H. Buford, the president of the Urban League of Metropolitan St. Louis and a supporter of Mr.

Bosley. Mr. Harmon, 57, who worked his way through the ranks of the Police Department during a 22-year career, was a popular chief who was considered to be effective fighting crime and challenging a department promotion system that depended on political connections. He resigned in 1995 after four years in the job, following a battle with Mayor Bosley over control of the department.

During the primary, support for Mayor Bosley was fervent among blacks. The St. Louis American, which calls itself "The Black Weekly," said Mr. Harmon was "a more subdued, palatable candidate propped up by business and white voters." The article carried the headline, "South Rises Again for Harmon," a reference to a largely white area of the city.

Judi Roman, Mr. Harmon's campaign manager, responded: "South St. Louis did turn out for Clarence, but it was not a racial issue for them. The issue was that they felt they had been disenfranchised by the Bosley administration."[131]

"For the first time, we had a Mayor sensitive to North St. Louis and its problems: schools, crime, the infrastructure of the inner city," translated, means: we had a black mayor who put the interests of the black people of North St. Louis - the very people responsible creating bad schools, the crime, and the breakdown of the infrastructure of the inner city - first.

It was Freeman Bosley Sr., whose comments on public caning, who was also speaking directly to this demographic reducing the civilization whites had created in St. Louis to nothing more than the

---

[131] http://www.nytimes.com/1997/03/10/us/racial-split-in-a-primary-disturbs-core-of-st-louis.html

civilization (or lack there of) black people's racial cousins create in Africa.

It was his son, the first black mayor St. Louis, who sided with those who were (to paraphrase the words of Bosley Sr.), "spoiling the city landscape, costing thousands of dollars to clean up and discouraging white people from moving into a neighborhood because it signals that black gang activity takes place there."

In actuality, that represented his constituents.

Public canings represent one of the first steps to returning civilization to inner-cities (urban environments), where the behavior of blacks has driven away the people capable of sustaining western civilization: white people.

Depo-Provera, of course, represents the first step to ensuring the problem is fixed in only one generation.

September 10, 2014
Metropolitan St. Louis: The heartland of America, exposed for those to see the true content of black people's character...

Amos Brown, longtime agitator for all things black in Indianapolis, called the Indianapolis Metropolitan Police Department (IMPD) an "occupying army" when describing their interactions with blacks.

Not to be outdone, but the city of Ferguson's police department (recall: in 1970, the city was 99 percent white and today, is roughly 27 percent white) has been labeled an "outside armed force" by a black St. Louis politician. [Clay tells Congress Ferguson police are "outside armed force", St. Louis Post-Dispatch, 9-10-14]:

> The Ferguson Police Department is an "outside armed force," Rep. William Lacy Clay. D-St. Louis says.
>
> The congressman made that observation in a speech on the

House of Representatives floor earlier this week about the Aug. 9 shooting death of Michael Brown, 18, by Ferguson officer Darren Wilson. Local authorities are investigating the shooting, and the Justice Department is conducting separate investigations into the shooting, and into the patterns and practices of the Ferguson Police Department.

"The pain that has enveloped that community since the tragic police shooting of Michael Brown on Aug. 9 has stirred the conscience of our nation, and has forced us to confront some very difficult truths," Clay said.

"The hard reality that I observed with my own eyes is a deep sense of outrage and anger that is present, not just in Ferguson, but in many communities across this country," Clay said. "And that pain is most deeply felt by millions of Americans of color, both young and old who know from decades of sad experience, that far too often, local law enforcement agencies and the justice system do not view them, or treat them, as equal citizens, who deserve due process and equal protection under the law."

Clay went on to say he has "little confidence in" the local investigation into the shooting. "There are many hard lessons to be learned from Ferguson, and I fear that there may be more to come," Clay said, adding that "we have too many unarmed black men who interact with police and wind up dead."[132]

What's funny is unarmed black men and women successfully drove away not only white people, but the civilization they created, in not just Ferguson but all throughout metropolitan St. Louis.

Unarmed black men and women also drove away businesses and convinced property appraisers to drop the value in both private and commercial real estate.

And as a false narrative surrounding the events between Officer

---

[132] http://www.stltoday.com/news/local/govt-and-politics/gateway-to-dc/clay-tells-congress-ferguson-police-are-outside-armed-force/article_a2209fbd-fe0c-5b64-8d03-4f347d1e2339.html

Darren Wilson and Michael Brown spreads throughout the black community with a ferocity not even replicated by the Ebola Virus, a picture of the incongruent reality of Post-Racial America emerges. [Crime Commissioner responds to his e-mail about possibly burning Ferguson City Hall, Fox2Now.com, 9-10-14]:

> An e-mail conversation, shared with FOX 2, reveals inflammatory comments between respected African American leaders. One leader responded by e-mail, saying `right on` to apparent words of violence.
>
> The conversation is contained in a 38 page email sent to all St. Louis Media. It's titled 'Civil Disobedience Shutdown of Interstate 70,' then this comment 'Anything short of arresting that White cop for murder is an insult to Black people and Ferguson city Hall and Police department needs to burn to the ground!!!'
>
> Tony Thompson, founder of Kwame Construction and member of the Regional Crime Commission wrote those words. Activist Eric Vickers responded, 'Right On!'[133]

What's truly hilarious in this scenario is blacks have already threatened further violence in Ferguson (a town that is 68 percent black today, though it was less than .1 percent black in 1970) if the consequences of their actions aren't... un-consequenced. [Ferguson Protesters: Rebuild Our Looted Businesses, "Or It's Gonna Be Hell to Pay" (Video), Gateway Pundit, 8-24-14]:

> CBS interviewed three young men in Ferguson, Missouri this week.
>
> One protester Gunny warned officials:
>
> "To be honest, if they don't come and restore these neighborhoods for these people, like when you gotta go travel miles to Walmart and to get gas and stuff like that, it should be right here. If they don't restore this community for people who stay here it's gonna be hell to pay...

---

[133] http://fox2now.com/2014/09/09/crime-commissioner-responds-to-his-e-mail-about-possibly-burning-ferguson-city-hall/

> A second protester chimed in:
>
> Yeah, that's why people looting, because they can't get no jobs.[134]

That's not why you can't you jobs; vocationally speaking, black labor is only valuable in corporate America as a buffer against EEOC lawsuits or via public jobs in local, state, and federal government. Don't worry though: the soon-to-be food desert called Ferguson will be the beneficiary of millions of federal dollars in aid to help the city recover from the August 2014 black insurrection.

Or, if we are to believe the hundreds of blacks who packed the first city council meeting since Michael Brown attacked Officer Darren Wilson – earning his justice in the process – the insurrection might not be over. [Hundreds attend Ferguson's first city council meeting since Michael Brown shooting, Fox2Now.com, 9-9-14]:

> "How are you getting Ferguson residents involved with trying to be unified?" asked one speaker.
>
> One speaker promised more demonstrations if he didn't see officer Darren Wilson face charges for the shooting death of Michael Brown.
>
> "You all might as well bring back the army because there's going to be chaos in the street again," said the young man.[135]

Chaos in the streets again?

Sigh.

The truth doesn't matter to those who support the idea Michael Brown was executed without provocation.

All that matters is a black man was killed by a white police officer, reinforcing their belief an uninterrupted line of white supremacy

---

[134] http://www.thegatewaypundit.com/2014/08/ferguson-protesters-rebuild-our-quiktrip-or-there-will-be-hell-to-pay-video/

[135] http://fox2now.com/2014/09/09/hundreds-attend-fergusons-first-city-council-meeting-since-michael-brown-shooting/

connects the 2014 Ferguson Police Department to Jim Crow, lynching, the Confederacy, and the German Nazi Party.

Never mind the horrendous casualty list racked up by black on black homicide/crime in metropolitan St. Louis, the real crime is the impermanent natures of the economic conditions whites create in suburbs (such as Ferguson) that immediately depart with them once white flight from black crime begins.

Without a tax-base to pay for basic civilizational needs (police, fire department, road maintenance, parks, and basic civic improvements required in a budget each fiscal year), you'll see massive property depreciating and an eroding business footprint: exactly what is happening in Ferguson since blacks became a clear demographic majority.

If police are an "occupying army" and an "outside armed force" depriving black people of basic liberties, then it's time for police to stop patrolling majority black areas.

Metropolitan St. Louis: The heartland of America, exposed for those to see the true content of black people's character...

September 12, 2014
This week's sign the black people are among us: The Ferguson Adolescent Six

The apocalypse already happened.

We're living in the aftermath of the end times.

Proof?

Get out of the way Jena Six.

Make room for the Ferguson Adolescent Six. [Black kids from the Ferguson block where Mike Brown lived star in a powerful video calling for 'white people to own up and face racism', Daily Mail, 9-10-14]

> - A T-shirt company promoting race equality released a video on Tuesday with children from Ferguson, Missouri aimed at calling attention to racism
> - FCKH8.com is a 'for-profit T-shirt company with an activist heart' that donates $5 out of every $13 dollars spent on T-shirts to charity
> - FCKH8.com recruited six children who lived on the same block where teenager Michael Brown, 18, was shot in the face by police officers
>
> A T-shirt company promoting race equality released a video on Tuesday with children from Ferguson, Missouri aimed at calling attention to the racism that still exists in America today.
>
> FCKH8.com is a 'for-profit T-shirt company with an activist heart' that donates $5 out of every $13 dollars spent on T-shirts to charities working to fight racism.
>
> The Blaze reports that the T-shirt company recruited six children from Ferguson, Missouri who lived on the same block where teenager Michael Brown, 18, was shot in the face by police officers.
>
>
> The video begins by saying that Ferguson is the place, 'where white police shot an unarmed black teen in the face.'
>
> The shooting spawned a nationwide discussion about the prevalence of racism in the modern day despite having a black president in office and supposedly living in more accepting times.
>
> In the background a kid can be heard yelling that the incident is, 'a national disgrace.'

The video goes on to point out things that white people allegedly say about racism and their belief that it no longer exists.

'But is racism still a thing?,' a kid asks pretending as though they were ignorant.

'All this focus on race makes me uncomfortable.'

'Try being black,' pipes an adorable little boy.

'It's you people who are making this about race,' say one kid,

'I don't see color,' mocked another.

'You people are just playing the race card,' said a kid pretending to be a jaded white person.

'Some of my best friends are black.'

Later in the video a white man appears in the video and talks about how fighting racism is about joining together.

'Racism is not over but I'm over racism,' says the T-shirt and the message the children are trying to send to racist America.[136]

It's hard to imagine eternal damnation being any worse than life in Black-Run America (BRA), where the FCKH8 video is basically a microcosm for 24/7/365 white guilt drip that is the modern entertainment/corporate/military/academic/government mission.

September 16, 2014

---

[136] http://www.dailymail.co.uk/news/article-2750204/T-shirt-company-recruits-black-kids-Ferguson-block-Mike-Brown-lived-join-make-powerful-video-calling-white-people-face-racism.html#ixzz3D9EJUgAK

How Will Future Generations Ever Believe This Story?

An honor student.

At a 99 percent black high school.[137]

Who wanted to be president.
An innocent bystander to the carnage that is the environment black people, in the absence of whites, create.

Actually, it's the environment blacks create regardless if whites are absent or present, quickly helping convince the latter racial group to pack their bags.

But back to the honor student, who calls St. Louis 'home'... [Honor student loses eye in drive-by shooting, Fox2Now.com, 9-16-14]:

> A man is still on the run after a drive-by shooting at a corner store in St. Louis.
> He hit an unintended target: Latasha Williams, 14.
>
> Friday had been a happy day for Williams, a Vashon freshma, her sister, Daja, 12, a 7th grader.
>
> "Everyone was giving her dollars and telling her good job," said their aunt, Shantell Barge.
>
> Progess reports had just come home from school and people around the neighborhood were rewarding the girls for their high marks.
>
> They went to the M.V. Market at 20th and Ferry in North St. Louis to buy snacks to celebrate around 8:30 Friday night.
>
> "It's not even decent for kids to be in the park," said their mother, Donnitta Turner, referring to the violent

---

[137] http://www.movoto.com/schools/saint-louis-mo/vashon-high-school-292928002011/

neighborhood. "They can't walk around this neighborhood like we grew up. It was better when we grew up. We could be outside. We could play. We can't even do this out here. It's sad. Something's got to give," Turner said, tears rolling down her cheeks.

The gunman pulled up in a red Monte Carlo, rose through the sun roof, and started shooting.

There were 53 shell casings on the ground when the shooting stopped.

Daja took cover under a parked car. Latasha was already inside.

"I climbed under the car as far as I could get. I'm looking out the corner of my eye and I'm looking at all of the gunshots bouncing off the ground…the next thing you know my step sister is screaming, 'Tasha's hit. Tasha's hit, call the police'," Daja said.

"It just feels like I'm dreaming, but I'm not," said the girls' mother.

Latasha was hit in the arm and in her face: a bullet where her eye used to be.

"That's the only store the kids have to walk to and get candy. Unfortunately, there's people out there all the time. When the bad guys come shooting, they're shooting for them but they're shooting at all the kids at the same time. Unfortunately my niece lost her eye due to being inside the store just trying to get some snacks," Barge said.[138]

Gun violence (fatal and non-fatal) is an activity the black population of St. Louis has a near monopoly on, with the parks of the city no-go areas for black children because of the ~~KlanNazis~~ ~~Tea Party Members~~ ~~Republicans~~… blacks. [Vashon High School freshman loses eye in shooting at St. Louis corner store, St. Louis Post-Dispatch, 9-16-14]:

---

[138] http://fox2now.com/2014/09/15/honor-student-loses-eye-in-drive-by-shooting/

St. Louis police have made no arrests in the shooting that wounded Latasha and injured a man, 32. Multiple shots were fired into the store, leaving a constellation of bullet holes in the shop's facade.

Now, Latasha's mother is asking for the shooter to come forward or for people to help police solve the crime.

"This gun stuff has got to stop," she said. "There are innocent kids being hurt."

Latasha, the oldest of seven siblings, has experienced violence in her family before.

Her father, Marvin Williams, was 21 when he was fatally shot in St. Louis on March 21, 2005. Police said then that they believed the shooting was gang-related.

Turner said she has already broken the lease on the family's apartment near North 20th Street and Salisbury Street, near Hyde Park, and is looking to move her family as soon as possible. She no longer thinks it's safe.

"It's bad over there and I refuse to raise my kids down there," Turner said. "It's shots every single night."[139]

So her father was a black gang-banger, who brought potentially seven black children into the world...

And the mother is now going to move her brood from St. Louis to a "safe" city (majority white) to raise her bastard children...

This one story perfectly captures the insanity of the pro-life movement, ensuring a pro-death movement permeates wherever Donnitta Turner, LaTasha William, and Turner's six other children migrate to...

This one story perfectly captures the insanity of modernity, an epoch we can not hope to change or reverse to some magical 1950s-esque

---

[139] http://www.stltoday.com/news/local/crime-and-courts/vashon-high-school-freshman-loses-eye-in-shooting-at-st/article_3151005b-5fc6-528c-99d6-c31d908941bb.html

existence, but only survive.

And if we survive, future generations will be hard pressed to believe people like LaTasha, Donnitta, or those who fired 53 rounds on a random Friday night and only hit two people could ever have lived.

As dragons were in tales of a pre-medieval Europe that never existed, so will the horror stories of a world once populated by LaTasha's and Donnitta's (for only they could give birth to men such as the gang-banger Marvin Williams, who was 16 when LaTasha was conceived) be interpreted by generations still unborn.

September 17, 2014
Black Terrorism in St. Louis: "If Darren Wilson gets off, you all better bring every army you all have got. 'Cause it's going down."

First, blacks in Ferguson threatened "it's gonna be hell to pay" if the conditions of post-riot city aren't restored to the conditions of the city when it was overwhelmingly white. [Ferguson residents frustrated over lack of opportunity, CBS News, 8-22-14]:

> Gunny: "To be honest, if they don't come and restore these neighborhoods for these people, like when you gotta go travel miles to Walmart and to get gas and stuff like that, it should be right here. If they don't restore this community for people who stay here it's gonna be hell to pay..."[140]

Blacks have no purchasing power, meaning even stores like Walmart are incapable of staying open in a city without a white population (or even Hispanic) to sustain it.

---

[140] http://www.cbsnews.com/videos/ferguson-residents-frustrated-over-lack-of-opportunity/

Were Ferguson to magically go back to its demographic breakdown in 1990 (73 percent white versus 27 percent white today), the neighborhoods currently "blighted" by a 67 percent black population could be restored; property value would magically increase; tax-revenue would grow, meaning streets would be paved and parks would be improved for children to enjoy the outdoors; and precious Walmart would return.

Now, blacks have threatened the city of St. Louis (giving new weight to the term black-mail) with massive violence if the lynching of Darren Wilson - you know, the man who executed angelic Michael Brown in cold blood - doesn't commence soon. [Fury of Ferguson descends on St. Louis County Council, St. Louis Post-Dispatch, 9-17-14]:

> "If Darren Wilson gets off, you all better bring every army you all have got. 'Cause it's going down," said one speaker.
>
> The fury of Ferguson descended on the seat of St. Louis County with a vengeance Tuesday night with demonstrators unleashing a torrent of chants, invective and threats at a County Council that listened for two hours in stunned silence.
>
> Protesters demanded the arrest of Darren Wilson, the police officer who shot 18-year-old Michael Brown to death on a Ferguson street five weeks ago, the removal of County Prosecutor Robert McCulloch from the Brown case, the resignations of County Police Chief Jon Belmar and Ferguson Police Chief Thomas Jackson and accountability from the elected county legislative arm.
>
> Council Chairwoman Hazel Erby twice threatened to end the meeting prematurely if the demonstrators — who interrupted speakers, including eight residents appealing to the council on zoning and other matters — didn't cease.
>
> Undeterred, the audience loudly cheered speakers who likened Wilson and other law enforcement officials to "war criminals," compared St. Louis County government to the Ku Klux Klan and drew analogies between the St. Louis region and Jim Crow laws.

> "You are ISIS to black people," one speaker told council members.
>
> The audience jeered a woman who voiced support for the police. She received a police escort from the building after the meeting.
>
> Speakers also threatened to shut down St. Louis Cardinals and Rams games this Sunday, disrupt weekend grocery shopping trips throughout the area and mount massive demonstrations if the Cardinals reach the World Series.
>
> Lastly came the foreshadowing of further violence if Wilson is not charged and convicted.
>
> "If Darren Wilson gets off, you all better bring every army you all have got. 'Cause it's going down," said one speaker.[141]

"If Darren Wilson gets off, you all better bring every army you all have got. 'Cause it's going down."

Oh, but it already went "down."

Recall, the black insurrection in Ferguson required a military-style response because the first night of lawlessness nearly saw innocent employees of a QuikTrip executed.[142] ["Snitches Get Stitches" message spray painted on burned-out QuikTrip, Fox2Now.com, 8-11-14]:

> An employee who was working the Quik Trip that was looted and burned told a terrifying story of survival. The 18 year old man didn't want to be identified but he did say, "Terrifying very, very, terrifying. Madden says: tell me what was going through your mind. Worker: I thought I was going to die tonight, I really thought I was going to die tonight.
>
> His mother added, "I'm very thankful that he's alright."

---

[141] http://www.stltoday.com/news/local/fury-of-ferguson-descends-on-st-louis-county-council/article_ca03267a-d87e-5399-9bd0-3bb95b50339f.html

[142] http://stlouis.cbslocal.com/2014/08/11/quiktrip-employee-workers-hid-in-back-room-as-ferguson-store-was-looted-set-on-fire/

The worker said he was at the register when the looters rushed the store. He and his two fellow workers locked themselves in a back room. One signaled the company's alarm system. They got a phone call telling them to stay put, that the police were on the way. But after ten or twenty minutes they decided it was best to escape, fortunately before the fire started.

The workers said, "One of the employees said we can get a way out of here and so we grabbed jackets to cover our uniform and we ran out of there, out the back door."

He said when he got outside he could see the looters keeping police at bay. He was glad he did not stay put and he was told to do, "If we would have stayed put we would have died."[143]

The black insurrection in Ferguson saw scores of business looted, but the real violence started immediately succeeding the lethal encounter between Officer Darren Wilson and Michael Brown. Multiple gun shots were fired by the irate black crowd at the police who gathered around the lifeless of Brown, in the already economically lifeless (remember, there's no Walmart!) city of Ferguson.[144]

The scene was so intense, it took hours before the funeral home director[145] dispatched to claim Brown's body could finish his job. [Why was Michael Brown's body left there for hours?, St. Louis Post-Dispatch, 9-14-14]:

'KILL THE POLICE'

A St. Louis County first precinct dispatcher was initially bewildered by the requests for backup. "We just called Ferguson back again, and they don't know anything about it,"

---

[143] http://fox2now.com/2014/08/11/quiktrip-sprayed-with-graffiti-set-on-fire-during-overnight-looting-near-ferguson/

[144] http://fox2now.com/2014/08/10/report-michael-brown-protesters-damage-police-vehicles-on-west-florissant/

[145] http://fox4kc.com/2014/09/08/funeral-director-explains-why-it-took-so-long-to-remove-michael-browns-body-from-street/

she said at one point.

A Ferguson dispatcher first told the ambulance district someone had been Tased.But at 12:10 p.m., county police began to flood the scene with cars: By 1 p.m., they had dispatched more than a dozen units, according to the county log. By 2 p.m., a dozen more, including two with police dogs.

And the scene was about to get much more turbulent.

At 2:11 p.m., Ferguson police logs captured reports of shots fired. At 2:14 p.m., ambulance dispatch noted additional gunshots, then a Code 1000, calling all available jurisdictions to help. Over the next 20 minutes, the first precinct dispatched more than 20 units from at least eight different municipal forces, from Bel-Ridge to St. John to Velda City.

At some point, Chief Jackson said he urged crime scene detectives to hurry up their work. "We've got to expedite," Jackson said he told them. "They said, 'OK, we're expediting.' But then we had a shooting over here, crowd's coming in, and it's really not secure there."

About 2:30 p.m., Calvin Whitaker, the livery service driver, arrived to pick up Brown's body. One end of Canfield was blocked off by police and emergency vehicles. At the other end, a crowd stood in his way. "They were screaming, 'Let's kill the police,'" he said. People flung water bottles at his black SUV, he said, cussed at his wife and called them murderers.

A police officer told them to stay in the car. "You guys do not have vests," he told them. "The best thing for you to do is get down." Whitaker and his wife reclined their seats and hunkered down.

Police dogs, newly arrived, pushed the crowd back some, Jackson said. But when the dogs stepped back, the crowd surged forward, he said, even angrier than before. Jackson began to circle the perimeter with Brown's mother.

McSpadden pleaded with the crowd, Whitaker said. "'All I want them to do is pick up my baby,'" he remembers her saying. "'Please respect him. Please move back.'

She would get a crowd moved back, and then another group would move up."

The scene was so tense, commanders in charge stopped the investigation at points and directed investigators to seek cover. Detectives also were pulled away to help manage the crowd.

At 2:45 p.m., four more canine units arrived. At 3:20 p.m., tactical operations officers — the county SWAT team — began pulling in

Finally, about 4 p.m., police officers gave the medical examiner investigator, then Whitaker and his wife, the go-ahead to take Brown's body to the morgue.

Whitaker moved behind the barriers that had eventually been put up around the body. Police stood shoulder to shoulder alongside Whitaker's cot and lined the path to his vehicle holding up sheets to block the public's view.

Whitaker, 42, said he has transported hundreds of bodies over the years under contract with the city of St. Louis and St. Louis County. "That is the worst situation I've ever been in," he said.[146]

Put Stephen King, Robert Kirkman (creator of *The Walking Dead*), and George Romero in a room and these writers of horror would be incapable of replicating the frightening reality that Ferguson has exposed since the events of August 10th.

In a country where the rule of law has collapsed into a scenario of "whatever the black man demands, will be our command" mindset, the lawlessness of Ferguson exposes the truth behind preppers addiction to preparing for the end of civilization; in the heartland of America, we see the seeds of civilizations demise already producing an inhuman crop of insurrectionists, unaccountable to any law of the

---

[146] http://www.stltoday.com/news/local/crime-and-courts/why-was-michael-brown-s-body-left-there-for-hours/article_0b73ec58-c6a1-516e-882f-74d18a4246e0.html

already dispossessed white man. [New Black Panther Leader: Officer Darren Wilson Wanted "Dead or Alive", Gateway Pundit, 9-14-14][147]

And those few business owners remaining behind enemy lines in 67 percent black Ferguson know better than to rebuild from the looted and broken buildings housing their meal ticket. [In Ferguson, still-boarded windows signal fears of more trouble, St. Louis Post-Dispatch, 9-14-14]:

> Looters who broke into John Zisser's tire store on the first night of rioting in Ferguson cost him about $100,000 in damage and lost merchandise.
>
> That included $30,000 to replace a dozen 9-foot-tall windows and several glass doors.
>
> Zisser has restocked the tires, wheels and other goods. But he has not replaced the windows.
>
> "What's the hurry?" he said last week. "Everyone knows it's foolish to do anything before the grand jury comes back."
>
> Zisser and owners of other riot-ravaged businesses in the Ferguson area are looking toward a St. Louis County grand jury like forecasters eyeing a gathering storm.
>
> On Tuesday, Adolphus Pruitt, St. Louis head of the NAACP, spoke at a news conference in Ferguson where community activists and religious leaders demanded Wilson's immediate arrest. "We are not going to be satisfied with a nonindictment," Pruitt said.
>
> On Wednesday, Pruitt elaborated.
>
> "A nonindictment from St. Louis County does not have to be the final say. A second grand jury can be impaneled. There can be a subsequent federal or state investigation. We need to get that message out to the protesters between now and the grand jury's ruling," he said.

---

[147] http://www.thegatewaypundit.com/2014/09/new-black-panther-leader-officer-darren-wilson-wanted-dead-or-alive/

But Pruitt also has heard the word on the street.

"If Wilson is not indicted, we are going to have our hands full in trying to maintain civility. Folks are going to go back on the street, and they are going to react to their despair, at least in the short term. That discussion is resonating, and I have heard it."

Zisser, 54, of Kirkwood, has owned and operated Zisser Tire and Auto Repair on West Florissant Avenue in Dellwood since 1987. He put the prospect of a nonindictment in blunt terms.

"Everyone around here knows that if that grand jury doesn't indict that cop, it will make the previous riots look like a cakewalk," he said.

Not a window was broken at the bar on Chambers Road, but owner Toni Downs is playing it safe.

"My insurance agent told me that looting is considered terrorism, and my policy didn't cover terrorism," Downs, 58, of Ferguson, said last week.

Downs said that nearby business owners have confided in her that if rioting resumes, they will not stand idly by.

"I think you're going to see people with guns guarding their businesses next time," she said.[148]

"My insurance agent told me that looting is considered terrorism, and my policy didn't cover terrorism."

To answer Gunny's question as to why 67 percent black Ferguson will never, ever be rebuilt (unless whites return in sufficient numbers to price Section 8 Voucher holding blacks out): business owners can't operate in a war zone, where Plexiglas isn't sufficient in ensuring their investment.

---

[148] http://www.stltoday.com/news/local/metro/in-ferguson-still-boarded-windows-signal-fears-of-more-trouble/article_ae95966d-b87d-53c6-9345-7d03e0b4b8d0.html

Terrorism.

This is what is breaking out in America's heartland.

A black insurrection.

"It's gonna be hell to pay.." if you don't rebuild and, "If Darren Wilson gets off, you all better bring every army you all have got. 'Cause it's going down."

Why be worried about ISIS?

According to Toni Downs insurance company, the real terrorists threatening not just America's economic vitality, but actual existence as a nation (where the rule of law survives) are already here.

September 18, 2014
What the Black Man Demands, Becomes Our Command
Capitulation.

Surrender.

Raid a QuikTrip and then burn it down, the state will inevitably bow down to your demands. [Nixon creates 'Office of Community Engagement' in wake of Ferguson, St. Louis Post-Dispatch, 9-18-14]:

> Gov. Jay Nixon today announced the creation of a state "Office of Community Engagement," which will focus on issues in minority and low-income communities in the wake of the Ferguson riots.
>
> Nixon appointed former Missouri state Sen. Maida Coleman as director of the new office. Former St. Louis City Municipal Judge Marvin Teer was appointed deputy director and general counsel.
>
> Coleman will be paid $120,000 annually and Teer will be

paid $110,000 annually.

> "Across our state, Missouri communities are facing serious issues involving race, educational and economic opportunities, and poverty," Nixon said in a written statement. The new office, he said, "will be responsible for facilitating meaningful communication about these issues that will yield concrete results ... and help to develop specific policies to address them."
>
> Under an executive order Nixon signed today, the new office will be housed within the state Office of Administration. Its duties will include "engaging communities, public and private sector leaders, clergy and citizens across the state in communication regarding critical issues affecting Missouri communities," according to the statement.
>
> The new office may make recommendations to the state Department of Economic Development, Missouri Community Service Commission, Missouri Housing Development Commission and other boards, commissions and agencies that administer programs designed to assist low-income individuals.[149]

Why might certain Missouri communities [black] be facing serious issues involving race, educational and economic opportunities, and poverty? Perhaps two stories from the past six years in St. Louis will help illustrate why the Office of Community Engagement is destined for failure. [Black leaders in St. Louis to recruit 'street teams' in anti-crime campaign, Missourian, 6-8-2008]:

> Black leaders who organized an anti-crime march that drew tens of thousands last weekend in St. Louis said Thursday they have begun recruiting "street teams" to mobilize in high-crime neighborhoods.
>
> Teams of men, including former gang members, will be

---

[149] http://www.stltoday.com/news/local/crime-and-courts/nixon-creates-office-of-community-engagement-in-wake-of-ferguson/article_b8896a73-510d-5ac2-ba73-2b6df60d04a8.html

assigned a city neighborhood to visit regularly for "real talk" with youth about teen pregnancy, drugs and gang violence, and to be role models for the rewards of education and employment. They'll also encourage residents to report crimes and suspicious behavior to police.

Other plans call for partnering with other groups to mentor young people, and holding regular neighborhood summits to get residents tackling their problems.

"We want to liberate our community, and help them know themselves," said Bishop Courtney Jones of Full Gospel Baptist Church Fellowship.

"Our kids like to talk real talk," Jones said. "We'll talk to them about having six or seven babies, the need for child support and the effects of drugs. This won't be surface stuff."

The announcement follows Sunday's much publicized black men's march in St. Louis to protest violence, especially black-on-black crime and the social ills that feed it.

The march was the launch for a plan dubbed "Call to Oneness" that black ministers, businessmen and community leaders have been working on since February. Its aim is to reduce crime and violence and resurrect struggling city neighborhoods.

The march succeeded in getting people's attention and demonstrated the black community is not complacent about its problems, said the Rev. F. James Clark of Shalom Church in Florissant, who heads the "Oneness" campaign.

Now, it's time to inspire and recruit people to get involved. At a meeting Monday night, the response was overwhelming, Jones said.

"This is not magic," Clark said. "This is going to take a whole lot of hard work." He added, don't expect results overnight. "We're in this for the long haul."[150]

---

[150] http://www.columbiamissourian.com/a/103427/black-leaders-in-st-louis-to-recruit-street-teams-in-anti-crime-campaign/

Has sustained violence in a majority white area ever necessitated the need for a march by whites to mandate the creation of a "Oneness" campaign?

No.

But perhaps this story will explain why poverty and a lack of economic opportunity exist in the majority black areas of St. Louis. [Thieves Cart Off St. Louis Bricks, New York Times, 9-19-2010]:

> By the time Raymond Feemster awoke to the pounding of firefighters at his door, flames were already licking his shotgun-style home. The vacant house next door, which neighbors said was frequented by squatters, had burst into flames and was now threatening to engulf houses on each side.
>
> Mr. Feemster, who gets around on an electric scooter, had to be carried out of the burning building, but today he considers himself lucky that the damage was contained to just two rooms.
>
> "My neighbor's house was completely destroyed," said Mr. Feemster, 58. "I guess it was one of the crackheads in that vacant house."
>
> Perhaps. But the blaze, one of 391 fires at vacant buildings in the city over the past two years, may have had a more sinister cause. Law enforcement officials, politicians and historic preservationists here have concluded that brick thieves are often to blame, deliberately torching buildings to quicken their harvest of St. Louis brick, prized by developers throughout the South for its distinctive character.
>
> "The firemen come and hose them down and shoot all that mortar off with the high-pressure hose," said Alderman Samuel Moore, whose predominantly black Fourth Ward has been hit particularly hard by brick thieves. When a thief goes to pick up the bricks after a fire, "They're just laying there nice and clean."
>
> It is a crime that has increased with the recession. Where

thieves in many cities harvest copper, aluminum and other materials from vacant buildings, brick rustling has emerged more recently as a sort of scrapper's endgame, exploited once the rest of a building's architectural elements have been exhausted. "Cleveland is suffering from this," said Royce Yeater, Midwest director for the National Trust for Historic Preservation. "I've also heard of it happening in Detroit."

After the fire that devastated much of St. Louis in 1849, city leaders passed an ordinance requiring all new buildings to be made of noncombustible material. That law, along with the rich clays of eastern Missouri, led to a flourishing brick industry here. Historians say that at the industry's height, around 1900, the city had more than 100 manufacturing plants, and St. Louis became known for the quality, craftsmanship and abundance of its brick.

"They love it in New Orleans and the South — wherever they're rebuilding, they want it because it's beautiful brick," said Barbara Buck, who owns Century Used Brick. "It really gives the building a dimension, a fingerprint."

Mr. Moore, who is drafting a bill that would increase the penalties for brick theft, said that while many thieves still used cables and picks to collapse a wall, arson had become the tool of choice. Thieves even set fire to wood-frame homes to create a diversion. Firefighters often knock down walls, making it easier for thieves to harvest the bricks.

"The whole block is gone — they stole the whole block," Mr. Moore marveled as he drove his white Dodge Magnum through his ward's motley collection of dilapidated homes and vacant lots. "They're stealing entire buildings, buildings that belong to the city. Where else in the world do you steal an entire city building?"

There are more than 8,000 vacant buildings in St. Louis, and more than 11,000 vacant lots.

The maximum penalty for brick theft here is a $500 fine or 90 days in jail or both. The city police said there were 34 brick-related thefts in the last year.

"You see these guys with mortar dust all over them, and they're stacking on a pallet, and they'll say, 'I'm just a day laborer working for that guy over there — whoa, where did he go?' " said Maribeth McMahon, a lawyer with the city counselor's office. "So this poor stiff, who's just trying to earn an hourly wage, gets a summons."

Ms. Buck, who said thieves often arrived at her brickyard with "bricks in the trunk of a Lexus," said she followed city ordinance and required brick vendors to produce a demolition permit to sell their bricks. A pallet of 500 goes for roughly $100, she said, but other less scrupulous buyers do not require permits.

Ms. Buck estimates that as many as eight tractor-trailer loads of stolen bricks leave the city each week for Florida, Louisiana or Texas, because "St. Louis brick is in such high demand."

The toll on the city's struggling north side has been particularly heavy. During a hard-luck tour of his ward last week, Mr. Moore pointed out several piles of rubble where houses once stood.[151]

Capitulation.

Surrender.

To a people willingly burning down the memory of what whites built in St. Louis; who can never hope to replicate what whites built in starting in 1849.

What the Black Man Demands, Becomes Our Command.

---

[151] http://www.nytimes.com/2010/09/20/us/20brick.html?_r=1&

September 21, 2014
"This is for Michael Brown," Scream Two Black Males in St. Louis as they rob Six Elderly Whites

You'll never see this story on CNN.

You'll never even see this story on Fox News. [Gunmen mentions Michael Brown as he robs three couples leaving a restaurant, St. Louis Post-Dispatch, 9-21-14]:

> St. Louis Metropolitan Police are investigating an armed robbery of six people who were walking from a restaurant in the 1100 block of Mississippi Avenue at 11:11 p.m. on Saturday.
>
> Police said the three couples, all of them from 59 to 61 years old, had just left a restaurant and were walking north on the west side of Mississippi when they were approached by two men. One of the men pointed a silver gun at the group and demanded their belongings.
>
> After the second man grabbed items from the group, the first man said, "This is for Michael Brown," according to a police account. Both men then fled on foot.
>
> One man was described at thin build about 5-feet-7 inches tall wearing a white tank top and blue jeans with medium length twisted braids armed with a small silver handgun.
>
> The other man also had a thin build and was about 5-feet-8 inches tall, wearing all black clothing and a black ski mask. Both were black men in their early 20s.
>
> Anyone who may have information regarding the armed robberies are asked to call CrimeStoppers anonymously at

866-371-8477.[152]

September 24, 2014
There's Always Something There to Remind Me...

A "sacred site" to some people...[Ferguson residents rebuild Michael Brown memorial after fire, St. Louis Post-Dispatch, 9-24-14]:

> The last thing this city needed was another flash point, but it got one early Tuesday when one of two Michael Brown memorials burned.
>
> Like the shooting of a black teenager by a white cop that inspired the shrine, its destruction touched off anger and controversy.
>
> Memorial items had been arranged near a concrete light post along Canfield Drive, where Brown was shot. A larger memorial several feet away, in the middle of the street, where Brown died, was not damaged.
>
> Rumors coursed through an outraged crowd of about 100 who gathered at the scene early Tuesday that an outsider had intentionally set the blaze.
>
> "There is no doubt about it," said David Whitt, 34, leader of a group of activists who call themselves the Canfield Watchmen. "Someone waited until everyone was asleep and set it on fire."
>
> Terrell Marshall, of Ferguson, said nothing was amiss when he drove past at 5 a.m., but when he drove by again at 6 a.m., the memorial was fully engulfed.
>
> Markese Mull, 39, who lives in the nearby Canfield Green

---

[152] http://www.stltoday.com/news/gunmen-mentions-michael-brown-as-he-robs-three-couples-leaving/article_d711821e-f3a9-513b-b942-64bab194c683.html

apartments, said several police cars arrived around 6:45 a.m., and "one cop got out and tried to stomp it out."

Eventually, Ferguson firefighters doused the flames.

By 8 a.m., the collection of stuffed animals, baseball caps, Michael Brown posters, apparel, votive candle jars and dead flowers was reduced to a heap of ashes.

For weeks after the shooting of Brown by Ferguson police Officer Darren Wilson, burning candles have been part of the memorials. Empty, overturned votive candle jars were lying next to the burn site. Pools of melted wax had hardened around the shrines.

But Whitt and others angrily discounted the possibility that a tipped-over candle was to blame. "There is no way a candle did this; someone used gasoline," Whitt said.

Others said they had smelled gasoline while the fire was burning.

One resident collected ashes in bags, but Whitt said his group would not allow police to examine the scene.

"They had their chance this morning, but they left," he said. "If they were to come back, they would just say, 'The scene is compromised now.'

"It doesn't matter anyway. We don't trust them. This is our home and we don't want them here."

In a press release, Police Chief Thomas Jackson said the cause of the fire is unknown and under investigation. He asked that anyone with information, or photos or videos of the fire starting, contact police. By noon Tuesday, residents had rebuilt the shrine with a blanket, a new collection of stuffed animals, T-shirts, flowers and several unlit votive candles next to the soot-stained pole.

About 75 people gathered, joined hands and prayed. They ended by raising their hands and shouting "We are Mike Brown," and, "We're young, we're strong, we're marching all day long."

The memorials have attracted a steady stream of visitors since Brown's death on Aug. 9. Some just cruise slowly past in vehicles. Others park and approach the sites.

Roslyn Howard, 27, and Charisma Alexander, 29, both of Ferguson, visited last week. "She was curious about it, so I said, 'Let's stop by and say a prayer,'" Howard said.

They joined another visitor, Lakresha Moore, of Ferguson. The three held hands, bowed their heads and prayed before wiping at tears and returning to their cars.

Earlier, Bill and Ellen Hirzy, of Washington, D.C., took time out from visiting family in St. Louis to pay their respects.

Ellen Hirzy, 65, said, "I woke up this morning and said, 'I have to get over here.' I believe in making pilgrimages. At a place like this, you can absorb what happened."
Like many others who paused or prayed there, her husband was overcome with emotion.

"To think about what happened here," Bill Hirzy, 78, a retired chemist, said as he dabbed at tears. "There's a spiritual feelin about this place." "Instead of a stain on the pavement, Michael Brown needs to be a mark on history," Mull said.

Like others along Canfield Drive, Mull said he worries about the future of the makeshift memorials.

"This has become a sacred site for people here. We're afraid the city will send a truck some night and just scrape it off the street," he said.[153]

Michael Brown attacked a cop, after strong-arm robbing some immigrant for a few score worth of Swisher Sweets.

And he's a hero to a people incapable of assimilating to the society

---

[153] http://www.stltoday.com/news/local/metro/ferguson-residents-rebuild-michael-brown-memorial-after-fire/article_e8e2f039-4fd0-5c0a-ae04-474f4b1df194.html

white people once built in Ferguson (remember, the city was 99 percent white in 1970...).

You can bet tonight will be an interesting one in the St. Louis metropolitan area, the heartland of America.

September 26, 2014
K-K-K-Mart – Company to Close "Underperforming" Store in 67% Black Ferguson (Courtesy of an "Underperforming" Population)

One day, people will look on the events of Ferguson in roughly August - December 2014 and wonder why decent people ever put up with a population who sided with a strong-armed robbing, police attacking thug and continued to believe magically Republicans would ever stand up the insanity of the Department of Justice. [Federal investigators discuss Ferguson investigation, St. Louis Post-Dispatch, 9-24-14]:

> U.S. Department of Justice officials promised a frustrated group of Ferguson residents Wednesday night that the federal government will take seriously their allegations of racial profiling and brutality at the hands of north St. Louis County law enforcement.
>
> More than 300 people packed into a meeting room at St. Louis Community College at Florissant Valley for an update on the federal civil rights investigation Attorney General Eric Holder announced this month in the wake of the fatal shooting Aug. 9 of Michael Brown by Ferguson police Officer Darren Wilson.
>
> Holder said the Justice Department's Civil Rights Division will investigate whether Ferguson police have engaged in a pattern of civil rights violations.

Christy Lopez, a Justice Department deputy counsel, reiterated that point Wednesday in front of a mostly calm crowd.

The point of the meeting was to give an update on the Justice Department's investigation and give residents a chance to share their stories with federal investigators in one-on-one sessions.

"We are here to address patterns or practices of police misconduct," Lopez said. She said investigators are looking at "whether people's constitutional rights are being violated on a regular basis."

Much to the frustration of many in the audience, Lopez did not say much about whether the Justice Department was looking specifically into potential misconduct by Wilson.

"We cannot promise a federal indictment, but we can promise a federal investigation," she said.

That wasn't good enough for many people in the crowd.

Jammian Weaver, 35, of the Spanish Lake area, left before the one-on-one sessions.

Weaver, who said police roughed him up as a teenager when he was walking home from work, said he was skeptical of the Justice Department.

"I got no satisfaction tonight," he said. "I wanted to hear answers, and I didn't get that."

Bobby Johnson, 24, of University City, said he was hoping to hear more of what might happen to Wilson.

"If that was me that shot somebody who is unarmed, I'd be arrested on capital murder right away," Johnson said. "I want to know why police get special protection."[154]

---

[154] http://www.stltoday.com/news/local/metro/federal-investigators-discuss-ferguson-investigation/article_73b4c5fb-dab4-514a-90e8-3b8207785b03.html

> *"We cannot promise a federal indictment, but we can promise a federal investigation.."*

A federal investigation into what? Perhaps... why K-Mart is closing its store in 67 percent black Ferguson (obviously, a crushing blow to the civil rights of black people to mandate a business be forced to stay in open in an area where the preferred method of payment is EBT/Food Stamps). [Kmart to close store near Florissant, St. Louis Post-Dispatch, 9-25-14]:

> The Kmart store near Florissant will close as part of what the retailer said Thursday is its latest effort to cut costs by shutting down underperforming stores.
>
> A liquidation sale will begin Sunday and the store, located at 2855 Dunn Road, will close in early December, Howard Riefs, a company spokesman, said in a statement.
>
> About 100 employees, most hourly or part-time workers, are affected.
>
> The store is just off West Florissant Avenue, about 2 miles north of the QuikTrip store that looters ransacked and burned after a Ferguson police officer shot and killed unarmed teenager Michael Brown on Aug. 9.
>
> The store is within an 868.5-acre commercial and residential area Ferguson is proposing to annex. The Ferguson City Council approved the proposal in June, then submitted it to the St. Louis County Boundary Commission for consideration. If supported by the commission, the proposal would be submitted for approval by Ferguson voters and voters in the annexation area, which is north of Interstate 270.
>
> Riefs said in an email that Kmart's decision to close the Florissant store was "unrelated to any local events."
>
> "The store was underperforming," he said.
>
> The store opened in October 1998 in what had been a Venture store.
>
> No other Kmart stores in the St. Louis area, Southern Illinois

or the rest of Missouri are facing immediate closure, the company said. Earlier this year, Kmart announced closure of its stores in Collinsville and Ellisville.[155]

A publicly-held corporation should never be allowed to make a rational business decision and close the doors of a store failing to make a profit, if such a closing negatively impacts the black community (never mind the black community was the source of the store being in the financial red... instead of the financial black).

So... when will a federal investigation by the Department of Justice be launched into the pattern of businesses shuttering their doors in communities no longer reflecting the one they were originally intending to serve (recall, Ferguson was roughly 45 - 50 percent white in 1998)?

September 27, 2014
"Two Hand Touch" Was Never the Game

And so, the die is cast. If you understand what this article means, you understand the future is now.

The present dictates the future.

No article, no speech, no action can outline what's coming more clearly than this...[DOJ asks Ferguson chief to stop police from wearing 'I am Darren Wilson' bracelets on duty, St. Louis Post-Dispatch, 9-27-14]:

> The U.S. Department of Justice asked Ferguson Police Chief Thomas Jackson on Friday to prohibit police officers from wearing "I am Darren Wilson" bracelets while on duty in Ferguson.

---

[155] http://www.stltoday.com/business/local/kmart-to-close-store-near-florissant/article_4aa5f1ed-7296-58d1-8c1f-58025e984d8e.html

Christy Lopez, a deputy chief in the Civil Rights Division, told Jackson in a letter that residents had photos of officers, from unknown local agencies, wearing the bracelets.

"We are keenly aware of the importance of individual expression of opinions, even those that some find offensive, insensitive, or harmful," Lopez said in the letter.

However, she continued, "these bracelets reinforce the very 'us versus them' mentality that many residents of Ferguson believe exists."

This is at least the second letter from Lopez to Jackson this week. The first, dated Tuesday, urged Jackson to enforce department policies requiring officers to wear nametags.

"The lack of name plates," she wrote, "makes it difficult or impossible for members of the public to identify officers if they engage in misconduct, or for police departments to hold them accountable."

Jackson could not immediately be reached for comment about the requests.[156]

It is Us vs. Them.

It's always been that way.

It's just few people ever dared contemplate what 'us versus them' meant...

This game is not friendly.

It's not "two-hand touch."

The game is simply "Stand With Michael Brown" or else...

---

[156] http://www.stltoday.com/news/local/crime-and-courts/doj-asks-ferguson-chief-to-stop-police-from-wearing-i/article_a2cfe060-6252-5fa6-8639-6715f643c8f4.html

September 29, 2014
Most Iconic Photo from the Black Insurrection in Ferguson: Yelling "who's streets?!" to Ferguson police...

Weakness.

Cowardice.

Pusillanimity.

In the animal kingdom, a display of these traits - to a predator - represent grounds for immediate, unrelenting attack.

Easy prey. [In a Video, Police Chief of Ferguson Apologizes, New York Times, 9-25-14]:

> Chief Thomas Jackson of the police force in Ferguson, Mo., issued a stark apology to the family of Michael Brown on Thursday, saying in a videotaped statement that he was sorry for the death of their son and for the four hours that the body of the unarmed 18-year-old lay in the street after he was fatally shot by a police officer.
>
> In the video, released by a public relations firm nearly seven weeks after the shooting, Chief Jackson spoke for about two and a half minutes, occasionally glancing down at notes in his hand. He was not in police uniform but rather a reddish-pink polo shirt.
>
> "I want to say this to the Brown family. No one who has not experienced the loss of a child can understand what you're feeling," he said, facing the camera and standing in front of an American flag. "I am truly sorry for the loss of your son. I'm also sorry that it took so long to remove Michael from the street. The time that it took involved very important work on the part of investigators who were trying to collect evidence and gain a true picture of what happened that day. But it was

just too long, and I'm truly sorry for that."

He also extended his apology to African-Americans in Ferguson, who have accused the police department of racial profiling and mistreatment.

"I'm also aware of the pain and the feeling of mistrust felt in some of the African-American community toward the police department," Chief Jackson said. "The city belongs to all of us, and we're all part of this community. It is clear that we have much work to do. As a community, a city and a nation, we have real problems to solve."[157]

Michael Brown's parents, the odd couple of Michael Brown Sr. and Lesley McSpadden, were "unmoved" by this public display of cowardice and capitulation to the black mob. They want Officer Darren Wilson "in handcuffs."[158]
Weakness.

Cowardice.

Pusillanimity.

The results?

A black population holding all the cards on the monopoly on violence. [Shots fired at off-duty officer on I-70; suspects on the loose, FOX2Now, 9-28-14]:

> An off-duty St. Louis city police officer was shot at early Sunday morning on Interstate 70.
>
> Around 12:20 a.m., the officer was on I-70 near I-170 when three black male suspects fired shots into his personal car.
>
> The officer was hit by glass and suffered an injury to his arm. Police say the officer did not shoot back. The three suspects

---

[157] http://www.nytimes.com/2014/09/26/us/ferguson-police-chief-apology-michael-brown.html?_r=0

[158] http://www.ksdk.com/story/news/local/2014/09/27/brown-parents-unmoved-jackson-apology/16342191/

fled the scene in a black sedan.[159]

"... the officer did not shoot back."

In St. Louis, with the rate of black crime and black hatred of police, the odds are high a white officer of the law will fire back on a black suspect.
And it might be much, much sooner than anyone wants to admit. [8 protesters arrested outside of Ferguson Police Dept., FOX2Now.com, 9-29-14]:

> Moments became tense in Ferguson Sunday night as several people were arrested outside of the Ferguson Police Department. The arrests were a part of the latest round of protests over the shooting death of 18-year-old Michael Brown.
>
> Authorities say a total of eight people were taken into custody. They were charged with failing to disperse and resisting arrest.
>
> Nearly 150 people were protesting. According to a Ferguson police official, that crowd would not leave South Florissant Road.
>
> Ferguson police put out a call for back up around 10 p.m. after bottles and rocks were reportedly thrown at officers. County police, highway patrol, and officers from other municipalities responded.
>
> About an hour or so later, the arrests took place.[160]

Weakness.

Cowardice.

Pusillanimity.

---

[159] http://fox2now.com/2014/09/28/st-louis-city-officer-shot-at-on-i-70/

[160] http://fox2now.com/2014/09/29/8-protesters-arrested-outside-of-ferguson-police-dept/

The results?

Rocks and bottles being thrown at police, and gunshots being fired in their direction, all because the monopoly on violence is no longer in the hands of the state; the black insurrectionists have usurped this vise on violence.

At this Sept. 28 black display of power in Ferguson, a *Washington Post* writer/contributor named Robert Samuels "tweeted" a picture of menacing, thuggish, brutish blacks taunting a white police officer. It includes a caption that tragically captures the reality of life in 67 percent black Ferguson, where white police officers were left behind (by white flight) to try and keep alive/protect the civilization whites abandoned:

> Yelling "who's streets?!" To #ferguson police[161]

Weakness.

Cowardice.

Pusillanimity.

The results?

Detroit in 2014, the same situation Ferguson will find itself in by 2016 at the earliest.

---

[161] https://twitter.com/newsbysamuels/status/516423173223776256

October 1, 2014
The Bell [Curve] Tolls for St. Louis

Twenty years ago was 1994.
What a different country.

What a different world.

Back in 1990, Philadelphia experimented with Norplant to reduce the black underclass.[162]

Back in 1993, Baltimore experimented with Norplant to reduce the black underclass.[163]

Movies of white men standing up to injustice, violence, and the agents of decay were released, with 1993 seeing both *Falling Down* and *Tombstone* hit theaters.

But in 1994 it was the release of one simple book that literally set the country on fire, for it dared submit a theory as to why inequality persisted that could be smelled in the smoldering ruins of the QuikTrip in Ferguson, Missouri.

Transformed from a dispensary of sugary/high calorie goods with only the swipe of the EBT/Food Stamp Card (named the Missouri EBT Card) to the staging ground of the black insurgency in Ferguson - where Rev. Cecil Rogers made "daily pilgrimages"[164] to visit - it is

---

[162] http://articles.philly.com/1990-12-12/news/25920681_1_black-children-norplant-black-middle-class

[163] http://articles.baltimoresun.com/1993-10-01/news/1993274047_1_norplant-school-clinics-baltimore-school

[164] http://www.stltoday.com/news/local/crime-and-courts/burned-out-quiktrip-being-put-off-limits-as-ferguson-gathering/article_5c61c54f-1611-599f-b495-491858612597.html

the ruins of the Quiktrip that give life to the infamous chapter 13 of *The Bell Curve: Intelligence and Class Structure in America*.

Richard Herrnstein and Charles Murray wrote in the introduction to Chapter 13 these words:

> "The debate about whether and how much genes and environment have to do with ethnic differences remains unresolved."

The racial unrest in Ferguson and St. Louis put bed this debate, as the metropolitan area is a living, breathing experiment confirming a Darwinian Truth so obvious it scarcely needs reminding what line in *The Bell Curve* (from chapter 13) came to life during the black insurrection of August 2014:

> "It seems highly likely to us that both genes and the environment have something to do with racial differences."

You see, the QuikTrip in Ferguson is *The Bell Curve* personified, a monument to the real "Bell Curve Wars" playing out across all of America. "Snitches Get Stitches" was spray painted on the ruins of the QuikTrip, a reminder of the genetic and environmental realities behind the racial differences dividing whites and blacks in St. Louis. ["Snitches Get Stitches" message spray painted on burned-out QuikTrip, Fox2Now.com, 8-11-14][165]

The remains of the QuikTrip became holy ground for the black insurgents, but for those curious enough to desire seeing a real-life re-enactment of chapter 13 of The Bell Curve, a quick glance in the direction of the insanity originating from there in August 2014 would be all the evidence necessary to confirm Murray and Herrnstein's theory. [The QuikTrip gas station, Ferguson protesters' staging ground, is now silent, Washington Post, 8-19-14]:

> "This is our place. This is what we've got," Maria Chappelle-Nadal, a state senator who has been central in staging many of the daytime protests, said during an interview outside of the QuikTrip this week. This was their Tahrir Square, their

---

[165] http://fox2now.com/2014/08/11/quiktrip-sprayed-with-graffiti-set-on-fire-during-overnight-looting-near-ferguson/

Tiananmen Square. The place each night where they would make their stand.

"These people have no other place, so they've made it their own," said Chappelle-Nadal.

On the large metal post that once displayed the red and white QT logo, one person spray-painted "The QT People's Park. Liberated 8/10/14."[166]

But the burning of the QuikTrip (where a black family cleaning the debris of the store where chastised by other blacks with shouts of you "shouldn't be helping the white man," [Volunteers Clean Up at Ferguson QuikTrip, Get Yelled At for "Helping the White Man", RiverFrontTimes.com, 8-12-14])[167] represented "pushback" against the encroaching reality of the Bell Curve's truth behind the demise of once prospering Ferguson (99 percent white in 1970 versus 27 percent white today) into just another micro-Detroit. [This Looted QuikTrip Represents St. Louis's Racial Inequality, New Republic, 8-14-14]:

> The social and economic reality of St. Louis is pretty simple. Prosperity is white, and poverty is black. It has been this way for decades, and the contours of this reality has become self-reinforcing. White residents have built their own affluent enclaves farther and farther from the city's core, in suburbs like Chesterfield, some 30 miles from downtown, where brand-new, dueling outlet malls have opened for business. Black residents live in a belt of communities along the northern side of the city in townships like Ferguson, or Baden that were abandoned by white residents, where the quaint strip malls of yesteryear are largely abandoned and storefront windows are covered with plywood.
>
> The black community in urban and inner-suburban St. Louis

---

[166] http://www.washingtonpost.com/politics/ferguson-protesters-staging-ground-the-quiktrip-gas-station-is-now-silent/2014/08/19/a8e4382e-27db-11e4-958c-268a320a60ce_story.html

[167] http://blogs.riverfronttimes.com/dailyrft/2014/08/volunteers_clean_up_at_ferguson_quiktrip_get_yelled_at_for_helping_the_white_man.php

has suffered within the confines of this system. Missouri had the nation's highest black homicide rate in 2010 and the second-highest in 2011, according to Violence Policy Center. When a black teenager is murdered, it can rate no more than a 300 word story in the local newspaper. The city's school system is largely composed of dysfunctional barracks where kids are kept for the day. In 2011, The high school graduation rate for St. Louis city was about 50 percent (in the largely white and affluent suburb of Clayton, by contrast, it is 98.5 percent), according to a tally in the *St. Louis Post Dispatch.*

Cops throughout St. Louis and its suburbs have the unenviable task of policing this social order. Lower-middle-class police officers patrol the gutted city neighborhoods that other white St. Louis residents avoid. The officers get shot at, yelled at, and in return they use unnecessary violence to make their presence felt. The cycle of mistrust, resentment and hostility between police and the black residents of St. Louis has been building for decades, and now it is boiling over. When a police officer gunned down Brown, black witnesses nearby described the scene as murder—a young man with his arms up, compliant, shot in the face and chest. It was the catalyst to rise up against the tectonic inequalities of St. Louis.

Burning a QuikTrip is an easy way to express rage at the city, at its history, at the police, and the social order. The morning after the looting, a man who identified himself as DeAndre Smith stood in the QuikTrip parking lot as the building smoldered behind him.

"This is exactly what's supposed to happen, when there's injustice in your community," Smith told a videographer for the *St. Louis Post-Dispatch.*[168]

No, Mr. DeAndre Smith: this isn't supposed to happen in any civilized city in the world. The burning of the QuikTrip in Ferguson, Missouri - a suburb of St. Louis - occurred because the growing inequality between blacks and whites (poor vs. wealthy) is a testament to the

---

[168] http://www.newrepublic.com/article/119088/looting-after-michael-brown-shooting-exposes-st-louis-economic-divide

truths addressed in *The Bell Curve*.

Burn one store down; watch another close (driven away by the Visible Black Hand of Economics). [Near the Ferguson QuikTrip that burned, another quietly closes, St. Louis Business Journal, 8-19-14][169]

What Mr. DeAndre Smith can never comprehend is the symbolism of the looted and burnt-out QuikTrip in Ferguson as the perfect, "he who laughs last, laughs best" present for those defenders and believers of *The Bell Curve* 20 years after its publication.

So is the East-West Gateway Council of Governments study on inequality in St. Louis... [New report underscores racial inequities in St. Louis region, St. Louis Post-Dispatch, 9-24-14]:

> Too often in the St. Louis region, owning a home, holding a job or even living beyond your first year of life depends upon your race, according to a new study that details an old problem.
>
> The report's authors at the East-West Gateway Council of Governments emphasized Wednesday that research on segregation and disparity was underway well before rioting in Ferguson put the region's race relations under a national spotlight.
>
> Findings of a divide in prosperity, health and education touched off a frank discussion among elected leaders on the Gateway board regarding the role of race in the local job market and governance.
>
> "There is a boil-over situation that just takes place when people are not working," said East St. Louis Mayor Alvin Parks. "I'm frustrated and I see you're living the good life. Or you're living a good life and I'm living a bad life, and I feel as if I should have the same opportunity to live the American dream that you're living."

---

[169] http://www.bizjournals.com/stlouis/news/2014/08/19/near-the-ferguson-quiktrip-that-burned-another.html

Jobs should be more accessible to people of color, he said.

The "Where We Stand" report compares the St. Louis region with 34 other metropolitan statistical areas. It found this to be the sixth most segregated, "and tends to have a wider gap between whites and blacks than many of the peer regions on a range of social, economic and health indicators."

Among the findings, based on 2012 measures:

• The median household income was $59,041 for whites, $30,479 for blacks.

• The percent of white families living in poverty was 9.2 percent, of black families 30.6 percent.

• A black infant was 3.6 times more likely than a white one to die in the first year of life.

• Blacks were more than twice as likely than whites to have no health care coverage.

East-West Gateway has been publishing the "Where We Stand" editions since 1992.

Periodically, the agency provides updates on specific topic areas, including racial segregation and disparity.

"The story has not changed much over the past 20 years," said Mary Rocchio, lead author of the report and manager of policy research at East-West Gateway.

Still, Rocchio said she was surprised by the size of the gaps between blacks and whites on some measures.[170]

"The story has not changed much over the past 20 years," said Marcy Rocchio...

In another 20 years, it will remain unchanged (if any whites remain anywhere near the St. Louis metropolitan area to compare their

---

[170] http://www.stltoday.com/news/local/metro/new-report-underscores-racial-inequities-in-st-louis-region/article_b3c64bc0-6700-53d7-9b13-69d625f4acef.html

standard of living to the teeming black masses...).

In another 200 years, it will remain unchanged.

High rates of poverty, lower household income, lack of insurance, and grotesquely African-levels of infant mortality rates are benchmarks of the black community; the opposite describe the white community of St. Louis.

Recall the words from the New Republic article describing the racial reality, Bell Curve inspired world of St. Louis:

> Lower-middle-class police officers patrol the gutted city neighborhoods that other white St. Louis residents avoid. The officers get shot at, yelled at, and in return they use unnecessary violence to make their presence felt. The cycle of mistrust, resentment and hostility between police and the black residents of St. Louis has been building for decades, and now it is boiling over.

But the cycle has a starting point, and it's not white racism, Jim Crow, or white supremacy.

Black dysfunction/failure has an origin. A source.

To reinterpret the introduction to chapter 13 of The Bell Curve, "The debate about whether and how much genes and environment have to do with ethnic differences is settled."

Courtesy of the racial experiment still ongoing in America's heartland, St. Louis.

The Bell Curve tolls for St. Louis: There is no changing what is...

October 2, 2014
Ebola, Ferguson, and the American Colonization Society: "There is a moral fitness in the idea of returning to Africa her children..."

> *"There is a moral fitness in the idea of returning to Africa her children, whose ancestors have been torn from her by the ruthless hand of fraud and violence. Transplanted in a foreign land, they will carry back to their native soil the rich fruits of religion, civilization, law and liberty. May it not be one of the great designs of the Ruler of the universe, (whose ways are often inscrutable by short-sighted mortals,) thus to transform an original crime, into a signal blessing to that most unfortunate portion of the globe?" -- Henry Clay, who was one of the earliest members (and died its president) of the American Colonization Society, which wanted to repatriate blacks to Africa. Liberia to be exact, from which Monrovia (named after U.S. President James Monroe) is the capital.[171]*

Ebola.

Yes, it's here in America (though the CDC was already warning funeral homes in the U.S. on how to deal with Ebola on Sept. 29...).

But so are Latter-Day Liberians, the very people whose Liberian brethren brought an African disease to America.

Ebola was never the problem. [Ferguson, Mo. Emblematic of Growing Suburban Poverty, Brookings Institute, 8-15-14]:
> The New York Times and others have described the deep-seated racial tensions and inequalities that have long plagued the St. Louis region, as well as the dramatic demographic transformation of Ferguson from a largely white suburban

---

[171] http://www.abrahamlincolnonline.org/lincoln/speeches/clay.htm

enclave (it was 85 percent white as recently as 1980) to a predominantly black community (it was 67 percent black by 2008-2012).

But Ferguson has also been home to dramatic economic changes in recent years. The city's unemployment rate rose from roughly 7 percent in 2000 to over 13 percent in 2010-12. For those residents who were employed, inflation-adjusted average earnings fell by one-third. The number of households using federal Housing Choice Vouchers climbed from roughly 300 in 2000 to more than 800 by the end of the decade.

Amid these changes, poverty skyrocketed. Between 2000 and 2010-2012, Ferguson's poor population doubled. By the end of that period, roughly one in four residents lived below the federal poverty line ($23,492 for a family of four in 2012), and 44 percent fell below twice that level.

None of this means that there are 1,000 Fergusons-in-waiting, but it should underscore the fact that there are a growing number of communities across the country facing similar, if quieter, deep challenges every day.[172]

"Transplanted in a foreign land, they will carry back to their native soil the rich fruits of religion, civilization, law and liberty." Mr. Clay, those blacks who remained in America failed to enrich the soil with either religion, civilization, law or liberty (Ferguson in 2014 is proof of this).

Liberia? Take a look at the Vice Travel Guide to Liberia to see the blessings of religion, civilization, law and liberty the descendants of repatriated blacks to Africa from America kept alive...[173]

But back to Ferguson... [Ferguson Business Owner Calls Nighttime Protests 'Terrorist Acts', CBS St. Louis, 10-2-14]:

---

[172] http://www.brookings.edu/blogs/the-avenue/posts/2014/08/15-ferguson-suburban-poverty

[173] http://www.vice.com/the-vice-guide-to-travel/the-vice-guide-to-liberia-1

> A Ferguson business owner is calling the protestors who descend on his city at night "terrorists" and says Homeland Security should be called in.
>
> The anonymous caller to the Charlie Brennan show, who KMOX confirmed is a Ferguson small business owner, says the daytime protestors are fine, but that changes when the outsiders, including elected officials from outside Ferguson, arrive after dark.
>
> "The unpeaceful protesters come out at night, trying to harm or burn our businesses down or stop the businesses," the caller said. "And it's time that our government called this what it is, and this is a terrorist act."
>
> The business owner says a lot of windows have been broken, fires have been set and trash is left behind.[174]

Sure, Ebola is now in America (courtesy of blacks from Liberia...), but in Ferguson we see something far more dangerous has proliferated for centuries. A problem Henry Clay and the wise men of the American Colonization Society knew they could forever remove from our now Ebola-stricken shores...

And Ferguson is ground zero for something beyond Ebola...zombies aren't the problem. That's for fiction, scaring kids, and helping guys get to second base on dates at movies... [Ferguson spokesman clarifies 'evacuation' comments, St. Louis Post-Dispatch, 10-2-14]:

> Ferguson officials are considering a range of possible scenarios for what could happen after a grand jury concludes its investigation into the shooting death of Michael Brown.
>
> In an interview with St. Louis Public Radio, city spokesman Devin James said that if violence breaks out, the city needed to be ready. He mentioned an evacuation situation during the interview, but later sought to clarify that he had simply been discussing various hypothetical responses.

---

[174] http://stlouis.cbslocal.com/2014/10/01/ferguson-business-owner-calls-nighttime-protests-terrorist-acts/

"You know, if there is no indictment and there is an evacuation situation, we need to be prepared for that," he said during the radio interview. "If there is an indictment and there is celebratory unrest, we need to be prepared for that."

James said that if there was an evacuation, the city was considering how best to contact residents.

"Do we rely on a combination of media, do we introduce robo-calls, do we do text messaging, emails, you know, we're looking at all of the different tactics available," he said, "and just trying to see, you know, what is the best method to communicate with everybody in the event that something like that happens, and we need to either tell people to hunker down or get out or whatever."

In a follow-up statement emailed to reporters, James said residents had not been told to evacuate. "Part of our job is to make sure from a communications standpoint that we are prepared for anything with residents, businesses and the community being the priority," he said.

"So we are looking at all the communication tactics and resources available to reach as many people as possible and law enforcement is looking at all the possibilities a well. I was not implying that we have recommendations about evacuating or hunkering down and was simply speaking with the reporter about many scenarios that need to be considered."[175]

Ferguson has already been the scene of an evacuation for those hoping to perpetuate civilization. We call this "white flight" from the encroaching "black undertow" (blacks escaping the poorly run black municipality of St. Louis for the white-run city of Ferguson, only to import the same morality and vices that caused St. Louis to be poorly run...):

- In 1970, Ferguson was 99 percent white
- In 1980, Ferguson was 85 percent white and 14 black

---

[175] http://www.stltoday.com/news/local/metro/ferguson-spokesman-clarifies-evacuation-comments/article_7dd1f883-834c-535c-85cd-9b1ba05b6dd0.html

- In 1990, Ferguson was 73.8 percent white and 25.1 percent black
- In 2000, Ferguson was 44.8 percent white and 52.4 percent black
- In 2010 Ferguson was 29.3 percent white and 67.4 percent black[Chart: Inside Ferguson's Changing Demographics, Forbes, 8-19-2014][176]

Ebola was already in America.

Detroit fell victim to the disease.

Baltimore and Memphis as well.

Ferguson is on the verge of falling, with East St. Louis a reminder of what is to come for the former city...

Newark, Camden, Birmingham...

When Officer Darren Wilson is found by the Grand Jury to be innocent, you'll see the true reality of Ebola in America.

Henry Clay tried to warn us.

And as the Brookings Institute story cited above dares to warn us, there are 1,000s of Ferguson's in the waiting...

October 5, 2014
Finally, the St. Louis Symphony Succeeds in Minority Outreach!

For years, the St. Louis Symphony has been trying to attract a

---

[176] http://www.forbes.com/sites/niallmccarthy/2014/08/19/chart-ferguson-white-flight/

minority audience (as have orchestras across the country). From the St. Louis Symphony's web site:

> IN UNISON®
> Enriching people's lives through the power of music by providing experiences and opportunities that serve as a bridge between diversity, community and legacy.
> Our flagship diversity initiative, IN UNISON® was created in 1992 to provide high-quality musical resources to the African-American community, specifically through specialized outreach to member churches participating in the program. St. Louis Symphony musicians present free performances in at least half of the more than 40 member churches annually. Formed in 1994, the IN UNISON® Chorus is comprised of 120 people from throughout the African-American community performing as part of the STL Symphony's season – all three concerts featuring the IN UNISON® Chorus now attract capacity or near-capacity audiences. Additionally, the IN UNISON® program encourages young people of diverse backgrounds to study music and has, through the years, recognized them for their talent and hard work through the awarding of scholarships and awards.[177]

Some clown named Greg Sandow (a classical music critic) has a web site, where he quotes the community relations director for the St. Louis Symphony and the organizations to outreach to the black community:

> Kevin Smoot, Community Relations Director, St. Louis Symphony
>
> We have a partnership between the orchestra and principally African-American churches. We started in 1992, with five congregations. They were proposed through the black clergy coalition, which selected the initial churches. Today we have grown to 24 member organizations. We have a waiting list of ten churches.
>
> It's a mutually beneficial situation. There's no charge or fee.

---

[177] https://www.stlsymphony.org/en/community--education/in-unison/

One of the benefits is that each organization receives a one-hour free concert in church by Symphony musicians. They started off as purely classical. But we've broadened our horizons. Our musicians lead regular lives. Rather than a purely classically driven program, they'll play everything from Bach to Thelonious Monk. That's a great connector, breaking down barriers. Almost the entire orchestra is involved. They're willing to share their time and talents to go out into the community. A lot of them want to branch out and learn more about themselves, and by their nature they give anyway. We have a community partnership program, a voluntary program that the musicians can participate in. They acquire points by participating. If they get enough, they get time off. A large portion of our orchestra participates.

One of the benefits is that the organizations have to sell 100 tickets in the course of the year to the orchestral season. They're deeply discounted.

We also have the St. Louis Symphony In Unison Chorus, principally African-American, 120 voices. As a result of all this, the attendance base of minorities, principally African-American, has increased tremendously. Also hall rentals. There's broad participation across the board in virtually every facet of the symphony, even volunteering.[178]

"Deeply discounted" tickets for the orchestral season? It's obvious the "minority outreach" isn't working.

Until this weekend.

For the same reason the Ferguson StreetFest had to be cancelled [Ferguson StreetFest cancelled due to recent unrest, Fox2Now.com, 9-24-14][179], we now know how "minority outreach" is going to work for the St. Louis Symphony. [Michael Brown protesters interrupt St. Louis Symphony performance, Fox2Now.com, 10-4-14]:

---

[178] http://www.gregsandow.com/old/afamint.htm

[179] http://fox2now.com/2014/09/24/ferguson-streetfest-cancelled-due-to-recent-unrest/

It was a moment that many at Powell Symphony Hall did not expect.

Mike Brown demonstrators started singing and chanting just before the orchestra and chorus started performing a piece.

The incident happened around 8:45 on Saturday night inside Powell Hall.

'It was certainly unexpected. I think it took everyone in the hall by surprise,' said Erika Ebsworth-Goold, the publicist for the St. Louis Symphony.

She was backstage when it all took place.

She says the intermission was ending and the St. Louis Symphony and Chorus were preparing to perform Brahms' German Requiem when the demonstrators stood up and started singing.

'The orchestra had assembled, the chorus was on the stage, our soloists were on the stage, and so was our conductor. We were just getting ready to start when this happened,' explained Ebsworth-Goold.

She says the demonstrators were in different parts of the arena and that they were all paying audience members.

The group displayed banners regarding the mike brown case and chanted 'black lives matter.'

After a few minutes, demonstrators left the hall peacefully.

But before leaving, the group dropped red paper hearts over the balcony that read in part 'requiem to Mike Brown.'

There was some clapping in the hall during the demonstration both from audience members and performers.

'There were a number of patrons inside the hall who were apparently very moved by what these people had to say,' said Ebsworth-Goold.

Symphony officials call what happened a delay to the concert and not an interruption since the symphony and chorus hadn't resumed performing yet when the demonstration took place.

That is something they are grateful for.

As for potential security changes at Powell Hall, Ebsworth said, 'These were people who had paid money to come see the concert. They were patrons of ours, and we'll discuss it certainly but I can't see any major security protocol changes at this point.'

Ebsworth-Goold tells us there were about 50 demonstrators last night and there were no arrests.

The symphony had another performance at 3pm Sunday afternoon.[180]

So, did this Requiem for Michael Brown occur because of the St. Louis Symphony program with the black churches of St. Louis, which offers deeply discounted tickets to performances to blacks?

The answer is obviously yes.

Those preaching "Requiem for Mike Brown" asked the audience: "Whose side are you on?"

A terrifying question, when you consider the answer you give could result in the taking of your life (terrorism at its finest.. and you're worried about ISIS?).

Ebola isn't the threat to civilization in St. Louis...

---

[180] http://www.stltoday.com/news/local/metro/michael-brown-protesters-interrupt-st-louis-symphony-orchestra-concert/article_bfd2b377-8da4-56f8-aa8d-64bf714e0114.html

October 6, 2014
Law and Order or Africa? What the Situation in Ferguson Represents

It was about a month ago that death threats to city officials in Ferguson (almost all white officials) didn't warrant an investigation by the FBI or Department of Justice. [Ferguson police, city leaders receive death threats, KSDK.com, 8-18-14][181]

When you have an Attorney General - "I am the attorney general of the United States, but I am also a black man" - who admits he "identifies with Ferguson's mistrust of cops" you should know something is terribly, terribly wrong in America.[182]

Sure, he has "resigned," but Eric "My People" Holder is still the Attorney General of the Department of Justice.

It's why this article from 67% black Ferguson is so important in understanding where America is headed. It details the trials and tribulations one of the few black cops employed by the Ferguson Police Department is dealing with from "his community," who only a white person when he dons the police blue. [Black and in blue: A Ferguson police sergeant reflects on a tough time, St. Louis Post-Dispatch, 10-3-14]:

> Seeing that a fellow African-American police officer had endured his fill of racial slurs shouted by people of his own race, Sgt. Harry Dilworth tapped the man's shoulder and took his place facing protesters.
> Riots following the Aug. 9 shooting of an unarmed black teen by a white officer make it a tough time to be on the Ferguson police force — and for Dilworth it's tougher if the person in

---

[181] http://www.ksdk.com/story/news/local/2014/08/11/ferguson-police-city-leaders-receive-death-threats/13886027/

[182] http://www.thedailybeast.com/articles/2014/09/23/eric-holder-i-identify-with-ferguson-s-mistrust-of-cops.html

blue happens to be black.

Most of the insults he heard on the line that day are too graphic to print. Among the more polite are "sellout" and "Uncle Tom," Dilworth said. He had stood with two other black officers, one from the Missouri Highway Patrol and one from the St. Louis County police.

"We didn't blink," he recalled in an interview this week. "We didn't say anything to them. We stood there and took it. We all talked about it afterwards. I said, 'Don't address ignorance with ignorance.'

"But it's hard to hear that from the minority group that you are representing ... You tune it out, but psychologically you're dealing with scars. Some officers are going to see counselors. We're not robots."

Black and white officers alike agree that the blacks have been targeted more on the front lines of policing the troubles that followed Michael Brown's death. They feel caught between empathizing with a brother officer who used deadly force and understanding a community that is venting pent-up rage against police.

Dilworth, 45, wishes he could retire, but he feels a draw to stay in the community he has served for 21 years.

Even on ordinary calls for service, some taunt him with the "hands up, don't shoot'" gesture widely adopted by protesters.

"You can only take so much of this," Dilworth said, taking a reporter with him Wednesday to patrol the 6.2-square-mile city.

Dilworth had been at Fort Leonard Wood fulfilling his duties as an Army reservist the day of the shooting. He said his wife wishes he were back in Iraq or Afghanistan.

"She thinks I would be safer there," he said.

'IT'S DIFFERENT NOW'

Dilworth is the only black supervisor and one of four African-American officers on a force of 53 in a community where two-thirds of the 21,000 residents are black.

His teeth clenched as he drove past a protester holding a sign that read "Stop Killing Us."

He questioned why protesters don't hold such signs at the scenes of murders, such as the recent killing in St. Louis of Donnie White. Dilworth said he knew White, who was on the way home from work when he got caught in crossfire between suspected black gangs.

"We are not killing you; you are killing yourselves," he said, his voice rising inside his police SUV. "This is a systematic problem that's been going on for years. I want to tell them to wake up! And look at exactly what the problem really is! Look at the statistics. The number of officer-involved shootings is relatively low. I stand a better chance of being killed by you."

A call for a disturbance echoed on his radio. Foremost on his mind, he said: Are his officers going to be safe? If something happens, what will he tell the spouse?[183]

One of his officers had to have his family move "out of state" because of erroneously being misidentified as the shooter of Michael "Gentle Giant" Brown.

Sgt. Harry Dilworth is not worth putting on a pedestal and praising as some future non-white Republican candidate for office; his actions in defense of law and order are admirable, but not worth inflating to an absurd degree.

But it is worth remember he is a police officer, viewed by the black majority of Ferguson as upholding the white man's law in Ferguson.

---

[183] http://www.stltoday.com/news/local/crime-and-courts/black-and-in-blue-a-ferguson-police-sergeant-reflects-on/article_b71556de-68b1-566f-a6ce-cc02c01b8343.html

And the future isn't white; it's African.

Ask yourself this: would a white person be safer in Iraq right now or in East St. Louis (a 98 percent black city that represents Ferguson's future)?

And ask yourself this: how low can civilization fall in Ferguson while the dwindling white minority tries to placate their demographic masters? [Even before Michael Brown's slaying in Ferguson, racial questions hung over police, Washington Post, 8-13-14]:

> On Wednesday, Ferguson Police Chief Thomas Jackson acknowledged the problems facing his department and asked the community for help in restoring its trust.
>
> "Apparently, there has been this undertow that has bubbled to the surface," Jackson said at a news conference. "It's our priority to address it and to fix what's been going wrong."
>
> St. Louis is among the most segregated metropolitan areas in the nation. Ferguson, one of the 91 municipalities in largely white St. Louis County, has seen its population shift in recent years. About two-thirds of the city's 21,100 residents are black. That's a significant increase from 2000, when blacks made up just over half of the population. White residents, who had accounted for 44 percent of the population, now make up just under 30 percent.
>
> Yet the police force patrolling Ferguson has not changed along with the population. The police force has 53 members, and three of them are black. The city's mayor and police chief are white, as are most of the members of the Ferguson City Council.
>
> "I've been trying to increase the diversity of the department ever since I got here," Jackson said Wednesday. He pointed out that he had promoted two black superintendents.
>
> "Race relations is a top priority right now," Jackson said. He said his force is working with the Department of Justice's community relations office to improve how police interact

with the citizens. "I've told them, 'Tell me what to do, and I'll do it.'"[184]

The white police chief of Ferguson said, of his policy to the new black demographic masters of the city's fate, "Tell me what to do, and I'll do it."

The last white mayor of Ferguson, current Mayor James Knowles II, bragged on August 18 how the city had been rebuilt after two tornadoes and the city would heal from the madness of the black insurrection (all ostensibly in the name of "Justice for Mike Brown").[185]

But the city won't heal.

It won't rebuild.

As property values fall in Ferguson, the remaining whites will abandon their lost equity and vacate the city they called "home," turning over control of the beleaguered town to those who marched for Darren Wilson's head.[186]

With this, Ferguson will regress to the black mean: as we see in Detroit, Camden, Newark, Memphis, and East St. Louis, this mean roughly correlates to the conditions found in Africa.

For the conditions of a city, good or bad, are only a reflection of its majority population.

---

[184] http://www.washingtonpost.com/politics/even-before-teen-michael-browns-slaying-in-mo-racial-questions-have-hung-over-police/2014/08/13/78b3c5c6-2307-11e4-86ca-6f03cbd15c1a_story.html

[185] http://www.ksdk.com/story/news/local/2014/08/11/ferguson-police-city-leaders-receive-death-threats/13886027/

[186] http://www.nbcnews.com/storyline/michael-brown-shooting/michael-brown-activists-call-arrest-officer-darren-wilson-n218886

October 8, 2014
"Us" and "them," "we" and "they."

There's a quote from Kafka I came across years ago, reading, "In the fight between you and the world, back the world."

Those Who Can See know something is irreparably wrong with western civilization, but no political party in all the western world dares stand in defiance of the zeitgeist to promote the interests of the only group capable of actually perpetuating this civilization: white people.

The sons and daughters of Europe.

Yes, non-whites can assimilate to western civilization, but they cannot perpetuate indefinitely.

In America, millions of people hold some level of awareness of the problem, though it will take a dramatic example to graduate them into the ranks of *Those Who Can See*.

But it's beyond vital for those individual members of the informal *Those Who Can See* group to remember this quote, paraphrased from Kafka: "In the fight between you and the world, back the world until the "you" multiplies."

And though it might be unfolding in the smallest of municipalities, in a city long past its glory days, an isolated event between a white cop and a Swisher Sweet thieving black male is providing proof we are approaching the day when the "you" starts to multiply dramatically.

Though it goes against everything you've been taught/indoctrinated with by the state, public schools, the entertainment industry (both Hollywood and television), and the Republicans, Democrats, and Libertarians, once you break free there's no going back: white people have rights too; white people have interests; and, white people have a future. [St. Louis Cardinals fans taunt black protesters urging justice for Michael Brown, New York Daily News, 10-7-14]:

> Racial tension spilled over from Ferguson, Mo., into nearby

St. Louis on Monday night, where a handful of protesters urging justice for Michael Brown were met by mostly white Cardinals fans who taunted them with chants about poverty, Africa and in support of the white officer who killed the unarmed black teen.

The ugly confrontation was caught on video outside of Busch Stadium, where the Cardinals took on the Los Angeles Dodgers in a National League baseball playoff game. A group of protesters massed outside Gate 4, a smoking section outside the stadium, and began urging "Justice for Mike Brown!" as they hoisted signs and an upside down American flag.

"We're the ones who f-----g gave all y'all all the freedoms that you have!" a petite blond white woman, holding a beer and rally towel, yells at the protesters.

On Monday, the peaceful protests quickly turned ugly but not violent. Smokers clad in Cardinals jersey responded to chants of "Justice for Mike Brown!" with jeers of "Let's Go Darren!" in reference to Wilson. One fan taped over the name across the back of a Cardinals jersey and hand wrote "I am Darren Wilson."

"If they'd be working, we wouldn't have this problem!" yelled one elderly white man.

   Fans later started a chant of "Get a job!" and, in response to a chant of "USA!" one man yells "Go home" while a white woman, the same who spoke about giving freedom, chants back, "Africa!"

Another fan tells the protesters to pull up their pants.

   "Go tear your own neighborhood up, see what that does," one man taunts.[187]

Maybe it seems silly to ascribe any message from these comments from white St. Louis Cardinals fans to those agitating for justice on

---

[187] http://www.nydailynews.com/news/national/st-louis-cardinals-fans-taunt-black-protesters-urging-justice-michael-brown-article-1.1966149

behalf of a Swisher Sweet thieving black male, but it only takes one example for people to be pushed in the direction of *Those Who Can See*.

The Cosby Show make-believe world of "race is just a social construct" falls apart quickly, revealing the real world: one Cornel Wilde depicted in the 1966 classic *The Naked Prey*. [For some Ferguson whites, racial fault lines exposed by shooting come as a surprise, Washington Post, 10-8-14]:

> Alice Singen had always seen her home town as an integrated, harmonious place. Like many other white residents, she prided herself on staying here even when others began to leave.
>
> But since the death of an unarmed black teenager at the hands of a white police officer, some African Americans are calling it segregated and racist. Now Singen has found herself talking in terms of "us" and "them," "we" and "they."
>
> "I didn't have any problems with anybody or any color, and all of a sudden it feels like we are being held responsible for something that's not our fault," Singen, 70, said as she left Faraci Pizza, a 46-year-old Ferguson business that has become a focal point of racial tension. "I don't get it."
>
> That sense of shock is common here among Ferguson whites in the wake of 18-year-old Michael Brown's death and the explosive protests in the days that followed.[188]

"Us" and "them," "we" and "they."

"In the fight between you and the world, back the world..."

Well... it's not individuals we are talking about anymore.[Exclusive: Missouri police plan for possible riots if Brown cop not charged, Reuters, 10-8-14]:

---

[188] http://www.washingtonpost.com/national/for-some-ferguson-whites-racial-fault-lines-exposed-by-shooting-come-as-a-surprise/2014/10/07/a25d95c0-497f-11e4-891d-713f052086a0_story.html

Ferguson today is a city on the edge. While mostly black residents hold small protests outside the police station each night, gun store owners report a jump in sales to white residents. Local business owners in the area where Brown was shot complain about lost trade. Many storefronts remain boarded up with plywood.

Police and elected officials are meeting regularly with multi-racial citizen groups in a bid to improve community relations, tackle concerns about police discrimination, and avoid the turmoil that followed Brown's shooting. Civil unrest is still the "worst case scenario", Knowles said.

Adam Weinstein, co-owner of County Guns, said sales were up 50 percent since Brown's shooting, mostly among white residents fearful of riots who are buying Glock, Springfield and Smith & Wesson handguns, and shotguns. "They are afraid the city is going to explode," Weinstein said, a former member of the U.S. Navy and St. Louis firefighter with heavily tattooed arms.

At Ferguson Market and Liquor, where Brown appears on a surveillance video pushing a store clerk before walking out with an unpaid box of cigarillos on the morning of his death, most of the storefront windows have been repaired after being shattered in looting.

In August, after Brown was shot, the mood inside the store was fearful. Today, it is one of defiance. One of the workers, who asked not to be named, said he had brought his handgun from home to keep in the store. "I'm ready to shoot anyone looking for trouble," he said.[189]

No one wants trouble.

This experiment in manufacturing racial tranquility, forced by an overzealous federal government (the precedent for blaming the racial gap in achievement/segregation/poverty/and overall black

---

[189] http://www.reuters.com/article/2014/10/07/us-usa-missouri-shooting-plans-idUSKCN0HW1TF20141007?feedType=RSS&feedName=topNews&utm_source=twitter

failure being set by the Kerner Commission, which blamed white racism for black poverty/dysfunction/riots in 1968)[190] has failed... miserably.

The microcosm for the instability of the United States of America is found in the St. Louis metropolitan area, where a small town called Ferguson is a reminder the past 70 years of American history have been nothing but one failure after another.

What's better: whites in metropolitan St. Louis know this fact better than most of us could even fathom.

"Us" and "them," "we" and "they."

October 9, 2014
..."living in a powder keg and giving off sparks": Vonderrit Myers, Jr. and the True Face of Black St. Louis

"He was unarmed," Teyonna Myers said. "He had a sandwich in his hand, and they thought it was a gun. It's like Michael Brown all over again." [Police officer fatally shoots teenager in south St. Louis, *St. Louis Post-Dispatch*, 10-9-14]

No sandwich I've ever encountered at Subway, Quiznos, or Blimpie ever came with a semi-automatic option.

But 18-year-old Vonderrit Myers, Jr. obviously found a sandwich artisan with the ability to pack meats, cheeses, salts, lettuce, tomato, gun powder, three 9 mm caliber bullets, and some sort of firing mechanism into a delicious, but incredibly deadly meal.

---

[190] http://www.vdare.com/articles/white-girl-bleed-a-lot-how-black-crime-is-breaking-down-control-through-white-guilt

Vonderrit Myers was "no stranger to law enforcement," as he was a passenger in a high-speed chase in St. Louis on June 27, who ran from police (tossing a Hi-Point 380 semi-automic pistol into a sewage drain), was eventually arrested, and faced trial for these charges on November 17. [St. Louis Police Officer Kills Teenager in Shaw Neighborhood, Ignites Fresh Protests,*RiverFront Times*, 10-9-14]:

Court records show that Myers faced a felony charge of unlawful use of a weapon stemming from a June 27 incident. Myers also faced a misdemeanor charge of resisting and/or interfering with an arrest for the same incident.

He also wore, as one of the conditions for his bail, an ankle bracelet/monitor.

All in all, like 18-year-old Michael Brown, Vonderrit Myers was a pillar of the St. Louis black community:

A hero.
A good boy.
Who was turning his life around.

An Honor Student (actually, he was struggling in school and a poster child for why President Obama's "My Brother's Keeper" program was instituted).

Running from cops was "just what [black] kids do," in not just Memphis, but St. Louis as well.

No, Vonderrit Myers didn't have a sandwich in his hand. He had a stolen gun (a 9 mm Smith & Wesson) and fired it at a police officer:

The St. Louis Post Dispatch says Vonderrit Myers, Jr., who was shot and killed Wednesday night by an off-duty police officer, was shot five to seven times.

The shooting happened around 7:30 p.m. on Shaw Boulevard. The officer was patrolling an area of the Shaw Neighborhood when this incident unfolded.

Vonderrit Deondre Myers, 18, was fatally shot Wednesday by an off-duty St. Louis police officer, Myers' attorney, Peter Cohen, said Thursday.

Dotson says while working security, the officers` attention was drawn to three African-American males near Shaw and Klemm. When the officer turned around in his car to approach the group, the young men started to run. The officer decided to follow the group in his car. After exiting his vehicle, he ran after a suspect through a gangway. That`s when the three suspects came together again.

According to the chief, one suspect approached the officer in an aggressive manner.

The officer told him to stop and surrender but the suspect kept coming at the officer. The two began to fight. The suspect`s hooded sweatshirt came off and he started running up a hill. At that point, the officer noticed the 18-year-old with a 9 millimeter handgun. Dotson says the suspect turned around and fired three shots at the officer. The officer fired back, shooting and killing the suspect.

As the *Gateway Pundit* noted, riots broke out with blacks in St. Louis immediately siding with Vonderrit Myers dead body and black elected officials working overtime to spread false rumors (obviously working overtime to incite furthering rioting and black terrorism):

An autopsy has shown that Vonderrit Myers Jr. was shot from five to seven times during a fatal encounter with an off-duty police officer Wednesday, police sources said.

Sen. Jamilah Nasheed suggested at a press conference earlier today that the teen had been shot in the back of the head, but medical examiners did not find any gunshots to the back of Myers' head, police sources said.

As Fox2Now and the *Gateway Pundit* both reported, the St. Louis County Emergency Operations Center has been activated as of today through next Tuesday courtesy of planned pro-Mike Brown, "Weekend of Resistance" (Ferguson October) activities by black agitators:

The St. Louis County Emergency Operations Center activates at 4pm Thursday through next Tuesday. It's in response to a planned protest calling for a "Weekend of Resistance" in response to police shootings.

Protesters will march to county prosecutor Bob McCulloch's Clayton office Friday afternoon, and gather for rally at Kiener Plaza downtown on Saturday.

It's only a matter of time before the first stories of "Justice for Mike Brown" or " Justice for Vonderrit Myers" attacks break out in St. Louis, with white people targeted because of black people's inability to cooperate with the police.

The St. Louis County Emergency Operations Center wasn't activated for Ebola, but for the physical manifestation of the virus: "Justice for Mike Brown" supporters and those who engage in the Ferguson-inspired "Weekend of Resistance."

October 10, 2014
Courtesy of the City of St. Louis Metropolitan Police Department's "Annual Report to the Community," We Know the Exact Percentage of Arrests Blacks Represent for Robbery, Murder, Assault, and Rape in St. Louis

A thick fog envelops all of America.

We all know it's there.

But no one will dare publicly mention it, so we continue searching for answers when the fog keeps us from simply seeing the solution: black crime - and the correct, rational fear of being the victim (or your incurring property damage/thefts at your property) of black crime - is choking the life out of our major cities.

This is the underlying reality of the Vonderrit Myers shooting in St. Louis, where an 18-year-old dead thug is now exalted as some hero of the black community for pulling a stolen gun on a white cop and firing three times in his direction (before the gun malfunctioned, obviously due to the 'ghetto' hold on the gun he employed).

Irresponsible (opportunistic) black leaders have seized on this continued unrest - criminality within the black community - to continue monologuing the white citizens of St. Louis as to their collective racist ways:

> Sen. Jamilah Nasheed had suggested at a press conference earlier Thursday that the teen had been shot in the back of the head, but the autopsy did not find any gunshots to the back of Myers' head.
>
> About two dozen protesters outside Police Headquarters on Thursday morning called for a Department of Justice investigation of Wednesday night's shooting.
>
> Identifying themselves as part of the Michael Brown Leadership Coalition, they also suggested that the governor appoint a blue-ribbon commission to look at this case.
>
> Members of the group said the focus should be on why the officer singled out Myers in the first place.
>
> "This was a case of racial profiling turned deadly," Nasheed alleged.
>
> Nasheed stood with Dotson and Mayor Francis Slay at a press conference recently calling for stiffer penalties against those carrying illegal guns.
>
> Minister Akbar Muhammad, international representative for the Nation Of Islam, said, "There is a culture of cover-up on the police department." He suggested that Dotson was supporting the officer Wednesday night before he talked to Myers' family and could possibly have had all the facts.
>
> "It makes it look like he was just defending himself? Give me a break," Muhammad said.
>
> An attorney, Jerryl Christmas, suggested, "There is no

epidemic of black officers shooting white kids, but there is an epidemic of white officers shooting black kids."

He said police are too quick to resort to deadly force.[191]

Let's take a look at how USA Today writer Yamiche Alcindor describes the situation in St. Louis, herself an activist for "Justice for Mike Brown" (obviously, an objective reporter...):

> Hollis described Myers as a "good kid" who was a high school senior and wanted to become an electrical engineer. "In life, all kids have their ups and downs," he said. Myers was wearing an ankle bracelet ordered by a court as a condition of bail in a previous gun charge, the *St. Louis Post-Dispatch* reported.
> According to the newspaper, Myers was to go on trial in November on charges of unlawful use of a weapon and resisting arrest. The case, according to court documents, involved a high-speed car chase and crash. Myers, who was a passenger, allegedly ran from police and tossed a .380-caliber pistol into a sewage drain, where police found it.
>
> Jerryl Christmas, an attorney for Myers' family, said police have not stated a reason that would have given the officer probable cause to pursue Myers and his friends.
>
> "It shows how anxious these officers are -- especially Caucasian officers -- to use excessive force toward African-American children," Christmas said. "Why are you even approaching this individual but for him being an African-American male with two or three other African-American males standing on the street?"
>
> People in Ferguson protesting Michael Brown's death have organized four days of activities in the area starting Friday.
>
> Myers' death has Stan Taylor, 37, a cellphone sales agent, thinking more violence will come.

---

[191] http://www.stltoday.com/news/local/crime-and-courts/teen-in-shaw-shooting-died-from-gunshot-to-right-cheek/article_2d5a8c2a-97db-5cec-a477-1130d7d26f7e.html

"They (police) are sparking war. It's going to be us against them," Taylor said. "Turning the other cheek is not getting the job done." [192]

Okay, so why are police so cognizant of blacks in the metropolitan St. Louis area (especially St. Louis)? Each year, the City of St. Louis Metropolitan Police Department, releases an Annual Report to the Community. This report breaks down violent crime and the overall percentage of the racial group arrested for each offense (note because of lack of trust with police, many violent crimes/homicides lack suspects. The black community would rather have criminals among them than in jail).

This data should help you understand why a white police officer correctly decided to confront Vonderrit Myers.

Remember, out of 318,000 people, St. Louis is 49.2 percent black 43.9 percent white (as of 2010 US Census).

For the sake of space, flip black to p. 20 to read the breakdown of arrests in St. Louis by race, courtesy of the City of St. Louis Metropolitan Police Department Annual Report to the Community.

A thick fog envelops all of America.

We all know it's there.

Until we dare confront this fog, our future as a nation will be anything but uncertain: it will nothing more than Detroit, East St. Louis, Memphis, Gary (Indiana), Camden, Birmingham, or Newark.

Violent crime in St. Louis is a one-race problem, that those white people still trying to keep civilization alive in the city do everything possible to keep out of their neighborhoods and communities. [Public police, private employer: A St. Louis oddity, St. Louis Post-Distpatch, 10-10-14]
This is why white people abandoned St. Louis (and hire off-duty white cops to patrol their neighborhoods); this is why white people

---

[192] Ferguson tensions rise after second shooting, USA Today, 10-10-14

abandon suburbs of St. Louis that attract black people fleeing the black crime of St. Louis; and the pattern continues...[193]

In closing, let's just quote James Kirkpatrick at VDare.com on the United States flag burning incident blacks participated in as they protested Vonderrit Myers death:

> Protesters in St. Louis, unhappy that blacks are not allowed to murder police officers, are now burning American flags as they riot in the city.
>
> It's worth noting that despite having the *de facto* support of the most powerful government in the world, the symbolic prize of the most powerful office in the world, the enthusiastic support of the Department of Justice, and the slavish support of the media, these African-Americans still feel oppressed and have no sense of allegiance or loyalty to the United States of America.
>
> Which of course raises the question–having already essentially dismantled the entire country in order to protect the self-esteem of nonwhites, what more is the historic American nation expected to do?[194]

What more are white people expected to do, Mr. Kirkpatrick?

Remain lost in the fog we all know is there yet refrain from pointing out exists (though we do hire off-duty cops to keep our neighborhoods safe, and if this fails retreat to the nearest all-white suburb to be freed from the type of community "Vonderrit Myers" and their enablers create).

More importantly: continue to allow blacks to monologue whites for their racist past and present, and ensure the future is one where white cops aren't even allowed to arrest black suspects (if white people are allowed to be cops at all).

---

[193] http://www.stltoday.com/news/local/crime-and-courts/public-police-private-employer-a-st-louis-oddity/article_f57f630d-cd97-516b-b619-1dc7fd2fea33.html

[194] http://www.vdare.com/posts/st-louis-protesters-burning-american-flags-now

October 13, 2014
More Than 90% of those Arrested for Weapons Offenses in St. Louis (1999 - 2012) are black: City is 49.2% black and 43.9% white

So there have been five fatal shootings of civilians combined in the city of St. Louis and county in 2014 by police.

All five involved black males. [St. Louis Area Police Now Have Five Fatal Officer Shootings Under Investigation for 2014, RiverFront Times, 10-9-14]:

> The fatal shooting of eighteen-year-old Vonderrit Myers by an off-duty St. Louis Metropolitan police officer Wednesday night has brought the number of fatal police shootings in 2014 that are currently under investigation in St. Louis city and county to five.
>
> All five of the deceased are black men under the age of 31. Two are accused of having a gun. One had a knife, as video evidence shows. And two were unarmed.
>
> The most attention has been focused on the shooting of Michael Brown, the unarmed eighteen-year-old shot and killed by Ferguson police officer Darren Wilson on August 9. A St. Louis County grand jury is considering whether to indict Wilson.[195]

Alright.

---

[195] http://blogs.riverfronttimes.com/dailyrft/2014/10/with_shaw_shooting_st_louis_area_now_has_5_fatal_police_shootings_under_investigation.php

Three had weapons; two had their fists.

None had sandwiches (sorry apologists for Vonderritt Myers). [Vonderrit Myers, Jr. showed off his guns before shooting, Fox2Now.com, 10-13-14][196]

During the Ferguson October marches, a rally was held with one area black 'reverend' unleashing on a system she believes is "guilty as hell." [Religious leaders call for continued Michael Brown protest, Fox2Now.com, 10-12-14]:

> One area pastor said many disenfranchised youth are tired of losing loved ones.
>
> "They are tired of lost opportunities and tired of lost hope," said Rev. Renita Lamkin, St. John AME Church in St. Charles. "They are sick of poor schools and bad policing policies and economic oppression. They are sick, and the whole damn system is guilty as hell."[197]

But what is the system guilty of? Executing black males with extreme prejudice? We already know the homicide rate in St. Louis is entirely due to the black population of the city. Blacks are executing other blacks with extreme prejudice in St. Louis. [Mother of murder victim calls for focus on black on black crime, Fox2Now, 9-1-14][198]

Remember, out of 318,000 people, St. Louis is 49.2 percent black 43.9 percent white (as of 2010 US Census).

Each year, the City of St. Louis Metropolitan Police Department, releases an Annual Report to the Community (check out p. 20 for the breakdown). This report breaks down violent crime and the overall percentage of the racial group arrested for each offense (note

---

[196] http://fox2now.com/2014/10/13/vonderrit-myers-jr-showed-off-his-guns-before-shooting/

[197] http://fox2now.com/2014/10/12/updates-fergusonoctober-interfaith-service-seeks-justice-for-michael-brown/

[198] http://fox2now.com/2014/09/01/mother-of-murder-victim-calls-for-focus-on-black-on-black-crime/

because of lack of trust with police, many violent crimes/homicides lack suspects. The black community would rather have criminals among them than in jail).[199]

And one of those crimes City of St. Louis Metropolitan Police Department tracks by race for is weapons arrests.

Yes, the Annual Report to the Community of St. Louis by the St. Louis Metropolitan Police Department details just who has been primarily responsible for keeping gun crime alive in the city.

Let's take a look at the data:

1999 – 1109 total Weapons arrests

white: 12.44%

Black: 87.47%

2000 – 967 total Weapons arrests

white: 10.55%

black: 89.14%

2002 - 844 total Weapons arrests

white: 9.83%

black: 89.93%

2003 - 766 total Weapons arrests
white: 10.7%
black: 89.16%

2004 - 655 total Weapons arrests
white: 12.75%
black: 86.94%

---

[199] http://fox2now.com/2013/07/19/st-louis-murders-remain-unsolved-because-lack-of-trust-and-fear/

2005 - 711 total Weapons arrests
white: 7.37%
black: 92.47%

2006 - 496 total Weapons arrests
white: 8.3%
black: 91.3%

2007 - 648 total Weapons arrests
white: 9.1%
black: 90.6%

2008 - 753 total Weapons arrests
white: 6.5%
black: 93.3%

2009 - 844 total Weapons arrests
white: 10.4%
black: 89.1 %

2010 - 821 total Weapons arrests
white: 7.7%
black: 92.3%

2011 - 857 total Weapons arrests
white: 8.6%
black: 91.2%

2012 – 817 total Weapons arrests
white: 9.9%

black: 89.7%

This data should sufficiently show the St. Louis Police Department is primarily encountering only dangerous, armed black males when they engage in community relations that end in a weapons arrest.

"The whole damn system is guilty as hell," for a reason Rev. Lamkin would never, ever admit: dangerous black males threaten to destabilize the civilization whites built in St. Louis and simply outlawing their ability to legally carry a firearm would immediately make the city infinitely safer.

Those blacks who carry illegal or stolen guns, like the late lover of sandwiches Vonderritt Myers, will immediately be thrown on death row: for blacks with illegal guns represent a menace to their community and a civilizational threat to the communities whites build (see: Detroit, Memphitws, Newark, Baltimore, Camden, ect.).

The system is guilty as hell for damning cops to a similar fate as Officer Darren Wilson; for daring to disarm a dangerous black male or simply ask them to walk on the sidewalk instead of the middle of the street can become the fodder for massive black agitation/riots/looting/violence.

Statistics don't lie; in the case of the black community defending blacks toting around ~~stolen guns~~ sandwiches, well, the latter group has no problem lying to keep dangerous criminals out of jails and walking the streets.

October 14, 2014
"Negro Fatigue" Settling in Across St. Louis Metropolitan Area, St. Louis Post-Dispatch Admits

A black mayor is an inevitability in Ferguson; the 67 percent black city today, that was 76 percent white in 1990 (99 percent white in 1970).

A black police chief and a majority black city council as well; after all, Ferguson is only 27 percent white and the city becomes 'blacker' as time marches forward.

But before this racial exchange of power occurs and the colonization of Ferguson by blacks into just another East St. Louis-style city is complete, whites are allowed a simple news story to air their grievances. [Weariness of Ferguson protests grows, St. Louis Post-Dispatch, 10-14-14]:

> Brian Fletcher loves Ferguson. He brags about it, he rattles off historical facts about it and, as the former mayor, he feels the urge to stick up for the city and its people.
>
> And right now, he says people are tired of the constant protesting, tired of the noise and tired of feeling intimidated.
>
> That's the exact reaction many protest leaders said they are hoping for.
>
> It's been nearly 70 days since Ferguson police Officer Darren Wilson fatally shot Michael Brown, 18.
>
> Since then, protests have sprung up around the region, spreading most recently to downtown St. Louis, St. Louis University, Webster Groves and also the Shaw neighborhood, where crowds have gathered to protest the fatal shooting of teenager Vonderitt Myers Jr. by St. Louis police.
>
> In one incident, video cameras captured a heated back-and-forth between protesters and Cardinals fans outside of Busch Stadium.
>
> But the epicenter of the unrest is in Ferguson, and Fletcher, like many others, says it's hard to remember what it felt like to live in Ferguson before the city became infamous.
>
> On a typical day in Ferguson, there's a persistent group of picketers along South Florissant Road, in front of the police station, holding signs with slogans such as: "Justice for All," and "Black Lives Matter."
>
> Ferguson resident Jill Hatcher said she used to drive by and honk her car horn in support.
>
> "Now I speed by with my windows up and my doors locked," she said.

Hatcher's fear stems from the events at night, when protesters sometimes march in the street drumming and chanting into the early hours.

Aside from the noise, there have been shots fired, attempted arson and some instances of looting.

A QUESTION OF RACE

Fletcher, who is white, also acknowledges that persistent racial tension underlies Ferguson's new reality.

"I think quite frankly, Caucasians are intimidated by protesters who think that if they can make Caucasians feel uncomfortable, they can change the rules. And it's working," Fletcher said.

A number of black people also feel uncomfortable. Pam Peters has lived in Ferguson for 37 years.

"I don't like the way people are talking about Ferguson now," she said. "We are good people. We are tired of the protests."

Peters said she didn't think Ferguson would ever go back to how it was before Brown's shooting.

"We just have way too many young people who are trying to stir the pot," she said. "If police stop them for no reason, that's not right. But, not to beat a dead horse, some of them bring it on themselves."[200]

No, it's going to be impossible to get out from under that, Mrs. Dubose. Get use to having no customers at your Natalie's Cakes & More store as the city's white population declines, unless you plan on accepting EBT/Food Stamps for your tasty treats.

---

[200] http://www.stltoday.com/news/local/metro/weariness-of-ferguson-protests-grows/article_d3260f13-d07d-592e-841b-3618d1ecbd5a.html

October 16, 2014
Visible Black Hand of Economics in Action: Many majority black St. Louis municipalities survive on court fines and fees

So the white political establishment has already capitulated in St. Louis to the black mob. [St. Louis to forgive about 220,000 warrants for nonviolent municipal offenses, St. Louis Post-Dispatch, 10-1-14]:

> Offenders of the city's municipal laws with outstanding warrants soon will get a free pass.
>
> St. Louis officials plan to announce that the city's municipal court will automatically clear outstanding warrants for nonviolent traffic violations and allow offenders to reset the court dates without a fee so long as they act by year's end, making it the most progressive warrant forgiveness program in the region.
>
> About 220,000 outstanding warrants issued before Oct. 1 in the city will automatically be forgiven, according to Jeff Rainford, the chief of staff to Mayor Francis Slay. He said the announcement was planned for today.
>
> Rainford said the novel approach comes from conversations in the wake of the unrest in Ferguson, where many advocates of the poor complain that some residents are burdened by steep court fines and saddled with warrants for minor offenses.
>
> "In light of Ferguson, we were thinking of how we can be more fair," Rainford said.[201]

"How can we be more fair."

---

[201] http://www.stltoday.com/news/local/crime-and-courts/st-louis-to-forgive-about-warrants-for-nonviolent-municipal-offenses/article_7f9dbef3-7409-5e81-ae28-3c79faa8b147.html

The most important question of modern America, a country completely gripped in the theocratic belief in Black-Run America's (BRA) moral authority.

Fair.

With your average black male being quite intimate with the judicial system, it's only fair to extend the "Ban the Box" campaign to the city Michael Brown and Vonderritt Myers called 'home.' [St. Louis city will no longer require job applicants to disclose felony convictions, St. Louis Post-Dispatch, 10-1-14]:

> Mayor Francis Slay announced on Tuesday that St. Louis will no longer require applicants for city jobs to disclose felony convictions.
>
> "Millions of Americans have been convicted of felonies. Many of them have paid their debt to society and are willing to earn a second chance," Slay said at a press conference.
>
> Some jobs are subject to regulations and the city is legally required to do background checks, such as at the airport or police department. Those checks will still take place, officials said.
>
> Slay said the city will do such screenings on a case-by-case basis but that job applications no longer will face a check-box asking them about their criminal history.
>
> "We would not hire a child molester for recreational programs," Slay said. "We would not hire an embezzler to handle money."
>
> The announcement comes as regional leaders grapple with the unrest in Ferguson after the shooting death of unarmed teenager Michael Brown. Protesters have used the situation to shine a light on problems such as racial discord, police tactics and poverty.
>
> Slay made the announcement while standing next to Jamilah Nasheed, a state senator who has appeared on the front lines of many of the Ferguson protests.

> "This is how you fight crime," Nasheed said. "You fight crime with jobs."
>
> Officials said some people may not apply for jobs thinking a conviction would automatically disqualify them.
>
> "If you get out of prison and you can't get a job, you can't provide for yourself or your family," Slay said.[202]

Fair.

"Ban the Box" to ensure fairness in job applications.

Why not just make it illegal to give black people tickets for nonviolent offenses?

Wouldn't that be fair?

Of course, and just the concept to introduce for white leaders hoping to curry favor with the black mob out for justice. [Court study shows fines weigh heavily on towns with larger African American population, Fox2Now, 10-15-14]:

> An independent study supports recent complaints that small, municipal courts in St. Louis County are often revenue raisers for towns in the northern part of the county.
>
> Better Together, a not-for-profit studying fragmented government in St. Louis County and City, issued the document Wednesday.
>
> "Our report indicates a systemic problem that allows for some municipalities to survive on court fines and fees. Further data shows this is largely done on the back of poor black communities," said Dave Leipholtz, an attorney and the Director of Community Based Studies. Leipholtz found some St. Louis County towns that budget for an increase in court fines and fees. In other cases the courts produce revenue well

---

[202] http://www.stltoday.com/news/local/crime-and-courts/st-louis-city-will-no-longer-require-job-applicants-to/article_fcd914e2-9df7-55b4-997c-52ac08f97a2a.html

beyond the cost of administering the judicial system.

Calverton Park topped the list at 66 percent of its general revenue derived from court fines and fees. Pine Lawn drew 48 percent and Normandy 40 percent. Twenty municipalities all north of Olive drew 20 percent or more of their general revenue from the fines and fees. Across St. Louis County communities averaged 13 percent of general revenue from the courts.

Not all of the fines are traffic related. Veteran municipal judge Frank Vatterott, who serves in Overland, said some fines come from prosecuting shop lifting and domestic abuse cases. But he agreed there are issues that need to be addressed to insure the municipal courts operate fairly and provide justice.

"I think it shows, unfortunately, for better or worse there are a lot of cities in the northern part of our county that exist on the traffic court. That's not healthy," he said.[203]

"Our report indicates a systemic problem that allows for some municipalities to survive on court fines and fees. Further data shows this is largely done on the back of poor black communities," said Dave Leipholtz..."

No, the systemic problem is that the black population in these cities lacks the ability to create any taxable wealth that can be used to fund a government and public services.

Literally, we have millions of unemployable black people bred via white tax dollars to... do... nothing but breed (and ultimately lock away into the prison system for crimes largely committed against their fellow blacks).

And no city illustrates the instability of the American Experiment better than this midwestern city dedicated to the promotion of fairness.

---

[203] http://fox2now.com/2014/10/15/study-many-north-st-louis-county-towns-balance-budgets-with-court-fees/

Consulting the 2009 New York Times Food Stamp Usage Across the Country interactive map, we learn this about the city of St. Louis (49 percent black and 43 percent white):

- As of 2009, 60 percent of blacks were on EBT/Food Stamps in the city of St. Louis
- As of 2009, 10 percent of whites were on EBT/Food Stamps in the city of St. Louis[204]

St. Louis County (different from the city of St. Louis) is just over one million people in population. It's home to Ferguson, that lovely post-white suburb boasting a growing, self-insufficient black population. [Ferguson: Gentrification and its discontents, Al-Jazeera, 8-16-14]

Of those one million people, 68 percent of the county's population is white and 23.7 percent is black. Consulting the 2009 New York Times Food Stamp Usage Across the Country interactive map, we learn this about the county:

- As of 2009, 38 percent of blacks were on EBT/Food Stamps in the city of St. Louis
- As of 2009, 4 percent of whites were on EBT/Food Stamps in the city of St. Louis[205]

"Our report indicates a systemic problem that allows for some municipalities to survive on court fines and fees. Further data shows this is largely done on the back of poor black communities," said Dave Leipholtz..."

It should be quite obvious these "poor black communities" in metropolitan St. Louis exist because of the hardworking white communities, who see their tax dollars redistributed to pay for the breeding of more black people.

"The Day the EBT Card Stops" will make the world George Romero created in *Night of the Living Dead* and *Dawn of the Dead* look like a

---

[204] http://www.nytimes.com/interactive/2009/11/28/us/20091128-foodstamps.html?_r=0

[205] Ibid.

Disney fairytale in comparison; and St. Louis will be the city (and metropolitan area) where the madness is most extreme.

Nature, unlike the white political establishment in St. Louis (and all of America), abhors fairness and equality.

In the end, her wrath will be most unkind.

Forgive outstanding warrants for failing to show up for court all you want.

"Ban the Box" all you want.

Refuse to ask why majority black communities lack the ability to survive without court fines and fees (a powerful reminder of the Visible Black Hand of Economics) all you want.

Mandating fairness, whatever the cost, is America's most noble pursuit.

In the end, the cost will simply be the civilization white people built in not just St. Louis, but all of America.

October 17, 2014
Repentance or the Guillotine: Multiple Faiths Converge on St. Louis to Demand White Police Atone for Their Sins

There is only sin in Black-Run America (BRA).

The sin of racism by whites.

Police departments across the collapsing, "hollowing out" landscapes of America primarily interact with black males, who commit the bulk of the crime in these nightmarish urban environments.[206]

Never mind black-on-black crime/robbery/homicide, the real sin is white cops daring to hold black suspects accountable for their actions (even when the black community only bothers to care when a Vonderritt Myers or Michael Brown is gunned down by cop simply trying to make their community safer by stopping the criminal activity a Myers/Brown is engaging in). [VIGIL HONORS SLAIN, COMFORTS THOSE WHO MOURN, St. Louis Post-Dispatch, January 1, 2002]:

> The Rev. Earl Nance, president of the St. Louis Clergy Coalition, said blacks must take more responsibility to help police fight "black-on-black crime."
>
> "I understand people who holler about the police," Nance said. "There are bad police officers, just like there are bad preachers and bad politicians. But I'd like to see more of these characters out there (protesting) on the streets when we kill each other."[207]

..."Blacks must take more responsibility," is a phrase that falls on deaf ears to 60 percent of the black community, is greeted with uncontrollable laughter by 35 percent of the black community, and is a statement of accountability 5 percent of the black community is incapable of comprehending.

Protesting black-on-black violence is counterproductive; the frequency of black-on-black violence being publicized by a rally or march and broadcast on the local network affiliates only confirms why white people live in suburbs far, far away from blacks and send their kids to "good schools " (devoid of blacks).

Which brings us to the most farcical moment of the entire farce of Ferguson.[Clergy-led protest raises questions over nature of repentance, St. Louis Post-Dispatch, 10-15-14]:

---

[206] http://www.stltoday.com/news/local/metro/census-shows-city-is-hollowing-out/article_4af01497-bca8-5b63-8cc6-1c724c11dd08.html

[207] VIGIL HONORS SLAIN, COMFORTS THOSE WHO MOURN, St. Louis Post-Dispatch, January 1, 2002

The rain pounding the pavement made no difference to those urging repentance.

With or without umbrellas, a gang of clergy from various faith traditions marched to the Ferguson Police Department on "Moral Monday," the last day in a weekend of protests dubbed Ferguson October. Clergy advanced on South Florissant Road determined to force one question on a community of officers: Will you repent?

They gathered in the parking lot of the police station and created a memorial to Michael Brown, the unarmed teenager fatally shot by Ferguson police Officer Darren Wilson on Aug. 9, by drawing a chalk outline of a body on the pavement. Candles were lit.

A line of police officers quickly formed a perimeter around a crowd of hundreds who had come in support of the clergy. Some guarded the police department's side door. Officers soon changed into riot gear, equipping themselves with shields and batons.

Then, in the midst of the unrelenting rain, one protest leader cried that officers would be given the chance to confess their sins and repent. One by one, clergy approached the officers on guard, asking them to — for at least a moment — forget their duties and reflect instead on America's system of racial injustice.

Others, however, said the protest reflected a more fire-and-brimstone kind of theology, with some in the crowd yelling "In Jesus' name, repent!," which sounded less like an invitation and more like a threat.

David Greenhaw, president of Eden Theological Seminary, who participated in the protest, said he, too, could have done without that part of the demonstration.

It was "dramatic but unrealistic to think that a police officer would offer their confession," Greenhaw said. "You know, I wasn't crazy about that. I didn't think that was the best element." Repentance, Greenhaw said, isn't "coercive, I think it's invited, and there was a coercive element." Greenhaw said the protest reflected a doctrinal divide in the theology of repentance.

Others said the call to repentance wasn't meant as a condemnation of any one individual but of American society as a whole. Before the march to the police station, clergy themselves were asked to repent for their complicity in a system of racial disparity that continues to hurt African-Americans.

Rabbi Susan Talve of Central Reform Congregation said the officers were "part of the system that use young black people as an ATM," referring to the disproportionate number of traffic tickets and fines inflicted on African-Americans. [208]

If racialized policing were occurring, the Department of Justice would immediately have suspended any and every officer engaging in such activities immediately. The only crime these clergy demanded repentance from white police officers for is that they were white at the time they arrested a black male.

Again: we are quickly approaching the day when it will be against the law for a white police officer to arrest a black person they suspect as having committed a crime.

Eight members of "a secretive unit of the U.S. Department of Justice called the Community Relations Service" have been on the ground in metropolitan St. Louis since August 10, when Darren Wilson defended himself from Michael Brown's unwanted advances.[209]

Eric "My People" Holder dispatched more than 40 FBI agents to canvass the neighborhood of Ferguson[210], where those unwanted

---

[208] http://www.stltoday.com/lifestyles/faith-and-values/clergy-led-protest-raises-questions-over-nature-of-repentance/article_6c644480-08e8-5cc3-a45c-d4414b153bd6.html

[209] http://www.stltoday.com/news/local/govt-and-politics/the-justice-department-s-soft-side-how-one-federal-agency/article_591a2e64-7dd1-5008-b300-0ab9ad8b9168.html

[210] http://www.justice.gov/opa/pr/attorney-general-statement-latest-developments-federal-civil-rights-investigation-ferguson-mo

advances by Michael Brown were permanently stopped; not to mention the legion of "prosecutors on the ground from the Civil Rights Division and U.S. Attorney's Office" Holder had on the ground probing for radicalized policing.[211]

They've found nothing to confirm that racialized policing is occurring in Ferguson or other communities in metropolitan St. Louis, outside of the frequent interaction the police have with black males when it comes to arresting suspects for violent crime, assaults, robbery, home invasions, homicide, rapes, and weapon offenses.

There is only sin in Black-Run America (BRA).
The sin of racism by whites.
Repent or else...

October 18, 2014
The Inevitable Michael Brown Riots: Does Darren Wilson's Testimony Represent a "Holy Grail" Racial Awakening for Whites?

Remember the end of *Indiana Jones and the Last Crusade*? Harrison Ford's character, Dr. Henry "Indiana" Jones, reaches for the cup of Christ (the Holy Grail); his extended fingers inches from grabbing the cup, as his father - played brilliantly by Sean Connery - holds onto his other hand.

"I can almost reach it dad," Indiana says to his father, the latter having obsessively spent his entire life trying to locate the cup.

"Indiana," his father cooly states, "Let it go."

The cup is lost forever, but the elder Jones' lifelong crusade was

---

[211] Ibid.

fulfilled; he saw the item that plagued his every thought, haunting his every dream.

It existed.

As Jared Taylor simply inquired in a recent video, do the facts of the events between Darren Wilson and Michael Brown in Ferguson even matter to blacks? [Ferguson: Do the Facts Even Matter?, American Renaissance, 10-16-14][212]

The answer, of course, is an emphatic 'no'.

Many white people, in not just America but the entire world, have looked on vainly for that one moment that will liberate us from the current paradigm we live, ushering in a new era where we are in control of forging our own future (instead of having a hostile managerial elite dictating that our past transgressions always overshadow the present and fundamentally stand in the way of us even having a future).

"The Holy Grail" moment that will open millions of eyes to a truth many individual white people wish they had never been exposed to, for the reality is no one will ever truly ascertain or pinpoint why some whites wake up to the nightmare of modernity and otherwise remain blissfully unaware of the dire predicament.

Perhaps there is no "Holy Grail" incident coming.

But with the hilariously inept reaction to the Ebola scare by the managerial leftist elite (their commitment to the destruction of the historical American population by mass immigration accentuated by an unwillingness to stop the African plague with a simple quarantine/flight restriction from infected nations) and the unraveling of the Gentle Giant narrative in metropolitan St. Louis should open up a few closed eyes.

Right? [*Police Officer in Ferguson Is Said to Recount a Struggle*, New York Times, 10-17-14]:

---

[212] http://www.amren.com/features/2014/10/ferguson-do-the-facts-even-matter/

The police officer who fatally shot Michael Brown in Ferguson, Mo., two months ago has told investigators that he was pinned in his vehicle and in fear for his life as he struggled over his gun with Mr. Brown, according to government officials briefed on the federal civil rights investigation into the matter.

The officer, Darren Wilson, has told the authorities that during the scuffle, Mr. Brown reached for the gun. It was fired twice in the car, according to forensics tests performed by the Federal Bureau of Investigation. The first bullet struck Mr. Brown in the arm; the second bullet missed.

The forensics tests showed Mr. Brown's blood on the gun, as well as on the interior door panel and on Officer Wilson's uniform. Officer Wilson told the authorities that Mr. Brown had punched and scratched him repeatedly, leaving swelling on his face and cuts on his neck.

This is the first public account of Officer Wilson's testimony to investigators, but it does not explain why, after he emerged from his vehicle, he fired at Mr. Brown multiple times. It contradicts some witness accounts, and it will not calm those who have been demanding to know why an unarmed man was shot a total of six times.

Mr. Brown's death continues to fuel anger and sometimes-violent protests.In September, Officer Wilson appeared for four hours before a St. Louis County grand jury, which was convened to determine whether there is probable cause that he committed a crime. Legal experts have said that his decision to testify was surprising, given that it was not required by law. But the struggle in the car may prove to be a more influential piece of information for the grand jury, one that speaks to Officer Wilson's state of mind, his feeling of vulnerability and his sense of heightened alert when he killed Mr. Brown. Police officers typically have wide latitude to use lethal force if they reasonably believe that they are in imminent danger.

The officials said that while the federal investigation was continuing, the evidence so far did not support civil rights charges against Officer Wilson. To press charges, the Justice Department would need to clear a high bar, proving that Officer Wilson willfully violated Mr. Brown's civil rights when he shot him.

The account of Officer Wilson's version of events did not come from the Ferguson Police Department or from officials whose activities are being investigated as part of the civil rights inquiry.[213]

What's so sad about this situation is the Attorney General of the Department of Justice, Eric "My People" Holder, obviously knew this truth before he went on his "deeply personal" sojourn to Ferguson ("I'm also a black man"), dispatched a legion of Justice Department Civil Rights investigators and more than 40 FBI agents to comb the St. Louis suburb for evidence of racism.

Just as in *Downfall*, somewhere Holder is portraying the endlessly parodied agitated Hitler scene...

Will blacks riot in St. Louis when the Grand Jury convened in the aftermath of the Darren Wilson/Michael Brown incident finds Mr. Wilson innocent of any guilt in the shooting?

May the odds ever be in our favor.

But know this: don't look at this event as one of those "Holy Grail" moments.

As Jared Taylor wisely pointed out, the facts in this case simply do not matter to black people: white people and blacks speak different languages in America, and no Rosetta Stone will ever translate our languages into peaceful discourse.

But *Those Who Can See* also speak a different language than your ordinary white person, for they have already had their Holy Grail moment of awakening.

---

[213] http://www.nytimes.com/2014/10/18/us/ferguson-case-officer-is-said-to-cite-struggle.html?_r=0

So come what may of the inevitable announcement by the Grand Jury that Darren Wilson is completely innocent, take a bit of wisdom from the final scene of *Indiana Jones and the Last Crusade:* "Let it go," when it comes to the notion the Holy Grail of racial awakening is coming.

You've already had this awakening.

For others, you can't show them what you've seen, because they wouldn't believe you if they saw it; they must see it for themselves.

But the one reassuring fact is unavoidable, once you've had your own personal "Holy Grail" moment: it does exist.

In the infinite potential interactions humans have one a daily basis, just one seemingly insignificant encounter can open an individuals eyes to a world they willingly remained ignorant of every moment prior until this briefest of instances.

But "let it go" when comes to a belief of a grand moment of mass awareness.

October 19, 2014
The Microcosm for the Nationwide War on Whites: The St. Louis Post-Dispatch confirms the role Section 8 Vouchers had in dismantling the civilization whites built (and fled) in Ferguson

It was never about "Mike Brown."

It was always about racial conquest; about the acquisition of power and the ability to exercise this political authority.

And if racial conquest is impeded from being implemented in any way, well, threaten violence, arson, and an insurrection. [Report: Michael Brown's blood found on Officer Darren Wilson's gun, car door, CNN, 10-18-14]:

> Angela Whitman, a Ferguson resident who was among activists meeting with U.S. Attorney General Eric Holder there in August, found the newspaper account of Wilson's testimony "so hard to believe."
>
> Whitman worried whether the revelation would provoke another round of racially charged protests akin to the violent demonstrations immediatelyafter Brown's August 9 death in the St. Louis suburb. Wilson is white; Brown was black.
>
> "This is not a black and white thing, this is about what's right and wrong. St. Louis is in trouble, because if this is what Darren Wilson said, and they believe him, St. Louis is going to burn," Whitman said.
>
> "I'm so frustrated with this. It's all for political gain. It's become no longer about Mike Brown," Whitman added.[214]

Is that a threat of domestic terrorism, Whitman?

"St. Louis is going to burn."

I'd say this is an admission of terrorism, but the black population has been terrorizing the white population for decades; if this wasn't the case white people wouldn't immediately put up a "for sale" sign in the yard at the first sign their community is going majority black.

The key to understanding the black insurrection in currently 67 percent black Ferguson, Missouri over the shooting death of Michael "No Angel" Brown by a white police officer can be found in this simple chronological exposé of the demographics of the city:

---

[214] http://www.cnn.com/2014/10/18/justice/michael-brown-darren-wilson-account/index.html

In 1970, Ferguson was 99 percent white; In 1980, Ferguson was 85 percent white and 14 black; In 1990, Ferguson was 73.8 percent white and 25.1 percent black; In 2000, Ferguson was 44.8 percent white and 52.4 percent black; In 2010 Ferguson was 29.3 percent white and 67.4 percent black[215]

Which brings us to this 1991 article from the St. Louis Post-Dispatch describing white people's decision to flee then 73.8 percent white Ferguson (to paraphrase Paul Revere: the blacks are coming, the blacks are coming!). [Whites Flock To Outlying Counties: Schools, Crime, Attitudes Cause Thousands To Abandon St. Louis, St. Louis Post-Dispatch, 4-15-1991]:

> Affordable housing, strong school systems and low crime rates have combined to form a powerful magnet to draw thousands of whites away from the city of St. Louis and St. Louis County and into once-remote areas of St. Charles, Jefferson and Franklin counties.
>
> Statistics from the 1990 census show that white population loss has been greatest in traditionally white, middle-class areas of south St. Louis and in middle-class sections of North County. The areas are the same ones that experienced dramatic increases in black population in the 1980s.
>
> The boom areas continue to be deep west St. Louis County, much of St. Charles County and Jefferson County."This is the smartest move I ever made," said Rick Clay, a father of three, who moved onto Lake Charles Drive near St. Peters in St. Charles County about a year ago.
>
> He said he had moved there from Ferguson, where he grew up."Schools were a big, big, big reason why we came here," said Clay, who is white. "And the area where I lived was deteriorating. That was the biggest thing."Greg Risinger is a white father of two who moved to St. Charles County from Ferguson about eight years ago.
>
> "We looked at the schools, we looked at the churches, we

---

[215] http://www.forbes.com/sites/niallmccarthy/2014/08/19/chart-ferguson-white-flight/

looked at Mid-Rivers Mall, and this is where we decided to live," he said. "People I went to grade school with are out here. We're real happy we made the move."

North County census tracts that experienced the largest losses in white population during the 1980s include: A tract bounded roughly by Interstate 270 on the south, the Chicago, Burlington and Quincy Railroad tracks on the north and east and Lewis and Clark Boulevard (Highway 367) on the west.

That tract saw the number of white residents drop to 10,937 from 13,121 - a loss of 17 percent. A tract bounded roughly by Interstate 270 on the north, New Halls Ferry Road on the west and Lewis and Clark (Highway 367) on the east. White population dropped by more than half - to 2,134 from 4,795.

A tract bounded by Interstate 270 on the north, Chambers Road on the south, Florissant Road on the west and Halls Ferry on the east. That tract saw its white population drop by 24 percent - to 6,145 from 8,113.

Other North County areas that showed dramatic white population loss included the city of Jennings, which saw its white population drop 32 percent, to 5,702 from 8,436; sections of Ferguson and parts of Normandy. North St. Louis County's loss, for the most part, has been St. Charles County's gain.

The county was the fastest-growing in Missouri from 1980 to 1990. Its population jumped by 48 percent - to 212,907 from 144,107. Whites make up 96 percent of the county's residents. 'We had 97 houses for sale 16 months ago, and we have eight left," said Marilyn Voorhees, a hostess for the Kingspointe development near O'Fallon, where houses are priced in the $60,000-to-$70,000 range.

"It's been incredible, even through this recession," she said. "The land is so cheap, the houses are so much more affordable."

Racial Considerations

Several whites interviewed by the Post-Dispatch said the

> movement of blacks into their old neighborhoods had had little bearing on their decisions to leave, but others acknowledged that it was a consideration.
>
> "We just felt kind of unsafe," said Carolyn Mooney, a white and the mother of two children. Her family moved to St. Charles County about a year ago from a town house in north St. Louis County."We were kind of the minority there. Neither my husband nor I are prejudiced, but we felt like a minority."Some whites offered stronger feelings."All the blacks were moving in, and my son was starting to play with them," said a woman who moved from North County into the High Sierra Subdivision of Jefferson County five years ago.
>
> She declined to give her name.
>
> We would have stayed, but we were scared. My husband wouldn't let me go out shopping at night."A white widow who lives in the lower Paddock Forest neighborhood north of Parker Road in North County said the racial change of the area was the major reason she had decided to put a "for sale" sign in front of the home where she has lived for 14 years.[216]

That article was published 23 years ago this past April.

This article, a story of the Section 8-ing of Ferguson,[217] was just published. [As low-income housing boomed, Ferguson pushed back, St. Louis Post-Dispatch, 10-19-14]:

> Flip the calendar back to the evening of Sept. 14, 2010, four years before the Michael Brown shooting, and take a seat in the blue-padded chairs here at City Hall.
>
> There was a meeting going on — one that would prove prophetic — about activity brewing on the city's far eastern flank.

---

[216] Whites Flock To Outlying Counties: Schools, Crime, Attitudes Cause Thousands To Abandon St. Louis, St. Louis Post-Dispatch, 4-15-1991

[217] http://www.stltoday.com/news/local/metro/why-did-the-michael-brown-shooting-happen-here/article_678334ce-500a-5689-8658-f548207cf253.html

Jammed full of high-density apartment complexes, the area stands in stark contrast to the historic downtown, which is the pride of city leaders and families trying to buck the sluggish trend of much of surrounding north St. Louis County.

The apartments came up during the meeting when then-Mayor Brian Fletcher asked for an update on the Responsible Landlord Initiative.

Ferguson, population 21,000, fretted a lot during the recession about foreclosures.

Now city officials had a jaw-dropping report in hand that mentioned 385 recommended evictions between January 2008 and June 2010.

"That's a lot of evictions," Fletcher said, according to a transcript of the meeting.

What's more, nearly half of the city's police calls were going to the apartment complexes. Places such as Oakmont Townhomes, Park Ridge Apartments, Northwinds Apartments, Versailles Apartments and Canfield Green, which would gain worldwide attention as the site of Brown's shooting by Ferguson police.

"Those are some really substantial numbers that we need to work on," Fletcher said.

"We need to get some police officers talking to the tenants."

City Manager John Shaw agreed: "There's definitely a problem there."

According to a Post-Dispatch analysis of Section 8 voucher data from the Department of Housing and Urban Development, the number of Section 8 voucher recipients has doubled in St. Louis County since the mid-1990s. That doesn't take into account other rental subsidy programs.

Factoring in all federal programs, there were roughly 13,000 households with subsidized housing in the county last year, including about 7,500 who used Section 8 vouchers, according to HUD estimates. By comparison, in the city of St. Louis, there were nearly 14,900 households living in subsidized units — about 4,700 used vouchers.

The data on Section 8 also show that the subsidies have tended to cluster in lower-income areas. Many inner-ring North County suburbs are disproportionately absorbing the tenants who have flocked to aging apartment complexes.

That includes Ferguson. A census tract that consists of a portion of Oakmont Townhomes and Northwinds Apartments and stretches eastward into unincorporated St. Louis County had more Section 8 renters in 2013 than any tract in the entire state, according to HUD estimates.

In that area, nearly 20 percent of the 5,000 people who lived there were in Section 8 units. More than half of those households had median incomes of less than $10,000; 57 percent were headed by one parent; and 99 percent were African-American.

According to records from the Housing Authority of St. Louis County, three of the top nine recipients of Section 8 payments from June 2011 to June 2014 were the owners of Park Ridge, Northwinds and Oakmont. Currently, more than 200 tenants in those complexes have vouchers.

In three census tracts that jut from the eastern portion of Ferguson into portions of Dellwood, Jennings and unincorporated North County, there were an estimated 745 Section 8 renters. That is more than in all areas of St. Louis

County south of Olive Boulevard.[218]

Section 8 Vouchers are nothing more than a form of biological warfare by the leftist, managerial elite against what remains of America's historic majority population: by moving blacks into formerly white areas, the managerial elite redistribute crime from failing urban cities (St. Louis) into the suburbs.

Crime follows, because crime only exists because of the people who commit (and propagate) it: read the *St. Louis Post-Dispatch* breakdown of the Section 8 Voucher scheme and you will see it's time white people petition the United Nations for ending the biological warfare the elites practice on their communities in America.

Now, when the pressure is at its zenith (the Darren Wilson/Michael Brown saga coming to an inevitable conclusion of the formers innocence being determined by a Grand Jury) courtesy of a population subsisting on Section 8 Vouchers and EBT card/Food Stamps, the transformation of Ferguson by the black undertow will be complete.

It was never about Mike Brown: it's about power.

Taking political power out of the hands of whites (forever) and giving it blacks: all while the managerial elite counts the money they earn from this Section 8 scheme...

Biological warfare is being waged in America: Thy name is Section 8 Vouchers.

Steve Sailer has dubbed "poor blacks" the biggest hot potato in America.

He is wrong. They are a population bred (subsidized by redistributed white taxpayer money) with only one goal: the complete dismantling of the civilization whites built and the dispossession of their political power as they scatter to new suburbs to live that will inevitably be targeted by Section 8 Vouchers for annihilation.

---

[218] http://www.stltoday.com/news/local/metro/why-did-the-michael-brown-shooting-happen-here/article_678334ce-500a-5689-8658-f548207cf253.html

"St. Louis is going to burn," warned (whined) some leftist to CNN, if Darren Wilson isn't brought to justice.

This admission of holding whites hostage unless blacks get their way isn't even in the Top 10 facts to discern from what you've read here.

That should provide sufficient evidence to show you how insane the situation is for *Those Who Can See* in 2014 America.

October 20, 2014
The tragic consequences of ignoring the contents of The Bell Curve; for as life in St. Louis proves, the bell curve will not ignore you

Confession time.

The idea of black-on-black crime has never bothered me, nor has the tendency for the black community to practice "no snitching" and protect black criminals in their midst.

What does bother me is the loss of real estate due to high rates of black-on-black crime, requiring white people to vacate the land where this internecine fighting takes place for either residential or business purposes.

What does bother me is the loss of ability to utilize public transportation, for the fear of being the victim of a crime, living/shopping near a bus or metro/train stop offers too great a risk and too little a reward for riding.[219]

---

[219] http://www.riverfronttimes.com/2008-08-20/news/out-of-control-shoplifting-at-the-st-louis-galleria-violent-attacks-in-the-delmar-loop-is-metrolink-a-vehicle-for-crime/

It's sad individual black people lack the future time-orientation and impulse control to refrain from participating in the type of violence that destroys black lives and demolishes property value wherever a black community is found; but it's a fact of life in America that no matter the money pumped into an initiative to offer jobs training, midnight basketball, or whatever other "My Brother's Keeper" program promises to do, the violence remains.

Take this hilarious story out of metropolitan St. Louis, which lets slip one immutable truth of what the black undertow imports: the price per square foot in 67 percent black Ferguson (remember: Ferguson was 76 percent white in 1990) was already trending down before the Darren Wilson/Mike Brown encounter. [Riot or not, homes are selling in Ferguson, St. Louis Post-Dispatch, 10-19-14]

St. Louis has been called the ultimate Bell Curve City, and there's no greater social metric of this fitting moniker than the monopoly blacks have on ensuring the city has a homicide problem.

Because of high rates of black homicide in the city, the Families Advocating Safe Streets was founded with only one goal in mind: a support group for friends and relatives of black homicide victims. [FAMILES TO HUNT KILLERS GROUPS SAYS POLICE, MEDIA PAY LITTLE HEED TO BLACKS, St. Louis Post-Dispatch, November 8, 1993]:

> Four families of black murder victims have hired a private detective to find the killers of their loved ones, saying police and the media have not given them enough attention because of their race or social status.
>
> Families Advocating Safe Streets, a support group for friends and relatives of black homicide victims, called a news conference Sunday at Northland shopping center to denounce what its members consider to be less concern and effort by homicide detectives and news organizations when it comes to black murder victims.
>
> "There is some concern that there is not an equal sense of outrage with respect to black homicide victims," said William

Oliver, an assistant professor of criminology at the University of Missouri at St. Louis. Oliver cited the flurry of attention that the media and police gave a double homicide this year in Ladue and the disappearance of a white waitress who worked at Union Station.

"Those cases received a great deal of attention, as they ought to have received," Oliver said. "On the other hand, there haven't been any black cases resulting in such scrutiny." He then introduced two mothers whose children were murdered.

One, Patricia Fedrick, said she did not even know if homicide detectives were still investigating the death of her son, Demetrius, 18.

He was shot in the head three months ago as he waited for a bus at Kingshighway and St. Louis Avenue. Homicide detectives could not be reached to comment Sunday.

Fedrick said she last heard from police two weeks ago. Police offered her moral support and said they would put their best detectives on the case, she said, "but as far as concrete, tax-paying actual facts, I haven't received any."

Demetrius Fedrick apparently was killed over a gold bracelet. "My son worked two jobs, graduated high school and started trying to become a man, but he was robbed of that also," his mother said.[220]

Supply and demand, in action: the supremely high rate of homicide in the black community of St. Louis leaves police jaded to trying to solve a seemingly insolvable problem versus the extreme rarity of white homicide in the city leading to immediate calls to solve the horrible crime (if black homicides were actually considered "horrible" by the black community, then they work overtime to end the so-called 'senseless' killings).

When taxpayer funded police departments have overwhelmed

---

[220] **FAMILES TO HUNT KILLERS GROUPS SAYS POLICE, MEDIA PAY LITTLE HEED TO BLACKS,** St. Louis Post-Dispatch, November 8, 1993

(and overburdened) with trying to investigate homicides of blacks and navigating the murky waters of a black community protecting suspects because they don't trust the police, you'll have the problems the Families Advocating Safe Streets runs into every single day of the year.

And every year the organization holds a vigil to read the names of those murdered during the prior in St. Louis, with the true casualty being the actual city of St. Louis. [VIGIL HONORS SLAIN, COMFORTS THOSE WHO MOURN, St. Louis Post-Dispatch, January 1, 2002]:

> The Rev. Earl Nance, president of the St. Louis Clergy Coalition, said blacks must take more responsibility to help police fight "black-on-black crime."
>
> "I understand people who holler about the police," Nance said. "There are bad police officers, just like there are bad preachers and bad politicians. But I'd like to see more of these characters out there (protesting) on the streets when we kill each other."[221]

No matter the promises made year after year, the same theme runs through each vigil. The same common dominator.['Let's try to get it straight': Speakers at annual vigil implore community to work harder to curb violence that claims lives, ST. LOUIS POST-DISPATCH, January 1, 2008]:

> Veteran activist Anthony Shahid said, "What's happening in our community is that we are losing our black youth like it's going out of style."[222]

No, the real cause for concern is how many sections of the city of St. Louis become uninhabitable to a family in search of a peaceful community to raise their children or a business looking to relocate in search of higher profits. [Homicides are down, but the pain lives on: FAMILIES GATHER AT ANNUAL CANDLELIGHT VIGIL., ST. LOUIS

---

[221] VIGIL HONORS SLAIN, COMFORTS THOSE WHO MOURN, St. Louis Post-Dispatch, January 1, 2002]:

[222] ['Let's try to get it straight': Speakers at annual vigil implore community to work harder to curb violence that claims lives, ST. LOUIS POST-DISPATCH, January 1, 2008

POST-DISPATCH, 1-1-2012]

> "IN AN IDEAL WORLD, THIS VIGIL WOULD NOT BE NECESSARY, BUT HERE WE ARE," MAYOR FRANCIS SLAY TOLD A CROWD OF ABOUT 100 MOURNERS, OFFICIALS AND PREACHERS GATHERED SATURDAY AT WILLIAMS TEMPLE CHURCH OF GOD IN CHRIST IN THE 1500 BLOCK OF UNION BOULEVARD.
> SLAY CALLED ON RESIDENTS AND FAMILY MEMBERS TO TEACH YOUNG PEOPLE "THE VALUE OF LIFE."
> MOST OF THE HOMICIDE VICTIMS WERE YOUNG AFRICAN-AMERICAN MEN KILLED DURING SHOOTINGS.
> JAMES CLARK OF BETTER FAMILY LIFE, A NONPROFIT JOB TRAINING AND SOCIAL SERVICES PROVIDER, TOLD THE GROUP THAT BLACK-ON-BLACK VIOLENCE HAS BECOME "TOO SERIOUS FOR WORDS" AND THAT ACTION IS NEEDED.
> "WE CANNOT TALK OR RALLY OUR WAY OUT OF THIS ONE," HE SAID. "LAST TIME AROUND IT WAS US VERSUS THEM. THIS TIME IT'S US VERSUS US. ... IT'S TIME TO PUT DOWN THE PISTOLS."[223]

So it never gets better and though the Families Advocating Safe Streets offers a great photo-op for white politicians and public servants to cozy up to the black community, the violence continues to drive away any of the civilization that only the former racial group and create/sustain/proliferate in St. Louis.

Conversely, the violence of the black community is only a problem as long as its primary source, the black population, goes unaddressed. [Mourners and community leaders gather for annual candlelight service for victims of homicides, St. Louis Post-Dispatch, 12-31-13]:

> St. Louis Mayor Francis Slay began his remarks by recalling city's 119th victim this year, Clara Jean Walker, who was inside her home Sunday when she was killed by a stray bullet that rocketed through a window.

---

[223] Homicides are down, but the pain lives on: FAMILIES GATHER AT ANNUAL CANDLELIGHT VIGIL., ST. LOUIS POST-DISPATCH, 1-1-2012

> "It's a tragedy that never should have happened," Slay said. "All of us should pledge to do everything we can to reduce the senseless shooting and violence. That includes telling police anything and everything we know about the person or people who were on Ms. Walker's street" or in any crime.
>
> "St. Louis is awash with guns," the mayor said. "This has got to stop." Of the 120 murdered in the city in 2013, 98 were men. At least 105 were African-American.[224]

Guns don't kill people, Mayor Slay.
A gun is an inanimate object, similarly to how a formerly robust community that goes from majority white to majority black is no longer animated with commercial life or blessed with rising property values.

Which brings us to a story that defines the Bell Curve City. [Brother and sister die in shootings blocks away from each other, Fox2Now, 10-19-14]:

> A Berkeley family is reeling from two separate murders. St. Louis Metropolitan Police say 35-year-old Margaree Dixson was shot and killed Saturday night. Her brother, 29-year-old Jermaine Jones, died at an area hospital a few hours later. He was also the victim of gunshots.
>
> Dixson's body was found near the intersection of Lillian and Plover. Officers were called for a shooting at approximately 11:40p.m. Saturday. Police say she was shot in the head, chest, arms and hand. Witnesses heard several gunshots.
>
> Approximately 2 ½ hours later, police responded to a shooting near Saloma and Wren. Jones was shot multiple times and taken to an area hospital where he died Sunday morning. According to police, Jones' acquaintances were standing with him when shots started coming from an unknown male. Police recovered two firearms from the victims' vehicle.

---

[224] http://www.stltoday.com/news/mourners-and-community-leaders-gather-for-annual-candlelight-service-for/article_18b1465d-6bca-55bc-b027-0f3fcddbd66a.html

> Family members did not want to speculate on a motive for the shootings but they are pleading for help and calling for an end to violence.
>
> "There's too much violence going on," said Nicole Rice, sister of Dixson and Jones. "I can't sleep. I can't think. It can't work. I can't do anything wondering if my son will be a victim to the streets."
>
> "When you lost two kids at one time it's tough," said Ann Carlson, family friend. "I mean the same night, back to back, it's painful.
>
> She said family members are now left to care for the victims' children without any money.
>
> "They don't have any insurance," said Carlson. "If anybody could help them or help us out, it will help."[225]

The idea of black-on-black crime has never bothered me, nor has the tendency for the black community to practice "no snitching" and protect black criminals in their midst.

What does bother me is the loss of real estate due to high rates of black-on-black crime, requiring white people to vacate the land where this internecine fighting takes place for either residential or business purposes.

No white community in America has ever founded anything resembling the Families Advocating Safe Streets group in St. Louis as blacks have done, a reminder of the tragic consequences of ignoring the contents of *The Bell Curve;* for as life in St. Louis proves, the bell curve will not ignore you.

---

[225] http://fox2now.com/2014/10/19/woman-found-shot-to-death-in-st-louis-alley/

October 22, 2014
The Ferguson Narrative Unravels: Can we cancel the whole "judging by content of character" truce now?

So what have learned in the past few days that we didn't already know?

Basically everything those nefarious white racist supporters of Darren Wilson believed has turned out to be true. [Evidence supports officer's account of shooting in Ferguson, Washington Post, 10-22-14][226]

Knowing an unarmed black teen can be lethal - just ask Yen Nguyen, whose 72-year husband Hoang was killed from a single punch by Elex Murphy (a black male) in St. Louis during a "Knockout Game" incident gone wrong - the revelation Michael Brown kept charging at Darren Wilson should put to bed the belief the former wasn't a threat. [Source: Darren Wilson says Michael Brown kept charging, St. Louis Post-Dispatch, 10-22-14][227]

The city where the propensity for the "Knockout Game" to be played - "Knockout king is a thrill," the kid told her. "It makes you want to keep doing it every day"[228] - was christened the 'spirit of the times' by the *St. Louis Post-Dispatch* on November 1, 2011.[229]

---

[226] http://www.washingtonpost.com/politics/new-evidence-supports-officers-account-of-shooting-in-ferguson/2014/10/22/cf38c7b4-5964-11e4-bd61-346aee66ba29_story.html

[227] http://www.stltoday.com/news/local/crime-and-courts/official-autopsy-shows-michael-brown-had-close-range-wound-to/article_e98a4ce0-c284-57c9-9882-3fb7df75fef6.html

[228] http://www.stltoday.com/news/local/crime-and-courts/article_81940695-c26e-5a8d-b3bc-33adc1aaa7b8.html

[229] http://www.stltoday.com/news/opinion/columns/the-platform/article_6ead38ce-6e93-5a70-8ced-a970686038f6.html#ixzz1cTKfTKDU

It's time to realize the harsh truth of what the Darren Wilson/Michael Brown encounter represented: an 18-year-old black male participating in the 'spirit of the times' on Wilson's face and him using lethal force to make sure he didn't share the same fate as Hoang Nguyen.

But these facts don't matter.

To blacks and their "whites-in-skin-color-only" (WISCO) sympathizers, no amount of evidence will ever convince them that Darren Wilson didn't execute the 'Hands Up, Don't Shoot' Gentle Giant in cold blood.

So the city must burn. [Ferguson turns into tinderbox once again after new details leaked, Fox2Now, 10-22-14]:

> One protester put it succinctly:
>
> "If there is not an indictment, excuse my French, all hell is going to break loose."[230]

But we already knew this, when a black protester at a Ferguson City Council meeting in mid-September promised "If Darren Wilson get off y'all better bring every army y'all got. Cause it's going down." [231] But what if "all hell" had all broken lose in 67 percent black Ferguson (99 percent white in 1970; 86 percent white in 1980; 76 percent white in 1990; 44 percent white in 2000; and 27 percent white today), and the shooting of Michael Brown was just a symptom of the hellish conditions created by the black majority in a city whose racial character had undergone a dramatic change since white flight turned into a full-on sprint in the mid-1990s?

---

[230] Ferguson turns into tinderbox once again after new details leaked, Fox2Now, 10-22-14

[231] http://www.thegatewaypundit.com/2014/09/ferguson-mob-threatens-stl-county-leaders-if-darren-wilson-get-off-yall-better-bring-every-army-yall-got-cause-its-going-down/

NPR and the WISCO commentators there can whine about the decline of Ferguson and its increasingly untenable housing situation, but the reality is the rapid collapse of the city was already in place before the first "Justice for Michael Brown" march took place.[232]

We already knew majority black North St. Louis was home to real estate long-time white residents (who still had fond memories of when white kids trick-or-treated safely in all-white neighborhoods, now streets with boarded up houses) couldn't give away. [Blame poverty, age for weak North County home market, St. Louis Post-Dispatch, 8-18-2013][233]

But did you know the metropolitan St. Louis area, courtesy of the black population, is home to one of America's hot spots for 'underwater' mortgages? [St. Louis is hot spot for 'underwater' mortgages, St. Louis Post-Dispatch, 5-9-14]:

> Metro St. Louis is a national hot spot for "underwater" mortgages, according to a new study, and the problem is particularly acute in north St. Louis County.
>
> Half or more of homeowners with mortgages owe more than their homes are worth in ZIP code areas covering Bellefontaine Neighbors, the Spanish Lake area, Berkeley and Jennings. The same is true in Cahokia, Ill., according to the study by the Haas Institute in Berkeley, Calif.
>
> In all, 16 St. Louis-area ZIP code areas ranked among the nation's worst in terms of homeowners stuck with their houses due to mortgage debt. Of that number, 11 were in North County, three in St. Louis city and two in the Metro East area.
>
> People who owe more than their homes are worth can't sell unless they can bring a big check to the closing, or convince

---

[232] http://www.npr.org/2014/10/20/357612090/unrest-in-ferguson-may-speed-up-decline-of-real-estate

[233] Blame poverty, age for weak North County home market, St. Louis Post-Dispatch, 8-18-2013

the bank to take less than it is owed. They are said to be "underwater" or "upside down" on their loans.

They are roughly twice as likely as others to default on their mortgages, leading to foreclosure. Some argue that stressed owners are less likely to improve their homes, or even maintain them, and that can affect the surrounding neighborhood.

Eric Repke is trying to escape an underwater loan on his house near Hazelwood Central High School. He bought the home in 2006, paying $146,000, and he still owes $110,000.

"I decided in 2011 not to make a major new investment in it, like a new kitchen or new floors," he said.

Then he took a job in O'Fallon in St. Charles County, and found himself commuting an hour to work. "I'm a father, and I don't want to spend all that time on the road," he said.

So, he moved his family close to his work and put his house on the market in March. "The highest offer we got was for $70,000," he said. That offer was from an investor who wanted to rent it out.

While paying for two homes, he's hoping to persuade Bank of America to accept less than it is owed — a so-called short sale.[234]

Remember, "Fifty percent of the town's 6,321 homeowners owe more on their mortgages than their homes are worth, a situation called being underwater. Nationally, 17 percent of homeowners are underwater." [Another Shadow in Ferguson as Outside Firms Buy and Rent Out Distressed Homes, New York Times, 9-3-14][235]

Though equality is mandated by the federal government, the free market does not bend to the whims of an overzealous ideology based on lies: the Visible Black Hand of Economics ensures nature returns

---

[234] St. Louis is hot spot for 'underwater' mortgages, St. Louis Post-Dispatch, 5-9-14

[235] http://dealbook.nytimes.com/2014/09/03/another-shadow-in-ferguson-as-outside-firms-buy-and-rent-out-distressed-homes/

to an economic situation clouded by an insane belief in racial egalitarianism, proven by the market forces showing a majority black city isn't conducive to appreciating home valuations. ['It's like modern day slavery:' The alarming Ferguson statistic plaguing many, KMOV.com, 10-21-14]:

> FERGUSON, Mo. (KMOV.com) -- The Ferguson police shooting that killed Michael Brown has put the north St. Louis County town under a microscope.
>
> The community faces enormous challenges including a housing crisis that has homeowners struggling to hang onto their homes.
>
> Six years since the height of the housing crisis, much of the country has recovered. But Ferguson has not.
>
> In the neighborhoods near Brown's memorial, boarded up houses dot the streets.   Fifty percent of homeowners are underwater, meaning they owe more on their mortgages than the homes are worth. The national average is 17 percent. Melody Wade works full time but is still three months behind on her mortgage. "It's like modern day slavery," Wade said Tuesday. "Like you're working for free. No matter what you do you're never, ever going to get out of this."[236]

Remember, home "Sales are down 32 percent in Ferguson since the shooting [of Michael Brown], more than the 13 percent drop for all of St. Louis County, in what has been a down year for home sales across the region," but more than 50 percent of the existing mortgages were underwater in the 67 percent black city prior to the shooting... courtesy of the black undertow phenomenon.

Despite the evidence Darren Wilson is guilty of nothing but protecting himself from the same fate of Hoang Nguyen ('the spirit of the times', right *St. Louis Post-Dispatch* editorial writers?) Missouri Gov. Nixon has capitulated to the black mob and announced a Ferguson Commission that will:

---

[236] 'It's like modern day slavery:' The alarming Ferguson statistic plaguing many, KMOV.com, 10-21-14

My charge to the Commission through Executive Order will be three-fold:

1. First, to conduct a thorough, wide-ranging and unflinching study of the social and economic conditions underscored by the unrest in the wake of the death of Michael Brown;

2. Second, to tap the expertise needed to address the concerns identified by the Commission – from poverty and education, to governance and law enforcement;

3. And third, to offer specific recommendations for making this region a stronger, fairer place for everyone to live.[237]

Gov. Nixon, *The Bell Curve* is a book you should immediately purchase and pass out to members of this Commission, if you intend an "unflinching study of the social and economic conditions" genesis, for it's in the genetic makeup of the people who call these communities home.

The quality of a neighborhood, good or bad, is simply a reflection of the majority racial population who lives there.

Remember: Consulting the 2009 New York Times Food Stamp Usage Across the Country interactive map, we learn this about the city of St. Louis (49 percent black and 43 percent white):

- As of 2009, 60 percent of blacks were on EBT/Food Stamps in the city of St. Louis
- As of 2009, 10 percent of whites were on EBT/Food Stamps in the city of St. Louis

St. Louis County (different from the city of St. Louis) is just over one million people in population. It's home to Ferguson, that lovely post-white suburb boasting a growing, self-insufficient black population. [Ferguson: Gentrification and its discontents, Al-Jazeera, 8-16-14]

Of those one million people, 68 percent of the county's population is white and 23.7 percent is black. Consulting the 2009 New York

---

[237] http://governor.mo.gov/news/speeches/ferguson-commission-announcement

Times Food Stamp Usage Across the Country interactive map, we learn this about the county:

- As of 2009, 38 percent of blacks were on EBT/Food Stamps in the city of St. Louis
- As of 2009, 4 percent of whites were on EBT/Food Stamps in the city of St. Louis

The Bell Curve, Gov. Nixon, will provide a quick discourse in why such a disparity in EBT/Food Stamp usage exists between black and white people, and it has nothing to do with racism or white supremacy (why would a white supremacist society voluntarily redistribute tax dollars to pay for the proliferation of black people?).

It's time to just come out and say what the entire black response (accentuated by the WISCO collaboration to turn Michael Brown into some kind of martyr) to the Darren Wilson/Brown interaction represents: the days of mandated truce of judging by content of character are over.

Over.

Darren Wilson is a hero, who was nearly knocked unconscious by Brown in his 'knockout game' style attack as he, a white cop, merely tried to arrest the black male suspect for stealing cigars.

A hero.

That he must hide, for fear of being lynched by a black mob and attacked viciously in the columns and newscasts of WISCO journalists, is the true "sign of the times."

October 23, 2014
'You can`t sell this s%$&": The Parable of "The Lion King" alive and well in Ferguson

What's that verse from the Bible? Let he who is without sin cast the first stone? ['It's murder and they will feel the wrath of God's vengeance': Michael Brown's family react angrily to leak of Darren Wilson's testimony, Daily Mail, 10-20-14]:

> The family of Michael Brown have said that the cop who shot him dead will 'feel the wrath of God's vengeance' after the officer claimed he was acting in self defense.
>
> Sheryl Davis, Brown's aunt, told MailOnline that she believes Darren Wilson committed murder and that he will suffer retribution in a 'mighty way'.
>
> She said that Wilson's actions were 'evil' and that he will be punished by a higher power for what he did - even if he is cleared.[238]

"Feel the wrath of God's vengeance..."

The world people like Michael Brown's family create is eerily reminiscent to the world the hyenas created after Scar took over the Pride Land in Disney's *The Lion King*; the delicate equilibrium of nature interrupted by something... unnatural, that was never intended to lead.

It's why white companies like Monsanto pledge $1 million to the 67% black city of Ferguson and Emerson pledges $4.4 million to "empower" black youth and fund scholarships in North St. Louis, where the majority black population lacks the ability to do such on their own.

As the black population of St. Louis continues to single-handily keep the body count ticking upward, the white police chief notes "What's the only thing that's changed since the middle of August?"[Body count in St. Louis poised to surpass 2013 total with two months left in year, St. Louis Post-Dispatch, 10-23-14]:

> "I believe there is some segment of the community that feels empowered by what's going on," Dotson said.
>
> Dotson compared the trend to dramatic increases in violent

---

[238] 'It's murder and they will feel the wrath of God's vengeance': Michael Brown's family react angrily to leak of Darren Wilson's testimony, Daily Mail, 10-20-14

crime in Cincinnati in 2001 when riots broke out there after a white police officer fatally shot an unarmed black teen.

"More people are committing crimes (in St. Louis)," Dotson said. "Something is different."[239]

The balance is gone; the hyenas have taken over.

Going back to the Bible verse quoted at the beginning, "Let he who is without sin cast the first stone," especially if it involves the Brown family fighting over who can legally peddle 'Michael Brown' swag to those forever chanting "Justice for Michael Brown" or "Black Lives Matter..." [Police investigating assault and theft following argument between Brown family relatives, Fox2Now.com, 10-23-14]:

> In a recent statement, Michael Brown's mother asked that her son not be part of self-serving business or political actions as she pleaded that he be remembered for the good. A reported assault and theft this past weekend may dramatically underscore that sentiment.
>
> It happened Saturday night, October 18th, at about 8:15 pm in the parking lot of Red's BBQ. It's the corner of Canfield and West Florissant, just blocks from where Michael Brown was shot and killed.
>
> Police sources tell us Brown's Grandmother, Pearlie Gordon, along with Brown's Cousin Tony Petty, were selling t-shirts and other Michael Brown merchandise.
>
> A police report describes a car pulling up and several people getting out. One of those people, was reported to be Michael Brown's Mom, Lesley McSpadden. A witness described McSpadden yelling 'You can't sell this s%$&" One of the relatives, who was selling, reportedly demanded McSpadden show a document proving she had a patent.
>
> The police report says that's when an unidentified person with McSpadden assaulted Petty so violently that it resulted

---

[239] Body count in St. Louis poised to surpass 2013 total with two months left in year, St. Louis Post-Dispatch, 10-23-14

in a 911 call. A witness tells Fox 2 that the weapon was a metal pipe or pole. The suspect reportedly struck Petty in the face. Medics then took him to Christian Northeast Hospital. The witness said the assault suspect grabbed merchandise and a box of cash believed to contain about $1,400.

It appears surveillance cameras could have captured the fight and be part of police evidence. Police report no arrests at this time.

We reached out to the local Brown family attorney, Anthony D. Gray and he declined to comment.[240]

'You can't sell this s%$&..."

Darren Wilson won't feel "the wrath of God's vengeance."

No.

Just like the world after Scar led a successful coup and took over the Pride Land in *The Lion King*, enabling the hyenas in the process, the world of Ferguson and St. Louis after the Michael Brown black insurrection is truly a revolt against nature. Thankfully, the Brown family squabbling over who is authorized to hawk $20 "Michael Brown" shirts is a powerful reminder of how out balance things are in metropolitan St. Louis.

A circle of insanity has usurped the circle of life in America.

October 26, 2014
"You can't go home again..."

First, President Obama sent three White House officials to attend

---

[240] Police investigating assault and theft following argument between Brown family relatives, Fox2Now.com, 10-23-14

Michael Brown's funeral.

Second, Attorney General Eric Holder came to Ferguson (a "deeply personal" visit, according to USA Today) and told a primarily black audience that though he holds the Department of Justice top spot, "He is also a black man."

It was also revealed Al Sharpton was "key advisor" to the White House on Ferguson, or "the man on the ground" for Barack Obama.[241]

Third, the Department of Justice asked the police chief of Ferguson to stop his officers from wearing "I am Darren Wilson" bracelets while on duty, only a week after Holder announced the DOJ "stands with the people of Ferguson."

Which people Holder referenced shouldn't be difficult to ascertain: the 67% of the city's population that is also, like Holder, a black man or woman.

Fourth, the Department of Justice top officials were furious leaks from the Grand Jury testimony of Darren Wilson were released as potentially "influence public opinion" in the direction of the white officer instead of the "black man," (like Obama and Holder) Michael Brown:

> A Justice Department spokeswoman responded in a statement to the Los Angeles Times: "The department considers the selective release of information in this investigation to be irresponsible and highly troubling. Since the release of the convenience-store footage, there seems to be an inappropriate effort to influence public opinion about this case."
>
> The reference to the convenience-store footage alluded to a video released by Ferguson police on the same day they disclosed Wilson's identity. The video showed Brown apparently intimidating a store clerk shortly before the shooting.

---

[241] Sharpton a key adviser to Obama on Ferguson, NY Post, 8-22-14

> Chris King, managing editor of the St. Louis American, a newspaper for black audiences, said law enforcement officials had offered him the leaks, saying "they had been briefed on the evidence and it didn't look good for Michael Brown supporters," but he declined and decried "third-party hearsay" in an editorial for the paper.

> "Tensions are so high that preparations for riots, if Wilson walks free, are discussed in sober terms in local and national media and on street corners," the American said in its editorial. "The editors of these powerful publications have shown a lapse in judgment and ethics that is not only shameful, but actually dangerous. We declare a mistrial in the court of public opinion."[242]

All of this "emboldening" of the black community by the Obama Administration and an overzealous black-centric Department of Justice has influenced blacks in Ferguson and metropolitan St. Louis to do something in retaliation to Brown's death.

If any mistrial in the court of public opinion has occurred in the case of Wilson and Brown, it's the Obama Administration, Eric Holder, and the media's failure to present the facts clearly and without prejudice ("I am also a black man...").

Thus, we get the most personal moment of this entire Ferguson Farce:

> Watch as the so called "peaceful" protesters in #Ferguson attack a young white man who "just wants to go home."

> The "protesters" continued to harass this young man all the way down the road while he was in his car.

> Thank God the police were there for protection.[243]

---

[242] http://www.latimes.com/nation/la-na-ferguson-leaks-20141022-story.html#page=1

[243] Ferguson "Peaceful" Protesters Attack Young White Boy in Street (Video), The Gateway Pundit, 10-25-14

What's the old saying? You can't go home again?

If you haven't figured out what the farce of Ferguson is all about yet, just watch the video below of the young white male trying to get home only to be caught in the madness of an Obama/Holder endorsed mob.

October 28, 2014
Does your conscience bother you? Tell the truth

Simple, eloquent, and to the point. From St. Louis Coptalk, a "message board ... provided for the use of law enforcement officers employed by the St. Louis Police Department and their supporters in the St. Louis Metropolitan area," we get this message:

> A Safety Message for Civilians
>
> Posted by A Concerned Cop on 10/26/2014, 8:29 pm
>
> If you don't have a gun, get one and get one soon. We will not be able to protect you or your family. It will be your responsibility to protect them. Our gutless commanders and politicians have neutered us. I'm serious, get a gun, get more than one, and keep one with you at all times.[244]

Oh, the people of St. Louis have guns.[245] As one of the co-owners of County Guns noted to the press, white people are buying up guns for fear, "the city is going to explode.":

> Ferguson today is a city on the edge. While mostly black residents hold small protests outside the police station each night, gun store owners report a jump in sales to white residents. Local business owners in the area where Brown was shot complain about lost trade. Many storefronts remain

---

[244] http://members.boardhost.com/stlouiscoptalk/msg/1414373341.html

[245] http://stlouis.cbslocal.com/2014/08/12/gun-sales-up-across-area/

boarded up with plywood.

> Police and elected officials are meeting regularly with multi-racial citizen groups in a bid to improve community relations, tackle concerns about police discrimination, and avoid the turmoil that followed Brown's shooting. Civil unrest is still the "worst case scenario", Knowles said.
>
> Adam Weinstein, co-owner of County Guns, said sales were up 50 percent since Brown's shooting, mostly among white residents fearful of riots who are buying Glock, Springfield and Smith & Wesson handguns, and shotguns. "They are afraid the city is going to explode," Weinstein said, a former member of the U.S. Navy and St. Louis firefighter with heavily tattooed arms.[246]

Fear of what's just beyond the horizon isn't exclusively for the white residents of metropolitan St. Louis. Recall, fear of black protesters convinced Walmart to lock up ammo at many St. Louis stores:

> Several Walmart stores in the St. Louis area have pulled ammunition from the shelves following recent protests.
>
> Monday night, demonstrators made their way into Walmart locations in Maplewood, Ferguson and Bridgeton, forcing the stores to close while several arrests were made.
>
> On Wednesday afternoon, the empty shelves at Maplewood looked like there had been a mass purchase of ammunition. But according to an employee, it was locked up in the back.
>
> "I can see why they would think that would be a concern if someone did break in in mass and loot the place and steal ammo," said shopper Tim Casey.[247]

Fear of what's coming in metropolitan St. Louis is palpable, scaring seven school districts into begging the St. Louis Prosecutor to release

---

[246] Exclusive: Missouri police plan for possible riots if Brown cop not charged, Reuters, 10-8-14

[247] Several Walmart locations locked-up ammunition during weekend protests, KMOV.com, 10-15-14]:

the grand jury findings until after school hours and kids are safely home:

> Seven school districts are asking St. Louis County Prosecutor Bob McCulloch to carefully consider when he releases the findings of the Michael Brown grand jury. They are raising safety concerns for students.
>
> A spokesperson says McCulloch has received this letter and is considering it.
>
> The letter was sent by the Riverview Gardens School District but was also signed by six other superintendents. The letter asks McCulloch to announce any grand jury decision either after 5p.m. on weekdays or on a weekend, preferably on Sunday.
>
> The letter is dated October 22nd.
>
> It references how the release of past information along with protests and the police response have forced road closures and made it difficult for students, parents and school buses to make it to campuses. The letter says school districts are expecting similar issues when the grand jury decision is announced and that information released during the school day has the potential to greatly affect school district operations.[248]

Remember: as a citizen of metro St. Louis, it will be your responsibility to protect yourself, your family, your property (be it private or commercial), and your business:

> A St. Louis property manager is warning businesses near the St. Louis County courthouse to prepare for "civil unrest" in the wake of the imminent grand jury decision in the Michael Brown shooting.
>
> Public demonstrations and random acts of violence have

---

[248] Multiple school districts write county prosecutor regarding grand jury decision, Fox2Now.com, 10-27-14

plagued the St. Louis area since August, when a white police officer shot and killed an unarmed, black teenager in the North St. Louis suburb of Ferguson, MO.

The warning to businesses came by way of a letter, dated October 21, addressed to "all tenants" in The Boulevard shopping center in Richmond Heights, MO. The shopping center is less than a mile and a half from the site of the grand jury proceeding in Clayton, MO.

The Pace Properties Manager disclosed that the property management team "met with local authorities/police recently to discuss their plans and recommendations for dealing with possible demonstrations and civil unrest after the grand jury decision is announced on the Michael Brown shooting."

The term "civil unrest" is used multiple times throughout the letter.

The note also lays out the priorities of police in the event of any riots:

"The number one concern of public safety officials in the event of demonstrations or civil unrest will be the safety of citizens. Protection of property will be a secondary consideration."

The letter further notes that "authorities anticipate that the grand jury's decision will be announced in November, at the earliest." This fits with other media reports which also predict a November announcement.[249]

On the Thomas Jefferson Memorial in Washington D.C. reads an inscription worth remembering, not for what's written, but what is left out. It's a quote from Jefferson on slavery located on the northeast interior wall. It reads: *"Nothing is more certainly written in the book of fate than these people are to be free."*

But it omits the next sentence: *"Nor is it less certain that the two*

---

[249] Exclusive: St. Louis Businesses Warned of 'Civil Unrest' After Grand Jury Decision, CNSNews.com, 10-27-14

races, equally free, cannot live in the same government."

And ultimately Thomas Jefferson's unheeded warning is the primary lesson of the Ferguson Fiasco and the great scandal behind the collapse of the city of St. Louis.

Whatever comes of the grand jury's decision in the case of Officer Darren Wilson, know the book of fate Thomas Jefferson cited didn't lie when he read from it then; and the chaos St. Louis Coptalk warned about, seven school districts fear is coming and the "civil unrest" businesses are preparing for now *was also noted* in the same tome.

October 29, 2014
Bell Curve City and Section 8 Housing: Spread of Vouchers in Ferguson and Metropolitan St. Louis Prove the Government has Declared War on White America

A couple years ago, Darnell Xavier "Chuckie" Vaughn was arrested in Minnesota for the murder of two black women in Ferguson, Missouri. Turns out, his father and mother (Darwin Vaughn and Lois Adams), as well as his friend DeAndrew Galmore helped him escape and they were arrested as well.[250]

But it's the story surrounding the murder perpetrated by Vaughn, published by a local St. Louis news affiliate, which details a world only black people are capable of collectively creating:

> Police have identified the two young women who were found shot to death in a Ferguson apartment early Friday morning.

---

[250] http://www.kmov.com/news/crime/Man-wanted-in-killing-of-2-Ferguson-women-arrested-in-Minnesota-168929116.html

> The victims have been identified as Tasheerra Johnson, 29, and Claudia Williams, 30. Police said Johnson and Williams were found dead Friday morning at the Oakmont Townhomes Complex in the 1600 block of Northwinds Estates Drive.
>
> Officials said family members discovered the bodies just after 6 a.m.
>
> Investigators said the victims apparently died from gunshot wounds. Police said a baby was also found the apartment and was not harmed.
>
> Officers say a vehicle belonging to one of the victims was reported missing, but has been located in Madison County, Illinois. Officials did not elaborate further on the vehicle's exact location.
>
> Several neighbors told News 4 the complex is notorious for having guns fired. One lady said she's made several complaints and has been robbed, but nothing has been done. She said since this recent incident, she plans on breaking her lease.
>
> News 4's Laura Hettiger called the management property asking about gunshots, but the person who answered the phone said they had no comment and hung up on her.
>
> Ferguson Police are urging anyone with information on this case or the missing vehicle to contact authorities.[251]

Perhaps the story of Darnell Xavier "Chuckie" Vaughn[252] and the violence at Oakmont Townhomes Complex illuminates why the mayor of Ferguson noted this about the relationship of the white police force to the 67 percent black population of the city:

> "The African-American community - youth in the African-

---

[251] Police identify 2 women found shot to death in Ferguson apartment, KMOV.com, 8-31-2012

[252] http://www.kmov.com/news/crime/Man-wanted-in-killing-of-2-Ferguson-women-arrested-in-Minnesota-168929116.html

American community in particular - has something against law enforcement in many ways," Knowles said.
"They don't like law enforcement, and they don't think law enforcement likes them."[253]

No, not perhaps. Oakmont Townhomes in Ferguson (along with Northwinds Apartments, where Michael Brown called "home") has more Section 8 voucher holders/rents than any tract in the entire state of Missouri. And it's 99 percent black. [As low-income housing boomed, Ferguson pushed back, St. Louis Post-Dispatch, 10-19-2014]:

The data on Section 8 also show that the subsidies have tended to cluster in lower-income areas. Many inner-ring North County suburbs are disproportionately absorbing the tenants who have flocked to aging apartment complexes.

That includes Ferguson. A census tract that consists of a portion of Oakmont Townhomes and Northwinds Apartments and stretches eastward into unincorporated St. Louis County had more Section 8 renters in 2013 than any tract in the entire state, according to HUD estimates.

In that area, nearly 20 percent of the 5,000 people who lived there were in Section 8 units. More than half of those households had median incomes of less than $10,000; 57 percent were headed by one parent; and 99 percent were African-American.

According to records from the Housing Authority of St. Louis County, three of the top nine recipients of Section 8 payments from June 2011 to June 2014 were the owners of Park Ridge, Northwinds and Oakmont. Currently, more than 200 tenants in those complexes have vouchers.

The concept of income inequality is just the economic expression of

---

[253] http://www.wjla.com/articles/2014/08/racial-tensions-are-not-new-in-st-louis-suburb-where-unarmed-black-teen-michael-brown-was-fatally-sh.html#ixzz3HZeNBEmx

blacks collective genetic limitations when compared to what whites can collectively achieve: in the absence of the white population, which built Ferguson (the city was 99 percent white in 1970), the city took on the character - and its economic fortunes were built on - of the rising black demographic majority.

Remember: the true story of Ferguson is the represents the disastrous nature of the House of Urban Development (HUDs) strategy of dispersing black criminality from urban areas to the suburbs:

> In reality, crime only follows Section 8 tenants to the suburbs, according to a large body of research, including a 2011 HUD-commissioned study. That's precisely what happened in Ferguson, once a quiet, working-class St. Louis suburb.
> Michael Brown grew up in the Section 8 epicenter of Ferguson, a small southeast corner of the city that includes several sprawling apartment complexes catering to subsidized poor renters. That area accounted for a whopping 40% of all robberies and 28% of all aggravated assaults reported in the city between 2010 and 2012, according to local crime data.
>
> An official with the St. Louis County Housing Authority, which administers Section 8 vouchers in Ferguson, confirmed that the area's a hotbed of crime. "We get plenty of complaints, and we refer them to the police," Susan Harrod, director of assisted housing, told me.
>
> The St. Louis Post-Dispatch and other press outlets have reported that Brown lived with his grandmother at the Northwinds Apartments, which, according to housing authority data obtained by IBD, has the greatest number of Section 8 tenants of any apartment complex in Ferguson. The county subsidizes 58 of the 438 units there.
>
> Northwinds also happens to be a nest of criminal activity.
>
> "I was robbed at gunpoint while holding my infant child right in front of my apartment ... worst experience of my life," said one former tenant. "I had my home invaded four times," said

another resident. "The crime is really bad. We have neighbors that stand around all day and sell dope.

"Almost everyone out here is on Section 8 and doesn't work," another Northwinds renter complained. "This isn't the apartment for working-class people. They break into people's houses and cars.

The complex reportedly had more than 50 units broken into in a single year.

Tenants have also complained about rapists entering through windows, and shootings virtually every weekend. Some move their mattresses to the floor, below their bedroom window, to dodge stray bullets at night. Last month, daytime gunshots from inside Northwinds cut short reporters' interviews with residents about the Brown case.

Males aren't the only perps. At an adjacent apartment, Canfield Green, where Brown was shot, a female tenant reportedly once chased a boyfriend across the parking lot and tried to attack him with a butcher knife. In another recent incident there, a woman traded blows with a young mother holding a baby on her hip. Packs of girls are known to roam the property, beating victims with socks packed with rocks.[254]

This is the world the black population of Ferguson, imported to the city via Section 8 Vouchers (which enrich property firms located in states such as Maine)[255], creates: cruel, violent, and one where citizens sleep on the floor to dodge stray bullets.

Again: the economic and moral conditions found in 67% black Ferguson is nothing more than the collective genetic expression of the majority demographic found there. This is why property values have dropped in Ferguson and North St. Louis, with the rising percentages of blacks convincing white residents its time to get out

---

[254] LBJ's War On Poverty Lies Beneath Ferguson Tragedy, Investors Business Daily, 9-3-2014

[255] http://www.pressherald.com/2014/08/20/maine-property-firm-remains-committed-to-chaotic-ferguson/

of the city before all mortgages go underwater.[256]

With all this stated, let's take a look at William Lacy Clay's denunciation of municipal courts in the St. Louis area, which he claims are little more than "ATM machines for local government.":

> U.S. Rep. William Lacy Clay called for the U.S. Department of Justice to review St. Louis area municipal courts that he says targets minority and low income residents as "ATM machines for local government."
>
> The request comes after Better Together, a group advocating for city-county consolidation, issued a report documentinghow municipalities use court fines and fees to get revenue from their residents. For example, the group found that St. Louis County's 90 municipalities made up 34 percent of all municipal fines and fees in the state of Missouri.
>
> "The very disturbing findings in the Better Together report indicate that municipal courts in both the City of St. Louis and many jurisdictions in St. Louis County often function as little more than municipal ATM machines," said Clay, who represents north St. Louis County. "They repeatedly victimize local residents, many of whom are African American, who have modest resources that might be better spent on essentials for their families."[257]

Money to pay for government has to come from somewhere, right? Roads and maintaining/improving existing infrastructure, schools, police, the fire department, and paying for a modest number municipal employees requires tax revenue, which the black population of St. Louis County's 90 municipalities aren't capable of producing (crime suspects, unfortunately, is not something this population lacks in producing).[258]

---

[256] St. Louis is hot spot for 'underwater' mortgages, St. Louis Post-Dispatch, 5-9-14

[257] Clay calls for federal review of St. Louis area municipal courts, St. Louis Post-Dispatch, 10-29-14

[258] http://www.ibtimes.com/ferguson-missouri-crime-stats-2014-blacks-arrested-4-times-much-whites-1658846

This black population, however, is capable of producing Michael Brown's, Vonderritt Myers', and Darnell Xavier "Chuckie" Vaughn's... the type of citizen that scares away legitimate businesses and drives down property values.

Your tax dollars go to fund the breeding, housing, and feeding of people like Darnell Vaughn and Michael Brown, both of whom called the largest tract of Section 8 voucher receivers in all of Missouri home.

October 30, 2014
Reverse Social Capital: The Hilarity of "Safe Zones" for Black Kids to Trick-or-Treat and Celebrate Halloween in North St. Louis

There's one day of the year that sociologists have failed to realize is the ultimate gauge in measuring social capital: Halloween.

Can your neighborhood pass the trick-or-treating test?[259]

If not, you obviously live in an all-black area, where boarded up houses, dimly lit streets, dead bodies in yards, and scary sights are a year around fact of life instead of front-yard Halloween decorations for the month of October as found in all-white communities.

Nothing builds community relations greater than the ability for parents to send their children un-chaperoned into the fall night and knock on strangers doors, ultimately receiving candy for their hard work.

Freely scavenging neighborhoods for the best houses to secure the best candy is a rite of passage for those children who had the

---

[259] http://www.vdare.com/articles/diversity-vs-halloween-can-your-neighborhood-pass-the-trick-or-treat-test

privilege of grown up in majority white communities, where the collective morality of individual white families enables an entire city to be a "safe zone" for trick-or-treating.

The same can't be said for majority black cities/communities, where the collective indifference of individual black families (sic) creates an environment unsuitable for children to play in the park or shoot hoops unsupervised, let alone trick-or-treat.

A writer at *The American Conservative* noted with great fondness the memories he had trick-or-treating in a much different Ferguson, Missouri than the one that now is hemorrhaging its white population (and thus the city's ability to keep the Halloween tradition alive):

> So here's a thought experiment: Imagine the neighborhood where you went trick-or-treating as a child, hurt your knee falling off the jungle gym, or went on your first shy date. Now imagine seeing it yourself one day, the eerily familiar backdrop occupied by violent mobs facing off against troops in camouflage amid clouds of tear gas.[260]

Ferguson is 67 percent black, a city remade in the image of its new majority demographic. With the continued fear of violence in Ferguson, even Halloween had to be sacrificed.[261]

And with this makeover in other parts of metropolitan St. Louis, particularly overwhelmingly black North St. Louis, you get the need for extraordinary measures to resurrect trick-or-treating traditions that vanished with white flight.

Enter the "safe zone.":

> For the seventh Halloween in a row, St. Louis Alderman Antonio French is helping to give hundreds of children a fun part of childhood.

---

[260] Ferguson Falls Apart: A former resident explains why the St. Louis suburb exemplifies a national loss of social trust., The American Conservative, 8-25-14

[261] http://www.ksdk.com/story/news/local/2014/10/16/i-love-ferguson-plans-alternative-halloween-event/17384957/

He's helping to organize a six-block "safe zone" for area children to trick-or-treat from 6 to 9 p.m. Friday. The location has varied from year to year, but this year's is the same as the last: the two blocks of Holly, Red Bud and Athlone avenues, bordering the southwest edge of O'Fallon Park.

There are about 250 houses in the area, and so far about 100 houses have signed up. Last year, about 1,000 children came to the area for trick-or-treating. The safe zones have become a project of The North Campus, French's tutoring and education program for children in several north St. Louis neighborhoods.

Commmitteewoman Laura Keys, who lives in the 4500 block of Athlone, said the safe zone was an expansion of an effort she made years ago to send letters to her neighbors and encourage her block to participate in Halloween. She remembers one elderly man telling her why he never wanted to give out candy.

"He talked about not feeling safe to open his door. If he doesn't feel safe, how many of my neighbors don't feel safe?"

She loves that French has expanded on the effort, she said, adding that she's putting the finishing touches on her Mad Hatter costume and has yet to drag her cardboard casket out of the basement.

"We do it up," she said of her family's decorations and costumes. "We have fog machines, we do the scary music." Her family tries to give out a lighted treat, such as glow necklaces or finger lights, to make children more visible.

North Campus provides candy to families who have signed up to give it out, and some families supplement with their own. A North Campus shuttle patrols the area, and St. Louis police keep an eye on it, too. Some volunteers will give out candy from the porches of some houses that are vacant but not necessarily abandoned, French says.

Last weekend, neighborhood children got together at The Sanctuary, another part of North Campus, and carved 50 pumpkins to decorate porches in the safe zone.

"It feels really good, to see kids walking up and down the street," French said. "It gets people feeling really good about their neighborhood."[262]

Sorry, but such measures are artificial, an ephemeral introduction of peace and stability in an environment where the collective genetic expression of black people permanently disables such activities from being replicated without mass intervention by the police, corporations, and altruistic white people.

Two blocks representing the artificial "safe zone" for black kids to trick or treat, whereas entire communities devoid of black people are safe for hordes of white kids to trick or treat without adult or police supervision to ensure no violence interrupts their fun.

But in the so-called black communities of St. Louis, no such environment can be duplicated.

The first year the "safe zone" was created in St. Louis for blacks to trick-or-treat, gunshots were heard in areas outside the designated safe areas...:

> This year Halloween fell on the weekend; me and Geto Boys were trick-or-treating, robbing little kids for bags," rapped Geto Boys emcee Bushwick Bill in the 1991 rap classic that featured frontman Scarface.
>
> Those few lines in the popular rap record spoke briefly to the ghastly, everyday realities of living in the 'hood n and not just on Halloween.
>
> Those everyday, scary news stories of crime in North St. Louis spooked 21st Ward Committeeman Antonio D. French into creating Safe Zone, four blocks of police-patrolled Halloween activities.

---

[262] Halloween 'safe zone' near O'Fallon Park gives kids of all ages a trick-or-treat experience, St. Louis Post-Dispatch, 10-30-14

Safe trick-or-treating last Friday spanned the 4400 and 4500 blocks of Anthone and Holly, bound by West Florissant (near O'Fallon Park) and Rosalie.

Kids went door to door worry-free, collecting their share of three 19 gallon containers of candy that were supplied by 21st Ward Democrats. Contributors, along with French, included 21st Ward Alderman Bennice Jones King, state Rep. Jamilah Nasheed and License Collector Mike McMillan.

One man's house in the 4500 block of Anthlone was dark and spooky with its front porch dreadfully decorated like a haunted house. Frightful music played, and the man scared children away after first giving them candy.

Front Yard Features provided its gigantic outdoor projection screen on a vacant lot in the 4500 block of Holly. Neighbors sat on haystacks to watch the featured horror flick, Scream.

One neighbor threw a Halloween party, inviting all neighborhood kids."Kids can run up to any house they want to, so it gives them what was taken away from them," said Linda Green, who lives in the 4500 block of Anthlone.

Gunshots rang out while Green talked, but she wasn't worried, knowing they weren't in the Safe Zone.

"It doesn't just make it safe for kids, but it also makes it safe for grownups who want to participate," Green said. "Cops put a stop to a lot of things that usually go on, and eyes are everywhere."

Resident Talvin Moore called the Safe Zone a beautiful thing. "With everything going on on the North Side, there are some bad people out there, but this is safe," he said.

Another Resident Terrence Little said, "The kids get to have fun like we did when we were growing up."

French said he collaborated with Laura Keys, an Anthlone resident who had organized safe trick-or-treating on her block for several years.

"My vision was to have a larger block and invite kids from all

> wards," said French, noting that some trick-or-treaters came from the county.
>
> "It got people out as a community, and people were sociable and got to know one another," French said.
>
> Another good thing, he said, was that families had a chance to enjoy the streets like they used to, instead of surrendering to criminals, as many inner city residents often do.[263]

Streets aren't surrendered to criminals. Communities whose infrastructure were built decades ago by whites are abandoned to blacks when the crime, vice, and violence they import into the city becomes an intolerable menace and impedes productive labor and living.

Ferguson is located in North St. Louis County; in 1990 the city was 76 percent white, while today it is roughly 28 percent white.

An article written in the St. Louis Post-Dispatch in April of 1991 reported on the coming of the black undertow into formerly white areas of metropolitan St. Louis (like Ferguson). This story foretold the doom of trick-or-treating in communities like the one lamented in the *American Conservative* piece cited above:

> Blacks - many of whom say they are fleeing drugs, crime and deteriorating housing - are continuing to leave north St. Louis and moving into historically white neighborhoods in south St. Louis and in north St. Louis County, 1990 census figures indicate.
>
> During the 1980s, the figures show, the number of blacks in north St. Louis dropped by about 27,000 - a number equal to the population of Kirkwood. Several North Side neighborhoods lost more than 20 percent of their population during the decade.
>
> "Moving here was a blessing," said Rhonda Williams, a 27-

---

[263] Committeeman creates Safe Zone for North Side trick-or-treaters, St. Louis American, 11-6-2008

year-old black mother of four children aged 5 to 9, who moved from the North Side into a South Side apartment near Nebraska Avenue and Wyoming Street in February 1990.

"Up there, there were just too many drugs; I had to get away," she said. Williams holds down jobs as a restaurant cook and as a packer for a chili company.

"If the drugs get worse down here, I'll move farther south," she said.

Like Williams, Rickey Grant Sr. also grew up on the city's North Side. And like Williams, he decided to leave.

Grant, 30, a black and the father of three, moved from the city's Fairground Park area two years ago into the Hathaway Trails Subdivision just north of Interstate 270 in North County.

"There was a lot of gang activity in the city," said Grant. "This is better here; I don't feel threatened here. I wanted my children to have better than what I had."

The census figures show that many of the heavily black neighborhoods of north St. Louis have been losing population at a staggering rate. At the same time, other parts of the city are becoming more integrated.

A census tract that takes in a portion of the Cabanne neighborhood (a tract bounded roughly by Page Boulevard on the north, Enright Avenue on the south, Goodfellow Boulevard on the west and Academy Avenue on the east) saw its black population drop by 29 percent - to 4,391 in 1990 from 6,150 in 1980.

Farther east, a census tract that takes in a part of the Vandeventer neighborhood (a tract bounded by Page and Enright, Taylor Avenue and North Grand Boulevard) lost 31 percent of its black population during the decade - to 2,977 from 4,310.Meanwhile, the black population of some areas of North County is steadily on the rise.

A census tract just north of Interstate 270 and east of Lewis and Clark Boulevard (Highway 367) has seen its black population nearly triple since 1980 - to 3,228 from 1,161. The area was 91 percent white in 1980; it was about 76 percent white in 1990.

Directly to the west, a tract bounded by Parker Road on the north, I-270 on the south, New Halls Ferry Road on the west and Lewis and Clark on the east, saw black population jump to 7,561 from 4,390. The percentage of blacks rose to 53 percent from 30 percent.

Other North County areas that showed sharp increases in black population included tracts that take in the city of Jennings and a section of the city of Ferguson.

Hugh Barlow, chairman of the sociology department at Southern Illinois University at Edwardsville, said the continuing migration of blacks into North County is both predictable and understandable.

"People tend to move into areas where they already know people and where they feel comfortable," he said. Barlow also said he has no doubt that there is some racial "steering" of black homebuyers into the area by real estate companies, although the realty companies adamantly deny it.

A local real estate executive who asked not to be identified called the continued movement of black families into North County "just a normal geographic movement of people from older, cheaper housing into newer, more expensive housing."

He said there is no reason to believe that the racial change will result in a deterioration of North County neighborhoods similar to the deterioration that took place in some areas of north St. Louis.

"That was a different time; those were different circumstances," he said. The people moving to North County are people wanting to upgrade their standard of living. They want to take care of their property, protect their equity."[264]

The only metric necessary to measure social capital is if your community can spontaneously hold trick-or-treating without the need to create artificial "safe zones," where police and adults designate a few blocks a momentary refuge from the everyday carnage of life normally found in the area.

Not one all-white (or overwhelmingly white) community/neighborhood/city in America has ever had the need to have a few blocks designated a "safe zone" for trick-or-treating.

In St. Louis, areas devoid of whiteness and overflowing with black pride lack the basic neighborly congeniality to keep a grocery store open; how do you expect a 'food desert' to be a temporary oasis for nocturnal candy gathering?

Enter the 'safe zone'... yet another reminder the black people are among us.

October 31, 2014
The Coming Negrogeddon in Ferguson

Attorney General, Eric "I am also a black man" Holder, has already announced his intentions when it comes to reforming the Ferguson Police Department (one he continues to throw under a Rosa Parks' driven bus): racial demographic changes in Ferguson mean the city must see an immediate increase in black police officers.

Holder, whose advice to the person leaking information from the

---

[264] Migration: Blacks Moving To County, South Side, St. Louis Post-Dispatch, 4-14-1991

Michael Brown investigation was "shut up,"[265] has utilized the full resources of the Department of Justice (organizations include the civil rights division of the DOJ as well as the Orwellian Community Relations Services of the same government agency)[266] and an 'Always 1963 Birmingham Somewhere' media to upset and agitate the black people of Ferguson and metropolitan St. Louis.

He has created an "us vs. them" mentality (announcing, "This attorney general and this Department of Justice stand with the people of Ferguson")[267], one far worse than the one Christy E. Lopez - deputy chief of the special litigation section of the Justice Department's civil rights division - claimed Ferguson Police Department members wearing "I am Darren Wilson" bracelets could ever hope to create.[268]

To Holder, Ferguson is nothing more than the epitome of "demography is destiny," with his belief that Ferguson police need "wholesale change" a reflection of his discomfort in the lack of melanin found in the majority white force.

The hated white police chief of Ferguson, Thomas Jackson, showed more tenacity in attacking Holder than any member of the Republican Party has the entire time Mr. "My People" has been agitating for all things black as the Attorney General. [Ferguson Police Chief fires back at reports his department is disbanding, St. Louis Post-Dispatch, 10-31-14]:

Jackson called it "irresponsible" for Holder to comment about

---

[265] http://fox2now.com/2014/10/29/holder-tells-grand-jury-leaker-to-shut-up/

[266] http://krcu.org/post/whos-who-justice-agencies-investigating-ferguson

[267] http://www.cnn.com/2014/08/21/us/missouri-teen-shooting/

[268] http://www.nytimes.com/2014/09/27/us/ferguson-missouri.html?_r=0

conclusions Justice Department investigators analyzing his department have made while their investigation is ongoing, especially while "he is telling others to 'shut up' about leaks."

The entire *Farce of Ferguson* has been due to the Justice Department (with Barack Obama's blessing) acting irresponsible; and now, with the fear "All hell may break loose" in the likely-scenario Darren Wilson avoids any charges from the Grand Jury, the true scope of Holder's "irresponsible" actions are about to manifest in an orgy of black violence/insurrectionary activities local authorities prepare to confront. [Ferguson police brace for new protests by spending thousands on riot gear: St Louis County police has spent $172,669 since August on teargas, grenades, pepper balls and other civil disobedience equipment, The Guardian, 10-28-14]

In a city whose tax base has been eroding for years, the soon-to-be 90 percent black city (at 67 percent black now, Ferguson will see a mass exodus of the remaining 28 percent white residents hoping to make some profit on their property), the opening salvos of St. Louis' Negrogeddon have already seen blacks cause damage to Asian-owned stores.

But now, as Holder prepares to cement his true legacy as Attorney General (finally kicking-off that "conversation about race" he wanted nearly six years ago), the coming St. Louis Negrogeddon - all of the metropolitan area prepares to endure - could ensure the Ferguson blacks inherit is nothing more than Section 8 apartment complexes and an abandoned business district:

> Businesses in Ferguson say they are "going to wait and see" how to sustain what has been a tumultuous few months of riots and dramatically reduced revenue, with some local store owners saying customers are "too scared" to bring their business to the area.
>
> Local stores and businesses throughout Ferguson expressed feelings of frustration and uncertainty as many have

boarded-up windows, increased security measures and lost thousands of dollars in revenue amid protests stemming from the Aug. 9 police shooting death of Michael Brown. Many businesses said they will just have to wait and see what happens ahead of an expected November ruling on whether or not to indict officer Darren Wilson.

"We've lost $200 to $300 in business nightly, people are afraid to pick up in the night, after dark," said Tammy Cao of the Hunan Chop Suey Chinese Restaurant.

"People are too scared at night ... I guess we'll just have to wait and see."

She said the store has "paid $1,500 out-of-pocket for window damages" caused by rioters, because the $5,000 insurance deductible "did not add up."

"I know customers who have left the area ... I just want everything to go back to normal and everyone can do business again."

A return to normalcy is a sentiment echoed by many Ferguson businesses.

Zisser Tire & Auto said the rioters "knocked out 90 percent of our windows, which are still boarded up."

"We've just been trying to go to work, business as usual – nobody wants to take the boards down until we see what happens. It's more of the not knowing what's going to happen next."

Jenny of Don Henefer Jewelers said that although their store has not been directly harmed by the Ferguson protests or rioters, they now "put all the jewelry away at night."

The Swiish Bar and Grill owners have filed a lawsuit against the state of Missouri, St. Louis County, the Missouri State

Highway Patrol and the cities of Ferguson and Jennings for what they claim is more than $25,000 in lost revenue. Owners Chantelle and Corey Nixon-Clark told KTVI-TV they were forced to close their doors for weeks as a law enforcement command post was set up in the Jennings shopping center amid the riots.

Some store owners said that customer and business fears are a shared experience.

"I feel scared about my business," Rokhaya Biteye, owner of Daba African Hair Braiding in one of the modest strip malls that line West Florissant, told Reuters.

She said profits have evaporated to almost nothing since the shooting. In weeks prior, she generally pulled in about $800, but is now bringing in less than $100 each week.

"I don't think it will work anymore," she said, adding that she has no insurance.

Charles of Ferguson Burger Bar & More said that he has resolved not to make any added security provisions to the store because of his faith in a higher power.

"I'm going to leave it up to the man I put in charge originally, I'm going to leave it up to God," he said. "I'm not boarding up, I'm not closing."[269]

"Going to leave it up to God..."

The Christians trying to defend Constantinople from the Muslim hordes believed their city was to be protected by God as well: we call the city Istanbul now.

---

[269] Ferguson Store Owners: Customers 'Too Scared' to Bring Business to the Area, St. Louis CBS, 10-30-14

The Obama Administration, Holder's Department of Justice and the State of Missouri have already declared whose side they represent: Al Sharpton is, after all, is a "key advisor" to President Obama on all matters Ferguson.

Meanwhile, the St. Louis County grand jury is nothing more than an entity whose impending announcement puts them on an island of absolute certainty: Negrogeddon is coming to not just Ferguson, but the entire metropolitan St. Louis.

And this will be Barack Obama and Eric Holder's great legacy: the agitation of a racial crusade against law, order, and the white people of Ferguson and metro St. Louis.

November 2, 2014
"When the legend becomes fact, print the legend."

But... but... but, he was "unarmed":

> Justice Department investigators have all but concluded they do not have a strong enough case to bring civil rights charges against Darren Wilson, the white police officer who shot and killed an unarmed black teenager in Ferguson, Mo., law enforcement officials said.
>
> When racial tension boiled over in Ferguson after the Aug. 9 shooting, Attorney General Eric H. Holder Jr. traveled to the St. Louis suburb to meet with city leaders and protest organizers in an effort to bring calm. He assured them that the federal government would open a civil rights investigation into the fatal shooting of Michael Brown. But that investigation now seems unlikely to result in any charges.
>
> "The evidence at this point does not support civil rights charges against Officer Wilson," said one person briefed on the investigation, who spoke on the condition of anonymity because of the sensitivity of the case.
>
> Justice Department officials are loath to acknowledge publicly that their case cannot now meet the high legal threshold for a successful civil rights prosecution. The timing is sensitive: Tensions are high in greater St. Louis as people

await the results of a grand jury's review of the case.[270]

November 4, 2014
Living in Occupied St. Louis: 28th Annual Guns 'N Hoses police-fire charity boxing match canceled because of fear first responders needed to deal with black insurrection

Much is being made about the tape of FAA officials apparently agreeing to a No-Fly Zone over Ferguson,[271] restricting the ability of national and local media from showing overhead shots of the black insurrection in the city.

Less is being made of the events cancelled in Ferguson and the metropolitan St. Louis area, courtesy of the black insurrection and the continued threat of a reigniting of hostilities when Darren Wilson is found innocent by the grand jury.

Much less.

The threat of rioting, looting, and black-in-origin violence is an ever-present fear for those living in the occupied heartland of America, a city where a monument stands as a reminder of the opening to the "Gateway to the West" and "Manifest Destiny."

In 2014, the reality of "Manifest Destruction" (look no farther than the sorrowful conditions of 98 percent black East St. Louis) seems to be on the horizon, and thus all emergency personnel in the

---

[270] Federal civil rights charges unlikely against police officer in Ferguson shooting, 10-31-14

[271] http://www.bizjournals.com/stlouis/morning_call/2014/11/police-deny-ferguson-no-fly-zone-was-to-keep-media.html

metropolitan St. Louis area must be prepared for combatting the black insurrection:

> Citing concerns about simmering unrest in Ferguson, sponsors have postponed this year's 28th annual Guns 'N Hoses police-fire charity boxing match, scheduled for Nov. 26.
>
> The event, typically held on the night before Thanksgiving at the Scottrade Center, benefits BackStoppers, a nonprofit providing financial support for the families of fallen first responders. Organizers said they hoped to reschedule in the new year.
>
> The charity's executive director, Ron Battelle, said organizers are concerned that many of the participants and attendees may be called to duty to manage possible protests after a St. Louis County grand jury decides whether to indict Ferguson police Officer Darren Wilson in the Aug. 9 killing of Michael Brown.
>
> Officials have said to expect an announcement in mid-November.
>
> "To hold the event at this time could serve as distraction to the service of our first responders," said Battelle, a former chief of the St. Louis County Police Department.
>
> "The decision to postpone was made by the organization after much thought and deliberation. It takes into account the recently increased hours of first responders who attend the event."
>
> Work, not training, must come first, Battelle said.
>
> "We don't want to be a distraction to police officers, firefighters and EMS personnel who will be working long hours," Battelle said. "We don't want to take them away from their prime responsibility."
>
> There also were worries that a large gathering of police officers might become a magnet for demonstrations and potential clashes.

This year's president of the organization is Robert McCulloch, the St. Louis County prosecuting attorney, whose refusal to recuse himself from the Brown investigation has made him the subject of criticism. His father was a St. Louis police officer shot to death in 1964 while trying to arrest a kidnapper, and some Ferguson protesters have said that makes his involvement in the Wilson case a conflict of interest.

Last year's event drew about 17,000 people and raised $292,000. The series of boxing matches, pitting police officers against firefighters, is the BackStoppers' biggest fundraiser. It has raised about $4.4 million since 1987.[272]

Guns 'N Hoses is easily the coolest name in the history of fundraisers, and violates every politically correct norm of modernity. That such an event exists is cause to immediately pause and smile, knowing there exists something as manly and community-orientated as Guns 'N Hoses.

And the continued hatred of Robert McCulloch[273] by the local and national press (and every member of Organized Blackness)[274] is also a reminder God has a sense of humor: his father, Paul, was a member of the St. Louis Police Department, and was gunned downed by a black man in the infamous Pruitt-Igoe Development...[275]

Back in September, with the initial black insurrection still going strong, the city of Ferguson was forced to cancel StreetFest because of the fear of black violence/disruptions making the event unsafe for those still believing civilization can flourish in a majority black city:

> Ferguson city officials have decided to postpone StreetFest, a

---

[272] Officials postpone charity boxing event because of concerns about Ferguson, St. Louis Post-Dispatch, 11-4-14

[273] http://www.newsweek.com/ferguson-prosecutor-robert-p-mccullochs-long-history-siding-police-267357

[274] http://www.cbsnews.com/news/naacp-president-special-prosecutor-critically-important-in-ferguson/

[275] https://lareviewofbooks.org/essay/killed-robert-mccullochs-father

beloved fifteen-year-old festival in the city's historic CityWalk district, and residents are blaming disruptive and disrespectful protesters.

The music and food festival was supposed to happen this weekend and feature the first-ever Ferguson StreetFest talent show, a home-brewing expo, a washer tournament, pony rides and, of course, the popular Manly Man High Heel Keg Relay, where men race each other while holding kegs of beer and wearing pumps.

Brian Fletcher, a former mayor of Ferguson and leader of the "I Heart Ferguson" campaign, said he completely disagrees with the city's decision and called on officials to reinstate the community festival, even if it means ending the festivities earlier in the night." Our city and our citizens and businesses must not be held hostage," Fletcher wrote on the "I Heart Ferguson" website.

"Residents have been patient, courteous, understanding for five weeks. Ferguson has been maligned, ridiculed and called a 'suburban ghetto,' especially by the national media. That ends today." Fletcher said he blames "illegal protesters," not non-violent demonstrators, for causing the safety concerns that led to the festival's postponement." The actions of the protesters are costing our businesses their livelihood and our city taxes.

This is their goal," he writes. "They disrupt the peace of restaurants, the Farmer's Market and traffic. They are breaking the law."

Protesters marching and chanting at Ferguson's popular weekly farmers' market has been a sore spot for residents, many of whom mentioned the disruptions at Monday night's town-hall meetings, which were closed to media and non-residents.

Fletcher offers another example of a time when "illegal protesters" caused problems for Ferguson residents:

> This past Saturday, a very well known female co-owner of multiple Ferguson businesses was blocked on S.

> Florissant road. Her vehicle was surrounded by the so called peaceful protectors taunting, cursing, calling her a white bit**. She was brought to tears. They stood in middle of the street, surrounding her vehicle, not allowing her to move. For 25 minutes she was held against her wishes as a hostage, literally kidnapped. The police were down the street a bit further handling another similar incident were a motorist supposedly bumped a protestor who was in the street blocking his path. The mob then pounded on the vehicle causing $1500 in damage (according to a local auto firm). I ask you again, is this peaceful?

> Fletcher says he's calling on Ferguson residents to tell the city council not to postpone or cancel StreetFest. Instead, Fletcher suggests the festival could end at 6 p.m. instead of 10:30 p.m. so there is "no darkness of night cover for [protesters'] illegal actions."

> Fletcher also asked the council to designate one entry/exit point for the festival and to station plainclothes police officers for security.[276]

Somewhere, somehow, Paul McCulloch is smiling: his son - hated for daring to remember to his father, believing in the community of St. Louis, and siding with police over the black rebel forces of the "Justice for Mike Brown" movement - is poised to unlock a door the media, the entertainment industry, academia, and the entire federal government has tried to keep shut for decades.[277]

It's a door that opened briefly enough to expose a people whose actions prompted the cancellation of StreetFest in Ferguson, and postponed the 28th annual Guns 'N Hoses police-fire charity boxing match...

---

[276] Ferguson Postpones Popular Festival, Residents Blame "Illegal Protesters", River Front Times, 9-23-14

[277] http://www.stltoday.com/news/local/metro/st-louis-prosecutor-has-faced-controversy-for-decades/article_cdd4c104-6086-506e-9ee8-aa957a31fee5.html

A door to a world every working white American goes into debt to avoid living near (if you pay a mortgage, you are in debt) has been kept closed for decades, but once it opens those who witness what's on the other side will forever join the ranks of *Those Who Can See*.

Paul McCulloch ghostly hand could symbolically open this door.

November 6, 2014
Putting the "Black" in Blackmail: Don't Shoot Coalition Proposes "Rules of Engagement" for Police in St. Louis During Impending Black Insurrection

A hurricane isn't on the verge of unsettling life as we know it in the metropolitan St. Louis area.

The Bell Curve tolls for the civilization whites have created in St. Louis - and wherever they migrate to in the area - with an unnatural force on the verge of being unleashed, galvanized into agitation by an Obama Administration dedicated to preserving the memory of a Gentle Giant.[278]

Fear of the violence from those rioting to the war cry of "Black Lives Matter" has already convinced property management companies[279] to create contingency plans to protect both physical assets and their employees.[280]

---

[278] http://www.washingtonpost.com/news/post-nation/wp/2014/08/23/white-house-officials-to-attend-michael-browns-funeral/

[279] http://www.bizjournals.com/stlouis/news/2014/11/05/novelly-s-property-management-company-outlines.html?ana=twt

[280] http://www.bizjournals.com/stlouis/news/2014/11/04/clayton-tenants-

Those in Clayton, where demonstrations for "Justice for Michael Brown" have previously been held, are preparing an unprecedented emergency situation.[281]

Best yet, members of the pro-Michael Brown Don't Shoot Coalition[282] - a group consisting of organizations such as the Organization for Black Struggle, Sistahs Talkin' Back, Missouri Immigrant and Refugee Advocates, Drone-Free St. Louis, Coalition to Abolish the Prison Industrial Complex (CAPIC), and Amnesty International - have demanded the police of metropolitan be handcuffed with "Rules of Engagement" for dealing with the impending riots.

In a word, the Don't Shoot Coalition has firmly put the black in blackmail: black radicals defining what the ROEs should be concerning *their* protests:

> A coalition of roughly 50 groups concerned about the fatal shooting of Michael Brown on Wednesday asked police to agree to "rules of engagement" for the response to the upcoming grand jury decision about the shooting and announced their own plans.
>
> At a news conference in St. Louis, "Don't Shoot Coalition" members said they were offering training in de-escalation and for legal observers. They vowed to have at least two safe spaces set up in each anticipated area of protest activity, to offer sanctuary in houses of worship. And they said that had been attempting, unsuccessfully so far, to negotiate key elements with local and federal officials.
>
> The group said police should value safety first, and agree to a "de-militarized response" that would bar the use of armored vehicles, rubber bullets, rifles and tear gas.

---

warned-of-unrest-emergency-plan.html?page=2

[281] Clayton officials, businesses plan for emergency situations, KSDK.com, 10-30-14

[282] http://www.dontshootstl.org/#!members/c1jxp

The group is asking for advance notice of the public announcement of the decision, so that they can prepare. They are also asking police to respect the safe spaces and ensure protesters can reach them.

A St. Louis County grand jury has been considering whether Ferguson Police Officer Darren Wilson should face charges for the Aug. 9 shooting of the unarmed Brown, 18. St. Louis County Prosecuting Attorney Robert P. McCulloch said Tuesday night that the jury was still hearing evidence, adding that he didn't expect a decision until mid- to late November.

Coalition members said tensions were growing, fueled by three recent fatal police shootings and long-term problems that include racial profiling, a lack of diversity and accountability in law enforcement, inequality and a lack of trust in police and the judicial system. The group blamed police for escalating peaceful protests into violence, saying that given proper space, protesters have been self-policing.

People "are going to pour into the street," predicted Montague Simmons, chair of the Organization of Black Struggle, and no amount of force will prevent that. But he said that the coalition would engage in "peaceful, non-violent civil disobedience" in the tradition of Mahatma Gandhi and Rev. Dr. Martin Luther King Jr., and wanted police to use respect and a non-militarized approach to protesters.

Simmons said he expected Clayton and the Ferguson police station to be "natural gathering areas" after the decision is announced. "Every injury, every bullet that flies, every drop of teargas," he said, will be on the hands of elected officials if they fail to act.

Here are those proposed "Rules of Engagement":

Proposed Rules of Engagement

1) The first priority shall be preservation of human life.

2) Channels of communication will be established so that situations can be de-escalated if necessary.

3) Police will give protesters 48 hour advance notice before grand jury decision is announced.

4) Police will provide to the public information that makes clear the chain of command, who is making what decisions and the processes for deciding when the police response will be escalated.

5) Every attempt should be made to communicate with protesters to reach "common sense" agreements based on these protocols, both ahead of time and at the scene of protests.

6) Clear standards of professionalism and sound community friendly-policing will be maintained and adhered to at all times.

7) Police will wear only the attire minimally required for their safety. Specialized riot gear will be avoided except as a last resort.

8) Crowd control equipment such as armored vehicles, rubber bullets, rifles and tear gas will not be used.

9) Police or other government authorities will not interfere with the free flow of information through tactics such as limiting cell or internet access, interception of cell or other mobile conversations or unwarranted wiretaps.

10) Every attempt will be made to pinpoint arrests so that only individual lawbreakers will be arrested. "Kettling" and mass arrests will not be used.

11) Safe houses shall be considered sacred ground and only entered by police when called upon or if extremely necessary.

12) Media and Legal Observers shall not be considered participants in protests and shall be allowed to do their jobs freely.

13) Every attempt will be made to provide alternate routes or other means for non-involved persons to get to places of employment and meet other transportation necessities.

14) Strategically, police commanders will allow protests to take and occupy larger and more disruptive spaces than would normally be tolerated, and will allow occupation of those spaces for longer periods of time than would normally be tolerated.

15) Police will be instructed to be tolerant of more minor lawbreaking (such as thrown water bottles) when deciding whether to escalate the use of force.

16) Police rank and file will be instructed to provide every latitude to allow for free assembly and expression, treating protesters as citizens and not "enemy combatants."

17) Excessive force and other forms of police misconduct will not be tolerated.

18) Intimidation and harassment of protesters will not be tolerated. This includes pretextual pedestrian or traffic stops, contacting of employers or family members, pre—emptive arrests or detention of "leaders," publishing of private information and any other means of intimidation and harassment.

19) Bond for arrestees will not be set above the levels which would be considered average over the last two years, and arrestees will not be held for periods longer than average lengths of time. Medical care will be liberally made available. Attorneys will be able to travel to and meet with clients without impediments.[283]

Had Michael Brown not viciously assaulted Officer Darren, respecting rule no. 1 proposed by the Don't Shoot Coalition, none of this would be happening.

Basically, the Don't Shoot Coalition is asking the police - those tasked with maintaining the monopoly on violence to protect the law biding - to cede their authority to them, in essence granting them the ability to burn down the city without any threat of retaliation by law

---

[283] Group proposes 'rules of engagement' for grand jury announcement in Michael Brown case, St. Louis Post-Dispatch, 11-5-14]:

enforcement agencies.

Gregory Hood wrote the key words to understanding what must be done in the wake of the impending black riots in not just Ferguson, but all of St. Louis:

> But for the Ferguson police, no matter what they do, the aesthetics of helmeted men against "peaceful" demonstrators will convict them in the eyes of public opinion.
>
> And after the smoke clears, Attorney General Eric Holder will find some pretext to put the entire department in a Justice Department hammer lock, regardless of what anyone did or does.
>
> As only black politicians and commentators are allowed to notice, a large black population requires a police force that *is* essentially an occupation. Whites are at fault whether they provide too little law enforcement or too much.
>
> Perhaps the best thing the police of Ferguson could do is what the people and the media seem to want: walk off the job. Leave Ferguson to its fate. Let's see who needs whom.
>
> Perhaps the time has come for responsible whites to stop trying to save people who don't want to be saved.[284]

The Bell Curve tolls for the civilization whites have created in St. Louis; but the tolling of this bell will showcase the incompatible nature of the continued American Experiment.

---

[284] http://www.amren.com/news/2014/08/whos-to-blame-for-the-ferguson-riots/

November 7, 2014 An Open Letter to the White Residents of Metropolitan St. Louis

Though we'll likely never meet, since the events of August 9th I've watched the unfolding calamity in not just Ferguson, but the entire metropolitan St. Louis area, with great interest.

Having already read a great deal about St. Louis and the wonderful history of your city, the immediate reaction by the established national press and left-of-center magazines to side (canonize in the process) with the late Michael Brown - using the shooting of Brown as an opportunity to denounce the purportedly evil segregation of the region as the primary catalyst for disparities of outcome and inequality in the black communities - and portray the unnamed police officer in his shooting as a terrorist left me with only, simple conclusion: the soon-to-be named Officer Darren Wilson had done nothing wrong.[285]

Nor have the white residents of metropolitan St. Louis area done anything wrong in deciding to decamp from once prosperous neighborhoods, communities, cities, or counties when the presence of newly arrived black migrants from downtown St. Louis (many sporting shiny new Section 8 Vouchers) threatened the peace, prosperity and quality of life you were accustomed to and enjoyed.[286]

The social capital that was broken when this migration commenced was only possible due to the collective individual efforts of white people and white families, creating an environment where streets were safe for kids to play and businesses flourished; conversely, as

---

[285] http://www.newrepublic.com/article/119102/what-white-st-louis-thinks-about-ferguson

[286] http://www.stltoday.com/news/local/metro/in-valley-park-public-housing-means-less-crime-but-more/article_e1a296f4-e4e0-5527-a35d-f82435b45385.html

we see in 98 percent black East St. Louis, a city devoid of whites and overflowing with blacks equates to these individuals collectively creating a community where all trappings of modern civilization collapse.

Disappear.

Interestingly, wherever the former white residents of these decaying, now majority black suburbs (think Ferguson) retreat to, prosperity quickly follows.

In reading about your city and metropolitan area, a few anecdotes quickly put into clear focus why St. Louis is so special and a reminder of the dangerous folly in refusing to understanding the biological reality of race.

Back in 2008, the St. Louis Post-Dispatch reported an experimental ShotSpotter Location System[287], which can "detect how many shots were fired, which side of a building they came from and whether the shooter was moving," to aid police in fighting crime, was installed in area of St. Louis - Wells-Goodfellow - that is 97.5 percent black and .7 percent white:

> A $250,000 Justice Department grant paid for the pilot program in Wells-Goodfellow, where 14 homicides happened in 2007. The neighborhood is bounded by Martin Luther King Drive, Union Boulevard, Natural Bridge Road and the city limits.
>
> Police say they will seek to expand the system if it works well. It costs about $200,000 per square mile, according to ShotSpotter.[288]

Doesn't this one story speak volumes about who is causing the

---

[287] http://www.stltoday.com/news/local/crime-and-courts/microphones-hear-gunshots-call-police/article_b673cb02-05a2-11e1-8c26-0019bb30f31a.html

[288] http://en.wikipedia.org/wiki/Wells/Goodfellow,_St._Louis

violence in the city of St. Louis and why you would be against government programs granting Section 8 Vouchers to those living in public housing the ability to live near you?

Stories of black teenagers participating in group attacks on primarily white people (some of these blacks teens as young as 13 years of age, and pregnant)[289] happen with such frequency it hardly seems odd to learn Mayor Francis Slay stumbled upon such a 'knockout game' assault in 2011.[290]

For though we have never met, my thoughts and prayers have been with those white people of Ferguson that Eric "I'm also a black man" Holder's Department of Justice refuses to stand with; by extension, my thoughts and prayers are with all those white people of metropolitan St. Louis who understand there's something funny about Michael Brown's parents being upset the video of him participating in a strong-arm robbery[291] - mere minutes before he was confronted by Officer Wilson - was released, but something even funnier about Brown's mother fighting with his grandmother over who can sell (and profit from) "Justice for Michael Brown" t-shirts:

> FOX 2 has just obtained the incident report involving a reported assault and robbery first exposed in the Fox Files. Chris Hayes obtained it after a hearing in St. Louis County Court.
>
> It went to Court because Michael Brown's Mom, Lesley McSpadden, asked police not to release the incident report. The City Attorney for Ferguson, Stephanie Karr, wanted to be

---

[289] http://www.stltoday.com/news/local/govt-and-politics/nick-pistor/teenagers-including--year-old-pregnant-girl-in-custody-after/article_b1debbc9-638d-53a2-82f8-f043fe37d139.html

[290] http://stlouis.cbslocal.com/2011/10/25/st-louis-mayor-witnesses-aftermath-of-knockout-kings-attack/

[291] http://stlouis.cbslocal.com/2014/08/15/browns-family-upset-about-release-of-surveillance-video/

sensitive while still following the law. So she took it to Judge Maura McShane who said the report needed to be released, according to the law.

It involves a reported felony robbery with a weapon, October 18th in the parking lot of Red`s BBQ. It`s the corner of Canfield and West Florissant, just blocks from where Michael Brown was shot and killed.

According to the newly released Ferguson police report, several people, including Brown`s paternal grandmother, Pearlie Gordon, were selling 'Justice for Mike Brown merchandise.'

Then at about 1:20 pm, cars pulled up and 20-30 people 'jumped out' and 'rushed them.' One of those people was Michael Brown`s Mom, Lesley McSpadden, who is quoted yelling, 'you can`t sell this s%$&.'

The report says Brown`s grandma was 'repeatedly struck in the back of the head by an unknown subject' and 'knocked to the ground.' The report adds that McSpadden 'then ran up and punched (grandma).'[292]

It's a joke, this entire Michael Brown-inspired "Ferguson October" movement, but it's one you should stop laughing at: because soon Darren Wilson will be found guilty of absolutely nothing by the grand jury and a hurricane will be unleashed upon not just Ferguson, but all of metropolitan St. Louis.

And as those people smart enough to see this impending crisis forming know, there's a storm coming:

> And as the nation awaits that decision, those on the ground are making preparations. "We've been doing board-ups for

---

[292] http://fox2now.com/2014/11/05/police-investigating-assault-felony-robbery-following-fight-among-michael-browns-family/

probably the past month, the phone's been ringing off the hook," said Brian Krieger, owner of American Board Up and Construction Services in St. Louis. "I've already purchased 500 sheets of plywood."

He said he expects work to increase in the coming days as businesses, especially those in the Ferguson area, take precautions for the announcement.[293]

Godspeed white people of metropolitan St. Louis.

There's a hurricane coming into your region.

Judging by the rates of segregation in your area (what I'd deem "common sense economic decisions based on the empirical evidence observed through simply noticing"), you've been prepared for something of this nature for a long time.

Best wishes,

Paul Kersey

November 10, 2014
In this last of meeting places/ We grope together And avoid speech/ Gathered on this beach of the tumid river

Nevil Shute's *On the Beach* is a story worth remembering as we watch with anxious anticipation how the scenario will unfold in Ferguson, Missouri.

---

[293] Ferguson Braces for Grand Jury Decision in Michael Brown's Shooting: Law Enforcement, Businesses Prepare for Possible Unrest With Decision on Whether to Indict Police Officer, Wall Street Journal, 11-7-14

In Shute's story a nuclear war between the United States and the USSR has completely destroyed the world, save for the residents of Australia (and New Zealand). The deadly radiation from this conflict, however, is traveling from the northern hemisphere to Australia, and the characters in his book spend their final moments on earth knowing they are doomed.

No deus ex machina shows up to grant them an extension of life, only the aftermath of an atomic conflagration.

Shute invites the reader to ponder the concept of being beyond salvation and knowing the date of their expiration.

For the civilization white people created in Ferguson (recall, the city was 99 percent white in 1970, just five years after the 630-foot Gateway Arch was completed), the On the Beach moment is close at hand in the 67 percent black city.

The last white mayor of the city, James Knowles, has already told CNN to "prepare for the worst" once the grand jury decision on Officer Darren Wilson becomes public knowledge.[294]

Gun sales are spiking in the area,[295] the group Mothers March for Justice has called for peace[296] and invoked pray for divine intervention, while Trayvon Martin's father has called for calm in Ferguson and an end to the [black-in-origin] "culture of violence" in St. Louis.[297]

"War," is what one black person is preparing for in Ferguson:

> Ronardo Ward, 33, is one of those hoping to maintain peace in Ferguson if Wilson isn't indicted.

---

[294] http://www.cnn.com/2014/11/06/us/ferguson-rules-protests/

[295] http://www.cnn.com/2014/11/10/us/ferguson-michael-brown-shooting/

[296] http://fox2now.com/2014/11/09/mothers-pray-for-peace-ahead-of-brown-grand-jury-announcement/

[297] http://fox2now.com/2014/11/08/tracy-martin-calls-for-calm-in-ferguson/

"We are getting prepared for war," Ward told CBS News. "And that's just crazy."

Michael Johnson, 42, believes many young people will rail against the "system."

"There's gonna be a lot of angry young people that's pretty much not gonna listen to the system anymore," Michael Johnson said. "Why should they?"

Protests have been going on for months following Brown's death in August.

"The destruction here symbolizes this community, and how fragile and crumbled things are here," Johnson told CBS News.

Despite the potential violence, Johnson doesn't believe Ferguson is ready to explode if Wilson is not indicted.

"I don't think it's going to be as bad as people want to make it out to be, but I think there's some tough times ahead," Johnson stated.[298]

Doom.

No hope of salvation.

"Prepare for the worst."

But the "worst" has always been with us, because we've refused to acknowledge the metaphorical atomic bombs from Shute's novel have already detonated in our world. The situation in Ferguson is a reminder the black undertow has no half-life, with the ability to be just as lethal in 2014 as it was two generations in North St. Louis in 1980.

The year St. Louis was crowned America's 'murder capital':

> St. Louis - Street violence - most of it in the blighted black

---

[298] Ferguson Resident: 'We are Getting Prepared for War', CBS St. Louis, 11-10-14

neighborhoods on the north side of St. Louis - has put this Midwestern river port on top the national heap in murder statistics.

Police recorded 230 murders in St. Louis in 1978, 46 for every 100,000 residents - highest ration in the nation and more than double the rate in New York City.

"A stickup in St. Louis used to be 'Your money or your life,'" said a cab driver.

"Now it's 'Your money AND your life.'"

St. Louis civil leaders say the predominantly black enclose on the north side, where murder is most frequent, have become virtual war zones.

St. Louis' chief prosecutor issued a public plea for help in curbing the violence. In an open letter to black church leaders, Circuit Attorney George Peach said 84 percent of the 285 persons slain last year were black.

In the cases that were solved, all the black victims were killed by other blacks, he added.

"With these harsh figures before us, it is not difficult to say that blacks are killing each other an alarming rate," Peach, who is white, said in his letter.

"The slightest arguments of result in bloodshed. We've got to stop the quick rush to the gun to settle disputes," Peach said.

The typical murder victim in St. Louis is a black male in his 20s, gunned down by a neighbor in a street near his home. In 64 percent of the killings a handgun is used.

The victim may have resisted a robbery, fought over money or been targeted by drug dealers.

"The law enforcement agencies take the attitude that, 'Well, there's another black killed. That's one less black we have to deal with,'" said state Rep. Fred Williams of St. Louis, who is black.

But Police Chief Eugene Camp commented, "You can't patrol against murder. if someone wants to kill somebody, how can we stop it?"

Black leaders say the business community has virtually abandoned the crime-ridden north side. What's left, they say, is unemployment and poverty.

St. Louis has lost 58,000 manufacturing jobs in the last 10 years. It stands to lose another 5,000 jobs over the next couple of years as General Motors abandons its north side assembly plant, the city's single largest source of tax revenue and one of its biggest employers. The operation will be relocated in rural Wentzville, 45 miles west of St. Louis.

"When an industry thinks about where it wants to relocate, it doesn't want to have its employees subjected to the kind of crime problems St. Louis has," said Williams.

Some police officers, unhappy with the department's failure to curb the murder rate, have organized the St. Louis Police Ethical Society. Its leader is Sgt. James Buchanan, a black who says the city should hire more black officers to try to deal more effectively with the crime in the black community.

St. Louis' population of 500,000 is more than 50 percent black. The police force of about 2,000 officers is 18 percent black. City officials say the cannot find enough qualified black officers.

Many murder investigations are hampered because witnesses decline to testy in court, and the reason, said Buchanan, is the unwillingness of some blacks to cooperate with white police officers.

"We could solve part of that if we had more black officers doing homicide investigations," Buchanan said, noting that of 16 detectives on the homicide squad, only two are black.

Peach said he didn't know what percentage of those arrested are never charged. But in "a pretty nice chunk" of cases where murder suspects are freed for lack of evidence, Peach said, the problem is a lack of willing or credible witnesses.

Peach said in many cases unwilling witnesses have an attitude of "to hell with the police, to hell with the courts."[299]

When this article was published in newspapers around the country back in 1980, the city of Ferguson was 85 percent white and 14 percent black.[300]

Many of those white people in Ferguson reading this story in 1980 probably smiled, noting exactly why they had been part of the white flight from St. Louis and how they now slept comfortably at night far from the sound of police sirens.

But the problems of St. Louis - detailed in this hilariously prophetic article for Ferguson's problems in 2014 - have migrated to Ferguson, precisely because the population responsible for creating the "virtual war zones" of 1980 have migrated to the suburb.

Just as the population responsible for creating a peaceful community (where nice, respectable affirmative action-enhanced or public sector employed blacks can raise their families away from the violence of blacks) migrated from Ferguson once it became impossible to maintain standards of civility.

Perhaps, like those characters in Shute's novel, the white people (and the civilization they birthed) of not just Ferguson, but all of America are doomed.

Or perhaps it's this *civilizational iteration* that is doomed, with just this nation ultimately doomed?

All in all, perhaps it's just a coincidence tomorrow is Veterans Day and the fear of roving bands of black insurgents/insurrectionists in Ferguson and metropolitan St. Louis (unleashed by the news Officer Darren Wilson faces no charges for his justified actions in the shooting death of 18-year-old Michael Brown) represent a power image for what exactly those brave - almost overwhelmingly white -

---

[299] St. Louis is U.S. 'murder capital', Associated Press, 4-5-1980

[300] http://www.nytimes.com/2014/08/13/opinion/racial-history-behind-the-ferguson-protests.html?_r=0

men gave their lives for: the right for black people to protest, whine, and even threaten mass violence until they get their way.

And forcing white people to continually pay for this unalienable right of eternal black grievance to perpetuate.

The dysfunction of the black community has its origin not in a political ideology, a lack of an embracement of free market principles, moral collapse, high rates of abortion, or the erosion of the nuclear family: the dysfunctions source is merely the individual black people who collectively are responsible for creating the conditions of the community.

It's not white people's fault that 67 percent black Ferguson is collapsing, just as it was not white people's fault that in 1980 predominantly black north St. Louis was - and still is - a "virtual war zone."

This civilization is doomed, but by no means does this fact doom the people whose collective will to power birthed it; there stands a monument to the vision of the white people who founded, explored, settled, and built this nation in St. Louis, and from the top of it one might be afforded a view of the suburb where it proves T. S. Eliot correct (cue up *The Hollow Men*):

> *This is the way the world ends*
>
> *This is the way the world ends*
>
> *This is the way the world ends*
>
> *Not with a bang but a whimper.*

November 12, 2014
Great Moments in Black History: The Time Black People Protested the Building of the Gateway Arch in St. Louis

Christopher Nolan did it.

Interstellar is spectacular and a movie made for a future we don't presently have, but will get the chance to secure.

From children being taught (in the movies fictional future) the Apollo 11 moon landing was a hoax to the book shelf notably displaying A. Scott Berg's *Lindbergh* biography, *Interstellar* is a movie made for those who have an atavistic reaction to Matthew McConaughey's monologue on the importance of the pioneering spirit:

> "We've always defined ourselves by the ability to overcome the impossible. And we count these moments. These moments when we dare to aim higher, to break barriers, to reach for the stars, to make the unknown known. We count these moments as our proudest achievements. But we lost all that. Or perhaps we've just forgotten that we are still pioneers."

It's fitting to remember to recall what the black population was doing when white America was looking to the sky in anticipation of the Apollo 11 mission on July 16: Ralph Abernathy Jr., the heir to the civil rights throne of Martin Luther King, was leading the Poor People's Campaign on a mule and buggy march across America.

As the Saturn V rocket prepared to launch into the sky, a rabble of blacks approached the space vehicle on a horse and cart to protest inequality and - in their eyes - a misappropriation of resources that could (and should) go to help the black underclass.

Easily, this is one of the most pathetic moments in the recorded history of humanity.

Prior to seeing *Interstellar*, a trailer for Selma played (yet another entry into the civil rights porn catalogue of making contemporary whites feel guilty for the actions of their ancestors; in the process creating animosity against every white who every existed among contemporary blacks).

The film will canonize the protest by blacks to be able to participate in a civilization they had no hand in creating, but - once unleashed via weaponized equality - whose hand was entirely responsible for the degradation of the civilizations white built. (see 2014 Birmingham, Selma, Detroit, Memphis, Camden, East St. Louis).

Which brings us to yet another Great Moment in Black History.

Just as the scene of a horse and buggy full of black people, juxtaposed with a massive rocket ship (Apollo 11) clearly served as a metaphor for the vast racial differences in intelligence, morality, and collective will power on July 16, 1969, the story of black people protesting the erection of the Gateway Arch in St. Louis is one worth remembering.

The Gateway Arch was built to commemorate westward expansion, Manifest Destiny and the (indomitable) pioneering spirit of the white men who tamed this country, building a mighty nation out of the wilderness of the territory acquired by Thomas Jefferson in the Louisiana Purchase of 1803.

It's a stunning monument, and an incredible feat of engineering brilliance. Charles Guggenhiem directed the brilliant *Monument to the Dream* (no, not Martin Luther King's...), which was a documentary telling the story of the building of the Gateway Arch. Nominated for an Academy Award in 1967, Guggenhiem's documentary unabashedly tells the story of a people still on a collision with space exploration and the successful landing on the moon.

The documentary is now known as the *Building the St. Louis Gateway Arch*.

But it was in 1964 black people would prove, once again, they must always be the center of attention.[301]

Though the Gateway Arch was designed by white men, with white engineers and architects trusted with completing the project, the lack of black participation was noticeable to those nascent members of Organized Blackness. In Jim Merkel's *The Making of an Icon: The Dreamers, The Schemers, and the Hard Hats who Built the Gateway Arch*, we are treated to a story of black defiance directly in the tradition of the mule and buggy march on the Apollo 11 launch site.

In a chapter titled 'Climbing to Equality', we learn:

> Shortly after noon on July 14, 1964, workers at the Arch grounds were opening their lunchboxes and preparing to eat bologna sandwiches, coffee, and maybe soup from a thermos. None of them was aware that the full force of the civil rights protests of the 1960s was about to break into what heretofore was the uncontroversial construction of the Gateway Arch.
>
> But civil rights activists had already turned attention toward what they saw as a lack of hiring of African-Americans during the monument's construction. It was only a matter of time before a highly publicized protest would occur there. By 1964, St. Louis was awash in protests. In August 1963, hundreds demonstrated against what they saw as racial discrimination at a local bank, the Jefferson Bank & Trust.
>
> African-Americans could only expect to work menial jobs, such as janitors. Many activists who were involved with those protests turned their attention toward the hiring of African-Americans at the Arch. Percy Green II, a leader of the Jefferson Bank protests, said activists thought there should be more hiring of blacks, since it was a federally funded project: "We didn't know why there weren't any black contractors as well as black employees."
>
> MacDonald Construction Co., the prime contractor for the project, indicated it hadn't found any qualified workers. The

---

[301] 50 years after Arch-climbing protest, 'We still have work to do' on minority hiring, St. Louis Post-Dispatch, 7-14-14

activists then started setting deadlines and making plans to do something big. Early in July, Green and a white protestor, Richard Daly, conducted what Green called a "reconnaissance" of the Arch grounds to determine whether they could execute their plan.

Then on July 14, they called a demonstration and a news conference for the east side of the Old Courthouse, within sight of the Arch. While reporters listened to Robert Curtis, an attorney and spokesman for the protestors, Green and Daly walked onto the Arch grounds, wearing work clothes.

As workers ate their lunches, Green and Daly scurried to ladders on the north leg and started climbing. When they reached 125 feet, they signaled people holding binoculars at the site of the news conference to indicate they'd climbed partway up one leg. Curtis then announced that two protests had climbed the north leg of the Arch. Quickly, the reporters left the news conference and dashed toward the north leg.

"We felt that that would be the only thing that would draw attention to the amount of racism (at the Arch) and how federal funds were being used to perpetuate it," said Green, who was 29 and the chairman of the employment committee for the Congress of Racial Equality (CORE), a local civil rights group.

By that time, the Arch was about 300 feet tall, but Green and Daly didn't want to higher. If they came close to the workers and there was an accident, they might be held responsible. From an elevator close by, police tried to talk them down. But they said they were staying until blacks started working at the Arch. The two were surrounded in kind of a cage, but there was reason to fear, and they acted cautiously. But they did plan to come down earlier.

Green had to get work at midnight. He figured that if he came down six hours after he made his climb he'd have time to make bail, go home, wash up, and get to work on time. They climbed down, were arrested, and went limp before the waiting police officers. They made bail, and Green got to work on time that night.

That night and the next morning, the papers, radio stations, and TV stations were full of stories about the protest. The National Park Service reacted by pushing for contractors to hire blacks and more black subcontractors.

More black workers did come on the job, to an extent, and three black-owned subcontractors were hired. "I'm satisfied that a token effort was made," Green said.

"There certainly was not sufficient number of blacks hired," But, he said, "Had it not been for our action, what little was done never would have occurred." Green went on to be arrested more than one hundred times for civil disobedience. He's been interviewed numerous times about what he did at the Arch. The protest and outcome still affect Green's viewpoint about the monument.

"This is a hell of a monument, but the question is, I wonder how many black people helped build it." He also thinks about those who lost their property when the lands were cleared for the Arch. They pyramids might be a great piece of architecture, but there was a great cost, Green believes.

"The only thing you say about those monuments is they put those cities on the map, but at what cost?" he said. "I think in terms of, you know, there are mucho injustices."[302]

"Mucho injustices..."

Nature is unjust, no matter the attempts by man to scuttle this immutable fact.

While our destiny is the stars, our immediate future is nothing more than the albatross of places like Selma, Ferguson, and the pathetic sight - memory - of the Poor People's Campaign of black people on a mule and cart demanding equality, justice, and the continuous penance by white people for their ancestors (supposed) sins and transgressions.

---

[302] Merkel, J. (2014). The making of an icon: The dreamers, the schemers, and the hard hats who built the Gateway Arch. St. Louis, Mo.: Reedy Press, p. 17-129

But there's a monument in St. Louis, not far from Ferguson, standing as a testament to the courage, fearlessness, and pioneering spirit of a people who tamed the North American continent and sent men to the moon with the slide rule.

The Spirit of St. Louis wasn't just the name of Charles Lindbergh's plane; it resides in all who watched *Interstellar* and realized the movie represents a revolt against the unnatural state of the modern world.

November 13, 2014
si vis pacem para bellum

Bram Stoker's classic *Dracula* is an epistolary novel, pieced together from diary entries from multiple individuals, letters, and even a captain's ship log (the demise of the *Demeter* easily being one of the more gripping examples of horror ever written) to give the book an air of authenticity.

Reading the fictional work, you're almost convinced you are inside the mind (and a captive of Dracula himself) of Jonathan Harker.

The horror the entire St. Louis metropolitan area now prepares for isn't the same as being held hostage in a dilapidated castle nestled in the Carpathian Mountains (with three hyper-sexual female vampires prepared to make a meal out of your neck), for its real.

Were a white supremacist novelist trying to piece together a fictional story of black dysfunction, dystopian state-mandated equality, and a media determined to deify a black criminal (damn the evidence!), the story of what's happening in Ferguson, Missouri would be too preposterous a plot to seriously rationalize as a tale worth telling.

Seriously.

But when you consider what's happening in Ferguson, piecing together news clippings to compile what reads like an unbelievable epistolary novel no sane publisher would ever sign to publish, you get a story - that like Grimm's Fairytales original endings - that won't have a happy ending.

Just read these headlines, ripped from the pages of local and national media outlets, to understand the insanity of the fiasco in Ferguson.

- [Feds bring impartial police training to St. Louis departments, St. Louis Post-Dispatch, 11-6-14]
- [Black Revolutionary Group Puts BOUNTY on Darren Wilson & FAMILY MEMBERS!, Gateway Pundit, 11-10-14]
- [Berkeley sends warning letters to residents about Brown grand jury ruling, Fox2Now, 11-12-14]
- [Conceal and carry permits have exploded across St. Louis area, Fox2Now, 11-12-14]
- [Some area churches will open their doors as sanctuaries for Michael Brown protesters, Fox2Now, 11-12-14]
- [Ferguson Resident: 'We are Getting Prepared for War', CBS St. Louis, 11-10-14
- [Ferguson activist: As grand jury decision looms, police plan 'to kill us in the streets', Raw Story, 11-10-14]
- Missouri State Senator Maria Chappelle-Nadal told CNN today that she was more afraid of the police in Ferguson than she was being shot at in a bunker in Baghdad, Iraq. "The world needs to know exactly what has been going on here in Ferguson. There have been several human rights that have been violated. The First Amendment starting with one. Being gassed. I was teargassed for three hours. Myself along with my intern. And the world needs to know this is what law enforcement did to us here. And, you don't see this all across America. *You don't even see this in Iraq or Afghanistan. Let me tell you. I've been to Iraq. And I've been fired at in a bunker in Iraq. And let me tell you I was more afraid in Ferguson, Missouri than I was in Baghdad, Iraq.*"[303]

---

[303] <u>MO State Senator Chappelle-Nadal: "I Was More Afraid in Ferguson, Than I Was in Baghdad"</u>, **Gateway Pundit, 11-11-14**

- Other businesses are also stockpiling plywood as a precaution and planning on shutting their doors after the grand jury's announcement.

A manager of a retail store in Clayton, near where protesters have marched in the streets in front of McCulloch's office, said the store has plywood available and will close temporarily for employees' safety when the grand jury announcement is made. The store manager spoke only on the condition of anonymity, fearing her store could be targeted during protests.

At Negwer Materials, a building supply distributor in Ferguson, the company has instituted a series of safety protocols in the wake of Brown's killing and protests near the business that include moving some equipment off-site on weekends and placing wooden barricades at times surrounding its property on Airport Road that prohibit entry.

The barricades are put in place when the company deems it's a "red" day on a scale of green, yellow and red, said president Scott Negwer. The color scale was put in place following the protests, and this is the first time in the company's 90-year history it has taken such measures.

"We are obviously very concerned about the possibility of something happening," Negwer said, adding there has been no damage to the property or other incidents tied to the protests. "It's fairly easy for us because we have the materials. I'm concerned, but not panicked."[304]

- Gun sales in Ferguson and surrounding areas have increased by 50 percent in recent weeks, as residents and law enforcement alike prepare for what might come from the grand jury's ruling of Darren Wilson, the police officer who shot teenage Michael Brown. "So maybe I get trapped here or something and have to have a John Wayne shootout," said Dan McMullen, the owner of an insurance agency located near the site of the August shooting death of Brown, CNN reported. "That's the silly part about it: Is that going

---

[304] Businesses brace for grand jury decision, St. Louis Post-Dispatch, **11-13-14**]

to happen? Not a chance. But I guess, could it? I'm the only white person here.'[305]

War is coming to Ferguson and the fear of an increasingly bellicose environment is rising throughout the entire metro St. Louis area: All because of one black male deciding he had the right to walk in the middle of a street and took offense when a cop asked him use the sidewalk.

Looting, riots, violence, a white "Justice for Michael Brown" sympathizer attacked by the very people he tried to march with (running from this colorful lynch mob and finding sanctuary in a Walgreens)... all because Michael Brown found it necessary to fail in the simplest of decisions to avoid scrutiny from law enforcement: cooperate with the police.[306]

So as an entire region prepares for war, we can cue up the Big'Mike Soundcloud for a soundtrack to the madness:

> Shit Talka:
>
> The chorus is taken from the popular song, "Bad Boys," but instead they sing, "shit talker, shit talker, whatcha gonna do? when a real killa killa come for you?"[307]

A real killer came for Officer Darren Wilson on the streets of Ferguson.

His name was Michael Brown.

Now, an entire metropolitan area knows if a "John Wayne shootout" happens, the only cavalary coming will be led (or answerable to) by an Attorney General who already came to Ferguson and said his blackness was on par with his duties as the head of the Department

---

[305] Ferguson on edge: Guns fly off shop shelves in case of 'John Wayne shootout', **Washington Times, 11-12-13**

[306] http://www.stltoday.com/news/local/crime-and-courts/man-beaten-at-ferguson-protest-strategy-meeting/article_ba9ebc92-cb6f-57d9-bc00-1c99edc3c99c.html

[307] 'Gentle Giant': Mike Brown's Explicit Rap Songs Praising Drugs, Drinking, Ho's & Murder, Clash Daily, August 16, 2014

of Justice...

Perhaps nothing will transpire in St. Louis once the Grand Jury's decision on Darren Wilson's fate is announced; but the fear of those aboard the doomed *Demeter* in Stoker's tale, knowing some shadowy figure threatened every member of crews life, is exactly the same fear felt by the white population of Ferguson and white residents of St. Louis (particularly business owners, who know looting and damage to their store might not be covered under existing insurance policies).

Maybe this fear is based on more fiction than fact... or maybe the nightmarish scenario of black mobs rising in St. Louis is far more believable than we even want to admit.

November 14, 2014
The "Justice for Michael Brown" Lynch Mob Target 78 Percent White Clayton to Fulfill Battle Cry of 'Loot... and rob them, not your own'

In a city where the suggestion of using drones to fight crime[308] isn't as outlandish as it seems (when police are forced to go undercover as pizza delivery drivers[309] because of crimes against those employed in this field, you know something is heinously wrong), the continued fear of Negrogeddon erupting in the St. Louis metropolitan area has sane individuals wishing such measures had

---

[308] http://www.kmov.com/news/local/St-Louis-Metro-Police-consider-use-of-drones-in-fighting-area-crime-227305821.html

[309] http://blogs.riverfronttimes.com/dailyrft/2012/11/fighting_crime_one_undercover.php

already been put in place.

Drones could help police immediately formulate plans to deal with those rioting by providing real-time aerial footage of the "Justice for Michael Brown" lynch mob as they march for... something.

More importantly, these drones could provide continuous feeds of video to document any rioter/looter/arsonist participating in violence and trying to seek refuge in one of the many churches that has sided with the black insurrection in St. Louis:

> Churches throughout the St. Louis region will offer "safe spaces" following the grand jury's decision on whether to indict Ferguson Police Officer Darren Wilson.
>
> Clergy are among those who are readying the community for what many are expecting to be a non-indictment of Wilson for the fatal shooting of unarmed teen Michael Brown Jr. on August 9 – and the unrest that is also expected to ensue.
>
> "The churches will have food available if people need to come in off the street and find respite," said Rev. Renita Lampkin, pastor of St. John AME Church in St. Charles, Missouri. "There will be people who will provide comfort and offer a sense of community."
>
> Four African Methodist Episcopal (AME) churches will serve as safe havens, including St. Luke's-Elmwood Park, St. James, St. Paul and St. Peters.
>
> On Friday, November 7, the Metropolitan Congregations United Clergy Caucus and Metropolitan Clergy Coalition announced that their confirmed safe spaces include Christ Church Cathedral, Washington Tabernacle Missionary Baptist Church, Samaritan UMC, First Congregational Church of St. Louis, Webster Groves Christian Church, Epiphany UCC

and Central Reform Congregation.[310]

These churches consider themselves "Holy Ground," with Greater St. Mark and St. John's Episcopal Church deciding police will not be allowed to enter once the "Justice for Michael Brown" brigade is unleashed via the grand jury finding Officer Darren Wilson guilty of...nothing:

> A group of organizers who have held trainings for least 600 potential protesters in the last week have a vision, and they say it's a non-violent one.
>
> "We as a community of people, we aren't going to use violent power," organizer Michael McPhearson told a group of about 100 who met in a hall on South Jefferson Avenue in St. Louis Thursday night. "We're going to use people power, to change things."
>
> They expected four areas to emerge as protester "hot spots" after the announcement: the Ferguson police station, the stretch of West Florissant Avenue near the QuikTrip that burned the day after the killing, the business district in Clayton, and the Shaw Neigborhood, where VonDerrit Myers Jr. was killed by a St. Louis police officer last month after the officer said Myers fired at him.
>
> Greater St. Mark and St. John's Episcopal Church at 2664 Arsenal Street are expected to open their doors as "safe spaces" for protesters, where they said police will not be allowed to enter. They also planned to "shut down" in Clayton at 7 a.m. on the first business day after the announcement.
>
> One instructor, who did not want to give her name, gave physical and mental health tips to the group. "The number

---

[310] Churches offer safe spaces, clergy train in 'de-escalation', St. Louis American, 11-13-14

one weapon of the police is fear," she said. She asked the crowd to repeat her sentence, and they did. She showed the crowd how to thump their own chests, echoing their own heartbeats, as a grounding tool. "That's going to make you feel human. And that's a dig at them, because they're trying to make you feel less human."

She used the acronym HALTS to help the potential protesters. H to remember to feed their physical hunger, A to help them remember to watch their anger, L to remember to go home or connect with others if they feel lonely, T for remembering to go home to rest if they're tired, and S to remember to not take things so seriously.

"It should be enjoyable, to tear down this system of oppression," she said. "Somewhat enjoyable. Gratifying is a better word." 311

When churches are publicly siding with an insurgency, you know the situation in metropolitan St. Louis is on the verge of erupting into a scenario where drones and undercover cops posing as pizza deliverymen are woefully inadequate.

Now the black mob is planning to target the city of Clayton, a 78 percent white city in metropolitan St. Louis having nothing to do with the situation in Ferguson. Home to the corporate headquarters of Enterprise Rent-a-Car, Heritage Home Group, Brown Shoe Company, Armstrong Teasdale (an international law firm), as well as the elite Washington University in St. Louis, Clayton is being targeted by the almost entirely black "Justice for Michael Brown" mob because the city is so white.

Which is why it could be the location of a large-scale incident, where those wooden shields of the black "Justice for Michael Brown" army

---

311 Organizers hold training for non-violent Ferguson protests, plan 'shut down' of Clayton, St. Louis Post-Dispatch, 11-14-14]:

are unleashed.[312]

Recall, when the madness began on August 11, black people were aghast 67% black Ferguson was the site of looting, rioting and arson.[313]

So, why not target 78 percent white Clayton? [Clayton Chief: Vital Services Will Not Be Interrupted, CBS St. Louis, 11-14-14]:

> The police chief in Clayton is reacting to demonstrators telling the media they will disrupt downtown Clayton on the first business day after the St. Louis County grand jury announces its ruling in the Michael Brown case.
>
> Chief Kevin Murphy issued a written statement, Friday, saying his department supports the right of demonstrators to be heard, but public health and safety must not be at risk.
>
> Murphy says plans are in place to make sure vital services are not interrupted. Below is the full statement:
>
> *"We are aware of recent media accounts announcing demonstrators' plans to disrupt downtown Clayton on the first business day after the Grand Jury announcement. We continue to support demonstrators' rights to have their voices heard, and part of our planning has involved maintaining the safety of demonstrators. At the same time, we cannot risk public health or safety. Organizations in downtown Clayton provide a wide array of critical services, including health care, employment services, transportation, public safety, child care, and social services for the elderly*

---

[312] Ferguson protesters are using wood meant to board up shops as shields: As stores are being boarded up in anticipation of unrest, some protesters have turned plywood into an act of protection and defiance., Washington Post, 11-13-14

[313] 'Loot ... and rob them, not your own'; Twitter users advise black people to loot white neighborhoods, Twitchy.com, 8-11-14

> *and disabled among others. These services support not just this city but also the entire county. We have plans in place to help ensure that these services aren't interrupted.*[314]

That 78 percent white Clayton would now be a target of the black mobs fury is proof this is no longer about "Justice for Michael Brown" but about getting revenge against whitey (sorry Angie Carron... bringing Yoga to Ferguson won't "heal" the city).

An honest Q&A session, conducted with the Don't Shoot Coalition by the St Louis Post-Dispatch, spelled out directly the racial angle the "Justice for Michael Brown" protesters have decided the movement must take: all because white people aren't impacted by some nebulous "unfair system.:

As we approach the grand jury decision after more than 80 days of protest, we understand that some members of the community are growing tired of civil unrest. They are asking questions about how it can end. Here are the Don't Shoot Coalition's answers to some of those questions.

Q: What good does it do to disrupt businesses and people's lives, when these people are not part of the problem?

A: Your question does not reflect the whole picture. This involves all of us. It's wrong to simply draw arbitrary boundaries around issues like fair policing, and decide that most folks are not involved. *Many people — especially white folks — feel they can ignore the problem. People who benefit from or are not impacted by this unfair system have a duty to speak up and not be complicit. Ferguson has shifted the boundary line. It is not enough to say, "I'm not racist" just because you have suppressed your conscious biases. The protests are designed to make people feel uncomfortable and spur us all to end society's*

---

[314] Clayton Chief: Vital Services Will Not Be Interrupted, CBS St. Louis, 11-14-14

structural biases.[315]

There's not one city in America where the fear of white people robbing pizza deliverymen necessitates police going undercover to put a stop to this crime epidemic; there's not one city in America where the fear of white crime caused the police chief to inquire about getting drones to patrol the city; there is one city in America where the black residents of the metropolitan area have decided to use the death of 18-year-old cigar stealing thug as the *Casus belli* for airing their racial grievances and hatred to their fellow citizens.

St. Louis.

The Bell Curve City.

November 15, 2014
St. Louis Prepares for War, though Air Force has long trained Trauma Surgeons (Prepping for War) in City: "Being here in the inner city prepares them for some of the blunt-trauma injuries they will see."

The calm before the storm.

A few more days of relative peace.

For beyond the horizon, the clouds of war move toward St. Louis.

As earlier as November 17 (Monday), the grand jury decision on whether or not to charge Darren Warren could unleash a force far more destructive than Zeus' fictional Kraken in 2010's *Clash of the*

---

[315] Q&A for people tired of Ferguson protests, St. Louis Post-Dispatch, 11-14-14

Titans.:

> While the St. Louis region awaits the grand jury decision in the shooting death of Michael Brown, area hospitals have been meeting to prepare for anything. DePaul Hospital received a few patients in August when the looting and demonstrating occurred in Ferguson. They, like other hospitals, are preparing for the worst to serve anyone in need of medical attention.
>
> Because of recent events in Ferguson, SSM Health Care has set up an incident operation center at its headquarters to support the incident commands at the seven SSM hospitals in the area. Mike Harris, the Network Emergency Preparedness Manager said, "We're not expecting the world to fall apart but were going to be ready for it if it does."
>
> The hospitals are members of a group called STARRS, the St. Louis Area Regional Response System. Pam Walker the St. Louis City Health Director said, "We really work hard to always be ready. So whether it's Ferguson, losing power, a big storm coming through, or a terrorist attack, we have a huge hospital system in our grasp."[316]

But St. Louis has long been a war zone: a city where violent crime (perpetrated almost entirely by individual black males, whose collective inability to restrain from criminality compels both white flight and businesses to relocate elsewhere) happens with such frequency that bodies shredded by bullets or full of gashes from knife-inflicted wounds present Air Force trauma surgeons a "battlefield" scenario.

To be blunt, the Center for Sustainment of Trauma and Readiness

---

[316] Hospitals prepare to work together in wake of area-wide emergency, Fox2Now.com, 11-14-14

Skills (C-STARS)[317], offers Air Force trauma surgeons insight into a world white flight and segregation allow them to avoid: *"They typically don't get to see gunshot and stab wounds," said Capt. Scott Fallin, administrator of the St. Louis program. "Being here in the inner city prepares them for some of the blunt-trauma injuries they will see."*:

> ST. LOUIS • Air Force Dr. Dan Bruzzini sits behind a one-way mirror prepared to provide a handful of military medical personnel a glimpse of what they can expect once deployed to "bad-guy land."
>
> On a table in the adjacent room, a sheet covers a $250,000 mannequin-like machine that resembles a young child with a bad belly wound and a less obvious head injury.Bruzzini keys a microphone. The simulation begins.
>
> "There's been an explosion at a downtown marketplace," he says over an intercom. "Expect casualties in 30 to 60 seconds."
>
> He says medics have found a 6-year-old boy under a collapsed wall. At Bruzzini's command, the team removes the sheet. For the next 20 minutes, using a computer program that manipulates the boy's vital signs and other body functions, Bruzzini throws a series of medical problems at the team. The strain is obvious as they struggle to keep the "patient" alive.
>
> It's a feeling Lt. Col. Bruzzini knows well. He based the scenario on an experience of his in a six-month Afghanistan tour in 2007.
>
> For several years now, St. Louis University Hospital has been among the final stops for many Air Force and Air National

---

[317] http://www.sluhospital.com/en-US/ourServices/medicalServices/Pages/USAFTraumaTrainingPrograms.aspx

Guard medical personnel headed to combat zones. Here, Bruzzini and more than a dozen other Air Force and Air National Guard doctors, nurses and technicians teach an intense two-week program designed to prepare the students for the serious injuries they are certain to treat in Iraq and Afghanistan.

"You have to give people the tools, the training and the experience beforehand," said Bruzzini, 42, of Webster Groves. "Otherwise, you're setting them up for failure."

The partnership between the Air Force and the hospital came about because of, in part, the downsizing of the military medical system that began more than a decade ago. The cuts closed military hospitals. As a result, most Air Force medical personnel now tend to work in smaller clinics and treat few serious injuries.

"They typically don't get to see gunshot and stab wounds," said Capt. Scott Fallin, administrator of the St. Louis program. "Being here in the inner city prepares them for some of the blunt-trauma injuries they will see."[318]

Hospitals are already prepared for whatever the "Justice for Michael Brown" mob sends their way, courtesy of a black population in metropolitan St. Louis that has long been engaged in an internecine war against itself (and the unfortunate white people who happen to be victims of - so called - "random" knock out game attacks or gun violence).

It's important to note one of the only ways to bring the black community together (and stop the violence - momentarily - in their community) is for them to find common ground in standing behind a black criminal who they feel was "executed" by a white cop.

---

[318] SLU's 'battlefield' helps train military personnel, *St. Louis Post-Dispatch*, 2-22-2011

Damn the evidence and testimony (with seven or eight blacks in Ferguson testifying to the grand jury on behalf of the Darren Wilson account of his encounter with Michael Brown, who all now live in fear of "snitches getting stitches") proving Michael Brown deserved to be face down in the streets of Ferguson; the 2008 "A Call to Oneness" in St. Louis, where 20,000 blacks marched to end black-on-black violence in St. Louis, has finally found grounding in the "Justice for Michael Brown" movement.[319]

What do you mean "A Call to Oneness?" Well, it's yet another great moment in black history (just a notch or two below the black community in St. Louis providing a "battlefield" worthy of Air Force trauma surgeons to prepare for the conditions found in the theater of war):

> El Howard, 13, sat with his sisters on the wooden steps of their four-family flat on Newstead Avenue in St. Louis on Sunday. They talked about what they see on the sidewalks around them — syringe needles, beer bottles, drug pushers and crime scenes. They can't walk anywhere without being asked for money. They are never out past dark.
> But on this day, the siblings saw something different — thousands of people, mostly African-American men, peacefully marching down their street, calling for an end to violence. The miles of marchers pointed to the sky and chanted, "One, one, one," prompting those lining the streets to join in.
>
> As the last of them made their way past, El thought about what he had seen. The teen looked up and said: "It's inspiring."

---

[319] http://www.washingtonpost.com/politics/new-evidence-supports-officers-account-of-shooting-in-ferguson/2014/10/22/cf38c7b4-5964-11e4-bd61-346aee66ba29_story.html

The march was part of an initiative, "A Call to Oneness," organized by local church leaders along with civic, public and private institutions. Organizers wanted to march through crime-plagued areas and send a positive message to young black men.

"When you are one of the cities which leads the nation in homicides, you don't have many options in terms of thinking about doing something," said the event coordinator, the Rev. Freddy James Clark. "When we march through north St. Louis, we hope to create a moral climate. We hope to reclaim, through the vehicle of reconciliation, respect for the other and sanctity of life."

There was no official count, but organizers estimated that they had surpassed their goal of 20,000 participants. The procession stretched the entire length of the nearly two-mile route, which started near Page Boulevard and Kingshighway and ended at Tandy Park in front of Sumner High School.

The initiative grew out of a chat between Clark and Eric C. Rhone, a board member of the Regional Chamber and Growth Association. Disgusted over the grim statistics, they realized it was time to stop waiting for others to fix the problem. The march was the culmination of three days of workshops and discussions over issues facing African-American men. Organizers were planning a meeting Thursday night to plan their next step.

The march came at the beginning of summer, when crime rates usually rise, and after a deadly couple of months that put the city's homicide pace far above last year's. During one day in May, five people were murdered.

Many along the route said the march helped restore the sense of pride and community they felt when the Annie Malone May Day Parade followed the same streets. Two years ago, that parade moved downtown for more space.

"Things like this in the community, in the 'hood' as we say, remind us that we need to fight together ... that we're not just one person trying to fight this big old problem," said Thomas Maxwell, 56, who lives in Dellwood but grew up near the march route.

Those reminders are important. Fighting a drug problem, he said, he was homeless for three years and spent 18 years in prison for robbery. He now has custody of two of his children and plans to become a counselor.

"Things like this gave me strength to get back in there and struggle," he said.[320]

If you can't laugh, you'll never understand the joke.

Those marching for "Justice for Michael Brown" do nothing more than resurrect the exact same spirit that compelled the Civil Rights agitators in Selma, Montgomery, Birmingham, Little Rock, Atlanta, Greensboro, and other southern cities to rebel against a system only hoping to keep 2014 Detroit from ever happening.

But 2014 Detroit did happen, proving the fears of those daring to defend the legitimacy of a system designed to perpetuate a civilization only whites are equipped with maintaining... correct.

And now, with an entire metropolitan region fearful of violence that could destabilize life in St. Louis, only one fact is clear: in 20 years, the "Justice for Michael Brown" crowd will be considered natural Republicans by white conservatives.

But St. Louis will still provide an environment where the Air Force trains trauma surgeons for the rigors of war, for the exact same

---

[320] Anti-violence march in city draws 20,000, ST. LOUIS POST-DISPATCH, 06/02/2008

reason black people occasionally organize to march against crime, gun violence, and homicide in the city... *"Being here in the inner city prepares them for some of the blunt-trauma injuries they will see."*

November 16, 2014
Ferguson a New Bethlehem?: When Gold, Frankincense, and Myrrh were replaced with Swisher Sweets, Skittles, and Arizona Watermelon Fruit Juice Cocktail

Gold, frankincense, and myrrh.

The Gospel of Matthew in the New Testament of the Bible tells us three wise men visited the newborn Christ in Bethlehem, presenting the King of Kings with gold, frankincense, and myrrh.

Some members of the cloth in metropolitan St. Louis would have you believe Ferguson is a suitable location for a modern-day Bethlehem, with the gifts of gold, frankincense, and myrrh replaced with the more appropriate presents of Swisher Sweets, Arizona Watermelon Fruit Juice Cocktail and Skittles:

> FERGUSON • About 120 people who attended a Mass for peace and justice Sunday morning at Blessed Teresa of Calcutta Catholic Church here were challenged to do more than just pray about the unrest in their community.
> The Rev. Robert "Rosy" Rosebrough compared the attention on Ferguson with the focus on the small town of Bethlehem

after Jesus Christ was born there in a manger.

"All of the world media has started to come back to Ferguson, waiting for the grand jury decision," he said. "They want to know what we are going to do, whatever the decision is."

Rosebrough urged churchgoers to take Jesus "out of the manger and into our hearts, not just in prayer but in effecting justice," particularly as it relates to education. The parish includes four school districts — Riverview Gardens, Normandy, Ferguson-Florissant and Hazelwood.

"When children have a good education, they have a chance to make a difference," he said. "How do we as parishioners of Blessed Teresa help effect changes in education?"

Rosebrough said Ferguson could be a new Bethlehem, an example of people who "stretch their arms out to the needy and make a difference through their actions."

Blessed Teresa of Calcutta and another Ferguson parish, Our Lady of Guadalupe, dedicated their Masses Sunday to the peace and justice message. Catholics from other parishes were invited to attend one of those Masses to show support for the community.[321]

Ferguson as a new Bethlehem?

Perhaps this 67 percent black suburb of St. Louis (strangely, the city was 100 percent white in 1970, begging the question of what attracted blacks to migrate to the Ferguson in the first place...) can be the Tigris and Euphrates of a new civilization, birthed from the ruins of a failed experiment that would continue to have us believe Michael Brown is a suitable replacement for ol' J.C.

---

[321] Engage Christ in prayer and promote justice, Ferguson priest urges attendees at Mass, St. Louis Post-Dispatch, 11-16-14

So in honor of Officer Darren Wilson, SBPDL encourages you to go out and participate in the continued deification of Michael Brown by joining in a 21st century reenactment of those three wise men who long ago traversed the Middle East, "bearing gifts we travel so far": buy some Swisher Sweets cigars (sorry, no strong-arm robbing your local convenience worker), a bag of Skittles, and an Arizona Watermelon Ice Tea.

Pay homage to our new King of Kings!

November 17, 2014
State of Emergency Declared in Ferguson: But the Battle for Black Empowerment is Already Won

With the announcement the Missouri National Guard has been activated by Gov. Nixon, only the dullest of minds would still believe the grand jury plans to charge Officer Darren Wilson.[322]

Like those poor, still human characters in *The Walking Dead*, trying to survive the aftermath of a zombie apocalypse simultaneously clinging to the illusion civilization will one day make a comeback, the white citizens of Ferguson and metropolitan St. Louis must begin to seriously assess the future for civilization in the region.

But it won't.

The Ferguson of 1970 (when the city was basically 100 percent

---

[322] http://www.ksdk.com/story/news/local/2014/11/17/mo-national-guard-on-standby-for-grand-jury-decision/19182985/

white) is never coming back.

The Ferguson of 1980 (when the city was 86 percent white) is never coming back.

The Ferguson of 1990 (when the city was 76 percent white) is never coming back.

Hell, the Ferguson of 2000 (when the city was 44 percent white) is never, ever coming back.

The now 67 percent black city of Ferguson will quickly become a 90 - 95 percent black city, with those few remaining white residents walking away from their severely underwater mortgage (recall: BEFORE the Darren Wilson/Michael Brown incident, 49 percent of mortgages were underwater and 38 percent of homes were below market peak), searching for some semblance of the community they once knew to exist in the city they now vacate.[323]

With Ferguson and other North St. Louis communities collapsing (with the collapse correlating exactly with the rise in the black population and decline in the white population, the latter responsible for creating the prosperous conditions which attracted the former)[324], the sad reality of the what riots, continued unrest in the name of "Justice for Michael Brown," and violence could do to an already precarious housing market should punctuate this fact: there's no civilization returning to Ferguson when the dust settles and those Ferguson insurrectionists stop - in the words of President Obama spoken privately to protest leaders on Nov. 5th -"staying on course in terms of pursuing what it was that he knew we were

---

[323] http://www.stltoday.com/business/local/st-louis-is-hot-spot-for-underwater-mortgages/article_1a9b46b5-38f4-5b93-b4b4-e895f8e0bab5.html

[324] http://www.stltoday.com/entertainment/movies/joe-williams/spanish-lake-director-charts-social-changes/article_9b5d9d7c-2174-5614-a738-328e33687d84.html

advocating."[325]

Those black participants in the "Justice for Michael Brown" farce have already won, even before Officer Wilson's fate is known. The National Guard being called out doesn't matter; a buildup of Homeland Security vehicles doesn't matter; all that matters is that, to paraphrase Obama, the course of what blacks are pursuing and advocating" in Ferguson and St. Louis stays true.[326]

Power.

Supplanting white political power with the mighty black fist of racial power.

Though not one elected white official in the entire state of Missouri (hell, in all of America) advocates explicitly - or implicitly - on behalf of white people and the civilization only they can create/sustain, whenever a black person is elected to office the expansion of black political power has increased.

Every action of this black official is explicitly to concentrate power in the hands of the black community.

It only takes a few stories to showcase the abandonment of political power by whites has already started in Ferguson and St. Louis, even before the grand jury's decision on Darren Wilson is made public.

> 1. The city of Ferguson, where white families once watched their children play Little League baseball and soccer games in a field where gun battles between blacks force the cancellation of sporting events, has joined forces with

---

[325] http://www.nytimes.com/2014/11/17/us/groups-in-ferguson-prepare-for-grand-jury-decision.html?_r=0

[326] http://stlouis.cbslocal.com/2014/11/17/is-the-department-of-homeland-security-in-town/

President Obama's My Brother's Keeper community challenge. The future of Ferguson is nothing but black, blacker, and blackest, so allocating resources into anything but black betterment programs would be misappropriation of the dwindling tax revenue the city produces. Summits for black youth are already being held, focusing on helping our ebony friends strive for attaining "six goals for youths: school readiness; reading at grade level by third grade; graduation from high school; completion of college or other postsecondary training; employment out of school; and safety from violent crime."[327]

2. Ferguson instituted a warrant forgiveness program[328], which St. Louis quickly adopted[329], because of the inability for individual black people to show up for their court dates and pay fines. Though the crimes were nonviolent in nature, the broken window principle of fighting crime was completely abandoned in allowing individual blacks who broke to a collective "get out of jail free card"... all because of the unrest unleashed in the aftermath of Michael Brown's death.

3. A program to hire more black police officers - as noted in this St. Louis Post-Dispatch story of 2013[330], a task of Herculean proportions in St. Louis - will be implemented in not just Ferguson, but the city of St. Louis as well.

Officer Wilson's fate is still (somewhat... never mind the national guard being put on alert) unknown, but the capitulation by the white minority in Ferguson is far, far from over:

---

[327] http://www.stltoday.com/news/local/metro/ferguson-summit-tackles-ways-to-help-black-youth-succeed/article_2bf1d802-7009-5c9b-a130-5cab05aad9b6.html

[328] http://stlouis.cbslocal.com/2014/10/13/ferguson-warrant-recall-program-extended-indefinitely/

[329] http://www.stltoday.com/news/local/crime-and-courts/st-louis-to-forgive-about-warrants-for-nonviolent-municipal-offenses/article_7f9dbef3-7409-5e81-ae28-3c79faa8b147.html

[330] http://www.stltoday.com/news/local/crime-and-courts/minority-recruitment-advancements-are-a-challenge-for-st-louis-police/article_8dcad127-ca8c-5cca-85b5-a72ab0577c01.html

First, the city of Ferguson gave Mario Jones a $300 fine. Then officials offered him a paintbrush instead.

Jones, 18, on several Saturdays made his way to Ferguson's old fire station, hovered over plywood panels with a cup of bold blue paint and worked with volunteers and other young people to create a mural that could bring a message of unity to the fractured city.

Jones was assigned to a pilot program in Ferguson that offers community service hours to teenagers facing misdemeanor charges. City leaders now are looking to expand the program rapidly as they try to reduce resentment between police and the local communities, where animosity has festered for years.

It is one of the small changes they hope will make a big difference in Ferguson and help to prevent the scenes of violence and looting that occurred after the death of Michael Brown.

Still, the fear of more unrest seems to mount by the moment as the city waits for a grand jury decision on whether to indict Darren Wilson, the police officer who killed Brown. An announcement is expected any day.

For many, the death of Brown, 18, was the final straw.

Residents have long accused police departments in north St. Louis County municipalities of slapping them with unjustified arrests and tickets bearing fines they could not afford to pay.

According to city leaders, 40 warrants are issued each month for teenagers who didn't show up in court for traffic violations.[331]

---

[331] Ferguson tries to offer youth with fines an alternative, hopes to help heal broken

What's next? Release all of those black people held behind bars?

Back in 1904, the Louisiana Purchase Exposition (commonly known as the St. Louis World's Fair) was held in the city of St. Louis, to commemorate Thomas Jefferson's purchase of the Louisiana territory from France.

Fitting that this occurred because of the loss of revenue France incurred via the black rebellion on the island of San Domingo, where every white person was slaughtered during the black insurrection. This island is now known as Haiti.

Lost White Tribes: The End of Privilege and the Last Colonials in Sri Lanka, Jamaica, Brazil, Haiti, Namibia, and Guadeloupe offers a glimpse into a world free of white privilege, and the type of intrusive law enforcement activity blacks find so disagreeable in 67 percent black Ferguson; where white people are sufficiently and correctly displaced of any and all power.

Just as is occurring in North St. Louis and Ferguson.

From Orizio's book we learn the Haitians instituted discrimination within their constitution:

> From the Haitian constitution of 1805:
>
> Article No. 12- "No white person, of whatever nationality, may set foot upon this territory as a land owner or master, nor may such persons in future acquire any property whatsoever."
>
> Article No. 13- "The preceding article does not apply to white

---

city, St. Louis Post-Dispatch, 11-16-14

women who have been naturalized by the government, nor to their eventual offspring. The provisions of this article also include those of Polish and German birth whom the government has naturalized.

Like those poor, still human characters in *The Walking Dead*, trying to survive the aftermath of a zombie apocalypse simultaneously clinging to the illusion civilization will one day make a comeback, the white citizens of Ferguson and metropolitan St. Louis must begin to seriously asses the future for civilization in the region.

But as we learn in season two of *The Walking Dead*, the disease turning the dead into zombies is a burden even the living carry. Every one is infected already, with the hope of a cure for the ailment one far below that of merely surviving each day in the post-apocalyptic world.

No matter where white people try and go, hoping to rebuild a Ferguson, a Clayton County, a Detroit, or a Birmingham, the federal government will gladly ensure the same people responsible for the demise of the city you fled have the legal right to do it to your new home.

Though few will admit it, the fate of the famous Shelley House - from the 1948 Supreme Court case, Shelley vs. Kraemer - at 4600 Labadie Avenue in North St. Louis is the fate of the entire civilization white Americans built out of the wilderness of the North American continent.

The virus of white guilt and a slavish devotion to equality, like the zombie virus infecting the living in *The Walking Dead*, sadly resides in us all; though the antidote to this virus might just be the collapse of the American Experiment.

Ironically, a monument to the greatness of those white pioneers who dared build a civilization out of an untamed wilderness stands in St. Louis. The Gateway Arch will stand a silent witness to the insanity of a people devoted to furthering black empowerment, without ever realizing such a concept is a naturally occurring EMP on civilization wherever this political power is unleashed.

Be it Detroit, East St. Louis, North St. Louis or Ferguson, the end result is the same; and those white people who still have fond memories of these cities or regions as being safe havens for raising a family will search vainly for a place to resurrect the community they still cherish.

Our job, all along, has been to survive the unraveling of the American Experiment.

November 18, 2014
What does 'Stay the Course' and 'The Struggle Must Go On' Mean?: President Obama and Eric "My People" Holder Officially Side with Ferguson Mob

'Stay the course' said President Obama to high-profile Ferguson protesters who met with him in a secret confab on November 5th.[332]

'Stay the course'.

What 'course would this be, Mr. President?

A 'course' where, "we're not going to get change in this society unless white people are just a little bit afraid."[333]

Perhaps a 'course' where the Attorney General of Department of

---

[332] http://www.nytimes.com/2014/11/17/us/groups-in-ferguson-prepare-for-grand-jury-decision.html?_r=0

[333] http://www.breitbart.com/Big-Government/2014/11/17/Organizers-Train-Newly-Minted-Protesters-in-St-Louis

Justice compares the not-so-gentle-giant Michael Brown to Emmet Till, stating, "The struggle must go on."[334]

Would the mission of 'stay the course' be the same as discussing plans for those high-profile Ferguson protesters to "target white areas?"[335]

The myth of the majority of the black Ferguson protesters (emboldened by creepy online activists rebelling against a "system" completely on the side of supposed protesters, as outlined in this brilliant James Kirkpatrick piece)[336] as being "peaceful" is immediately dispelled when you recall the man tasked with retrieving Brown's body in the middle of the street was greeted with gunshots, an angry black mob, and forced to hide in his car for hours.

Calvin Whitaker, a funeral director charged with moving bodies in St. Louis County, has probably seen his fair share of horrific crime scenes courtesy of the low impulse control blacks display on a daily basis.

But what he encountered on August 9 *started the course* of events President Obama pleaded with protesters in that secret meeting to stay on and accentuates the reality of Holder's "the struggle must go on," comment.

Arriving at 2:25 p.m. to find a "tumultuous, angry crowd," Whitaker and his wife related this scene:

> "It was very hectic, you could cut the tension with a knife," Whitaker tells *Fox2Now*. "Police could not control the crowd."
>
> At one point, Whitaker heard gunshots nearby, just as

---

[334] http://www.realclearpolitics.com/video/2014/11/17/eric_holder_likens_michael_brown_to_emmett_till_the_struggle_goes_on.html

[335] http://www.thegatewaypundit.com/2014/11/caught-on-tape-ferguson-activists-discuss-plans-to-target-white-areas-video/?PageSpeed=noscript

[336] http://www.vdare.com/articles/manufacturing-dissent-the-ruling-classs-saul-alinsky-strategy-in-ferguson-mo

Jackson told reporters in the days after Brown's shooting. Whitaker and his wife don't carry bullet-proof vests, so police told them to "hunker down" in their car to keep safe.

"There were times when we feared for our lives," Whitaker says. He and his wife stayed in the car for two hours waiting for police to control the crowd. "It took so long because we could not do our job. It was unsafe for us to be there...There was nowhere for us to go."[337]

This was the moment where the 'course' was chartered for wherever the farce in Ferguson is headed, a final destination of which no one knows for sure.

In a city where the propensity for black males to wear their pants low prompted one black alderman to propose a bill fining these belt-less individuals $100 for every fashion fail, it should have been obvious one unfortunate encounter between a white police officer and black male would set off a chain of events beyond the control of logic or reason and into a realm where (with apologies to Arthur Conan Doyle), *"once you eliminate the impossible, whatever remains, no matter how improbable, must be the truth."*[338]

Welcome to life in Bell Curve City.

St. Louis.

The probability a white police officer would encounter a black male engaged in some form of criminality and that this event would then end in questionable circumstances immediately causing hundreds of black people to storm out of their apartments and demand justice was actually quite high in St. Louis, considering how often white police arrest black males in the city.

And with Section 8 Vouchers redistributing the lower class black proles from downtown St. Louis into formerly all-white suburbs,

---

[337] http://blogs.riverfronttimes.com/dailyrft/2014/09/funeral_director_explains_why_michael_browns_body_stayed_in_the_street_for_hours.php

[338] http://news.stlpublicradio.org/post/100-fine-sagging-pants-yes-under-proposed-st-louis-bill

it's axiomatic white police in these cities will have more than their fair share of opportunities to become intimate with individual black criminals.

The extreme buildup of quasi-military machinery and weaponry in advance to the grand jury announcement of whether Darren Wilson will/or will not face charges for the death of Michael Brown is not unprecedented in St. Louis.

Back in 2011, the city of St. Louis Police Department unveiled a refitted Brinks Trunk to use as a crime deterrent. Far more hilarious than the "Pants Up, Don't Loot" billboard put in Ferguson, the St. Louis Police Nuisance Abatement Vehicle' represented an absolutely awesome force in trying to slow down the social capital destroying force known as the legitimate fear of black criminality:

> Police are also planning to deploy the Armadillo in the U-City Loop, if needed to quell unruly crowds.
>
> "We can take the vehicle and park it right in the heart of the Loop in the city of St. Louis and if anything happens we have it right on video tape," Spiess said, "So, it really gives us an advantage in that regard."[339]

Only one year later, a massive gathering of teens (media code word for "blacks") proved the necessity for the Nuisance Abatement Vehicle existence: 200 - 300 black youth, energized by the warm weather, congregated at the Delmar Loop and engaged in roving fights, punctuated by intermittent gunfire.[340]

Though the trouble was brushed off as "an anomaly," the mere fact the Nuisance Abatement Vehicle had been in the arsenal of the St. Louis Police for more than a year prior to the incident - *to combat such an eventuality* - showcases the black mob wasn't an aberration.[341]

---

[339] http://stlouis.cbslocal.com/2011/08/18/st-louis-police-preparing-new-vehicle-to-fight-crime/

[340] http://www.stltoday.com/news/local/disturbance-on-delmar-loop-last-night/article_622e4368-7c14-11e1-9f1b-001a4bcf6878.html

[341] http://www.stltoday.com/news/local/metro/trouble-in-loop-was-anomaly-

The 'course' was set long before Darren Wilson pulled his SUV up to a stop next to a doped up Michael Brown and asked him to get out of the middle of the road.

The 'course' was set long before Officer Paul McCulloch was gunned down by a black criminal in the infamous Pruitt-Igoe Housing Complex in St. Louis, an incident which would prompt black leaders to call for his sons removal from the grand jury deciding the fate of Darren Wilson himself.

Perhaps even the fate of the civilization whites created in St. Louis...

The 'course' was set even before J.D. and Ethel Shelley tried to purchase the house on 4600 Labadie Avenue.

W.E.B. DuBois himself would be proud to see Eric Holder in the office of Attorney General, unrelenting his quest that, "The struggle must go on."

For just as Union soldiers sang *John Brown's Body,* those clinging to the delusions of homicidal abolitionist see in "Michael Brown's Body" an opportunity to exact justice against those they deem standing in the way of true progress: white people.

This is the 'course' President Obama referred to in the secret meeting on November 5th; this is "the struggle that must go on" Holder referenced.

Never, for one moment, believe the majority of those seeking justice for Michael Brown desire peace, for in the minutes after his death a crowd of unfriendly blacks emerged from their Section 8 Voucher furnished dwellings demanding the blood of the Ferguson Police Department.

Agitated by those passing down the message of 'stay the course' to key Ferguson protest leaders, you should be quite capable with ascertaining what will happen when Darren Wilson is found innocent by the grand jury.

officials-say/article_0b6ce699-d202-5733-9211-66eab93aa4b6.html

But... "the struggle must go on."

November 19, 2014
'Social Justice' Rolls On: St. Louis Mayor Francis Slay Concedes to the "Rules of Engagement" Dictated by the Black Insurrectionist Don't Shoot Coalition

There's something absolutely hysterical in the news Mayor Francis Slay of St. Louis has agreed to many of the demands the Don't Shoot Coalition... demanded.

With black protests/rioting/looting/violence a foregone conclusion at this point, the group put together a 19-point "Rules of Engagement" they demanded law enforcement in the city must abide by, and the white mayor of St. Louis happily consented to them.[342]

In effect, he ceded the city of St. Louis and the future of the metropolitan area, over to the black mob (fueled by an unrelenting hatred of the civilization white people built, passed down to their progeny - white privilege - and dared to protect by passing laws that have a disparate impact by individual blacks incapable of collectively following them).

A region whose violence is already scaring away conventions,

---

[342] http://news.stlpublicradio.org/post/dont-shoot-coalition-calls-police-rules-engagement

concerts, football games, and other economically-need events (because unlike the majority of the black residents of St. Louis and St. Louis County, these events have a positive economic impact on the region).[343]

About the only economic activity this black mob, who basically just received the keys to the kingdom with Mayor Slay's decision to negotiate with the black terrorists masquerading as "Justice for Mike Brown" militants, creates is in convincing unarmed white people to buy weapons[344] (perhaps white people will be able to live out their "John Wayne shootout" fantasy...).[345]

The so-called 'oppressed' now are in control of the city:

> St. Louis Mayor Francis Slay has requested 400 members of the National Guard to help in the city after the grand jury's decision is announced in the Michael Brown case.
>
> He has also agreed to some of the Don't Shoot Coalition's proposed rules of engagement.
>
> In a letter to the St. Louis Board of Aldermen and the Public Safety Committee, the mayor said he considers "rules of engagement" a military term, and would prefer to call them "rules of conduct."
>
> He has agreed to let protesters occupy public spaces and even be "disruptive but not violent."
>
> "Like blocking the street or blocking a sidewalk for a specific

---

[343] Ferguson echoes through St. Louis convention business, St. Louis Post-Dispatch, 11-18-14

[344] http://www.dailymail.co.uk/news/article-2840348/Gun-sales-Ferguson-spike-staggering-700-residents-wait-Officer-Darren-Wilson-indicted-shooting-dead-unarmed-teenager-Michael-Brown.html

[345] http://www.cnn.com/2014/11/10/us/ferguson-michael-brown-shooting/

period of time," Slay told KMOX.

He also agreed not to shut down safe houses – where protesters meet to strategize.

The mayor wrote that the city will use the Guard troops to patrol with officers who are not at organized protests, and will assist individual officers to patrol and watch for random acts of violence or property damage.

Concerning the use of protective gear, the mayor said officers will be in normal uniform and only switch to protective gear if public safety becomes a concern.

"We have met many dozens of times with each other, with federal, state and other local officials, with protest leaders and protesters themselves. ... I am absolutely convinced that the leaders of the demonstrations and the vast majority of demonstrators themselves are committed to non-violence," the mayor said in the letter. "Change is necessary, inevitable and irreversible."[346]

You can read the full letter from Mayor Slay, ridiculously addressing the demands of the Don't Shoot Coalition as if they represented an opposing general (instead of fighting for the same team/ the same system), here.[347]

The list of 19 "Rules of Engagement" demands should have been greeted with thunderous laughter from those elected officials tasked with protecting the civilization whites created in St. Louis, for they must answer to those owning property (be it commercial or private) and trying to operate revenue - and tax - producing businesses in both the city of St. Louis and St. Louis County or else

---

[346] Mayor Slay: 'Disruption' Will be Allowed in St. Louis, CBS St. Louis, 11-19-14

[347] https://cbsstlouis.files.wordpress.com/2014/11/letter-from-mayor-slay.pdf

they've effectively dissolved their governmental duties.

But they, as this *Washington Post* article notes, negotiated on many of the 19 points crafted by the Don't Shoot Coalition.[348]

Not only this, but the Dean of the St. Louis University School of Law wrote a letter, titled "Ferguson Support," where he stressed the schools commitment to educating another generation of lawyers on to 'social justice'... :

> The events of Aug. 9, 2014 in Ferguson, Missouri brought a national spotlight to the St. Louis region and many members of the SLU LAW community have stepped up, participating in the frontlines of this crisis and taking a role as advocates to help educate and bring our city together.
>
> In the month since the death of Michael Brown, I have seen our Jesuit mission in action at the School of Law and have been heartened to see our community come together to help work toward solutions in Ferguson, but I am not surprised. The pursuit of justice for those unable to seek it on their own is woven into our fiber. We teach the basics of legal process and critical analysis essential to effective lawyering.
>
> We feel it is within the mission of our law school and Saint Louis University to educate another generation of lawyers committed to social justice, to being men and women in service to others. As our region begins the process of healing and reform in the wake of Ferguson, I am confident the public at large will come to better know our mission. Below are examples of it in action.
>
> Best wishes,

---

[348] http://www.washingtonpost.com/politics/police-in-st-louis-agree-to-rules-of-engagement-for-protests-after-grand-jury-decision/2014/11/18/75107438-6f5a-11e4-893f-86bd390a3340_story.html

Michael A. Wolff Dean and Professor of Law[349]

Social Justice, or, a movement that serves to continuously erode the very fabric of civilization white people dared quilt centuries ago, until the moment arises when all evidence of its glory every existing are gone.

Those "Justice for Mike Brown" protesters, who hilariously are now in control of St. Louis' fate, wrote a letter to the *St. Louis Post-Dispatch* declaring their intentions, with facts, logic, and reason completely absence from their manifesto.

Save one.

The collective hatred of the type of civilization white people create in their absence, where life, liberty, and social capital flourishes:

> WHY WE ARE HERE
>
> And make no mistake: Our cause is a call for basic human decency. All children deserve to live their lives in a way that allows them to fully achieve their potential. So we protest, we march and we stand because that opportunity was violently taken from Mike.
>
> We are here to demand that human life has profound value, no matter its trappings, skin color, ZIP code or gender. We are here to focus the spotlight on the unnecessary loss of human life. Stories about assumed chaos after the return of the grand jury's decision ignore the primary and central fact: an unarmed child was killed far, far too young.
>
> We implore those that scorn and dismiss our protest to walk in our shoes. In too many communities, unarmed black youth, particularly males, are stripped of life and liberty by

---

[349] Ferguson Support: A Message From the Dean, November 18, SLU.edu

police officers. Many, far too many, of those unarmed children. And in our peaceful grief, we were met with weaponry meant only for times of war, and invective accusing Mike and our movement of thuggery that justified the violence.

The disruption we have therefore intentionally created reflects the disruption of life we will no longer tolerate. So, if we disrupt the status quo now, know that is an intentional choice. We seek to nonviolently mirror this violent, intolerable disruption of life in our communities. If this were your constant reality, we believe you would make the same choice.[350]

These are the people, courtesy of Mayor Slay and the numerous police departments who decided to work with the Don't Shoot Coalition, caving to their demands, that now control the city of St. Louis, Ferguson, and the fate of yet another major metropolitan region of America.

The only comparison one can make is the monologue from Bane in Christopher Nolan's *The Dark Knight Rises* movie. Though most critics didn't understand the villain was engaging in a bit of satire - since his true goals where the complete annihilation of Gotham City - and was instead unleashing a socialist, French Revolutionary-style of misery upon the city, in actuality Bane simply unleashed agents of destruction using the rhetoric of those who babble for "social justice" and write illogical manifestos for the St. Louis Post-Dispatch.

Allow us to quote Bane:

> "Behind you stands a symbol of oppression, Blackgate Prison... We take Gotham from the corrupt, the rich, the oppressors of generations who kept you down with myths of

---

[350] Opinion: Bringing attention to persistent injustice, St. Louis Post-Dispatch, 11-18-14

opportunity, and we give it back to you, the people. Gotham is yours. None shall interfere, do as you please. Start by storming Blackgate and free the oppressed. Step forward, those who would serve, for an army will be raised. The powerful will be ripped from their decadent nests and cast out into the cold world that we know and endure. Courts will be convened, spoils will be enjoyed. Blood will be shed. The police will survive as they learn to survive true justice. This great city... it will endure. Gotham will survive."

Your average black person believes Darren Wilson executed Michael Brown as he ran home to continue his crusade of curing cancer; your below average black person believes every black person locked in a jail cell is there because of corrupt, racist judicial system; your exceptionally below average black person believes Barack Obama is a God, descended from the black people who built the pyramids during some great Nubian epoch.

Your above average black person works to incite all of these types of blacks as their army to one day convene courts to erase all vestiges of 'white privilege' and enjoy the spoils of their conquest.

It's just too bad so few black people, who steadfastly believe Egyptians of antiquity were black and erected the pyramids, will ever consider how these ancient Nubian engineering prowess doesn't translate into blacks today being able to maintain the existing infrastructure of cities they inherit via white flight.

Oh well. As long as we all learn to survive the "true justice" of the perpetual revolution in America: the quest to lower quality of life and all standards governing merit until those pesky racial inequalities dissolve away.

St. Louis' political establishment, by negotiating with the Don't Shoot Coalition on any of their demands, has ceded the city and county to the black insurrectionists.

November 20, 2014
Ferguson War Journal (The Black Occupation): Day 104 – Families of Nearly All-White Ferguson Police Department in Virtual Hiding, Facing Death Threats and Assault

The city of Ferguson, once an all-white suburb 15 miles away from downtown St. Louis, is 67 percent black (and rising); much to the chagrin of news outlets everywhere, the police department still reflects the old Ferguson with 94.6 percent of its force being white.[351]

With the National Guard called in to protect key government buildings and important (tax-revenue producing) shopping centers in downtown St. Louis, the troubles in a suburb with roughly 21,000 people threaten to destabilize the entire metropolitan region.[352]

But of course, when 60 percent of the black population (as of 2009) in the city of St. Louis and 38 percent of the black population in St. Louis County are on EBT/Food Stamps, the reality of how stable the region was before the Michael Brown/Darren Wilson encounter immediately comes into question.

With the black occupation (what some call the "Justice for Mike

---

[351] http://www.newrepublic.com/article/119070/michael-browns-death-leads-scrutiny-ferguson-white-police

[352] http://www.bizjournals.com/stlouis/news/2014/11/20/guard-to-protect-government-buildings-shopping.html?ana=twt

Brown" movement) of Ferguson now at Day 104 - how "peaceful" this insurrection can be deemed is questionable, since, save the owners of Ferguson Burger Bar who have, "put... faith in God for nothing to happen" - the one question on unfortunately few people's minds is how the families of the almost entirely white Ferguson Police Department are coping.[353]

Considering their loved ones put on the FPD uniform every day to patrol a city under siege by a movement despising the fact they even exist - an FPD who have been forced by the Department of Justice to remove "I am Darren Wilson" bracelets,[354] lest they want to foster an 'us vs. them' mentality - it should be obvious they too are under duress:

> Wives and children of many police officers are in virtual hiding, as some face assault and death threats.
>
> Fox Files investigator Chris Hayes talked with the wife of a Ferguson officer who said she's not leaving town, because she fears people aren't hearing the whole truth about her husband's Department.
>
> During the spring of 2014, the City of Ferguson commissioned a study to find out what residents thought about City services, including the Ferguson Police Department. It's data that some fear could be met with threats of violence, at a time when police families are already telling their sons and daughters, 'Don't tell anyone you're the child of a police officer.'
>
> The police wife said, 'We don't have answers for them' as she broke down. Then she continued, 'It's very frightening. Most people who have a family member who's a police officer are very proud of what they do.'
>
> She remains proud, in hiding. We protected her identity for

---

[353] http://www.ksdk.com/story/news/local/2014/11/19/ferguson-business-refusing-to-board-windows/19247743/

[354] http://www.stltoday.com/news/local/crime-and-courts/doj-asks-ferguson-chief-to-stop-police-from-wearing-i/article_a2cfe060-6252-5fa6-8639-6715f643c8f4.html

her safety. She continued, 'This is real and people actually do know how to find us and they do want to harm us.'

She's received many strange calls, including this message, just before I met her, (Unknown caller) 'Would you rather hear me coming out, coming out and robbing your house? And it would be like, it'd just be like silence man, you couldn't hear nothing."

She talked about looking over her shoulder, 'Did they follow me here? Did I do a good enough job after work today of taking different routes, on my way home. Just letting my younger daughter leave the house...'

She says some families are leaving town. She says she's decided to stay for Ferguson Police officers, but also for Ferguson residents, who ranked the police department as one of the best city services.

It's in a survey no one's talked about, headed by a Professor at University of Missouri-St. Louis. It's from May of 2014, before any unrest, when the City of Ferguson wanted to know what residents thought about annexing an area north of 270.

Researchers asked registered voters and 61% of them said they believed Ferguson was "moving in the right direction." Then citizens ranked city services, putting police third after the fire department and trash service (above six other departments like "code enforcement" and "streets," at the bottom).

When you break it down by ward, even the area surrounding Canfield where Michael Brown died, 69% of those residents rated Ferguson Police good or excellent. Only 4% scored Ferguson police as poor.

The police wife fears the public is not hearing everything. When people complained about militarization of police, she said it wasn't Ferguson police with the heavy gear. She said, 'They didn't have the equipment they needed.' Not even helmets, until families pooled their money to buy them.

> Now she wonders if the Department of Justice also only hears those screaming loudest. She added, 'Well, it appears the DOJ made up their mind before they ever got started.' She continued, 'I'm very worried about what's going to happen to the citizens and what's going to happen to the businesses and what's going to happen to the police officers. This is a good community with a long history and they love their community.'[355]

There can be no doubt the Department of Justice's Community Relations Services, with 'mediators' in the city of Ferguson for most of the occupation, have decided from day one Darren Wilson deprived Michael Brown of this right to exist while being black.[356]

Such is one of the highest, most noble rights in all of America.

Though this right is not enjoyed by one of the few black officers on the FPD, Sgt. Harry Dilworth. In a featured piece at the St. Louis Post-Dispatch, this officer found out his loyalty to the blue of the Ferguson Police Department meant being seen as an Uncle Tom to those black insurrectionists attempting to exert control over the city:

> Dilworth, 45, wishes he could retire, but he feels a draw to stay in the community he has served for 21 years.
>
> Even on ordinary calls for service, some taunt him with the "hands up, don't shoot"' gesture widely adopted by protesters.
>
> "You can only take so much of this," Dilworth said, taking a reporter with him Wednesday to patrol the 6.2-square-mile city.
>
> Dilworth had been at Fort Leonard Wood fulfilling his duties as an Army reservist the day of the shooting. He said his wife wishes he were back in Iraq or Afghanistan.
>
> "She thinks I would be safer there," he said.

---

[355] A police wife fears for family, fights for department, Fox2Now.com, 11-19-14

[356] http://www.wnd.com/2014/11/ferguson-stirred-up-by-feds-community-relations-service/

'IT'S DIFFERENT NOW'

Dilworth is the only black supervisor and one of four African-American officers on a force of 53 in a community where two-thirds of the 21,000 residents are black. His teeth clenched as he drove past a protester holding a sign that read "Stop Killing Us."

He questioned why protesters don't hold such signs at the scenes of murders, such as the recent killing in St. Louis of Donnie White. Dilworth said he knew White, who was on the way home from work when he got caught in crossfire between suspected black gangs.

"We are not killing you; you are killing yourselves," he said, his voice rising inside his police SUV. "This is a systematic problem that's been going on for years. I want to tell them to wake up! And look at exactly what the problem really is! Look at the statistics. The number of officer-involved shootings is relatively low. I stand a better chance of being killed by you."[357]

His wife thinks he, as black police officer in Ferguson, would be safer back in the war zone of Iraq or Afghanistan.

How do you think the wives and family members of white police officers in Ferguson feel?

Oh wait, they are in hiding...

The war goes on, with the truth of what happened on August 9th obfuscated by the powerful racial animosity of the black rabble toward whites (or anything deemed defending so-called 'white supremacy', such as the police) who hold Ferguson and all of metropolitan St. Louis hostage.

---

[357] http://www.stltoday.com/news/local/crime-and-courts/black-and-in-blue-a-ferguson-police-sergeant-reflects-on/article_b71556de-68b1-566f-a6ce-cc02c01b8343.html

November 21, 2014
An Open Letter to Officer Darren Wilson

Dear Officer Wilson,

We've never met, though were we to brush against one another in a crowded store or pass one another one the street, I'm quite positive we'd smile at one and instinctively nod a sign of respect to each other.

From the moment you pulled your SUV slowly up to the jaywalking Michael Brown and Dorian Johnson to right now, you've unwittingly become a pariah to a world you probably never knew existed.

The intense hatred and scorn directed your way for an incident most supporters of Michael Brown reflexively believe to have been nothing more than you executing an innocent black male (whose hands were up...) is largely due to the media, the Obama Administration, and the Department of Justice deciding your fate was sealed the moment his lifeless body fell on Canfield Drive.

You've been the subject of a Star Chamber, sentenced in the court of public opinion before any evidence could be presented to absolve you from the guilt of Brown's death; in fact, if a video of the altercation existed showing Brown to assault you, go for your gun, then charge at you after you told him to remain still, well, even this bit of visual evidence would be considered a distortion of reality by his out-for-your-blood followers.

But I stand by you, Darren Wilson.

The *Washington Post* sent nine reporters to locate some shred of proof you had uttered something racial in the past to prove you had prejudicial thoughts when you pulled your SUV up to Wilson and Johnson.

Nine reporters.

They dug up nothing.[358]

The city you served has become a war zone, with the already depreciating property values prior to your altercation with Brown drifting closer to a scenario when homeowners simply must walk away from their completely capsized mortgages.[359]

Boarded up businesses on West Florissant are reminders the owners of these stores are aware those marching for Michael Brown aren't peaceful, but a bellicose group of mendacious individuals clinging to a delusional belief you represent all that is wrong with society.

Boarded up businesses throughout Clayton, downtown St. Louis and other communities of Greater St. Louis are a reminder of how deep the lies of your guilt have been willingly consumed by the black community, and the fears the owners of these stores have when the black mob/rioters are loosened by the grand jury's decision to not to charge you with anything.

But I stand by you, Darren Wilson, just as others on the police force you proudly served donned (to the Department of Justice's immediate disapproval) "I am Darren Wilson" bracelets. Mind you, a DOJ that plays by its own set of rules in Ferguson...[360]

I stand by you, against those who stood outside the Ferguson Police Department on November 20th shouting, "What do we want? Darren Wilson! How do we want him? Dead!" [361]

Though you and fellow police officers in metropolitan can't force

---

[358] http://www.washingtonpost.com/national/darren-wilsons-first-job-was-on-a-troubled-police-force-disbanded-by-authorities/2014/08/23/1ac796f0-2a45-11e4-8593-da634b334390_story.html

[359] http://www.stltoday.com/business/local/st-louis-is-hot-spot-for-underwater-mortgages/article_1a9b46b5-38f4-5b93-b4b4-e895f8e0bab5.html

[360] http://fox2now.com/2014/11/20/department-of-justice-investigators-in-ferguson-appear-to-be-breaking-their-own-rules/

[361] http://www.nationalreview.com/corner/393195/ferguson-protesters-erupt-outside-police-department-what-do-we-want-darren-wilson-how?

white people to commit crime, the Department of Justice mandated "impartial police training" classes after your altercation with Brown, so police can have, "enhance ... understanding of how bias — including implicit or unconscious bias — affects officer behavior, and the impact that biased policing has on officers and the community."

The statistics culled from police arrests in the city of St. Louis showcase why an officer, such as yourself, might take notice of black males walking in the middle of the street.

The City of St. Louis Metropolitan Police Department, releases an Annual Report to the Community. This report breaks down violent crime and the overall percentage of the racial group arrested for each offense (The breakdown can be found on p. 20).

Remember, out of 318,000 people, St. Louis is 49.2 percent black 43.9 percent white (as of 2010 US Census). And guess what? Another one of those crimes City of St. Louis Metropolitan Police Department tracks by race for is weapons arrests (you can find the data on p. 227).

But why bring any of this data up? Ferguson is 15 miles away from downtown St. Louis, right?

Well, thanks to the joy of Section 8 Vouchers, the population responsible with making St. Louis one of America's most dangerous cities has found a new home in Ferguson.

Mr. Wilson, where you aware of the racial history of Ferguson? Let me elaborate:

- In 1970, Ferguson was 99 percent white
- In 1980, Ferguson was 85 percent white and 14 black
- In 1990, Ferguson was 73.8 percent white and 25.1 percent black
- In 2000, Ferguson was 44.8 percent white and 52.4 percent black

- In 2010 Ferguson was 29.3 percent white and 67.4 percent black[362]
-

Which brings us to 2014 and the situation of today. The violence was so bad in the Section 8 Voucher saturated apartment complex Michael Brown called home that some tenants would sleep on the floor for fear of being shot in the night.[363]

Such is the conditions of an inner-city, where the urban nightmare of daily gun shots is the very fear that once drove whites to move to Ferguson; it's now the sound of gun shots in Ferguson driving whites from the city in search of a new home.

Such is the reason why the Section 8 Vouchers successfully redistributed the crime normally found in downtown St. Louis to once peaceful communities like Ferguson.

Your city, Officer Wilson.

Now, with citizens of metropolitan St. Louis searching for some form of security to protect their homes, be it cameras or guns, a series of events you unwittingly started when you confronted Brown and Johnson is coming to its finality: threats of violence have escalated from just those protesters demanding your head, but now, to as one of the most popular doomsday scenario/prepper sites reports: Rioters To Target Whites: "You Will Never Be Safe… Not You, Not Your Children"[364]

SHTFplan.com has a simple moniker: "When it hits the fan, don't say we didn't warn you."

Well, Officer Wilson, the shit has hit the fan in St. Louis.

But I stand by you.

---

[362] Chart: Inside Ferguson's Changing Demographics, **Forbes, 8-19-2014**

[363] http://news.investors.com/090314-715932-great-society-housing-programs-of-1960s-helped-create-inner-city-despair.htm#ixzz3HO7kGJN7

[364] https://www.shtfplan.com/headline-news/rioters-to-target-whites-you-will-never-be-safe-not-you-not-your-children_11202014

Our Attorney General, Eric Holder, has issued police guidance on how he hopes they treat the protesters[365] he's helped influence from the earliest stages of this fiasco in Ferguson; nearly a score of churches in St. Louis will operate as safe houses for those protesters,[366] engaged in violence and open defiance of the laws governing civilized society, to seek shelter from legal scrutiny; and "rules of engagement," crafted by the Don't Shoot Coalition and demanded the police adhere to during the arrest, have been agreed upon.[367]

As the Gateway Pundit reported, those rules include:

> Highlights from today's presser:
>
> ** Police will allow protest mob "to occupy larger and more disruptive spaces than would normally be tolerated."
>
> ** Safe houses will be considered "sacred ground."
>
> ** Excessive force and other forms of "police misconduct" will not be tolerated.
>
> ** Intimidation and harassment "of protesters" will not be tolerated.[368]

Yet not a finger is lifted when masked blacks, brandishing semiautomatic weapons, threaten people in St. Louis if you, Officer Wilson, aren't indicted:

> A group of black protesters holding weapons put together a

---

[365] http://www.stltoday.com/news/local/govt-and-politics/with-ferguson-decision-looming-holder-issues-new-police-guidance/article_535b777a-19e9-504d-811f-d97517d8ab1f.html

[366] http://www.stltoday.com/lifestyles/faith-and-values/churches-to-serve-as-safe-spaces-after-ferguson-grand-jury/article_48dcdbdc-587f-5507-8997-017513dc3c72.html

[367] http://www.stltoday.com/news/local/crime-and-courts/police-officials-respond-to-rules-of-engagement-sought-for-ferguson/article_3f747e2c-eca1-529e-ac3c-f2aa4d2df0f8.html

[368] http://www.thegatewaypundit.com/2014/11/st-louis-mayor-commissioner-dooley-release-rules-for-police-officers-during-riots/

video this week threatening to kill "mother-f*ckers" if Officer Wilson is not indicted.

It's hard to understand but at one point they say, "Niggas aint out here playin no more." And, "We gonna bring it to your front door."

The men display several guns in the video.[369]

This, Officer Wilson, is the state of metropolitan St. Louis on November 21, 2014.

And it should be obvious to you now that the fractured state of race relations in the metro area was always bubbling below the surface, ready to erupt when the right set of events triggered it: those set of events being your altercation with Michael Brown.

But this hatred and racial resentment is largely a one-way street, with the black population of St. Louis resenting the type of civilization whites create in their absence; the safe schools whites maintain and sustain in the absence of black pupils; the appreciating property value majority white communities in the absence of apartment complex replete with Section 8 Voucher holding blacks who once called the urban war zone (a war zone of their creation) home.

Officer Wilson, we've never met, and odds are we will never have the opportunity to look one another in the eyes and shake hands.

But the atmosphere you accidentally unleashed on August 9th was always prepared to engulf metropolitan St. Louis with just the slightest release of the racial resentment blacks harbor toward whites; black-on-black crime/homicide is of no concern to this community, when they've willingly swallowed the poisonous, egregiously offensive and inaccurate lie, that you executed Michael Brown for the mere crime of walking while black.[370]

---

[369] http://www.thegatewaypundit.com/2014/11/breaking-video-masked-ferguson-protesters-with-guns-threaten-police/

[370] http://fox2now.com/2014/09/01/mother-of-murder-victim-calls-for-focus-on-

Michael Brown lost his life on August 9th because he decided to try and take your life, Officer Wilson.

Never forget this.

And never forget that I stand by you.

As do tens of thousands of people in metropolitan St. Louis; hundreds of thousands in Missouri; and millions around America.

Respectfully yours,

Paul Kersey

November 22, 2014
The situation in 67% black Ferguson is no longer an American problem: it's an African problem

Just as Budweiser is no longer an American company, the situation in 67 percent black Ferguson and the metropolitan area of St. Louis is no longer an American problem: it's an African problem.

With the increasingly volatile situation bordering a layer of hell even Virgil kept Dante from seeing, the anthem of the African protests has a four letter word pervasive in the Justice for Michael Brown lexicon:

> "F— the police" and shouting "We don't give a f— about your laws like you don't give a f— about our lives."[371]

---

black-on-black-crime/

[371] http://www.nationalreview.com/corner/393294/ferguson-protests-grow-

The Bell Curve City is on the cusp of a nuclear meltdown, with these words from a *New York Times* profile on the Ferguson protesters illustrating a hatred that borders on judging entirely by the color of skin:

> When violence broke out over the summer, Richard Clark, 30, said he stayed away because he did not want people to think, "See, that's what we thought they were — animals."
>
> But he said he felt that blacks continued to be treated as animals, so the more confrontational approach might be necessary. He was willing to die for the cause, he said, if it meant a better life for his two daughters. Still, he said, he was not sure how far he was willing to go.
>
> "You just don't know what the hell you going to do until you're put in that position," he said.
>
> Brian Curtis, 24, knows exactly what he thinks should happen if Officer Wilson is not indicted. It would mean that peaceful protests were not working, he said, and that a more assertive, even violent, approach was necessary.
>
> "I'm following the crowd," Mr. Curtis said. "If we don't get no justice, we got to start taking matters into our own hands. They want to go loot, we can go do that. They want to break stuff out, we can go do that, too. Something got to be done to make our voices heard."

"Your voices heard?"

Haven't the black voices of Barack Obama and Eric Holder been sufficient in denoting who is in charge in Ferguson and determined to see racial justice to its glorious fruition? Mr. Curtis -- your voice is echoed in the words and actions of Obama and Holder who have

---

larger-we-dont-give-f-about-your-laws-ryan-lovelace

both decided Officer Darren Wilson's actions on August 9th represent a moment to reignite the struggle for instituting black supremacy in America.

A story in the Christian Science Monitor showcases the solidarity blacks across America have with the deceased Michael Brown and the great antipathy they feel toward the Anglo-Saxon system of justice (you know innocent until proven guilty...:

> One mid-September poll of St. Louis County residents, for example, found 7 in 10 blacks saying Wilson should be charged with a crime and an equal share of whites saying the opposite. Ferguson, part of the St. Louis metro area, is in the county.
>
> In a broader nationwide survey, taken around the first week of September, 91 percent of blacks said Wilson should be charged, while only 42 percent of whites said that.[372]

Ninety-one percent? You can bet Obama and Holder are part of this 91 percent. Holder's sympathies are 100 percent on the side of the Ferguson protesters, those "animals" who are prepared to do whatever it takes to "make our voices heard."[373]

And black leaders in St. Louis and Missouri are letting slip the reality of what "make our voices heard" means.

The Gateway Pundit reported the leader of the Congressional Black Caucus is threaten push-back if Wilson isn't indicted:

> Rep. G. K. Butterfield, the new leader of the Congressional

---

[372] http://www.csmonitor.com/USA/2014/1121/How-differently-do-blacks-and-whites-view-Ferguson-Here-are-the-numbers.-video

[373] http://www.washingtonpost.com/world/national-security/holder-frustrated-with-mo-governor-over-actions-before-ferguson-grand-jury-decision/2014/11/21/d61b43cc-717e-11e4-ad12-3734c461eab6_story.html

Black Caucus, called on the grand jury to indict Officer Darren Wilson in the shooting death of Michael Brown or there will be pushback.

Via GotNews:

> "I was a judge for fifteen years as you know and I presided over many grand juries. So I would certainly hope that the grand jury in Ferguson, Missouri will find that there is sufficient evidence to conclude that a crime probably was committed. To lay out that crime and to let a jury of twelve in Missouri decide the guilt or innocence of the police officer. But if they turn their back on justice I'm fearful that there will be pushback from those who are concerned about it. And, I'm one of those who's concerned about it. There will be pushback. We'll be asking questions. I would hope that any demonstrations that take place in Ferguson, Missouri would be peaceful and nonviolent. And I would hope that law enforcement would not inflame citizens who might want to express their First Amendment right."[374]

"Inflame citizens?"

Isn't it obvious the Anglo-Saxon concept of "innocent until proven guilty" is lost on the mind of Africans who are determined Officer Wilson must pay for his sins (and in turn, whites must make more concessions to black people convinced white supremacy is the basis for inequalities existing between the two communities)?

One member of the cloth, a black bishop for the Church of God in Christ, is threatening to move the church's convention elsewhere if justice is not found for Michael Brown. Damn the evidence the grand jury is presented, the only type of justice satiating black people will be racial justice (it should be noted those working in the restaurant

---

[374] http://www.thegatewaypundit.com/2014/11/black-caucus-leader-warns-st-louis-county-jury-to-indict-officer-darren-wilson-video/

industry in St. Louis are delighted to hear the Church of God in Christ is looking for an alternative town to host their convention, for those attending the black theological convention are notoriously bad tippers):

> Bishop Charles E. Blake Sr., the Church of God in Christ's presiding bishop, last week sent a letter to Missouri Gov. Jay Nixon, outlining concerns over Michael Brown's death — and threatening to move its annual convention elsewhere.
>
> "We feel especially obligated to urge that steps be taken to ensure that there will be justice in the Michael Brown shooting and that necessary systemic changes will be made," Blake said, according to the St. Louis Post-Dispatch.
>
> Brian Hall, chief marketing officer for the St. Louis Convention and Visitors Commission, told the Post-Dispatch that the church's annual convention led to $98 million in expenditures in the region in the past five years.[375]

Bishop Blake put out a hilarious "Pastoral Statement" which basically amounts to trying to racial extort the white community of St. Louis for the actions of one white police officer daring to defend his right to live and exercising his right to discriminate against the deceased Michael Brown, who had designs of taking his life on August 9th. Because Wilson lived, whites in St. Louis County must pay (according to Bishop Blake):

> We call on the Justice Department to oversee the restructuring of the Ferguson police department, with special attention to the grievous lack of representation of blacks on the force. And we encourage the DOJ to continue its investigation into possible civil rights violations in the Michael Brown case.

---

[375] http://www.bizjournals.com/stlouis/morning_call/2014/11/church-of-god-in-christ-threatens-to-pull.html

> We call on local clergy to continue to minister to the needs of the community. The church must become more involved in championing their cause. We urge pastors to begin to minister, mentor and monitor youth involved in or at risk for violent behavior.
>
> Finally, we call on the business community and philanthropists to support the creation of jobs for young black men and women in Ferguson and throughout St. Louis County and city. They should support the efforts of clergy working with the youth from the poorest neighborhoods in the area.
>
> Under God's providence this tragedy can become a door of opportunity. Thus, what was intended for evil can become a source of blessing.[376]

"Intended for evil?"

You mean the actions of Michael Brown, who refused to comply with the request of Officer Wilson to get out of the middle of the road and walk on the sidewalk\and then tried to deprive the white policeman of his personal sidearm?

Just as Budweiser is no longer an American company, the situation in 67 percent black Ferguson and the metropolitan area of St. Louis is no longer an American problem: it's an African problem.

The reaction by blacks to the situation in Ferguson, not just in St. Louis but all of America, should provide a powerful reminder the reaction to Darren Wilson being found innocent of any crime by the grand jury will ignite a reaction nationwide.

To borrow an adjective from Richard Clark, the response will be "animalistic."

---

[376] http://www.cogic.org/blog/uncategorized/pastoral-statement-on-ferguson/

It will be a purely African response.

November 23, 2014
May the Odds be Ever in Your Favor: Former Navy SEALs Hired to Get Guns and Gold out of St. Louis

Gun sales in St. Louis spiked on August 11.[377]

Gun sales in St. Louis spiked even further on August 19.[378]

Gun sales spiked the farthest around mid-November.[379]

With the St. Louis metropolitan-area held hostage by the fear of spontaneous blackness, erupting in a fury of racial rage when Darren Wilson is found innocent by the grand jury, security companies are seeing unprecedented requests for their services to install cameras at both commercial buildings and private residences.[380]

Terrorism.

Plain and simple.

---

[377] http://www.bizjournals.com/stlouis/news/2014/08/12/gun-stores-see-sales-spike-in-wake-of-ferguson.html

[378] http://www.washingtonpost.com/blogs/the-fix/wp/2014/08/20/gun-sales-are-up-near-ferguson-but-not-farther-away/

[379] http://www.usatoday.com/story/news/nation/2014/11/20/gun-buyers-st-louis/19311107/

[380] http://fox2now.com/2014/11/20/security-companies-busy-protecting-home-from-possible-unrest-in-ferguson/

The scenario still unfolding in Ferguson and metropolitan St. Louis can only be described as terrorism: the fear of white residence, owners of capital (be it large commercial real estate or small businesses), and property owners grows exponential as the "Justice for Michael Brown" mob grows more belligerent and bellicose.

Terrorism.

Enough to convince the political leaders of Clayton, a roughly 8 percent black city in metropolitan St. Louis, to enlist a private army to protect private citizens, the city's infrastructure, and private property (primarily commercial, but also private) from the people who have cultivated the war clouds on the horizon.

A number of local and out-of-state private security companies are seeing massive requests for protection from such companies as Wells Fargo, Bank of America, and Trader Joe's, but rules governing how security personnel licensing requirements are secured through the St. Louis County Police Department will not be relaxed.[381]

Thus, the reason the *Wall Street Journal* profiled one local St. Louis construction worker (on November 6) entrepreneurial enough to understand the coming black riots in the city represent a more lucrative market than those business owners prepare for impending inclement weather:

> And as the nation awaits that decision, those on the ground are making preparations.
>
> "We've been doing board-ups for probably the past month, the phone's been ringing off the hook," said Brian Krieger, owner of American Board Up and Construction Services in St. Louis. "I've already purchased 500 sheets of plywood."
>
> He said he expects work to increase in the coming days as businesses, especially those in the Ferguson area, take

---

[381] http://www.stltoday.com/news/local/crime-and-courts/police-refuse-to-waive-security-guard-rules-to-meet-ferguson/article_8e6fbe20-aecb-567a-ad70-caf37db28a6d.html

precautions for the announcement.[382]

Terrorism.

When the black protests (rioting/looting/arson) started in early August, one private security firm was brought in to offer protection for journalists. With employees, having Navy SEAL and U.S. Ranger on their resume, the official Twitter for Asymmetric Solutions 'tweeted' this out:

> We've been to Baghdad, Kabul, KL, Manilla, Peshwar, Bogata. Never guessed we would deploy a high threat team in our own city. #furgeson
> — Asymmetric Solutions (@AsymmetricUSA) August 19, 2014[383]

Terrorism.

But Asymmetric Solutions wasn't done. They aren't done:

> Business owners in the St. Louis, Missouri area have hired private military contractors to transport guns and gold, fearing their shops will be targeted by looters if a grand jury does not indict Darren Wilson, the police officer who shot and killed Michael Brown in the St. Louis County suburb of Ferguson.
>
> "There's a lot of people that brought in a lot of money to have people secure their assets," said Stephen King, owner of Metro Shooting Supplies gun shop, a 15-minute drive from Ferguson. "Some of those people spent $10 an hour on security guards and some people have $1,000 a day private contractors."
>
> King confirmed that gun shops in the area are hiring private military contractors to escort the transport of their guns to secure locations. A private military contractor who spoke to

---

[382] http://online.wsj.com/articles/ferguson-community-braces-for-grand-jury-decision-in-black-teens-shooting-1415311318

[383] http://dailycaller.com/2014/08/21/military-security-contractor-deploys-high-threat-team-to-ferguson/

VICE News on condition of anonymity said that more than 300 private military contractors, or PMCs, have been contracted for work in direct response to Ferguson security concerns.

Jared Ogden, director of operations for Asymmetric Solutions, a private military contractor staffed by former special operations forces told VICE News his company was hired by businesses to transport "St. Louis-based company assets."

"We've got our hands in a bunch things" related to security in the Ferguson area, said Ogden, a former Navy SEAL who was featured on the National Geographic reality program, *Survival Alaska*.

"If you are a business owner and you are in the business of selling firearms and you're in an area where shops have been looted, burned down, property stolen, you now have the responsibility to society to ensure to do everything possible to make sure that those firearms do not get into the hands of the wrong people."

Missouri Gold Buyers & Jewelry, the largest precious metal buyer in the state, according to the company's website, has four shops in the St. Louis area, two of which are in North St. Louis County communities neighboring Ferguson. It was one of several area businesses looted following protests over Brown's death. In August, masked men shattered one of the back windows of the diminutive shop on Kingshighway Boulevard in St. Louis and got inside, but they were unable to break into the safe, according to the shop's owner, Mike Duke.

Duke is not taking any risks this time around.

"We got everything out last week, we put it back on Monday," said Duke, who had heard the grand jury decision would be announced on a Sunday. "This weekend it's going out again. A lot of it has already been moved." Moving his product back and forth comes at quite a cost, though exactly how much he wouldn't say.

"It's costing a lot of money," he said. "The worst part is the stores that are normally are producing cash in the North County stores, for the last three months, nobody's doing business in North County. Revenue's way down. It's horrible."

Duke said he employs Cook Security, a private security and surveillance company, to provide security for his shops and has recently hired 12 additional private security guards to protect his stores, and one to escort the transport of gold, diamonds and coins from the stores to a safe location.

He noted that the dollar value of the product being moved to secure offsite locations is in the millions.

"I'm not like a pawn shop, I don't buy TVs," he said. "I have precious metals. We have a law here that whatever you buy you have to hold for five days. So all those stores had those five days worth of business there. I'm a very large buyer so that's a large amount of money."

Ogden said the business owners' concerns are understandable, especially when it comes to the potential for stolen guns on the streets.

"If certain merchandise, like firearms, got into the wrong hands, it would be a catalyst to more violence," he said.

King plans to keep his gun shop open this weekend, and is ready to defend it if need be, though he is keeping quiet about the particulars of the store's security plans.

"We're going to have to do whatever we have to do legally to defend ourselves against some type of violent threat. It wouldn't be a brain surgeon that's going to be coming to our store to attack us," he said. "We know what we're going to do but they don't know, and that's the way we want to keep it."[384]

The Hunger Games was just a movie.

---

[384] Private Military Contractors Hired to Move Guns and Gold Out of Ferguson, Vice News, 11-21-14

What's happening in St. Louis is real.

And the only word does justice to what the black population is doing to Ferguson, the city of St. Louis, and those communities making up the County of St. Louis: Terrorism.

November 25, 2014
It's a very, very mad world, mad world

It's hard to put into words the shock of seeing the President of the United States publicly side with the black riots/looting/arsonists in Ferguson.

But the head of the executive branch of the United States government did just this when he said those angry over Darren Wilson escaping indictment (performing some legal Houdini act, aided by white supremacy in the eyes of those still clinging irrationally to the false Ferguson narrative of a cop executing the black equivalent of Andre the Giant's character in *The Princess Bride*) were merely engaging in, "an understandable reaction."

"An understandable reaction..."

Perhaps President Obama found inspiration in the command of Michael Brown's stepfather encouraging the black mob in Ferguson to, "burn this bitch down!"[385]

Telling some white Quisling (the Quisling as mentioned in Max Brooks novel *World War Z*, who pretends to be a zombie and ultimately gets eating alive by the horde they march with...) on MSNBC that, "This is St. Louis's race war," Missouri State Sen. Maria

---

[385] http://www.thesmokinggun.com/buster/ferguson/burn-this-bitch-down-879056

Chappelle-Nadali warned those whites still believing character judgments are the best course of action in pursuing interracial relations.

When, in fact, Chappelle Nadali and her army have already judged you by the color of your skin: if it resembles Darren Wilson, then you are their enemy:

> "We didn't have a race war like other cities throughout the U.S. This is our race war."[386]

Those other cities as to having a race war transpire go unmentioned, but judging by the condition of Newark, Baltimore, Detroit, and Birmingham (those locations where a one-sided war was waged on the whites who built the very civilization blacks could only envy and watch crumble away once they became in demographic control), St. Louis and Ferguson are headed to a similar in the hands of black political control.

Which brings up the primary question going unanswered as of yet: why was Ferguson allowed to burn last night?

We know firefighters were being shot at by those race warring blacks, in a hilarious reminder the events of *American History X* have a real-world basis for fact; thus the conflagration of black racial hate toward symbols of white capitalism (structural racism to the enlightened masses at MSNBC and CNN) in Ferguson went up in flames after being thoroughly looted.[387]

But why-oh-why did the National Guard not intervene to provide much needed support to those outgunned police in Ferguson? The St. Louis Post-Dispatch reports:

> As ruins of about a dozen businesses here smoldered today, an "extremely frustrated" Mayor James Knowles III was

---

[386] http://www.breitbart.com/Breitbart-TV/2014/11/24/State-Senator-This-Is-St-Louis-Race-War

[387] http://hosted.ap.org/dynamic/stories/U/US_FERGUSON_PROTESTS?SITE=AP&SECTION=HOME&TEMPLATE=DEFAULT&CTIME=2014-11-25-03-48-15

asking what happened to onetime plans to shield vulnerable businesses with a protective line of Missouri National Guard members.

"The National Guard was not deployed in enough time to save all our businesses," he said in a press conference just after 2 p.m., calling the delay "deeply disturbing."

Earlier, in an interview, the mayor said: "What should have happened last night? They should have had National Guard troops protecting the hard targets in Ferguson and allowed law enforcement to pursue a very mobile crowd of looters and arsonists. That's the problem. They (the police) could not secure the commercial districts."

Knowles added, "I don't believe we've seen the commitment from the state we hoped to get. And knowing that there's so many people out there who committed a crime, who committed destruction, who aren't going to be held accountable, because law enforcement was overwhelmed — it makes me concerned for the nights to come."

St. Louis city officials said they requested 400 Guard troops, which were deployed by Police Chief Sam Dotson to protect government buildings and businesses. They delivered what a mayor's aide said was a good result.

Nixon's office has not responded to requests for comment today, but announced that he will hold a press conference with Guard leaders at 3 p.m. at the University of Missouri-St. Louis.

Lt. Gov. Peter Kinder, a Republican, said the governor, a Democrat, owes an explanation for an "inexplicable" decision to hold back on Guard help.

He said Knowles called him after being unable to reach Nixon. "How does the governor of Missouri not answer the calls, the pleas, of the mayor on the ground?" Kinder asked.

Earlier today, Ferguson Police Chief Tom Jackson raised the question of whether the Guard plan was changed to add to outside political pressure for him to resign.

"I can't say that for sure; there was a period of time that passed (between the formation of the original plan and pressure for his resignation)," Jackson said. "I can't speak to other people's motives."

He said he was assured weeks ago that Ferguson would get as many Guard soldiers as needed to secure the businesses, so officers could concentrate on police duties, like answering calls for service.

Then, he said, the plan was changed without explanation.

"I thought, 'Holy crap, are we going to have enough people to protect the businesses in our major corridors?' I was assured we'd have plenty of law enforcement to handle those tasks. And we got overwhelmed and overrun."[388]

Do we need to even venture a guess as to where the order for the National Guard to stand down came from, ensuring the black insurrectionists in Ferguson had an opportunity to light the flames of race war so many blacks in Missouri seem excited to see ignited?

Any guesses?

How about a three word hint...

"An understandable reaction..."

And now those white people remaining in Ferguson and metropolitan St. Louis know how Charlton Heston's character felt in *The Omega Man*: "Oh my God! It's almost dark. They'll be waking up soon."

And those waking up will be the army Chappelle Nadali hopes to usher in a race war to take not only Ferguson, but all of St. Louis in a similar manner to how Detroit and Birmingham fell.

---

[388] http://www.stltoday.com/news/local/crime-and-courts/ferguson-officials-where-was-the-national-guard/article_343a2224-4d61-54fb-b5ac-a13ea99951f7.html

November 27, 2014
"You Say You Want a Revolution... well, you know, your EBT Card has got to work."

While the family of the late Michael Brown continues to squabble over who has the right to sell(and profit from) quickly produced merchandise in his honor, a story has broken serving as the most appropriate metaphor for the age of Black-Run America.[389]

BRA, for short.

As the original story of the fatal encounter between Brown and Officer Darren Wilson continues to look more and more like a piece of Swiss cheese (showcasing the utter nefarious nature of the media, the vast majority of blacks who sided with Brown by immediately judging his skin color, the Obama Administration, and the Department of Justice), a more hilarious development has arisen to bring much needed levity to the farce in Ferguson.[390]

It was reported two members of the New Black Panther Party - Brandon Orlando Baldwin and Olajuwon Davis - tried to purchase .45 ACP guns under "false pretenses." It turns out our intrepid NBBP friends also tried to buy ingredients for making a bomb.

The FBI arrested these two would-be DuoBombers and the story quietly went away.[391]

---

[389] http://www.breitbart.com/Big-Government/2014/11/26/Michael-Brown-s-Mother-Step-Father-Under-Investigation-For-Violent-Confrontation-Over-Justice-For-Mike-Brown-Merchandise

[390] http://bigstory.ap.org/article/078c82ad45ff4ec6aa1c7744dfa7df14/grand-jury-documents-rife-inconsistencies

[391] http://www.reuters.com/article/2014/11/22/us-usa-missouri-shooting-

Until today.

Now, before we get to the hilarious part of this story, let's remind the reader of two pertinent facts:

Consulting the 2009 New York Times Food Stamp Usage Across the Country interactive map, we learn this about the city of St. Louis (49 percent black and 43 percent white):
- As of 2009, 60 percent of blacks were on EBT/Food Stamps in the city of St. Louis
- As of 2009, 10 percent of whites were on EBT/Food Stamps in the city of St. Louis

St. Louis County (different from the city of St. Louis) is just over one million people in population. It's home to Ferguson, that lovely post-white suburb boasting a growing, self-insufficient black population. [Ferguson: Gentrification and its discontents, Al-Jazeera, 8-16-14]

Of those one million people, 78 percent of the county's population is white and 23.7 percent is black. Consulting the 2009 New York Times Food Stamp Usage Across the Country interactive map, we learn this about the county:

- As of 2009, 38 percent of blacks were on EBT/Food Stamps in St. Louis County
- As of 2009, 4 percent of whites were on EBT/Food Stamps in St. Louis County

Ninety percent (90 percent!!!) of black children will have been on EBT/Food Stamps by the time they reach 20 years of age.[392]

And now, comes the story celebrating the sheer horror of modern America, yet hilariously shows how this situation could immediately

---

explosives-idUSKCN0J602N20141122

[392] http://www.nytimes.com/2009/11/29/us/29foodstamps.html?pagewanted=all&_r=0

be rectified:

> Two men indicted last week on federal weapons charges allegedly had plans to bomb the Gateway Arch — and to kill St. Louis County Prosecuting Attorney Robert McCulloch and Ferguson Police Chief Tom Jackson — the Post-Dispatch has learned.
> Sources close to the investigation were uncertain whether the men had the capability to carry out the plans, although the two allegedly did buy what they thought was a pipe bomb in an undercover law enforcement sting.
>
> The men wanted to acquire two more bombs, the sources said, but could not afford to do it until one suspect's girlfriend's Electronic Benefit Transfer card was replenished.
>
> An indictment, with no mention of bombs or killings, was returned in federal court here Nov. 19 and unsealed Friday upon the arrest of Brandon Orlando Baldwin and Olajuwon Ali Davis. Their addresses and Baldwin's age were not available; Davis is 22.
>
> The arrest came three days before McCulloch revealed that a grand jury would not indict Ferguson police Officer Darren Wilson in the controversial killing of Michael Brown. The announcement triggered looting and multiple arsons in Ferguson.
>
> The charges say that between Nov. 1 and Nov. 13, at the Cabela's store in Hazelwood, Baldwin claimed to be buying two Hi-Point .45-caliber pistols for himself when they were really for another person. Brandon also is known as Brandon Muhammad, according to court documents, and Davis now goes by the last name Ali, his attorney said. Each faces a charge of aiding and abetting the making of a false written statement made in connection with a firearms purchase.[393]

Ah, the all-powerful EBT card! A simple device allowing blacks access to a world their abilities and intelligence deprives them

---

[393] Alleged plot included bombing Arch, killing St. Louis County prosecutor, Ferguson chief, St. Louis Post-Dispatch, 11-27-14

from... accessing. It's the great equalizer, for without the EBT/Food Stamp card, one wonders how 60 percent of blacks in St. Louis and 38 percent of blacks in St. Louis County would eat?

Or those would-be black revolutionaries acquire the necessary components to make more bombs:

> The men wanted to acquire two more bombs, the sources said, but could not afford to do it until one suspect's girlfriend's Electronic Benefit Transfer card was replenished.[394]

Today, Darren Wilson is enjoying a Thanksgiving meal with his new bride and family; while the Michael Brown continues to battle one another over who has the right to peddle poorly made "Justice for Michael Brown" or "Hands Up, Don't Shoot" merchandise.

Odds are, the Michael Brown family is eating Thanksgiving courtesy of the EBT card as well, just as the bulk of those chanting "No Justice, No Peace" in Ferguson and other parts of the St. Louis metropolitan area owe their holiday meal to...

"You Say You Want a Revolution... well, you know, your EBT Card has got to work."

Those desiring an end to BRA need only push for one, simple move: turn off the EBT card for a day.

November 28, 2014
Will the last white person to leave Ferguson please turn the lights off?

There's something about this story that's just... funny:

---

[394] Ibid

Welcome to "Ferghanistan."

Tragic before-and-after photos show the devastation to restaurants, shops and small businesses that were trashed, looted and torched by the raging mob of rioters in Ferguson, Mo.

Nearly every building along South Florissant Street — where the Ferguson police station is located — was ransacked after the announcement that a grand jury had declined to indict Officer Darren Wilson in the fatal shooting of Michael Brown.

Among the stores damaged were Advance Auto Parts, Fashion R, TitleMax Title Loans, Clean World Laundromat and Little Caesars pizzeria.

Others included Walgreens, Beauty Town, Family Dollar, and O'Reilly Auto Parts — many of which were owned by minorities, KMOV-TV reported.

Residents were left stunned by the wreckage.

"Speaking your mind — that's America. You are supposed to be able to protest peacefully and make your point. But this . . ." said the distraught manager of Little Caesars, where a dozen people lost their jobs after the place was gutted, the Daily Mail reported.

Other residents said the devastation in their suburban St. Louis city was so bad it looked like "Ferghanistan" or war-torn Iraq, the paper said.[395]

"Ferghanistan?"

Why demonize the good people of Afghanistan with such a demeaning reference to Ferguson?

The British, Russians, and Americans have been trying to invade and conquer Afghanistan for over two centuries, while white people have been fleeing the ever-growing presence of blacks in Ferguson,

---

[395] Before-and-after photos show destruction in Ferguson, NY Post, 11-27-14

turning the city into Fergetroit.

And the value of homes in Fergetroit (recall: a *St. Louis Post-Dispatch* article - published on May 9, 2014 - noted 49 percent of mortgages in 67 percent black Ferguson were underwater, while 38 percent were below market peak; the damage to real estate value was done long before anyone had ever heard the names Michael Brown or Darren Wilson) is quickly approaching the infamous $1 amount for homes in nearly all-black Gary, Indiana and Detroit, Michigan:

> Dennis Norman, a broker and partner for MORE, said homeowners in a position to sell will watch to see if burned-out buildings in Ferguson's business district are repaired.
>
> If that rebuilding effort does not materialize, "that might be when they all decide to jump on the bandwagon and get out," he said.
>
> The commercial market seems likely to remain jittery, too. Pope has been unable to find a buyer for a Ferguson building with 12 apartment units and ground-floor retail space - even before protesters this week smashed the windows of the retail shops.
>
> "If I had to sell it today, I'd probably have to give it away," he said.[396]

The world found in Fergetroit is one that only the growing black population there - migrants from the "hollowing out," black-in-origin war zone of St. Louis - could create.[397]

Will the last white person to leave Ferguson please turn the lights off?

---

[396] Come spring, 'For Sale' signs expected in U.S. riot-hit town, Yahoo! News, 11-28-14

[397] http://www.stltoday.com/news/local/metro/census-shows-city-is-hollowing-out/article_4af01497-bca8-5b63-8cc6-1c724c11dd08.html

With the city now Fergetroit, it's time to just smile and realize yet another American municipality serves as a glaring case study in the reality of racial differences.

November 30, 2014
Roads? Where we're going, we don't need roads.

Remember, Al Sharpton was noted as a "key advisor" to President Barack Obama on all things Ferguson by the *New York Post*.

This makes his declaration, from Ferguson on Sunday November 30th, that, " "Justice will come to Ferguson," and, "We're not gonna stop marching and protesting until we do," all the more interesting.[398]

But not as interesting as the other "advisors" who arrived in Ferguson recently:

> Following a night of arson fires and bashed storefronts that hit close to home, Greg Hildebrand stood naked Tuesday, drying off from a needed shower, when he noticed somebody on the rooftop.
>
> "I opened the window and said, 'Hey, can I help you?'" said Hildebrand, 35, a website developer.
>
> The man said he was security and would be up there at night with others to protect the pocket of second-story apartments and lower-level storefronts near the Ferguson Police

---

[398] http://www.stltoday.com/news/local/metro/rev-al-sharpton-to-mcculloch-battle-for-justice-in-ferguson/article_33854153-3f00-5779-9cd8-bfb16d5fc97d.html

Department. A day earlier, rioters had broken out windows below Hildebrand's apartment in the 100 block of South Florissant Road and torched a nearby beauty supply store.

"I am in the middle of a difficult spot," Hildebrand said. "I feel a lot better having those guys up on the roof."

But he wasn't clear exactly who "those guys" were or where they came from.

Puzzled and alarmed protesters have wondered, too — some accusing the mysterious guards in military fatigues of being in the Ku Klux Klan.

In fact, they are volunteers affiliated with a 35,000-member national organization called Oath Keepers. Yale Law School graduate and libertarian Stewart Rhodes said by telephone from Montana that he founded the group in 2009 to protect constitutional rights, including those of protesters confronted by what he described as overly militarized police.

Police questioned group members early in the week and allowed them to stay. But Saturday, after media inquiries, St. Louis County police officers ordered the Oath Keepers to leave the rooftops.

Threatened with arrest for operating without a license, the volunteers argued but eventually left their positions early Saturday, Rhodes said.

"We are going to go back as protesters," Rhodes said Saturday afternoon.

Rhodes, who said he is Mexican-American, stressed that Oath Keepers is not anti-government. He said the volunteers handling rooftop security in Ferguson were current or former government employees and first responders, many who have intense military, police and EMS training.

"We thought they were going to do it right this time," Rhodes said of government response to the grand jury decision released Monday in the Michael Brown case.

"But when Monday rolled around and they didn't park the National Guard at these businesses, that's when we said we have got to do something.

"Historically, the government almost always fails to protect people," he added.

"We were sick in our gut we couldn't be here sooner," said John Karriman of Joplin, Mo., a state leader of Oath Keepers who teaches police tactics. "We are here to volunteer our time and make sure everybody stays safe."

Another leader, who would give only his first name, Sam, described himself as a weapons engineer from the St. Louis area who has done security contracting for the U.S. government. He said he was motivated to help after seeing a CNN story featuring extensive damage to Natalie's Cake's & More, which also helped generate thousands of dollars in donations for the small business.

Sam said he contacted owner Natalie Dubose and told her he was going to secure her store and others.

"She started crying," Sam said.

Oath Keepers boarded up a bunch of the storefronts and started night rotations on several rooftops. Sam said he vetted volunteers to ensure there weren't any "racists" or "people with an ax to grind." He said he picked volunteers who "have seen the elephant and are calm under fire."

Fearing more arsonists, Oath Keeper volunteers kept buckets of water, fire extinguishers and other nonlethal weapons on the rooftops. Some are also armed with rifles that aren't available at Walmart and Cabela's.[399]

Are you beginning to realize where all this "Ferguson" nonsense is heading?

In *Back to the Future 2*, we got a glimpse of a future American city,

---

[399] Police shut down mysterious 'Oath Keepers' guarding rooftops in downtown Ferguson, St. Louis Post-Dispatch, 11-30-14

Hill Valley (set in 2015), where flying cars and hover boards were the norm; in our world, the city of 67 percent black Ferguson looks like the dystopian world of 1985 Hill Valley created by the movies antagonist, Biff Tannen.

It was a copy of *Grays Sports Almanac: Complete Sports Statistics 1950-2000* that was the catalyst for the collapse of Hill Valley into the chaos, violence, and vice Marty McFly encountered in an alternate 1985; it's the absence of white people and the growing black population (whose crime and social capital disabling culture only they can create being the catalyst for white flight) there responsible for the crumbling community of Ferguson.

Back in 1985, the city of Ferguson was around 85 percent white; if you were to go back in time and show citizens of the city then images and video of the city now, would they believe you?

December 1, 2014
Hammer Time (After Months of Being Told They Could be the next Michael Brown, Black Youths Avenge Him)

It was a slap in the face when black members of the Washington Redskins[400] raised their hands in solidarity with the spirit of Michael Brown in mid-August; it was an outright declaration of war when black members of the St. Louis Rams decided to embark in keeping alive the fictional myth of the Gentle Giant on November 30th, when they too raised their hands in solidarity.[401]

A number of rappers joined forces to rhyme the Michael Brown-inspired "Don't Shoot" (the forensic evidence showing Brown tried to steal Officer Darren Wilson's gun obviously inadmissible in the court of black logic/opinion).[402]

Black public school students in metropolitan St. Louis have been fed a constant diet of "white police are out to get you" and "white racism" is behind your pitiful existence. Clergy United for Peace has been conducting workshops in public schools on how black students should deal with the situation in Ferguson, "urge[ing] the teenagers to express themselves in a nonviolent way if the grand jury chooses not to indict Wilson.

(Rev. Robert) White advised them to "get mad, just don't seem it":

> The question has become a common one posed to black high school students when the shooting death of Michael Brown is

---

[400] http://espn.go.com/nfl/story/_/id/11375414/eleven-washington-redskins-players-show-solidarity-ferguson-missouri-protest

[401] http://www.sportingnews.com/nfl/story/2014-11-30/hands-up-dont-shoot-ferguson-missouri-michael-brown-darren-wilson-st-louis-rams-protest-tunnel-video

[402] http://www.billboard.com/articles/columns/the-juice/6229479/the-game-diddy-rick-ross-michael-brown-tribute-song-dont-shoot

discussed. But the responses aren't always as predictable.

"How many of you had that thought it could have been me?" said the Rev. Robert White, a St. Louis pastor, to nearly 50 students in the library of East St. Louis High School Thursday.

About 30 hands shot up.

"That's interesting," White said. "I see females with their hands up."

"Tell me," he said to a girl at a front table. "Why are you saying that could have been you?"

"Because I'm black," Monecia Hudson, a junior, told him. "It really doesn't make a difference what gender you are. Police — they don't care who you are. If they feel you're doing something wrong they're going to do whatever they feel."

In high schools across the St. Louis area — particularly at those with high percentages of African-American students — conversations like this one are exposing levels of vulnerability that black students are feeling three months after Brown's shooting.

Pastors and educators are concerned. White and other members of Clergy United for Peace, which formed after Brown's shooting, are going into schools to help educate students about the legal process, including the role of a grand jury. They want young people to talk openly about their fears, frustrations and other feelings, but also be fully aware of the law.

"How many of you think Darren Wilson should be indicted?" asked the Rev. Michael Robinson.

About half the hands went up. Several said they weren't sure.

One East St. Louis student asked why a police officer would shoot someone repeatedly. Another asked why police Officer Darren Wilson hasn't been arrested.[403]

---

[403] Clergy reach out to wary high school students in wake of Brown shooting, St.

Officer Darren Wilson wasn't arrested, nor charged with any crime by the grand jury because he did nothing in confronting Michael Brown or subduing the charging, attacking, violent Gentle Giant.

But as this article makes clear, Clergy United for Peace was going around metropolitan St. Louis public schools (particularly those with high black populations) basically telling them they could be next in joining Michael Brown in the afterlife, courtesy of a trigger-happy, racist white cop.

Which brings us to the story of the young blacks wielding hammers mob in St. Louis and their fatal encounter with a white man who just happened to be a Bosnian immigrant:

> A 17-year-old St. Louis man has been charged with first-degree murder and armed criminal action in the bludgeoning death of a Bosnian immigrant.
>
> Police say Robert Mitchell along with two other teens, both juveniles, attacked the 32-year-old man with hammers early Sunday. He was pronounced dead at a hospital. Mitchell and one of the juveniles are black and the other teen is Hispanic, according to police.
>
> A police spokeswoman said investigators do not believe race played a role in the bludgeoning death of a Bosnian immigrant early Sunday, but declined to say what authorities believe is the motive in the killing.
>
> Many at the scene of the murder near Gravois Avenue and Itaska Street speculated that the four men who beat Zemir Begic, 32, to death with hammers targeted him because of his Bosnian descent.
>
> But detectives do not believe Begic's Bosnian heritage or the color of his skin served as a motive in any way, police spokeswoman Schron Jackson said.
>
> Witnesses told police that the victim and the suspect exchanged some words as Begic was walking past them on

---

Louis Post-Dispatch, 11-14-14

the way to his car, Jackson said.

Someone then hit Begic's car with something or kicked it, and Begic stopped his car, got out and exchanged words with the suspects once more. That's when he was attacked, Jackson said.

"We think it was wrong place, wrong time," Jackson said.

Homicide detectives do not believe the suspects took anything from the victim during the attack.

Jackson said Chief Sam Dotson noted that none of the suspects appear to have anything in their criminal backgrounds to suggest they would do something of this magnitude.

Dotson said more than one hammer was used in the killing, but he would not say how many.

Police arrested two suspects, ages 15 and 16 Sunday. Mitchell turned himself in to police Sunday night. Detectives believe they know who the fourth suspect is, but have not yet made an arrest, Jackson said.[404]

"We think it was wrong place, wrong time..."

A possible explanation for the Darren Wilson/Michael Brown encounter; an implausible explanation for a black/brown coalition - injected with lethal doses of "the white man is keeping me down" pep talks from organization like the Clergy United for Peace - encountering a white man and beating him to death as they randomly carried hammers.

They were actively seeking the right place and right time to exact racial revenge for Michael Brown.

And they got racial revenge on Zemir Begic, a man they didn't know was Bosnian, but soon introduced their hammers to because he was

---

[404] Fatal hammer attack on Bosnian immigrant not racially motivated, St. Louis police say, St. Louis Post-Dispatch, 12-1-14

white. As Bob McCarty reports:

> Conversely, a video shot by a resident of South St. Louis' Bevo Mill neighborhood reveals heretofore-unpublished details about what happened near the intersection of Gravois Avenue and Itaska Street before the attack that left Zemir Begic, 32, dead.
>
> At the 45-second mark, the woman who recorded the video — whose name I will not share for reasons of her personal safety — says, "And, of course, it's a white kid, right after black people running up and down the street saying, 'Eff the white people, kill the white people.' This is what we have."[405]

Thanks President Obama and Attorney General Holder; thanks Washington Redskins and St. Louis Rams; thanks Clergy United for Peace; thanks CNN, MSNBC, and the St. Louis Post-Dispatch for peddling lie after lie after lie in an effort to turn an 18-year-old Swisher Sweet liberating thug into the second coming of Jesus Christ.

Zemir Begic represents the consequences of persisting in living by lies and disseminating a false narrative surrounding the life of anything-but-angelic Michael Brown.

His death, at the hands of black (and a brown) youths, is an indication we are witnessing the Birth of a New Nation; one conceived in the notion *Django Unchained* offers a worthy glimpse in how one must deal with the white man.

December 2, 2014
Please Rod Serling, Tell us we are Just in the Twilight Zone...

An "occupying force" is how Attorney General Eric Holder describes

---

[405] http://www.bobmccarty.com/2014/12/01/exclusive-hammers-attack-video-from-south-st-louis/

the police of every community in the United States of America.

Parody?

No.

Treason?

No.

Something far, far worse. No matter the forensic evidence or sworn testimony presented to the grand jury deciding the fate of Officer Darren Wilson, the head of the Department of Justice has determined in a highly racial prejudicial manner Michael Brown was executed; thus, all cops are - via guilt by association - in the same shoes as Wilson.

Speaking in the "City too busy to hate (Atlanta)," Holder has just delivered what can only be described as the speech declaring war on law and order in favor of allowing the barbarians the freedom to plunder, loot, riot, and rape without pesky police interference:

> Like you, I understand that the need for this trust was made clear in the wake of the intense public reaction to last week's grand jury announcement. But the problems we must confront are not only found in Ferguson. The issues raised in Missouri are not unique to that state or that small city. We are dealing with concerns that are truly national in scope and that threaten the entire nation. Broadly speaking, without mutual understanding between citizens – whose rights must be respected – and law enforcement officers – who make tremendous and often-unheralded personal sacrifices every day to preserve public safety – there can be no meaningful progress. Our police officers cannot be seen as an occupying force disconnected from the communities they serve. Bonds that have been broken must be restored. Bonds that never existed must now be created.
>
> But the issue is larger than just the police and the community. Our overall system of justice must be strengthened and made more fair. In this way, we can ensure

> faith in the justice system. Without that deserved faith, without that reasoned belief, there can be no justice. This is not an unreasonable desire – it is a fundamental American right enshrined in our founding documents.
>
> There can be no question that Michael Brown's death was a tragedy. Any loss of life – and particularly the loss of someone so young – is heart-rending, regardless of the circumstances. But in the months since this incident occurred, it has sparked a significant national conversation about the need to ensure confidence in the law enforcement and criminal justice processes. The rifts that this tragedy exposed, in Ferguson and elsewhere, must be addressed – by all Americans – in a constructive manner. And it is deeply unfortunate that this vital conversation was interrupted, and this young man's memory dishonored, by destruction and looting on the part of a relatively small criminal element.[406]

Hmm... let's take a quick look at the loss of another man whose death will never be described as either a tragedy or heart-rendering. No significant national conversation will occur, because such discussion would spark a fire in a few inquisitive minds - capable of independent thought - showcasing the deep reality of the source of crime and racial hostilities/resentment in America.

And it ain't white people or the "occupying force" of cops compelling black people to pick up hammers and attack people... just white people being in the 'wrong place, at the wrong time' when blacks decide to use those hammers in exacting justice in a form of non-verbal racial dialogue AG Holder will never, ever comment on (with his silence speaking volumes to his condoning of such actions):

> One teen was charged with murder, two more were held and a fourth was sought Monday as officials spent another day trying to quell speculation that the bludgeoning death of a Bosnian immigrant was racially motivated.
>
> "There is no evidence that this was a crime occasioned by the race or ethnicity of the victim," Mayor Francis Slay declared

---

[406] Attorney General Eric Holder Delivers Remarks During the Interfaith Service and Community Forum at Ebenezer Baptist Church, Justice.gov, 12-1-2014

in a formal statement. He added, "Speculation that this attack had anything to do with the Ferguson protests is absolutely unfounded."

Police have been saying the same thing about the killing of Zemir Begic, 32, who was beaten to death with at least two hammers near Gravois Avenue and Itaska Street about 1:15 a.m. Sunday.

According to court documents, members of the group yelled at Begic, his fiancée and two others as they walked to Begic's car. As the vehicle drove away, one teen jumped on the back and began beating on it. Begic stopped and got out, and one of the men taunted him to fight before all four attacked — and continued to beat him after he fell to the ground.

"We think it was wrong place, wrong time," police spokeswoman Schron Jackson said.
Detectives do not believe the attackers took anything but Begic's life. He died at St. Louis University Hospital, suffering injuries to his head, abdomen, face and mouth.

Jackson said there was nothing in the suspects' criminal backgrounds to suggest they would do something of this magnitude.

Slay wrote: "I don't know what happened to them or to their families to lead these young people to commit such a horrific crime. It's disturbing. We do not know their past. Their futures, though, will be as grim as the judicial system can make it."[407]

Wait... the suspects in the lynching of Begic had criminal backgrounds?

"Detectives do not believe the attackers took anything but Begic's life?"

"Their futures, though, will be as grim as the judicial system can make it."

---

[407] St. Louis mayor, police say race played no role in hammer slaying of Bosnian immigrant, St. Louis Post-Dispatch, 12-2-14

You mean a judicial system administered by an Attorney General who tells an almost entirely black audience the police of America represent an "Occupying Force" in the black community?

Please tell me Rod Serling is about to appear, reminding us this is just the Twilight Zone, instead of a world where Michael Brown continues to be the poor, innocent victim and Officer Darren Wilson a reminder of a sinister, white supremacist dry-run to liberate our inner-cities of more angelic black lives (that really, really, REALLY matter...).

Treason in Black-Run America (BRA) is the act of noticing that the life of Zemir Begic mattered, and those callous detectives declaring his "life" was the only thing the black attackers took is a reminder of the true evil no one dares confront.

The "Occupying Force" isn't the police; it's white guilt occupying us in a forceful manner from ever giving voice to the reality of our dispossession.

December 3, 2014
Why Aren't the Oath Keepers Protecting Officer Darren Wilson?

So the story should be all over, right?

Officer Darren Wilson has resigned from the Ferguson Police Department, the latter, tax-payer supported organization now committed to recruiting exclusively black people to replace white people as officers of the (Eric "My People" Holder approved) law.

Wilson, the six-year law enforcement officer, wrote this letter to define his reasons for resigning:

> In a telephone interview Saturday evening, Wilson said he resigned after the police department told him it had received threats that violence would ensue if he remained an

employee.

"I'm resigning of my own free will," he said. "I'm not willing to let someone else get hurt because of me."

Wilson's resignation letter reads, in part:

"I have been told that my continued employment may put the residents and police officers of the City of Ferguson at risk, which is a circumstance that I cannot allow.

For obvious reasons, I wanted to wait until the grand jury made their decision before I officially made my decision to resign. It was my hope to continue in police work, but the safety of other police officers and the community are of paramount importance to me. It is my hope that my resignation will allow the community to heal."[408]

Honor and a duty to protect his fellow officers (almost all white people) from racial reprisals... the more we learn about Officer Wilson the more we understand why his fellow officers wore - to the chagrin of the Department of Justice - "I Am Darren Wilson" bracelets.

Well, now we learn something else:

Darren Wilson has lived in the shadows for nearly four months, changing residence from house to house, spending spare time in dark movie theaters, in hopes he won't be spotted.

But he has not sneaked around alone. He has had protectors.

Fellow officers have been by his side day and night, as deadly threats have driven the former Ferguson police officer into hiding, after he shot unarmed teen Michael Brown in August.

"Fraternal Order of Police members from the surrounding

---

[408] http://www.stltoday.com/news/local/crime-and-courts/darren-wilson-resigns-from-ferguson-police-department/article_a8cfa6e7-408c-520c-b9d2-de2a75e8983d.html

area volunteered and have provided him with security from that time, right up until the present," FOP spokesman Jim Pasco told CNN.

They had to, because Ferguson police were either "unwilling or unable" to protect Wilson, Pasco alleged. It was the department's duty, he said. "That's what the police department's supposed to do."

CNN has reached out for comment on Pasco's claim to the Ferguson police department but has not heard back.

The volunteer officers are guarding Wilson in their off-duty time — without pay, Pasco said.

Sitting duck

Early talk of cyberstalking drove Wilson underground.

He was pushing a lawn mower days after the shooting, when he was told his home address was circulating online. He realized he was a sitting duck.

"He had to leave the grass, literally, half mowed," his lawyer, Neil Bruntrager told CNN. Wilson stuffed belongings into bags, and three hours later, he began a life out of sight.[409]

It should be noted the Ferguson Police Department has been targeted for racial cleansing by Eric "I'm also a black man" Holder, and the Department of Justice has its 'Eye of Sauron' focused directly on the small suburb of St. Louis for any sign of racial profiling or anti-black sentiments.[410]

In the eyes of the state-aligned media organs (CNN, MSNBC, ABC, NBC, CBS, FOX), daring to consider the forensic evidence and non-discredited eye-witness testimony of his lethal encounter with Michael Brown conclusively supports Darren Wilson is tantamount

---

[409] Off-duty cops protect Darren Wilson, as death threats come in, Fox2Now.com, 12-3-14

[410] http://www.businessinsider.com/eric-holder-ferguson-police-should-consider-becoming-more-racially-diverse-2014-8

to the most shocking display of anti-black thought since George Zimmerman stalked Trayvon Martin for execution.

The Ferguson Police Department has all but decided to abandon the hiring of white males (or white women), instead embarking on a holy racial crusade that St. Martin Luther King would deem almost adequate in addressing historical racial inequities.[411]

Almost, because white people are still employed by the Ferguson Police Department.

Why the Oath Keepers have yet to offer to protect Darren Wilson (and his pregnant wife from death threats) goes without question; for if the threats against Officer Wilson's continued employment with the Ferguson Police Department were credible enough for him to resign (to protect the lives of his former colleagues), then the threats that persist against his life *since* he has resigned should warrant protection from the Oath Keepers.

Right?

Though the Oath Keepers are back guarding the war zone that is the business district in Ferguson - whose members "laughed" at the St. Louis County ordinance initially causing them to abandon their voluntary defense of the city - they should be protecting Darren Wilson and looking to secure him future employment within their connected ranks.[412]

After all, some individual demanded they be removed from Ferguson (hint: Eric Holder, the same person who was distressed with Gov. Nixon calling up the National Guard and declaring a state of emergency in Ferguson prior to the grand jury's findings); *Bearing Arms* reports those Oath Keepers trying to stop looting/rioting/arson from the "burn this motherfucker down" inspired rebel army (a racial-influenced rant from Michael Brown's

---

[411] http://www.npr.org/blogs/thetwo-way/2014/11/30/367548761/ferguson-largely-peaceful-after-officers-decision-to-quit

[412] http://www.stltoday.com/news/local/crime-and-courts/oath-keepers-are-back-on-the-rooftops-in-ferguson-despite/article_18757380-b471-5a6f-848c-a4dfe9805ed6.html

step-dad Louis Head) had guns of the government trained on them:

> "We had an alarming incident that happened last night with our team spotting what looked like a fed three-man sniper team moving into a nearby house on higher ground, and then pointing their rifles at our team of American combat veterans, while our team was guarding the buildings against looters."
>
> Rhodes said the team even observed the state highway patrol snipers deploy onto the roof of a nearby fire hall and point rifles at them.
>
> "Our team leader called Unified Command to find out what was going on and then local police responded," he explained.
>
> He said that the local police were unaware of what the federal government were doing and that there was no coordination. "The local police are on our side and expressed gratitude for us being there, but the Feds are trying to run us out."
>
> The federal government is trying to badmouth this organization of ex-police and ex-military, even called them a "domestic terrorist" group.
>
> There has not been independent verification of the presence of federal and state law enforcement officers attempting to intimidate the Oath Keepers, though the obscure fig leaf of a law that the government used to threaten the group shows that someone worked very hard to find a dubious excuse to bring pressure to remove the group of guardians.[413]

Does there need to be an "independent verification" of this claim, when it's known Eric Holder was livid over the deployment of a heavy police presence in Ferguson during the August looting/rioting of the city by blacks, uttering the immortal, "get those damned tanks out of there" regarding the use of wrongly-criticized military vehicles (the lack of these vehicles when Ferguson burned on

---

[413] http://www.nydailynews.com/news/crime/michael-brown-stepdad-eyed-ferguson-riots-report-article-1.2030219

November 24th testament to the obvious necessity of such armaments to deter black looting/rioting/arson/violence)?[414]

We live in incredibly dangerous times, when the Office of the Presidency of the United States of America and the Attorney General of the Department of Justice have publicly sided with Michael Brown and given tacit approval of the rebel army that just burned much of the business district in Ferguson to the ground.

Darren Wilson's life (as well as the life of his wife and unborn child) is still threatened, though he resigned from the Ferguson Police Department that will soon resemble the police force of Port-au-Prince, Haiti (the city will sprinting to look like the ruined capital of that black republic as well); it's time the Oath Keepers volunteer to defend him and his wife from the credible threats against his life.

The story in Ferguson should be over, but it's only just beginning.

December 4, 2014
"To Whatever End..."

"The days have gone down in the west. Behind the hills, into shadow. How did it come to this?"

Not everyone wishes the same fate of Zemir Begic.[415]

Not everyone is willing to submit to the mob:

> A man was arrested during protests Wednesday evening in the Central West End after he drove through the crowd and later waved a gun at protesters.

---

[414] http://www.zerohedge.com/news/2014-08-18/ferguson-curfew-cancelled-national-guard-arrives-holder-demands-remove-damn-tanks

[415] http://www.upi.com/Top_News/US/2014/12/01/Bosnian-community-in-St-Louis-outraged-over-fatal-hammer-attack/5831417454845/

The incident happened during a day of demonstrations that brought protesters to several sites in and around St. Louis.

In the incident Wednesday night, a protest leader said four protesters were hit. A police spokeswoman said nobody was seriously hurt.

The incident happened around 8 p.m., after about 75 protesters gathered in Maryland Plaza and were beginning to lay down for a "die-in" in the street.

As they did, a man driving a Town and Country minivan drove through the intersection and accelerated through the crowd. One woman was seen crouching on the hood of the minivan as the van continued forward. She fell off as the vehicle rounded a curve.

Protesters chased and then surrounded the minivan, and the driver waved a black handgun at them. At one point, protesters broke out the van's back window. The van was dented, and police recovered a rock from the back seat. Police took the driver, a 57-year-old man, into custody.

Leah Freeman, police spokeswoman, said it was unclear whether the protesters jumped onto the motorist's vehicle or if the motorist drove toward the protesters in an attempt to get through the crowd.

Police detained the man Wednesday night released him. Police did not identify him. Police are still investigating "due to contradicting statements from the driver and indivuals at the scene."

About 8:30 p.m., the protesters moved on to Chase Park Plaza, where they flooded the lobby, and then briefly shut down the intersection of Lindell Boulevard and Kingshighway. Police stood by. The protesters continued marching through the neighborhood for another hour or so.[416]

---

[416] Motorist hits crowd members, pulls gun at Central West End protest, St. Louis Post-Dispatch, 12-4-14

We are witnessing a revolution born before our eyes, hideously growing into a creature few dare even contemplate to what size it might mature. Those who stand in its way will either suffer the fate of Zemir Begic or be hauled into custody by the police as this 57-year-old white driver did.

John Derbyshire noted the lyrics of one the late Michael Brown's freestyle rap recordings, "Luh Vee K-Loc" (posted onto SoundCloud on August 5, 2014... only four days before his fatal decision to rob a store and assault Officer Darren Wilson) included this prophetic line:

> I'm a count this money While I smoke some laugh[?].Run up all me p*ssy n*ggers Amen jus' 40 cal.I can torch 'em bad. Eh chewa honey bounce, baby, there's a Glock in your face. And you betta not make a sound.I only like white men on my money down[?]I ain't racist really But, n*gger, I'm down with black and brown. Those who are last shall be first, Whites on the bottom now![417]

Look at those last few lines from the SoundCloud recording of Big'Mike "Luh Vee K-Loc": "But, n*gger, I'm down with black and brown. Those who are last shall be first, Whites on the bottom now!"

Inevitably, the wrong motorist will be stopped, his or her car surrounded by those protesting for 'Justice for Michael Brown' or 'Justice for Eric Garner' (or 'Justice for [insert overweight dead black name here]'), and the situation will end in a scenario the media and the Obama Administration have been working overtime to create: more martyrs for the cause of racial justice to triumph and a white, gun-owning suspect to crucify for daring to use lethal force from becoming the next Zemir Begic.

'To whatever end" indeed.

---

[417] http://www.vdare.com/posts/radio-derb-is-on-the-air-michael-brown-rap-singer-whites-on-the-bottom-now-etc

December 5, 2014
#WhiteLivesMatter – Remembering Megan Boken

Never, ever forget the callous words of St. Louis Police spokesman (woman for those gender-supremacists) Schron Jackson, when she described the rationale behind Zemir Begic's murder. The *St. Louis Post-Dispatch* reported her describing the circumstances surrounding his lynching, by four black youth armed with hammers, thusly:

> "We think it was wrong place, wrong time," police spokeswoman Schron Jackson said.[418]

How many... how many other homicides of white children, grandchildren, brothers, sisters, mothers, aunts, fathers, uncles, grandmothers, and grandfathers have been described in a similar manner by a police spokesman when the suspect in the murder happened to share the same racial background of the killers of Begic?

"...*wrong place, wrong time.*"

That any person reading this could have a family member or friend whose final moments on this earth are described in a similar manner by a police spokesperson (quickly printed by the local newspaper and buried forever before further examination) is sorry reminder that life as a white person in 2014 Black-Run America - BRA - is the, "...*wrong place, wrong time.*"

Which brings us to remember another white St. Louis resident who found herself in a situation not unlike the one Begic unwittingly encountered: the 2012 murder of Megan Boken.

---

[418] http://www.stltoday.com/news/local/crime-and-courts/mayor-police-say-race-played-no-role-in-hammer-slaying/article_e2254f3d-6ea6-5265-973c-e0eccd4ece61.html

At the time a recent St. Louis University graduate, Boken would be murdered by two black males in broad day light (at roughly 2 p.m.) for no other reason than her killer just wanted to rob her.[419]

Jonathan Esters and Keith Perkins (who strike an uncanny resemblance to the hypothetical son President Barack Obama never had...) were those two black males.[420]

In attempting to steal her phone in a brazen, daylight robbery, they stole her life (the *Daily Mail* described it as a "robbery gone wrong").[421]

Her final moments on earth went from engaging in a casual conversation with her on a cell phone to fighting for her life in what would be remembered as... a "robbery gone wrong":

> Dave Marzullo, a police spokesman, said earlier that there was no evidence Boken knew her assailant.
>
> "We don't know whether the suspect was in the vehicle and got out and shot her or if he opened the door and shot her. There are conflicting statements," Marzullo said. But "we are investigating this as an attempted robbery."
>
> Boken, who graduated from Saint Louis University last year, was shot roughly two miles from where she was to play that afternoon in an alumni game on the university's campus.
>
> Boken was talking to her mother when "the phone went static" about the time of the gunfire, her former coach, Anne Kordes, told the Chicago Tribune. Friends grew nervous after

---

[419] http://www.stltoday.com/news/local/crime-and-courts/from-aug-former-slu-volleyball-player-shot-and-killed-in/article_a3193e9e-e999-11e1-a39e-001a4bcf6878.html

[420] http://www.stltoday.com/news/local/crime-and-courts/second-man-pleads-guilty-in-central-west-end-killing-of/article_1d88a316-60f4-5988-adf1-84003b18a202.html

[421] http://www.dailymail.co.uk/news/article-2192843/Megan-Boken-2-suspects-arrested-Saint-Louise-University-volleyball-stars-murder.html

> Boken failed to appear for the game and they learned from her mother that "something weird happened" during their phone conversation, Kordes said.
>
> "I think everybody was in a frantic mode wondering where she was. Parents were out combing the neighborhoods," she said.[422]

"...wrong place, wrong time."

"...robbery gone wrong."

Back when this story first broke, the current mayor of St. Louis, Francis Slay (who was so quick to declare no racial angle to the hammer execution of Zemir Begic by four blacks), said this of Boken's murder:

> "Nothing irritates me more, nothing worries me more when I go to sleep at night and when I wake up every morning than to think about these thugs that are out there, trying to victimize innocent people in our city," St. Louis Mayor Francis Slay said.

Just who are those thugs terrorizing St. Louis? Each year, the City of St. Louis Metropolitan Police Department releases an Annual Report to the Community. This report breaks down violent crime and the overall percentage of the racial group arrested for each offense. For our purposes, we'll look at the yearly breakdown of those arrested for aggravated assault, robbery, murder, and forcible rape (the data goes from 1999 - 2012, omitting 2001 with 2013 yet to be made available to the public).

Remember, out of 318,000 people, St. Louis is 49.2 percent black 43.9 percent white (as of 2010 US Census).

The breakdown is available on p. 20.

Those thugs worrying you at night, Mayor Slay, out there victimizing the city of St. Louis are almost invariably of the same racial

---

[422] Police question person of interest in death of volleyball player Megan Boken, FoxNews.com, 8-23-12

background as the killers of Begic in 2014 and Boken in 2012.

For those protesting police and demanding #BlackLivesMatter, take a good look into data combed from the SMLPD Annual Report to the City to understand why the black community is the only one needing a community relations pipeline with police: without a black community in St. Louis, it's hard to imagine the city needing much of a police force at all.

For then, homicides brushed aside by police spokesman as either the victim being in *"...wrong place, wrong time,"* or a case of a *"...robbery gone wrong,"* would no longer be part of the vernacular.

RIP Megan Boken.

RIP Zemir Begic.

December 8, 2014
The St. Louis Post-Dispatch Disables Reader Comments, Ensuring the One-Way (DOJ-approved) Lecture on White Privilege Can Continue

It has to be a monologue.

A one-way street.

No conversation, just dictating.

Deviation from the goal of ascribing all blame for black dysfunction on "deeply rooted" white racism and white privilege (the latter evil a reason to excuse the black riots/arson/violence in Ferguson) will not be tolerated in polite, Eric Holder-approved discussions.[423]

---

[423] http://time.com/3605606/ferguson-in-defense-of-rioting/

When the Department of Justice wasn't demanding white Ferguson Police Officers remove "I am Darren Wilson" bracelets[424] (creating in the words of DOJ official an "Us vs. Them" mentality), they were busy conducting seminars equating vestiges of white privilege in the less than 27 percent white St. Louis suburb with the declining conditions of the city:

> When Department of Justice officials arrived in Ferguson, Mo., one day after the death of Michael Brown, it wasn't just to conduct an investigation on potential civil-rights violations. In fact, officials from one Justice Department office were conducting meetings with Ferguson residents to educate them on subjects such as "white privilege."
>
> The DOJ's Community Relations Service arrived in Ferguson purportedly to lessen the tension between protesters and city officials. But sources who attended the DOJ's private gatherings with Ferguson residents tell NRO that the Justice Department also sought to educate and question the community about the issues of white privilege and racism. The political nature of the Justice Department's intervention in Ferguson may not be exclusive to its interactions with residents; it also might have affected its ongoing investigations into the Ferguson Police Department and officer Darren Wilson.
>
> As investigators combed through Ferguson, DOJ's Community Relations Service began holding the town-hall meetings, which excluded press and everyone from out of town. Ferguson resident Audrey Watson, 47, attended one of the meetings. She says federal officials organized the attendees into small groups and asked questions such as "What stereotypes exist in our community?" "How does white privilege impact race relations in our community?" and "Is there a need for personal commitment to race relations?"
>
> Hundreds of people attended the fall meetings, including

---

[424] http://www.stltoday.com/news/local/crime-and-courts/doj-asks-ferguson-chief-to-stop-police-from-wearing-i/article_a2cfe060-6252-5fa6-8639-6715f643c8f4.html

Ferguson mayor James Knowles III, who says many people at the initial meetings were angry and screaming. Knowles says the Community Relations Service officials told him they had previously responded to Trayvon Martin's death in Sanford, Fla., and that they were there to help. During the meetings, he says, the DOJ officials talked about underlying racism that people may not perceive, and the issue of white privilege.

"I mean, I think it was really just trying to get people to understand what that [white privilege] means, because the average white person wakes up and says, if you're just a middle-class white person, you say, What privilege do I have?"

Knowles says. "But until you really understand the systemic issues and maybe some of those not-visible things that exist in society, which affect African Americans or other persons of color, you may not really understand what that is."[425]

Systemic issues?

The virus of 'white privilege' has invaded the minds of so many white people, willing to believe any excuse for the collective depravity of black individuals that completely dismantles all social conditions required to be deemed a 'community', except the most obvious: genetic differences.

The Lessons of Ferguson, as the *St. Louis Post-Dispatch* would have you believe, are the inevitable rise of the voiceless to the terrible, terrible legacy of slavery, opposition to poor performing black schools, lack of economic activity in majority black municipalities, and a lack of racially-proportional democratic representation.[426]

Never mind the obvious reason majority black schools are academic wastelands (because of the individual black students collectively

---

[425] The Department of Social Justice: Federal officials lectured Ferguson residents about "white privilege.", National Review, 12-8-14

[426] http://www.stltoday.com/gallery/news/opinion/columns/kevin-horrigan/horrigan-lessons-from-ferguson/collection_bd76d75c-a210-5dde-b44d-1371a283d47f.html#16

performing poorly on tests designed with white students in mind, dropping out school, and assaulting fellow students and teachers)[427]; never mind the obvious reason businesses close in once-flourishing majority white cities now economically blighted when the population is majority black (because black people lack purchasing power necessary for maintaining a business district and attracting investors outside of check cashing and title loan stores); basically, the insidious residue of white privilege covering contemporary whites - like Bill Murray after encountering Slimer in *Ghostbusters* - is the primary reason the near majority of mortgages in Ferguson were underwater even before Michael Brown challenged Officer Darren Wilson with, "What the fuck are you gonna do?"[428]

And because the continued lecture against 'white privilege' and 'white racism' must be conducted by only those who agree all ills in the black community (sic) have a Klansman as a source to blame, the *St. Louis Post-Dispatch* has taken the cowardly steps to disabling all comments on items published in the opinion section.

After inviting readers to start a conversation on race ("Let's have this conversation. Let's talk about race."[429]), the editorial board at the paper decided the one-way monologuing on a race was a better policy:

> For the next two months, we are turning off the comment function on all editorials, columns and letters in the opinion section.
>
> Why?
>
> Ferguson.
>
> Last Sunday, we challenged our region to have the serious discussion on race that it has been avoiding for decades. Such difficult discussions are made more challenging when, just to

---

[427] http://www.stltoday.com/news/local/education/normandy-high-the-most-dangerous-school-in-the-area/article_49a1b882-cd74-5cc4-8096-fcb1405d8380.html

[428] http://www.vox.com/2014/11/25/7287443/dorian-johnson-story

[429] Editorial: Race. Something to talk about, St. Louis Post-Dispatch, 11-29-14

present a thoughtful point of view, you have to endure vile and racist comments, shouting and personal attacks.

Ever since newspapers started putting stories on the Internet, there has been a vigorous debate within the industry about the effect of reader comments. The Post-Dispatch has made efforts to improve the level of discussion in comment sections, but there are wins and losses.

There are positive moments, such as when readers last week left touching tributes in comments about sports columnist Bryan Burwell after he lost his battle with cancer. But there are other instances where comments deteriorate into racist remarks or demeaning discussion that has nothing to do with the original story or editorial or column.

Recently, the news service Reuters decided to get rid of comments on its stories. The online startup Vox doesn't allow commenting.

We intend to use our opinion pages to help the St. Louis region have a meaningful discussion about race. So we are going to turn off the comments in the editorial section for a while, and see what we learn from it. (Comment will continue on news articles). Comments might return to the opinion pages. Or we might find that without them, the discussion — through letters, social media conversations and online chats, rises to a higher level.

That's the goal.

Also, starting this week, we plan a weekly live chat to discuss the various issues surrounding Ferguson. Details will be posted on our website and social media platforms.

To be clear: It's not that we don't want to hear from those who disagree with us.

Quite the contrary. Every day we publish letters from people criticizing our editorials, and we engage in discussions on Twitter and Facebook about the things we write. We believe those venues offer a safer, more civil place to talk about the racial injustice that dominates the Ferguson discussion.

Let's give civility a try.[430]

Civility?

You mean sticking with a narrative that inevitably led to black people burning down the business district of Ferguson and attacking a white man and killing him with repeated hammer blows.[431]

Every failure of the black community is racially motivated on the part of whites hoping to forever oppress a people whose primary contribution to life in St. Louis is the need for more police to patrol their crime-infested streets and neighborhoods... right, *St. Louis Times-Dispatch*?

Everything involving black people in St. Louis is racially motivated until it isn't, as in the time the *St. Louis Times-Dispatch* labeled the uniquely black Knockout Game just part of 'the spirit of the times':

> It's hard to judge how bad a problem the so-called "knockout game" really is. But because it has resulted in the death of 72-year-old man, left at least a half a dozen other people injured and reinforced fears about the safety of city neighborhoods, it's bad enough.
>
> Roving bands of teenagers slugging people just for the hell of it? That takes us into "A Clockwork Orange" territory.
>
> It has reached the point that it has triggered an all-out response by the St. Louis Police Department. Top investigators and a special police squad have been assigned. A prosecutor has been designated to focus on the cases.
>
> Reporter Denise Hollinshed of the *Post-Dispatch* talked to some kids outside of Roosevelt High School, one of whom

---

[430] Editorial: No comments. An experiment in elevating the conversation, 12-8-14

[431] http://www.stltoday.com/news/local/crime-and-courts/fatal-hammer-attack-on-bosnian-immigrant-not-racially-motivated-st/article_9f15bf49-c8b7-5bc3-8671-ac291f666084.html

acknowledged that he'd taken part in the "knockout king" game.

"Knockout king is a thrill," the kid told her. "It makes you want to keep doing it every day."

Sure, the kid said, he knew he could hurt somebody. But he added, "You don't know them, so why care about hurting them?"

That's a chilling statement. It reflects an almost sociopathic lack of empathy. On the other hand, the more you think about it, it perfectly captures today's zeitgeist, the spirit of the times.[432]

No, the 'spirit of the times' is the continued one-way conversation by those managers of the system of racial governance/bureaucracy known as Black-Run America (BRA), dedicated to the promulgation of only goal: *The proposition that all white people are endowed with white privilege by their ancestors, ultimately only capable of being removed by a stealthy course of action; nothing more than genocide.*

The goals of the revolution in San Domingo (Haiti) are being played out in America under the guise of whites atoning for the sins of their ancestors daring to create a country that every non-white in the world actively tries to immigrate to; the world those actively demanding white people acquiesce to by checking their privilege looks an awful lot like East St. Louis and Camden.

Never forget the goal of pushing 'white privilege' as a new paradigm in governing white relations with non-whites (past, present, and future relations, mind you) is to create a morality where the continued erosion of white political power is not only ensured, but the gradual disappearance of whites is all but assured.

---

[432] http://www.stltoday.com/news/opinion/columns/the-platform/editorial-the-knockout-game-and-the-spirit-of-the-times/article_6ead38ce-6e93-5a70-8ced-a970686038f6.html

December 10, 2014
Every White Cop in America Must Ask Themselves "Do I want to become Darren Wilson" when they Encounter Black Males

Buried in what would seem an innocuous story is an important point reinforcing the reality of police as guardians of the state:

> St. Louis County Police Chief Jon Belmar is concerned "a rift" could be created if police officers are automatically branded as racist by critics.
>
> Speaking to Fox News on Wednesday following a grand jury's decision not to indict a New York City officer in Eric Garner's death, Belmar said the mantra that police are bad is counterproductive.
>
> "I think it is because it's going to cause a rift at some point that may be very, very difficult for us to come back to. We are the 24-7 face of government here in law enforcement. We're looking to solve problems. We're looking to make sure that people understand we can't arrest our way out of a problem," Belmar said.[433]

"The 24/7 face of government."

An important, but correct point.

Until recently, Officer Darren Wilson was one of these representatives of the government in Ferguson. In late August, a total of nine (yes, nine) *Washington Post* reporters[434] were assigned the story of trying to uncover some dirt on Wilson to establish a background anecdote magically proving he had some reason racial

---

[433] Police Chief: Branding Officers as Racist is 'Going to Cause Rift at Some Point', CBS St. Louis, 12-4-14

[434] http://www.washingtonpost.com/national/darren-wilsons-first-job-was-on-a-troubled-police-force-disbanded-by-authorities/2014/08/23/1ac796f0-2a45-11e4-8593-da634b334390_story.html

reason to shoot Michael Brown... granting the Department of Justice the ability to charge Wilson with violating Brown's civil rights.[435]

Those nine reporters uncovered nothing in Wilson's past, save him being a solid police officer.

But nothing in Wilson's past matters now, save what transpired on August 9, 2014, for this incident will forever cloud his future courtesy of a racial lynch mob exhibiting a ferocity for revenge even Javert would find overwhelming.

Those revolutionary members of the 'Justice for Michael Brown' movement consider all police officers as complicit in his death [guilty-by-association] and Darren Wilson is just the extremely white-face representing the state's monopoly on violence.

And in the words of one press release released by a group of black lawyers attempting to revoke his police officer license, a face that looks like "a demon":

> The National Bar Association, led by an attorney for Michael Brown's family, says it filed a "lawsuit" with the Missouri Department of Public Safety demanding the revocation of Darren Wilson's police officer license.
>
> The department acknowledged receiving a document but said it is being treated as a complaint because the agency is not a venue for a suit. Spokesman Mike O'Connell said he could not reveal specifics from the document.
>
> Wilson, a white Ferguson police officer, fatally shot Brown, an unarmed black teen, on Aug. 9, triggering nationwide protests. Wilson resigned from the force Nov. 29, five days after a St. Louis County grand jury decided not to indict him in Brown's death.
>
> Neil Bruntrager, an attorney for Wilson, said that his being a police officer "is off the table forever" but that, "Keeping his license in good standing is a matter of pride." Bruntrager

---

[435] http://www.washingtonpost.com/world/national-security/federal-civil-rights-charges-unlikely-against-police-officer-in-ferguson-shooting/2014/10/31/56189d80-6055-11e4-8b9e-2ccdac31a031_story.html

added, "He didn't resign under any criminal charges and he didn't do anything wrong."

The association, which says it represents African-American lawyers and judges, is headed by Benjamin Crump, who represents Brown's family.

It press release said it filed the document "on the grounds that he committed a criminal act ..."

The release says Wilson's comment in a TV interview that Brown had "looked like a demon" led the association to "challenge his suitability to ever wear a badge and carry a gun ever again."[436]

Every white police officer in America is only a "one or two minute encounter with an unstable black male" away from sharing the fate of Darren Wilson, truly illustrating the utter instability of Black-Run America (BRA).

And what is his fate? *New York Times* reporters Julie Bosman and Campbell Robertson, though aware of the death threats to Wilson's life, published the street he lives on (sharing the house with his new, pregnant bride).[437]

Though being a police officer was "the job of his life," Wilson now enjoys the type of life ofeternally hounded George Zimmerman:

> Ferguson police officer Darren Wilson is married, expecting a baby and contemplating his future now that a grand jury has decided not to indict him in the shooting death of unarmed black youth Michael Brown.
>
> Since the shooting, Wilson has been in hiding. He described a solitary life with a small circle of people, much like the life described by George Zimmerman after he was acquitted of

---

[436] African-American lawyers group seeks to have Darren Wilson's police officer license revoked, St. Louis Post-Dispatch, 12-10-14

[437] http://dailycaller.com/2014/11/28/new-york-times-defends-its-decision-to-publish-name-of-darren-wilsons-home-street/

killing unarmed black teen Trayvon Martin in Florida.

"You have to take precautions, where you sit in a restaurant and where you drive," he said. "You have to make sure no one is following you."

If he goes out, he said, he has to be on guard for who is looking at him or looking too long.

Wilson said his conscience is clear. He said he would do everything the same if faced with Brown again.

"I did my job that day," he said.[438]

Darren Wilson did do his job on August 9, 2014; but because he did his job, he's now out of a job. With angry, racial-influenced mobs burning down buildings and beating people with hammers all in the name of exacting justice for the individual Darren Wilson briefly encountered in his final moments as an active-duty officer for the Ferguson Police Department.

The truly scary thought for every white police officer in America is when they pull up on a group of black males, with one or two matching the description of a recent robbery/assault/murder suspect and if their training will take over or will the legacy of Darren Wilson sneak into their mind?

Will this white police officer just keep on driving, allowing a potential black suspect to freely go on his/her way in committing another (perhaps more lethal) crime? Or will this white police officer approach the potential black male suspect and "in one or two fateful minutes" become the next officer having death threats Tweeted his way and *New York Times* reporters publishing his address?

The "rift" St. Louis County Police Chief Jon Belmar warned about goes far, far deeper than most people dare imagine.

And because of the intensity of black criminality,[439] coupled

---

[438] http://www.usatoday.com/story/news/nation/2014/11/26/darren-wilson-abc-interview/19522717/

[439] http://www.stltoday.com/news/local/crime-and-courts/article_937f845f-0802-5c0a-84b1-393598b43281.html#.VIi91WycynU.twitter

with unaccountable nature society holds black parents with maintaining some semblance of discipline over their children, the odds are extremely high another white police officer shoots innocent black youth incident will occur soon in either the city of St. Louis or metropolitan St. Louis.[440]

December 12, 2014
Ferguson is a reminder the American Dream is over; the American Nightmare is just beginning.

National Review published a profile of the last white mayor of Ferguson, current Mayor James Knowles III. In the piece, it ends with his eternal optimism that commerce will come back to the 67 percent black city of Ferguson, they'll be profitable (and produce tax revenue to support public services), and his belief homeowners will have peace in the city:

> "A lot of people talk about the new normal, and I'm not sure we know exactly what that is yet," he says. "But one thing that I'm confident of is that commerce will return and businesses will get back to a point where they're having regular customers and being profitable, and that homeowners will be able to have peace in their neighborhoods."[441]

Oh, there was a time when Ferguson had plenty of commerce, with businesses enjoying regular customers and growing profits, and homeowners enjoyed peace and stability: but this was when Ferguson was 99 percent white (1970); or 86 percent white (1980); or 78 percent white (1990). The existing housing stock is described by the *St. Louis Post-Dispatch* as, "a picture of pleasant suburbia, with

---

[440] http://www.ksdk.com/story/news/local/2014/12/09/stl-police-holding-parents-accountable/20161613/

[441] Meet the Mayor of Ferguson: What do you do as your town is being destroyed by violent rioters?, 12-12-14

trees lining streets in front of tract houses built during the 1950s and 1960s."[442]

But those who built the infrastructure of Ferguson and laid the foundation for a community flourish are scarcely represented among the demographic holding the majority today: The city is 27 percent white today, and the necessary ingredient for creating a stable, peaceful, prosperous community is in rapid decline, while a surplus of the people who helped chase away this former racial majority in Ferguson is only growing in demographic maturity.

It's fitting to note Ferguson was a "sundown town"[443] until the mid-1960s (when the city was 100 percent white), meaning black people were banned from the city after dark; if you watched how those black people behaved in the business district over Ferguson on November 24, 2014after dark, you'd see the wisdom of the city's forefathers making a posthumous point.[444]

But Ferguson is no longer a "sundown town," nor is it a city bursting at the seams with economic prospects (the latter a lesson in the necessity of the former). Only a few months in to 2014, the *St. Louis Post-Dispatch* noted 49 percent of the mortgages in Ferguson were "underwater" (negative equity), with 38 percent of homes below market peak.[445]

Once, the sky was limit for the prospects of a family in Ferguson; but that was when the city was nearly all-white or close to 80 percent white (from 1970 - 1990).

Now, no gutter is dirty or slimy enough for the depths for which a soon-to-be 100 percent black city will fall.

---

[442] http://www.stltoday.com/business/local/in-ferguson-optimism-about-the-city-s-revival-turns-to/article_3729e091-4a27-5ffe-b905-345f1c596bc4.html

[443] http://www.epi.org/publication/making-ferguson/#how-ferguson-became-ferguson

[444]http://www.usatoday.com/story/news/nation/2014/11/24/ferguson-grand-jury-deliberations/19474907/

[445] http://www.stltoday.com/business/local/st-louis-is-hot-spot-for-underwater-mortgages/article_1a9b46b5-38f4-5b93-b4b4-e895f8e0bab5.html

The prospects for the future of Ferguson the last white mayor touts, clinging to a delusion race-neutral theory for why the city collapsed with a ferocity tighter than Linus from *The Peanuts* does as he awaits The Great Pumpkin to arrive, Knowles would be wise to consider a few bleak statistics demonstrating the African-esque future for the once all-white suburb of St. Louis:

> Median family income was $44,000 in 2012, compared with $75,000 in St. Louis County as a whole and $59,000 for the state of Missouri. The town had a poverty rate of 20 percent, according to the census, compared to 7.8 percent for the county as a whole and 10.7 percent in Missouri.[446]

And, of course, the federal government in its infinite wisdom has seen fit to redistribute the black undertow from the city of St. Louis to Ferguson via Section 8 Vouchers:

> In Ferguson, 461 families are receiving federal subsidies, about 8 percent of the Section 8 vouchers issued by the Housing Authority of St. Louis County.[447]

With the influx of Section 8 Voucher holders (almost all black), the police have found themselves busy:

> In recent years, half of all police calls in Ferguson came from a cluster of complexes that include Park Ridge, Northwinds, Oakmont Townhomes, Versailles Apartments and Canfield Green, where Michael Brown was fatally shot by police in August.[448]

Ferguson has enjoyed a "higher underwater and foreclosure rates than the rest of the St. Louis metropolitan area for years," according

---

[446] http://www.stltoday.com/business/local/in-ferguson-optimism-about-the-city-s-revival-turns-to/article_3729e091-4a27-5ffe-b905-345f1c596bc4.html

[447] http://www.diversityinc.com/news/ferguson-housing-town-landlords-thriving/

[448] http://www.stltoday.com/news/local/crime-and-courts/state-treasurer-asks-for-review-of-subsidized-low-income-housing/article_eccb575e-cab2-540a-82ea-fd2c5bfe7565.html

Realtytrac Vice President Daren Blomquist, though the racial angle to this decline is politely never, ever brought up.[449]

And because of Ferguson's current demographic liabilities (a surplus of unproductive blacks and a dwindling number of tax-producing whites), the city must resort the same type of revenue-producing activity many attribute to the lack of trust between police and the nearly 70 percent black population:

> Ferguson, Missouri, which is recovering from riots following the August shooting death of an unarmed black teenager by a white policeman, plans to close a budget gap by boosting revenue from public-safety fines and tapping reserves.
>
> The strategy by the St. Louis suburb, which suffered a second round of violent protests last month after a grand jury refused to indict the police officer, may risk worsening community relations with increased citations and weakening its credit standing by reducing a rainy-day fund.
>
> To close a projected deficit for fiscal 2014, which ended June 30, the municipality will deplete a $10 million capital-projects reserve, Jeffrey Blume, Ferguson's finance director, said in a telephone interview. For the current year, the city is budgeting for higher receipts from police-issued tickets.
>
> "There are a number of things going on in 2014 and one is a revenue shortfall that we anticipate making up in 2015," Blume said. "There's about a million-dollar increase in public-safety fines to make up the difference."
>
> Revenue from violations, which already represents the city's second-largest source of cash after sales taxes, will rise to 15.7 percent of receipts in fiscal 2015, from a projected 11.8 percent this year, he said. In 2013, fines brought in $2.2 million, or 11.8 percent of the city's $18.62 million in annual revenue, according to budget documents.[450]

---

[449] http://stlouis.cbslocal.com/2014/12/11/foreclosure-filings-drop-in-st-louis-area-but-ferguson-remains-underwater/

[450] Ferguson to Increase Police Ticketing to Close City's Budget Gap, Bloomberg, 12-12-14

How many once prosperous suburbs of cities like Atlanta, Birmingham, Milwaukee, Detroit, Memphis, Chicago, Indianapolis, Charlotte, Baltimore, Cleveland, Cincinnati, Philadelphia, Washington D.C., Richmond, Kansas City (Missouri), Nashville, and Minneapolis find themselves in the precarious demographic situation of being the next Ferguson?

Ferguson is a reminder the American Dream is over; the American Nightmare is just beginning.

The wisdom of a people who declared Ferguson a one-time "sundown town" was supplanted by a suicidal devotion to the concept of racial equality. But each passing year, as the federal government (and state governments) becomes more explicitly anti-white, brings us more and more evidence disparities between the races have a biological source; and with each passing year, the wisdom of those men who once declared a city such as Ferguson a "sundown town" becomes hauntingly obvious.

December 15, 2014
The Tribe Has Spoken...

If this story doesn't put a smile on your face, then moments of elation are impossible for you:

> Activists connected to the Leadership Coalition for Justice (formerly called the Justice for Mike Brown Leadership Coalition) and the African People's Socialist Party announced Friday that they are convening a symbolic grand jury in January to decide for themselves whether former Ferguson police officer Darren Wilson should be charged with a crime for killing Michael Brown.
>
> The group organizing the symbolic grand jury is called the International People's Democratic Uhuru Movement, a group that seeks to liberate and empower people of African descent around the world.

"In the face of the inability of the justice system to work for our people and our community, in the face of the grand jury's inability to see what the whole world has been able to see about the murder of Mike Brown on August 9th ... clearly it is time for African people to begin to take matters in our own hands," said African People's Socialist Party leader Omali Yeshitela. "In that regard I'm here to announce that on January 3rd and 4th black people will have our own grand jury."

According to Yeshitela, the grand jury will be selected based on their reputations as upstanding members of the community and will make their decision following existing laws after being presented with the same evidence and testimony given to the official grand jury.

But, said Yeshitela, the "Black People's Grand Jury" will be open to the public and will look at the death of Brown in context of "the history of black people in this county, in this country, and see whether or not it is likely that Darren Wilson or any instrument of state power in this country would murder an 18-year-old unarmed teenager."

When asked about the goal of this grand jury, given that it will have no power to arrest or discipline Wilson, Yeshitela said that highlighting that lack of power was the whole point.

Yeshitela was joined Friday by Kennethia Miller and two other St. Louis women affiliated with Yeshitela's Uhuru Movement, which seeks (among other things) to put black people in charge of the hiring of police in communities where mostly black people live.

"We think it's extremely urgent that we hold the black people's grand jury and build a campaign for black community control of the police," Miller said. "As a mother, I'm outraged and deeply concerned about the ongoing law enforcement-based violence that's taken the lives of our children."[451]

---

[451] African Liberation Group Plans To Convene 'Black People's Grand Jury' Against

St. Louis averages roughly 33 firearms-related incidents each week,[452] with the nearly all of these shootings involving a black suspect. Miller isn't outraged or deeply concerned by these 1,716 firearm-related incidents that occur every year, which are instrumental in driving down property value and convincing the new owners of Budweiser - InBev - to completely divest from the city of St. Louis.

After the hostile takeover of the King of Beers in 2008, InBev cut roughly six percent of Budweiser's workforce,[453] a harbinger of the company moving all of the operations out of St. Louis. Only days ago, InBev announced Budweiser U.S. Sales and Marketing would move to New York City, a much more accessible (and safer) city than St. Louis.[454]

Remember: Just as 83 percent black Detroit has few corporations providing tax-revenue (as well as a minority of property-owners actually paying their property taxes), a Budweiser-less St. Louis will be reliant on a majority black population to provide the taxes to fund the public payroll and bankroll civic improvements...

Not to mention, the promise of pensions for those retired public employees evaporating as the new black majority can no longer sustain a first-world economy once taken for granted of when middle-class whites built and maintained it (the Visible Black Hand of Economics never fails to appear).

With the black population exclusively working to make St. Louis uninhabitable for the law-abiding (and eroding the opportunity for corporate growth - or chances of corporate relocation - in the city), no one should lament the call for a new, all-black grand jury.

Darren Wilson, St. Louis Public Radio, 12-12-14

[452] Outrage after bloody night in St. Louis leaves 18 shot, one stabbed, St. Louis Post Dispatch, 6-11-2013

[453] http://money.cnn.com/2008/12/08/news/companies/anheuser_job_cuts/index.htm?postversion=2008120814

[454] http://www.wsj.com/articles/anheuser-busch-inbev-moving-u-s-sales-marketing-hub-to-new-york-1418166755

Whatever outcome these black boobs deliberate upon, their findings will have no legal bearing on the case; however, no amount of evidence would ever convince them the actions taken by Officer Darren Wilson on August 9, 2014 represented the correct one.

From a purely racialistic (instead of legalistic) line of reasoning, they've already castigated Officer Wilson for the crime of murder their black comrade Michael Brown, damn the evidence! Moments such as this[455] represent a window into the future: a world where the evolution of Anglo-Saxon law (Magna Carta, English Common Law, the Bill or Rights, Habeas Corpus, etc.) devolves to the law of the jungle.

Because the law of the jungle quickly mandates tribes form for protection, so civilization can slowly be introduced to an area where it has all but disappeared:

> A city police officer stationed at City Hall when protesters showed up Friday to protest police brutality drew the attention of demonstrators because the officer wore a "Wilson" name tag on his sleeve in a show of solidarity with former Ferguson Officer Darren Wilson.
>
> Now that officer also has his department's attention.
>
> In an interview Friday, Chief Sam Dotson said the "officer clearly violated our policies and will be disciplined."
>
> "I couldn't be more disappointed," Dotson said. "We spend a lot of time working on professionalism and building a bridge in the community."
>
> Jeff Roorda, business manager for the St. Louis Police Officers' Association, said the officer at issue was transferred Friday from District 3 to District 6, which Roorda said has the highest crime in the city.

---

[455] African-American grand jury to examine evidence in the Michael Brown shooting, Fox2Now, 12-12-14

"For months, the U.S. Department of Justice has been calling violent protests where officers were shot at and had Molotov cocktails thrown at them 'constitutionally protected exercises of freedom of speech, freedom of assembly and freedom of expression,'" Roorda said.

"Now a police officer does nothing more than wear another officer's name on his sleeve, an officer who has been exonerated of any wrongdoing, and is being told that his passive statement is constitutionally prohibited free speech. There is something wrong with this picture."[456]

Oh, there is something incredible wrong with the picture of Ferguson, St. Louis, Missouri, and the United States of America in 2014.

Very, very wrong: That white police officers would still talk about building a bridge to the "community" (black community) and not completely abandon the task of trying to bring law and order to a people more inclined to practice the art of "no snitching" in protecting their criminals.

Never, ever stand in the way of those making hilarious demands for racially-exclusive courts, for it's only a positive step in the direction of racial separation.

December 16, 2014
If It Turns Out a Member of the Flood Christian Church Set it on Fire, Will Pastor Carlton Lee Apologize for Slandering "White supremacists?"

The property at 7413 W. Florissant Avenue, Saint Louis, MO 63136 doesn't look like much; or, it didn't look like much.

---

[456] St. Louis police say they'll discipline officer who wore 'Wilson' name tag at City Hall protest, St. Louis Post-Dispatch, 12-13-14

Built in 1946, this 2,670 square foot building was - only recently- the home of Flood Christian Church.

"Birthed" on Easter Sunday 2013, the Flood Christian Church is led by Pastor Carlton Lee and Lady Chanel Lee.

He told the *Washington Post* he poured his life-savings into buying the property for $160,000, but RealtyTrac shows the property was purchased in June of this year for $37,500 (with the average purchase property near 7413 W. Florissant Avenue $42,147).[457]

Regardless of the actual cost Pastor Lee paid for the property, the building burned on November 24.

You remember November 24? After months and months of black leaders - like the good Reverend Lee, who constantly was filmed or quoted by St. Louis media calling for "justice" - rallying the black community into a frenzy over the perceived execution of Michael Brown by Officer Darren Wilson, the
Negro Kristallnacht commenced.[458]

One of the buildings burned on November 24 was 7413 W. Florissant Avenue.

The home of Flood Christian Church, which has been named the church Michael Brown, Sr. "attended," though this designation is largely one of necessity...[459]

Fittingly, a mainstream media always on the ready to paint the Christianity of whites as a foolish, antiquated, intolerant faith has no problem publishing eloquent accounts about the Brown family

---

[457] http://www.renter.realtytrac.com/property/mo/saint-louis/63136/7413-w-florissant-ave/200733351

[458] http://www.stltoday.com/news/local/article_6a0138db-a055-5ea0-9ad6-484fbf0f20b9.html

[459] http://www.washingtonpost.com/national/the-brown-familys-pastor-tries-to-make-sense-of-fire-that-gutted-his-church/2014/11/28/15520f3e-7711-11e4-a755-e32227229e7b_story.html

church that was engulfed in flames on Nov. 24 (a night of rioting/looting/and arson the media and black leaders are entirely responsible for unleashing).

As we all know, Reverend Lee immediately absolved members of his flock or his black brethren in Ferguson for the guilt in his "church" burning. He pointed the finger of blame at 'white supremacists':

> White supremacists have destroyed the church attended by the father of slain Ferguson teenager Michael Brown, according to its pastor.
>
> The Flood Christian Church was burned to the ground on Monday. Its pastor Rev Carlton Lee told NBC news he did not believe that the destruction was part of the wider destruction after the grand jury's clearance of police officer Darren Wilson, who shot Brown. He said the church was targeted by people angry because of his support for the Brown family and his repeated calls for Wilson to be arrested after the shooting.
>
> "The police called me and told me the church was on fire," Lee said. "I was in complete disbelief. I didn't think anyone would set a church on fire.
>
> "I feel like one of my children has died. I put my blood, my sweat, my tears into this church, getting this church built from the ground up. To see that it was taken down in a few minutes is really heartbreaking."
>
> He had baptised Michael Brown Senior, his wife Cal and their children only the day before. Lee told ABC news: "Sunday, we do the baptism, Monday, the church is on fire. It just doesn't add up." Brown was "devastated again" by the news of the fire, he said.[460]

Those aren't flames you're smelling; it's the putrid stench of 100% bull $hi&.

---

[460] Ferguson church burning is white supremacist revenge attack, says pastor, Christian Today, 11-26-14

How can you anyone call the Flood Christian Church the "Brown family church" when he the father of the deceased Brown, Jr. *was only baptized the day before the church burned*?

The Bureau of Alcohol, Tobacco, Firearms and Explosives is investigating the fire, with $10,000 reward offered to anyone who will dare "snitch" out their fellow black person for starting the fire. Sorry, it's a "white supremacist" that *really* started the fire...[461]

With Pastor Lee playing the "white people burned my church down" card, admiring Social Justice Warrior's (SJW) in the media have helped ensure The Flood's GoFundMe page is overflowing with cash -- $88,000+ and counting.[462]

As long as white liberals think it's *1963 Birmingham Somewhere* or *Mississippi is still burning*, their checkbooks will be busy (and $88,000 from a GoFundMe page is a much better haul than the usual amount of offerings the 75 or so black people who attend the church on Sunday tithe the church...).

What's interesting is the church is located three miles away from the business district in Ferguson where the Negro Kristallnacht happened on November 24, the intensity of the protests/looting/rioting/and arson by blacks a testament to Pastor Lee's passionate belief in the injustice of the justice system (which he preached about and mugged for the cameras - while offering spiritual guidance to the Brown family - constantly since August 9).

Let's be completely honest about 'who' set fire to the property at 7413 W. Florissant Avenue: it wasn't white supremacists as Pastor Lee would have you believe, but in all likelihood a member of the Flood Christian Church.

---

[461] http://www.stltoday.com/lifestyles/faith-and-values/federal-officials-investigating-fire-at-church-connected-to-michael-brown/article_e4b41d11-a02d-5956-b396-b67b36302410.html

[462] http://www.washingtonpost.com/news/post-nation/wp/2014/11/30/brown-family-pastor-delivers-sermon-days-after-church-was-gutted/

December 18, 2014
The Food Desertization of Ferguson Well Underway: Big Lots Closing Up Shop in 67% Black City

In five years time, the small town of Ferguson will hardly be mentioned at all.

Instead, scores of other *once prosperous/now economically declining* cities (once meaning "all white," with now meaning, "boasting aging white, growing black population") will have usurped the energy of those demanding "Justice for Mike Brown" or hilariously asserting #BlackLivesMatter.

Never mind the cheapness of black life in a city such as Milwaukee or New Orleans (the latter city launching the "NOLA For Life" campaign to convince black people to stop killing other black people).

Or Birmingham, Nashville, Newark, Chicago, Camden, Baltimore, Rochester (New York), Philadelphia, or Minneapolis, where black life only matters when it is extinguished by a white cop or white property owner daring to defend their family or business.

But in five years time, when the 2020 U.S Census is being compiled and the city of Ferguson (100 percent white in 1970; 86 percent white in 1980; 77 percent white in 1990) registers an 85 percent black population - complete with an all-black city council, black mayor, black police chief, and woefully underfunded majority black police force - the victory over the perceived white supremacy Officer Darren Wilson embodied will be complete.

The consequences of this racial victory will be the creation of just another food desert, where liquor, title pawn and check cashing stores provide the bulk of the tax-producing economic activity in the city; but the political victory of establishing a city of the blacks, for the blacks, and by the blacks will be complete.

One can even envision a statue erected to the memory of Michael Brown in a prominent location of the city, commemorating his death as the moment racial vengeance could be exacted and political control of Ferguson in black hands could be established.

But for every action, there is an equal and opposite reaction.

Just as property values in Ferguson were declining as the black population increased, so to did a few keen observers note the long-term economic ramifications of the black insurrection on commerce.[463]

At the time of Brown's death on August 9, 2014, Ferguson was 67 percent black; with demography being destiny, the city's fate was already sealed, but the lack of black political control had yet to catch up to the white abandonment of the city.

And as the unrest grew in the hot summer of 2014, one business decided to pull up stakes. K-Mart, an embattled big box store (that might not even have one store opened in 2020 America), closed its Ferguson location: the long-term health of the store, built in a city to service a population that had long since abandoned Ferguson, wasn't looking to be in the financial black.

The economic conditions individual white people collectively create form something outside investors realize is the perfect reason for building a store or restaurant in this community: social capital.

Social capital can be defined simply as children and teenagers walking on the sidewalk instead of monopolizing the middle of the road and deliberately disobeying the law (Michael Brown would still be alive had he simply walked on the side of the road after stealing the Swisher Sweet cigars).

But the latter scenario is what birthed the "Justice for Mike Brown" movement, a clear reminder the health and vitality of a city is completely reflected in its demographic makeup.

And this demographic makeup of Ferguson (and the clear racial

---

[463] Some fear rioting may seal Ferguson fate for decades, USA Today, 11-30-14

dominance blacks will assert in the city) is a reminder of why companies are leaving:

> A major chain is shutting down its store in Ferguson.
>
> Big Lots is the second national chain store that has closed since the death of Mike Brown. Neither Big Lots, nor KMART, who previously announced the closure of its Ferguson store, are linking the shut down to the area unrest but some small businesses are feeling the pinch.
>
> "Once my lease is open I think I will have to move," said Binh Ho.
>
> Ho owns a nail shop near the Big Lots and said her business has been down 50 percent.
>
> Her neighbor, Salon Selective, also shut down.
>
> "I worked at Salon Selective and I lost my job. She closed up after the riots her clients did not want to come over here anymore because of all the things going on," said Carolyn Tidwell.
>
> The Kmart at 270 and West Florissant announced in September it would close. "It's really bad because we don't have anywhere to go as is if these things shut down where are we going to go we have nowhere else to go," said resident Sandy Rason.[464]

In five years, white faces in Ferguson will be as rare as their counterparts in present-day East St. Louis (98 percent black); in this nearly all-black Ferguson, the triumphant black majority will complain to their empowered black city leaders to do something about the city being just another food desert.[465]

After all, the Visible Black Hand of Economics will have driven away

---

[464] Big Lots announces closure of Ferguson store, says unrest not a factor, KMOV St. Louis, 12-17-14

[465] In Ferguson, there are no malls left to boycott, QZ.com, 11-30-14

all major chains from the city, save those immigrant-owned grocery stores interested in working behind plexiglas and subsisting on an EBT/Food Stamp carrying clientele.

Political control of Ferguson will be entirely in black hands, but never forget the concept of black power/empowerment is the ultimate EMP; Detroit is the roadmap for any neighborhood, community, city, municipality, or county that goes from being all-white to all-black.

Ferguson's fate is sealed, with companies that must answer to stockholders already seeing the black writing on the wall; but the truly scary thing about modern America is the vast number of neighborhoods, communities, cities, municipalities, and counties undergoing similar demographic transitions.

The concentration of political power into black hands is, almost invariably, the unleashing of an economic EMP on the city foolish enough to vote their own ruin into office.

For the more we attempt to believe race is a social construct, the civilization whites constructed inevitably collapses when blacks try and maintain it.

Ferguson is not immune to the biological reality of race, reflected in both K-Mart and Big Lots decision to abandon a city where the food desertization process is well underway

December 24, 2014
Through the years we'll always be together. If the fates allow...

In early December, three black males tried to rob Pooh's Corner in St. Louis. The bar in south city was a popular hangout for cops, a fact the three black males who tried to rob Pooh's Corner probably weren't aware of...

The tragedy is 63-year-old Diana Lawrence[466] is dead because of the actions of these three black males; luckily multiple patrons at the bar were armed, ensuring a greater tragedy was avoided:

> The former police officer was standing toward the back of the bar, nursing a can of Natural Light, when the crack of gunfire shattered the vibe.
>
> Three armed men barged into Pooh's Corner about 11 p.m. Dec. 2 and ordered everyone to the floor. At least one fired a shot into the ceiling.
>
> The former police officer at the bar shot his .357 Magnum snubnose at one of the robbers standing nearby, hitting him in the eye. The retired cop said the gunman collapsed, and he kicked a pistol away before emptying his cylinder at the muzzle flashes near the front door.
>
> "Instincts kicked in," said the former city officer, 65, of St. Louis. "All of that so-called training kind of evaporates, so I won't attribute it to training. I just attribute it to survival instincts."
>
> One of the armed robbers escaped the shootout and is still on the loose. The former officer, who served in the St. Louis Police Department for eight years in the 1970s, asked not to be identified because he fears retaliation against him or his family.
>
> It was the second time since 2008 that the ex-cop who tends bar part-time at the Carondelet neighborhood tavern opened fire to fight off would-be robbers. Five people were wounded in the latest gunfight at Pooh's Corner, at 6023 Virginia Avenue, including the ex-cop and two of the robbers. A bar patron, Diana Lawrence, 63, of St. Louis, died the next day from a shot to the back of her head. It is not clear who shot her, but witnesses have said Lawrence was sitting at a table with her back to the robbers when she was shot. Autopsy

---

[466]http://www.ksdk.com/story/news/crime/2014/12/03/multiple-people-shot-at-south-city-bar/19820261/

results are not yet available.

"I lost a dear friend," the former officer said. "I believe those men had murder on their minds."[467]

"The former officer... asked not to be identified because he fears retaliation against him or his family."

This comment is a reminder the black community of St. Louis immediately sides with those who break the law and will strive for retribution against those who dare impede their comrades ability to rob businesses like Pooh's Corner.
Keep this fact in mind when we consider the next "Justice for Michael Brown" mob target; those now agitating for violence against the cops in 82 percent black Berkeley (just another formerly all-white suburb blighted by now majority demographic) have 18-year-old Antonio Martin:

> A Berkeley police officer fired at least three shots at a suspect who pulled a gun on him, the St. Louis County Police chief said at a Wednesday morning news conference.
>
> Police Chief Jon Belmar said the officer was doing a business check at a Mobil on the run station about 11:15 p.m. Tuesday when the shooting happened.
>
> The officer saw two people on the parking lot in the 6800 block of North Hanley Road and began talking with them.
>
> Belmar said one of the people approached the driver's side of the vehicle.One of the individuals "produced a pistol with his arm straight out, pointing it straight at the officer kind of from across the hood," Belmar said.
>
> At that point, the chief said, the officer got his service revolver "and fired what we think is three shots."
>
> The officer, who is 34 and white, is a 6-year veteran of the department, Belmar said. He was placed on investigative leave, which is standard.

---

[467] Ex-St. Louis cop who opened fire on robbers at Pooh's Corner bar says 'instincts kicked in', St. Louis Post-Dispatch, 12-20-14

Belmar said one round struck the suspect, an 18-year-old black male, and one struck a tire of the police car. Police said they did not immediately know where the third round went.

From the videotape released by St. Louis County Police and Belmar's description, the officer was near the front driver's side of the vehicle and the suspect was on the other side, near the car's headlights, when the shooting occurred.

As the officer points his gun, he is backing away and loses his balance, Belmar said. As he fell, he dropped his flashlight and fired off at least three shots.

The suspect was pronounced dead at the scene by EMS units. Berkeley police called the county's crimes against persons unit at 11:45 p.m., and they arrived at the scene at 12:15 a.m., Belmar said.

The body, which was covered and concealed from the crowd by a partition, was removed from the scene at 1:40 a.m., Belmar said.

He also said the 9 mm gun found on the suspect had five rounds in the magazine and one round in the chamber. He also said the gun's serial number had been filed off.

Belmar declined to release his name at the news conference but said he had a criminal record, with charges including three assaults, armed robbery, armed criminal action and multiple uses of weapons since he was 17.

A woman at the scene overnight, Toni Martin, said it was her son, Antonio Martin, 18.[468]

To truly understand why the unidentified cop who saved numerous lives at Pooh's Corner on December 2 fears for his life, look no further than Martin's family scrambling to defend their son.

A son, mind you, who had a vast criminal record including assaults, armed robbery, and multiple uses of a firearm since he was 17...:

---

[468] Berkeley officer kills suspect who pulled gun; police say victim was 'known' to police, St. Louis Post-Dispatch, 12-24-14

Antonio Martin's extended family was in shock early Wednesday, as they waited for details to unfold about the fatal shooting of the 18-year-old at a Berkeley gas station.

"This doesn't make any sense for them to kill my son like this," Toni Martin-Green said early Wednesday from her home located near the University of Missouri-St. Louis campus. "I am trying to be calm."

Martin mainly grew up in the Hyde Park area of North St. Louis before moving with family to unincorporated St. Louis County a few years ago. Martin attended high school in Jennings before dropping out and had also been enrolled in the federal Job Corps program for a spell. He last worked at White Castle and wanted to go back to Job Corps, his father said.

Police say the man shot had a criminal record, with charges including three assaults, armed robbery, armed criminal action and multiple uses of weapons since he was 17.

Martin's parents acknowledged that their son has been arrested before and had "stumbled in the past."

"In the last year, he was really trying to find who he was. He was ready to take the world on," the father said. "He knew he had parents who loved him. He had that support."

"He was not a violent person, to our knowledge," he added. "Around us there weren't any pistols. It's hard to believe that."

His grandmother, Margret Chandler, was also in disbelief.

"When he was around me, he knew to do right," she said. "Why would he pull out a gun against the police? That's the thing I don't get. It just doesn't add up."[469]

---

[469] Parents of Antonio Martin say his fatal shooting 'doesn't make any sense', St. Louis Post-Dispatch, 12-24-14]

Well mom and grandma, when your son wasn't around he was doing everything he could except doing right; now, more violence is breaking in St. Louis because of yet another black male making a decision to directly challenge the states monopoly on violence.

And though the American state in 2014 is incredibly, over-the-top, anti-white, the police represent the one instrument standing in the way of a tidal wave of black criminality capsizing the entire nation into the orgiastic violence found on December 2nd at Pooh's Corner.

Hold your family a little tighter this 2014 Christmas Eve and remember each incident where a criminal black male dares challenge the authority of police (and their monopoly on violence) is another crack in the American Experiment's hull, proof our nation has "failed... for as we see a black community prepared to defend Antonio Martin's right to point a gun at a police officer, we view the dissolution of the American Dream and the birth of the American Nightmare.[470]

December 28, 2014
"White line's in the middle of the road, that's the worst place to drive."

So a memorial to a dead black male is sitting in the middle of Canfield Drive in Ferguson.

The middle of the road.

On the white line.

Where people drive cars.

As Roddy Piper's character in *They Live!* said, "White line's in the

---

[470]http://www.salon.com/2014/12/17/eric_holders_parting_shot_police_abuse_sca ndals_mean_the_nation_has_failed/

middle of the road, that's the worst place to drive":

> A Ferguson police spokesman was placed on unpaid leave after acknowledging remarks to a Washington Post blogger in which he called the Michael Brown memorial a "pile of trash," city officials said Saturday.
>
> One day earlier, the city stood behind the spokesman, Officer Timothy Zoll — claiming he had been misquoted — after an inquiry into the damaged memorial in the middle of Canfield Drive. But officials retreated in a one-page statement issued Saturday.
>
> Zoll was "confronted with the results" of a department investigation into the remarks attributed to him, city officials said.
>
> The officer "admitted to department investigators" that he made the statement attributed to him" and had "misled" superiors about the interview.
>
> The unpaid leave is effective immediately while disciplinary proceedings begin, according to the statement.[471]

What happened on August 9th in 67 percent black Ferguson has launched a revolution; I'm still not quite sure people understand just *who* will *ultimately* benefit from the actions of these revolutionaries...

December 29, 2014
An Advocate of All Things Black Compares his Community to the Flintstones and the White Community to the Jetsons... Without Getting the Joke

---

[471] Ferguson officer placed on leave over remarks about damaged memorial, St. Louis Post-Dispatch, 12-28-14

The black newspaper, *The St. Louis American*, published an article containing perhaps the greatest quote you'll ever, ever read.

Ever.

Courtesy of Families Advocating Safe Streets (one of those uniquely black organizations found in any urban area of America with a high percentage of violent blacks engaging in behavior contrary to the #BlackLivesMatter meme), we get the absolute best quote ever on the inherent reality of the Bell Curve.

Good luck finding it!:

> African Americans in St. Louis do not mourn only victims of police violence, as critics of the Ferguson protest movement frequently claim. In fact, this New Year's Eve will mark the 23rd annual prayer vigil for victims of violence organized by Families Advocating for Safe Streets.
>
> "It's for people who lost their lives to violence in the past year," said St. Louis Alderman Sam Moore, vice president of the organization.
>
> The 23rd annual prayer vigil will be held 4 p.m. New Year Eve's at William's Temple Church of God in Christ, 1500 Union Blvd. at Martin Luther King Boulevard.
>
> "We commemorate those who lost their lives," Moore said. "We light candles, read the names of all the victims and release 149 balloons – hopefully it's still at 149, but however many."
>
> When Moore was interviewed on December 18, and still at press time, there were 149 homicides in St. Louis in 2014. Of those 149 people killed in the city, two – Kajieme Powell and VonDerrit Myers Jr. – were killed by police officers.

"It's a travesty and a shame," Moore said. "We're continually trying to bring to the forefront that our problem is not just with police killing people."

But Moore and his organization, which was founded and is still led by Jeanette Culpepper, also work with police to solve homicides in the city.

"We go to the site where a murder occurred and pass out flyers asking people to give information about the murders," Moore said. "We tell them how to remain anonymous and ask people to come forward."

It is not easy, Moore said, because many people distrust the police – and fear criminals.

"People don't want to cooperate because there are repercussions," Moore said. "Witnesses get hurt and killed. But we hand out flyers telling them they can remain anonymous."

"If anyone lost a loved one, you'd want that same information about your loved one," Moore said. "We need to come together, come to a consensus and get these people off the street so we can have a safe environment."

The enemy on the street is formidable, Moore said, as he sees street criminals adapting to police better than the cops sleuth them.

"Criminals in my ward know the police patterns," Moore said. "They've gone wild. The mean streets of St. Louis have not been taken care of."

One crime story Moore does not buy is the reported racial tensions between blacks and Bosnians following the street murder of a young Bosnian man, allegedly by a group of black and Hispanic teens.

"I am sickened by what happened to the young man, the Bosnian man beat to death with hammers on the South Side," Moore said. "But to say blacks don't like Bosnians is a diversionary tactic. How do I know who a Bosnian is? We don't know who Bosnians are. It was an isolated incident."

Moore is focused on his North Side 4th Ward, which badly needs redevelopment.

There are seven empty lots on the very block where he lives. He offered pop cultural comparisons to describe North City's underdevelopment.

"We live like Flintstones compared to the Jetsons," Moore said. "The Jetsons go, 'Zip!' and are off into space, while we are still running with our feet on the ground holding up a log."

But even he was caught up in the excitement that swept the world, starting with protests in Ferguson and St. Louis. He said, "A lot of people never knew that black people in St. Louis had this kind of spirit bottled inside of them."[472]

Did you find it?

It might just be me, but I'd say Moore denigrated Fred Flintstone and the good citizens of Bedrock by comparing their harmonious community to the undeniably primitive conditions of heavily black North St. Louis -- conditions that are merely a reflection of the type of community the individual black people there can collectively create.

One fact can be sure: Bedrock didn't need a Families Advocating Safe Streets organization, even though dinosaurs roamed them...

---

[472] 23rd annual prayer vigil for victims, *St. Louis American*, 12-24-14

December 31, 2014
You grew up way too fast and now there's nothing to believe, And reruns all become our history

Ferguson War Journal: Day 144

In the past seven days, two attempted ambushes on police by blacks in St. Louis have failed.[473]

One, because Antonio Martin left the safety on his gun when he pointed it at a white cop.[474]

Two, because black people - luckily - are horrendous marksman.[475]

Only a day before Christmas, one of the so-called leading Ferguson "peace" protestors was arrested for trying to start a blaze at a QuickTrip (the gas station seemingly the Bastille of this revolution):

> One of the most frequently quoted and photographed Ferguson protesters was charged Saturday with setting fire to a Berkeley convenience store last week.
>
> St. Louis County police arrested Joshua Williams, 19, of St. Louis, on Friday after several local media outlets and store surveillance captured images of him trying to set a pile of

---

[473] http://www.stltoday.com/news/local/crime-and-courts/article_d45db16a-7422-5307-b81d-b45dbdc896ba.html#.VJr0gSC3E9A.twitter

[474] Berkeley Police Chief Frank McCall Said Antonio Martin's Gun Still Had The Safety On, Inquisitr.com, 12-30-14

[475] Six arrested after shots fired near looted Ferguson beauty supply store, KMOV.com, 12-30-14

> wood on fire outside the QuikTrip on North Hanley Road early Wednesday.
>
> Williams confessed to setting fires at the store in a videotaped interview, according to court documents.
>
> Williams has been quoted as an advocate for peaceful protests.
>
> An MSNBC profile of Williams in September quoted him as saying, "We have to come together as one and show them we can be peaceful, that we can do this. If not, they're going to just want us to act up so (police) can pull out their toys on us again."
>
> Later, he continued: "I learned that we have to stand up and that you can't get nowhere with violence but you can always move people without it."[476]

You can't get nowhere with violence...

Well, actually you can, but that's a lesson for another day.

Another time.

For now, let's remember the undeniably hypocritical war cry of #BlackLivesMatter and roll the ugliness of another year of black violence in St. Louis working overtime to make the city unsafe for civilization:

> April Fields' killer hid in the back seat of her car in January, then stabbed and strangled the 25-year-old woman after she dropped off her daughter at day care.
>
> Nick Kapusniak, 20, died in March in a drive-by shooting during a backyard party with his fraternity brothers.
>
> Kourtney Warren, 23, was killed Nov. 21 when an apparent drug deal erupted into a gunfight at a Phillips 66 gas station.

---

[476] Protester who advocates peace charged with setting fire at Berkeley QT, St. Louis Post-Dispatch, 12-24-14

Those people may not have been connected in life but are linked in death as part of a somber tally of about 190 people who died violently in St. Louis and St. Louis County in 2014. Their names will be read aloud tonight at an annual New Year's Eve vigil to remember those murdered in the area this year.

The 159 murders in St. Louis this year — through Tuesday — have made 2014 the most violent of recent years, with at least 39 more murders than last year. It's the highest yearly tally of criminal homicides since 2008, when the city recorded 167 murders.

University of Missouri-St. Louis criminologist Rick Rosenfeld said the increase in homicides in four north St. Louis neighborhoods alone — Wells Goodfellow, St. Louis Place, the West End and Kingsway East — accounted for most of the year's overall rise in murders.

"The homicide increase is highly localized," he said. "Most areas of the city saw no change over last year."

Police Chief Sam Dotson said he believed one of the reasons for the increase here since August could be what he has called the "Ferguson effect," the belief that criminals became more emboldened since the Aug. 9 killing of Michael Brown by a Ferguson police officer. Dotson said he believed crime rose in part because police were diverted from regular patrols to special details focusing on civil unrest.

Rosenfeld said he saw those links in the data. "If you're heavily involved in crime, you run a strong risk of being killed," he said. "If you're not, your risk is much, much lower."

Most of the victims were black and male, as were most of the suspects in cases in which a suspect description is known.

This month, Dotson asked the mayor to find money to hire 160 more city officers over the next two years. That followed the death of Bosnian immigrant Zemir Begic, 32, who was beaten to death by a group of teenagers with hammers in the Bevo Mill neighborhood Nov. 30. Three days later, a woman was killed and five other people were shot in an attempted robbery at Pooh's Corner, a bar in south St. Louis popular with retired and off-duty police.

Dotson also vowed to return to hotspot policing now that officers are spending less time focused on protests in the city.

Two-thirds of all murder cases in St. Louis are still unsolved. That includes the death of Kapusniak, a student at the St. Louis College of Pharmacy who was hit by gunfire from a car passing through an alley in the 2700 block of Accomac Street on March 1.

His mother, Renee Kapusniak, said she was concerned about the growing violence in St. Louis. Kapusniak said she last spoke with police a few months ago and was told there were no fresh leads. But she isn't giving up hope.

"With all the violence going on there, we do not want another family to live through what we're going through," she said Tuesday by phone from her home in Waukesha, Wis. "He was a young life who unfortunately was taken from us by a random act of violence, and it has to stop."[477]

The hallmarks of the black community: black violence[478] lowering property value, ensuring those home owners a wet time with their mortgage and negative equity.[479] With a fierce devotion to the code of "No Snitching,"[480] the bulk of violent black people who have engaged in homicidal behavior remain at large to do it again. The "code of silence" among black criminals and the black population that breeds, shelters, and protects them represents

---

[477] St. Louis homicides up more than 30 percent in 2014 to highest total since 2008, *St. Louis Post-Dispatch*, 12-31-14

[478] http://www.nytimes.com/2013/11/20/us/in-neighborhoods-like-north-st-louis-gunfire-still-rules-the-night.html?pagewanted=all&_r=0

[479] http://www.stltoday.com/business/local/st-louis-is-hot-spot-for-underwater-mortgages/article_1a9b46b5-38f4-5b93-b4b4-e895f8e0bab5.html

[480] http://fox2now.com/2014/08/11/quiktrip-sprayed-with-graffiti-set-on-fire-during-overnight-looting-near-ferguson/

a civilization-stunting phenomenon.[481]

Those white people daring to restore civilization to the vast acreage's of land overwhelmed by the black undertow become victims of the random violence that drove away whites decades ago.[482]

For decades, the black population in St. Louis has been solely responsible for the city having a high homicide rate as well as a nonfatal shooting problem. The streets of St. Louis and North St. Louis aren't violent; it's the black population of St. Louis and North St. Louis that makes these streets uninhabitable, even for ghosts.

So as 2014 comes to an end, the continued stagnation of human evolution via the toxicity of liberalism and its adherents steadfast (slavish) devotion to black improvement/empowerment means we will continue to more of the same in St. Louis - and all of America - in 2015.

But the day will come when this rerun ends.

Our task is not to speed up this moment's arrival, but survive until it arrives.

---

[481] http://www.stltoday.com/news/local/metro/girl-s-burial-spotlights-a-culture-of-violence/article_26bd5032-f188-514a-ba93-1e9ac727e745.html

[482] http://www.stltoday.com/news/local/crime-and-courts/st-louis-college-of-pharmacy-student-fatally-shot/article_72c4cee2-8257-5ef8-b9b3-e9ab261e51ef.html

January 5, 2015
Eastern Mysticism meets Pathological White Altruism: Brunch, Yoga, and the Hilarity of SWPLs

Yoga offers only one positive: hot girls in yoga pants..

Nothing more, nothing less.

An overlooked story from the Farce in Ferguson needs rehashing today, if only to remind people why scores of black people disrupting white people enjoying brunch in New York City is a cause for laughter instead of anger.

Restaurants with outdoor seating (where brunch can be pleasantly consumed) is an immediate indicator you are in a tony, majority white area, where the social capital collectively created by individual whites enables the type of status whoring completely absent in a majority black area.

The introduction of blacks into a community they had no part in building represents the tinder in ensuring all social capital is quickly consumed by the immediate regression to the black mean.

Which is why the story of Angie Carron must be told:

> As anticipation in Ferguson mounts, maybe the town could use a little yoga. Angie Carron wants to be the one to bring it there.
>
> The fifteen-year Florissant resident and owner of OM Turtle Yoga recently signed a lease for a second studio, an 1,100-square-foot space down the road from the Ferguson police station.
>
> "Everyone is like, 'Why Ferguson? Why now?'" Carron says.

"But truly, why not Ferguson right now? We all need to find our center, our peace, our balance, and I think this is a better time than any to bring our studio to Ferguson."

But it's not unreasonable to think opening a storefront in Ferguson is a risk.

Protesters have threatened other nearby businesses, and more demonstrations are likely if Darren Wilson, the Ferguson police officer who fatally shot eighteen-year-old Michael Brown, is not charged with a crime.

Andy Wurm's Tire and Wheel, directly across from Ferguson's police headquarters, offers one example. Although the majority of protesters cooperated a couple months ago when Wurm asked them to move off his lot, he says he received some threats of bricks going through his windows.

Faraci Pizza, a few blocks from the police station on South Florissant Avenue, has also been a target. Protesters who claimed to see the owner point a gun at them threatened to shut the restaurant down. The family that owns Faraci said they've lost a lot of business since August because people are afraid to come into Ferguson at night.

All the more reason to open a yoga studio, Carron says.

When she signed the lease for the Ferguson space, the former Express Scripts employee walked away from a six-figure salary, benefits and a 401K, deciding to focus her energy on operating the two studios full time.

"It truly is a mission," she says of her passion to help her students in the same way yoga has helped her. "I am blessed to work with all these people on a daily basis, and I want to bring that to Ferguson."

Before she decided to open a second studio, Carron's morning commute to Express Scripts took her down South Florissant Avenue past protesters and signs and boarded-up windows.

"There's a lot of passionate people in that town that want to see it grow," she says. "It just feels like yoga would be a good fit for helping the town rebuild."

She plans to open her second yoga studio location in early December.[483]

"There's a lot of passionate people in that town that want to see it grow..."

You mean like Michael Brown's stepfather Louis Head who shouted, "Burn this motherf---er down" and "Burn this bitch down"?[484]

He seems ardent in his steadfast belief in growing Ferguson, so it's axiomatic he was one of the first to sign up for a yoga lesson with Angie Carron's OM Turtle Yoga, right?

Were those black people who engaged in the #BlackBrunchNYC protest against white supremacy (never mind the white people eating brunch probably voted for both Barack Obama and Bill de Blasio) to see their movement spread, OM Turtle Yoga would be the perfect venue to voice concern with white supremacy and white racism in Ferguson.

Only a white racist would believe they alone could bring peace and balance to an unstable community, such as the 70 percent black community of Ferguson. After all, isn't that the type of white colonial mindset #BlackBrunchNYC is trying trying to fight?

If you can't laugh at what 2015 America represents, you have no hope of surviving its collapse.

For a society that bases the pursuit of yoga and brunching as worthwhile endeavors is one deserving of collapse.

---

[483] Yoga Instructor Hopes To Bring Healing To Ferguson With New Studio, *Riverfront Times*, 11-13-14

[484] Michael Brown's stepfather at rally: 'Burn this bitch down!', CNN.com, 12-8-14

January 6, 2015
... His truth is marching on.

The Battle Hymn of the Republic is the most vile song ever, ever composed. But it's a fitting tune to hear play silently in your head when you read the news of what happened in Portland, where a 100-year-old World War II veteran was to be honored.

Was to be honored is the key phrase, because more than 100 #BlackLivesMatter and "Justice for Michael Brown" protesters pushed their way into the event to make sure the 100-year-old veteran knew just who his (and his fellow soldiers) sacrifices went toward empowering.[485]

Those brave men who stormed Iwo Jima didn't do so to enable more than 100 black (and white) people to disrupt a centenarian from receiving the accolades and admiration he so richly deserved; nor did any veteran of the United States Military die so that a black person could bellow "down," and then proceed to watch a formally American city burn....

But such is life in 2015 America.

If any positive emotion toward the Old Republic was left, it's this story that would assuredly bring forth the same patriotism and passion which once compelled young men to follow a leader like George S. Patton to whatever hell he'd lead them toward:

> No one said anything to either man. No one gave an order, or even made a suggestion. But the two soldiers seemed to simply know what they had to do. Maj. Lance Dell and Sgt. 1st Class Eric Allison of the Missouri National Guard rescued a burned American flag.
>
> "They treated the flag like it was trash," Allison said. "It's not trash to us."

---

[485] Navy vet, 100, persuades protesters to let him speak: 'Give me a chance', Oregon Live, 1-3-15

In a demonstration on South Florissant Road in Ferguson on Dec. 4, several protesters wearing Guy Fawkes masks lit an American flag on fire. After letting it burn for a bit, they let it drop to the wet ground.

At that point — it could have been one or two seconds, it might have been 30 — two Missouri National Guardsmen in combat gear crossed into the fray of South Florissant.

With as much tenderness as can be mustered when covered in riot gear and hit by angry insults, Dell and Allison picked up the remains of the flag off the street, folded as much of it as they could, picked up smaller, charred pieces of fabric and then walked it inside for safe keeping.

Dell, 46, and Allison, 43, are full-time National Guard members, assigned to the 205th Military Police Battalion in Poplar Bluff.

Both men spent 13 months in Afghanistan around 2010, and Allison also spent 18 months in Iraq in 2004-05. They've served together long enough that they knew their thoughts were aligned when the flag was burned. They looked at each other and acted.

'WE LOVE THE FLAG'

Said Allison, "My dad used to tell me that you can't even count the people who gave their lives so we can fly that flag. We love the flag, or at least what it stands for."Dell noted that he and his men are well aware of the court rulings concerning flag burning.

"We know that it's a constitutional right to burn the flag," Dell said.

"But I knew we couldn't leave it just lying in the road."

Two weeks after the incident, the flag was still in the two soldiers' possession.

They're not sure what exactly will become of it, but Dell said anyone concerned should know that it will be handled "by the code."⁴⁸⁶

There is one place this flag will never call "home":

> From street-artist paintings on boards protecting store windows to signs bearing the now iconic statement, "Hands Up. Don't Shoot," cultural images from the Ferguson protests have become firmly established in recent Missouri history. So much so that the Missouri History Museum is gathering images and items cataloguing the unrest that followed the August shooting death of Michael Brown by a Ferguson police officer.
>
> The museum in St. Louis' Forest Park is in the process of gathering not only physical artifacts from Ferguson, but Twitter feeds, oral histories from protesters, residents and police, and even cellphone videos. It's all meant to give future generations a real-time perspective from those affected by the shooting and the aftermath that included protests, riots, and the strained relations between police and minority communities.
>
> This is a rare example of being at a point where history is made all around you," said Chris Gordon, Library and Collections director for the museum. "We're standing in the midst of it, and we haven't had that chance very often. Documenting everything we can -- getting all sides, all perspectives -- is very important."⁴⁸⁷

"...getting all sides, all perspectives -- is very important."

No story of the Farce in Ferguson is complete without understanding HUD's pernicious role in facilitating the black insurrection via Section 8 vouchers. Indeed, blacks emboldened with Section 8 Vouchers to rekindle those most hateful words in *The Battle Hymn of the Republic*('He is trampling out the vintage where the grapes of

---

[486] Amid protest in Ferguson, guardsmen rescued flag, *St. Louis Post-Dispatch*, 12-30-14

[487] Missouri museum collecting real-time history of Ferguson, Associated Press, 1-6-15

wrath are stored'*)* is a sick reminder of what the Affirmatively Furthering Fair Housing plan represents.

The charred remains of the flag Dell and Allison picked up on the streets of 70 percent black Ferguson echoes the words of Francis Scott Key, but with one important caveat: though the American flag might have still been there, Ferguson is now Africa in America.

January 12, 2014
#WhiteLivesMatter: Bobby Christman Gunned Down in "Most Heavily Patrolled Area of St. Louis" by Black Male

Years from now, those who knew him in life will still remember where they were when they heard he had been murdered (I'll never forget where I was when the news of Brittany Watts' murder broke).

Though 19-year-old Bobby Christman will be nothing more than a memory, the lesson his death tragically taught those who knew him will never be forgotten.

It will be a lesson haunting his family and friends for as long as they live; one noticeable in the blight and ruin of the once thriving city of St. Louis:

> "We had officers within a five to six block radius when this incident happened," said St. Louis Metropolitan Police Captain Michael Caruso.
>
> He said downtown is the most heavily patrolled area of St. Louis. He said the department would review its strategies following this shooting, but doubts anything could have been

done differently to prevent the shooting.

"Some criminals are just bolder than others," said Caruso.[488]

"We think it was wrong place, wrong time," police spokeswoman Schron Jackson said of the lynching of Zemir Begic by multiple black people. The St. Louis Post-Dispatch reported on the Begic slaying these callous words: *"Detectives do not believe the attackers took anything but Begic's life."*

Add to those words, "Some criminals are just bolder than others."

Dubbed an "isolated incident" by St. Louis Metropolitan Police Major Michael Caruso, the shooting death of the white teen by a black suspect could have been avoided if police were allowed to deal with black criminality realistically.

Or if sundown laws were still allowed to keep the primary racial group responsible for all of the gun crime in the city of St. Louis off of the streets after dark. A large police presence wouldn't be needed then to make the city as safe as the white suburbs for the nocturnal activities of whites in downtown St. Louis; that blacks are allowed to roam free is the reason St. Louis is incredibly dangerous and requires a massive police force to make whites feel safe from the threat blacks pose.

Instead, Bobby Christman is dead. As is the future of St. Louis:

> Incident: Assault 1st (Shooting)
>
> Location: 700 block of N. 15thDate/Time: 1/11/15 @ 00:43
>
> Victim #1: 19-year old white male
>
> Victim #2: 17-year old white male

---

[488] College student shot, killed near City Museum downtown, Fox2Now.com, 1-11-2015

Victim #3: 19-year old white female

Suspect: Unknown black male

Officers responded to the above location for a "shooting" and upon arrival, located Victim #1 seated in the front passenger seat of a vehicle, unconscious and suffering from a gunshot wound to the head. Victim #1 was conveyed to a hospital and listed in critical/unstable condition. Victims #2 and #3 stated all three victims were seated inside the parked vehicle when an unknown suspect approached them, opened a rear passenger door to their vehicle and produced a firearm. The suspect demanded the victims' property and grabbed Victim #3's purse. A struggle ensued over the purse and the suspect fired a shot, striking Victim #1. The suspect then entered the passenger side of a silver vehicle and fled the scene. The investigation is ongoing.[489]

The racial aspect of the murder of Bobby Christman is one most of media in St. Louis is actively leaving out of the stories they publish:

Police from St. Louis and East St. Louis traded gunshots Sunday night in Washington Park with suspects in the fatal shooting downtown earlier that day of a 2013 DeSmet Jesuit High School graduate, police said Monday.

Three suspects escaped on foot after leading police on a short car chase, Illinois State Police spokesman Lt. Dave Bivens said.

Bobby Christman, 19, of St. Louis County was shot during a robbery attempt as he sat in the front passenger seat of a car parked at Lucas and North 15th streets near the Washington Avenue restaurant and entertainment area, police said. A

---

[489] Teen Shot in Head by Purse-Snatching Robber in Downtown St. Louis: Police, River Front Times, 1-12-15]

woman, 19, was in the rear seat. Another teen, 17, also was in the car.

The suspect's vehicle pulled up next to Christman's car and a man got out with a handgun, police said. He opened the rear driver's side door of the parked car and tried to grab the woman's purse. She resisted, police said. Christman said something to the gunman, who then fired the shot that struck Christman, police said witnesses told them. The gunman then jumped back in a vehicle and fled.

St. Louis Police Chief Sam Dotson said the suspects were in a silver 2004 Chrysler Sebring carjacked downtown last week.

After Sunday's fatal shooting, city police tracked the car to the Washington Park area. About 6:30 p.m. Sunday, the car fled St. Louis and East St. Louis police and someone in the car fired shots at city officers. No officers were hit. Police returned fire but it is not clear if the suspects were wounded.

The suspects bailed out of the vehicle after a short chase and ran off near 50th Street and Caseyville Avenue in Washington Park. Police recovered the car and are analyzing it for evidence.

"They bailed out, ran, and the way (detectives) described it, it was a field of vacant buildings," Dotson said. "And so obviously, it's not our neighborhoods, we're not familiar with it. I think for an officer safety issue, the officer made the right choice not to pursue through an area he's unfamiliar with."

Dotson said officers are hoping the car will lead to the suspects in Christman's death.

Police said Christman was unconscious when they arrived at 12:43 a.m. Sunday. He was taken to a hospital, where he died about 6 p.m.

Christman lived in the 7100 block of Tournament Drive in south St. Louis County.

He was a sophomore at Southeast Missouri State University, where he was a member of Sigma Phi Epsilon Fraternity.[490]

Read that one more time: *"They bailed out, ran, and the way (detectives) described it, it was a field of vacant buildings,"* Dotson said. *"And so obviously, it's not our neighborhoods, we're not familiar with it. I think for an officer safety issue, the officer made the right choice not to pursue through an area he's unfamiliar with."*

Blight.

A "field of vacant buildings" courtesy of individual black people collectively making entire communities unsafe for businesses to operate or families to live in; and a perfect place for black suspects to hide or ambush police.

This is the reality of 2015 St. Louis, a microcosm for America's failed racial experiment.

Years from now, those who knew him in life will still remember where they were when they heard he had been murdered.

Though 19-year-old Bobby Christman will be nothing more than a memory, the lesson his death tragically taught those who knew him will never be forgotten.

---

[490] Police exchanged gunfire with suspects in car wanted in killing of De Smet grad, St. Louis Post-Dispatch, 1-12-15

January 14, 2015
The Standard Deviation Stands Alone (St. Louis' "Save Our Sons" Initiative to Uplift Blacks)

The Memphis Gun Down Program.

NOLA For Life.

Baltimore's Safe Streets (the motto: Stop Shooting. Start Living.)

Indianapolis' Your Life Matters Program.

Milwaukee's Homicide Review Commission.

President Obama's My Brother's Keeper Program.

Kansas City's No Violence Alliance.

What do all of these initiatives/programs have in common?

All are necessary because the standards of civilization collectively established by individual white males are a standard deviation greater than what individual black males can collectively achieve.

All are programs or initiatives requiring funding (be it in grant, government funds, or non-profit donation form...) because of the failures of individual black people to refrain from criminality, making the cities listed above dangerous places for both families and businesses.

With Obama's My Brother's Keeper Program, the reality of the dysfunction inherent in the black community can no longer be contained to "urban" environments: wherever blacks are found in America, the reality of the standard deviation separating them from the standards whites have established is easily discernible in every statistic measuring misery...

But no program or initiative comes close to the desperation found in the name of St. Louis *Save Our Sons*:

> Take 500 young men, jobless or underemployed, from north St. Louis County. Give them a month's training in how to land a job, keep it and get promoted. Then give them a job at a local company.
>
> That's the mission of "Save our Sons," an Urban League program that's landed $1.2 million in donations from big-name St. Louis area companies in the wake of unrest in Ferguson.
>
> Urban League officials came up with the idea after talking to young men on the streets.
>
> "Young people said they weren't being listened to. All of them to a one said we need jobs," said Urban League CEO Michael McMillan. Scholarships and job training were also on their list.
>
> The jobs issue is critical. The unemployment rate for black men in St. Louis County has run at triple the rate for whites. From 2011 to 2013, black joblessness averaged 17 percent against 5.8 percent for whites, according to the Census Bureau.
>
> Save Our Sons is running its first class of 20 young men, and more will be added over two years. Two St. Louis companies — who wish to remain anonymous — have promised to hire the first 40 graduates at jobs paying $10 per hour plus benefits, said Herta Shikapwashya, the Urban League vice president running the program.
>
> The classes have four components: how to get a job, keep it, get promoted and stay marketable. It teaches interview skills, how to impress a boss with good work, and how to network to find the next job.
>
> A good job is what Darryl George needs now. "I've been through a lot, and it's at the point where it's really changing my life," said George, 33, of Jennings. He just lost a temporary

job in a warehouse earning $8.25 an hour. That limits the child support he can pay for his two daughters, aged 13 and 11.

He hopes Save Our Sons, with its promise of training and a new job, will put him on a better track. "I want to make the community better," he said. "I want to be one of the people who come back and speak to the class once I get a job."

He said the program is open to men with problems, including "work issues, child support issues, a felony conviction."

Some of the biggest names in corporate St. Louis are chipping in the $1.2 million, including Wells Fargo Advisors, Monsanto, Emerson, Anheuser-Busch InBev, AT&T, Regions Bank and Reliance Bank. The NAACP is also contributing.[491]

The dysfunction found in the black community represents an incredible business opportunity for those hoping to find eternal employment. Job security in this growing field (explosive growth is forecasted for the next decade!) is easily the highest of any vocation, save that of the black conservative looking for employment in Conservatism Inc.[492]

But no matter the money invested, no matter the number of programs or initiatives, and no matter the desperation of the names of these organizations (S.O.S in St. Louis), the standard deviation will remain.

January 16, 2015
THE YEAR WAS 2081, and everybody was finally unequal.

The pursuit of equality mandates the elimination of freedom and the

---

[491] Program means jobs for north St. Louis County men, *St. Louis Post-Dispatch*, 1-14-15

[492] http://www.crainsdetroit.com/article/20141201/NEWS01/141209994/skillman-foundation-to-give-2m-to-help-young-men-in-detroit

implementation of unjust laws.

In essence, equality as the highest moral good is the embracing of injustice as the ultimate weapon to fight nature.

But nature will always win, no matter the effort to pretend she's not there.

It was only a few a days ago, in thinking about the majesty and true beauty of the Gateway Arch in St. Louis (easily the most powerful symbol of Manifest Destiny and Western Man's unabashed conquering of the North American continent) that a realization of what it truly represents hit me: the bell curve.

No matter the effort, no matter the number of programs or initiatives, no matter the number of zero's in the monetary investment, the failure for the black race to live up to the standards set by the white race in St. Louis seem inescapably connected to one unmentionable word: genetics.

Discrimination on the part of whites to hold blacks doesn't make any sense, considering the same drive, ingenuity and resilience of a people reflected off the Gateway Arch (remember, it was built to memorialize Manifest Destiny...) has now been handicapped to eternally help black people catch up...

The same problems blamed for high black homicide rates (and overall black failure when compared to white standards of civilization) at the time the Berlin Wall fell [are still blamed today when describing why heavily black North St. Louis is a food desert.[493]

Black failures then (and now) are blamed on unemployment, drugs, inadequate housing and lack of education are cited by those who try to find the reason for St. Louis' epidemic, as well as leaning on "hyper-segregation" and isolation from amenities, opportunities and resources, making it more difficult for them to get ahead in life:

---

[493] St. Louis Activists Struggle to End Violence's Toll on Young Black Men, Los Angeles Times, 12-31-1989

James Clark, vice president of community outreach for Better Family Lifesays he realizes there is a sub-culture in the urban core where "crime and violence is accepted."

He blames that on lack of education and respect. Better Family Life tries to give those boys and men a new vision of themselves to combat the message that they are nothing.

"So the first thing we do is we give them a thorough understanding that you are a child of God you have to be responsible to yourself, your family and your neighborhood," Clark said.

The current methods of hot spot policing from the St. Louis police department have been highly praised by outsiders, but Clark believes that is not what the community needs, suggesting hot spot resourcing would bear better outcomes.

"If we aren't literally in our neighborhoods going door-to-door doing assessments on everyone in the household and then delivering the resources to meet the needs of the individuals in the households this will only get worse," he explained.

The list of resources Clark seeks is long. He said, "We need prenatal care, we need alcohol and drug treatment, we need clinical evaluations, we need employment."[494]

In reality, Clark's idea is to retard the advancement of white civilization so black people can catch up (after all, when resources are redirected from one community to the other, the former community is left without any investments for its betterment).

St. Louis in 2015 is 49 percent black and 43 percent white; the black population is solely responsible with keeping St. Louis in the lead for most violent American cities (see p. 20).

This is why St. Louis Blues fans are scared of coming to

---

[494] Community Activist Sheds Light on Black Homicide Victimization in Missouri, CBS St. Louis, 1-27-14

downtown (the Blues are the National Hockey League franchise).[495]

This is why downtown St. Louis is a ghost-town at 5 p.m. on a weekday night:

> But Wednesday afternoon, I was strolling back to the newspaper when I happened to pass Copia Wine Bar and Restaurant, which occupies several storefronts — and 15,000 square feet — on the south side of Washington Avenue between 11th Street and Tucker Boulevard. Almost passed it, I should say. I decided to have a glass of wine.
>
> It was almost 5 o'clock. The place was nearly empty.
>
> Amer Hawatmeh owns and runs the place. He came over to chat. (All right. I've stopped for a glass of wine once or twice before.) "How's business?" I asked.
>
> "Terrible," he said.
>
> Lunch and dinner are down. Happy hour is way down. Parties have been hit the hardest, he said. He told me he had almost $225,000 in cancellations in November and December. Mostly holiday parties, he said.
>
> "Right now the weather is bad, but even before, you could see something was wrong. We used to look out the window and you'd think this was a major metropolis, but you don't see that any more. The street is empty."
>
> That is not exactly welcome news for an entertainment district.
>
> The future seems clouded. What will Ferguson do to the convention business? But that's the future. The present is troubled enough. Hawatmeh said he didn't know how long he'd be able to continue.
>
> I asked what he would do if he were in charge. "We need more police," he said.

---

[495] http://fox2now.com/2015/01/13/blues-fans-worried-about-security-in-downtown-st-louis/

"Visible police. I love the police. But you need to be able to see them. You know what I would do? Put them on horses. Get those horses from Forest Park and bring them here. If there is a crowd of people, and you have a policeman in the middle of the crowd, you can't see him. But if he is on a horse, everybody can see him."[496]

Downtown St. Louis would not be dying were it not for the consistent, persistent, and visible threat of black criminality (visible in the blight and abandoned buildings were commerce once flourished).

The government, both major political parties, academia, the media, and all major religions in America push equality with a ferocity even *Harrison Bergeron* would find shocking, but the reality of inequality remains obvious to anyone willing to consider an alternative to the madness of modernity: and this reality can be glimpsed in looking at the arch in St. Louis, a monument we will one day praise as commemorating the opening of the west to Manifest Destiny, but also to the reality of race.

For the Gateway Arch also is the perfect representation of the much denounced Bell Curve, a work whose primary theory does far more to explain the continued inability of the black race to achieve the standards of civilization set by whites than relying on the boogeyman of white privilege to explain away high rates of criminality, dysfunction, and food deserts wherever black people in America are found.

---

[496] Bill McClellan: Bring in the horses, downtown businessman urges, St. Louis Post-Dispatch, 1-16-15

January 20, 2015
George Soros, Barack Obama, and Eric Holder Walk into a Bar in Ferguson (While the Washington Post blames St. Louis gun violence on white people)...

> Matthias: We waited for you, Neville, so you could see this: The end. The end of all you done. You see, none of it was real. It was illusion. Your art, your science, it was all a nightmare. And now it's done. Finished. - *The Omega Man*

So George Soros spends $33 million to fund the Ferguson protests.[497] This was after Barack Obama sent three members of his administration to the ~~state~~ funeral of Michael Brown in Ferguson, thereby publicly siding with the 'Gentle Giant' (silently castigating Officer Darren Wilson by his actions).[498]

Of course, before George Soros could spend the $33 million, Attorney General Eric "My People" Holder went on a spiritual pilgrimage to Ferguson to cleanse his soul of whatever was left of his attachment to anything connected to 'whiteness'.[499]

---

[497] George Soros funds Ferguson protests, hopes to spur civil action: Liberal billionaire gave at least $33 million in one year to groups that emboldened activists, Washington Times, 1-15-15

[498] President Obama sending three White House officials to Michael Brown's funeral: Leading the group for Monday's service will be the chairman of the My Brother's Keeper Task Force, Broderick Johnson., New York Daily News, 8-24-14]

[499] [Eric Holder: 'I'm the attorney general of the US. But I am also a black man, The Guardian, 8-20-14]

Though Soros' $33 million investment in the Ferguson protesters was unknown until recently, the investment by the Obama Administration and the Eric Holder-led Department of Justice into the "Farce in Ferguson" was quite known.

And because of the Obama Administration and Holder's Department of Justice investment in Michael Brown's innocence in Ferguson, those white people in the roughly 70 percent black city decided to buy up firearms to protect themselves, their property, and businesses.

> Gun sales in Ferguson and surrounding areas have increased by 50 percent in recent weeks, as residents and law enforcement alike prepare for what might come from the grand jury's ruling of Darren Wilson, the police officer who shot teenage Michael Brown. "So maybe I get trapped here or something and have to have a John Wayne shootout," said Dan McMullen, the owner of an insurance agency located near the site of the August shooting death of Brown, CNN reported. "That's the silly part about it: Is that going to happen? [500]Not a chance. But I guess, could it? I'm the only white person here.'

Alright: why rehash all of this?

Because the *Washington Post* refuses to acknowledge that more than 90 percent of those arrested for weapons offenses in the city of St. Louis (since 1999) have been black:

> The firearms have been flying at County Guns. Located just a few miles from Ferguson, Mo., this small gun shop has seen a flood of customers looking to buy that first handgun or maybe a backup Glock for the car or Mossberg shotgun for home protection.
>
> "We have sold a boatload of guns in the last few months," owner Adam Weinstein said.
>
> Other gun shops near Ferguson have reported similar

---

[500] [Ferguson on edge: Guns fly off shop shelves in case of 'John Wayne shootout', Washington Times, 11-12-14]:

firearm frenzies. By every measure Missouri's gun sales have spiked since Aug. 9, when a white policeman shot and killed a unarmed black teenager in Ferguson, an incident that touched off continued protests and sporadic violence – and fed fear about personal protection.

Today, without doubt, there are many more firearms in and around Ferguson. More handguns. More shotguns. More assault-style rifles.

So what will the effect of all these new firearms be?

"I would expect some uptick in gun violence," said Daniel Webster, professor and director of Johns Hopkins Center for Gun Policy and Research.

He doesn't know how soon it will happen. Or how big the increase will be. But he believes the additional gun sales will have tragic repercussions.[501]

Funny: hammers have tragic repercussions. Just ask Zemir Begic.

White people bought guns throughout the St. Louis region because they correctly perceived a federal government - whose chief officer of the executive branch and attorney general of the Department of Justice both decided to side with Michael Brown in very public fashions - shockingly siding with the Ferguson mob.

Which, we would find out later, enjoyed $33 million from George Soros.

So the *Washington Post* believes the purchasing of guns by white people to protect themselves from the hate-filled Ferguson lynch mob (which the Obama Administration sided with...) will somehow increase gun violence in St. Louis in 2015, when virtually all fatal and nonfatal gun crime in the St. Louis metro-area is committed by blacks...

Of course, any plan to confront black criminality (more police) is

---

[501] Guns sales spiked after the Ferguson unrest. Will gun crime rise as well?: More firearms are on the streets now -- and, for some, that means more gun crime., 1-7-15

protested by the same Ferguson-influenced protesters who were financed to the tune of $33 million by George Soros... :

> While Mayor Francis Slay is pushing to hire more police officers, one group took to the steps inside city hall in opposition of the plan.
>
> Members of the Justice for Michael Brown Leadership Coalition believe hiring more police would equal harassment for low-income residents and minorities.
>
> "More police only means increased targeting of poor people and people of color," said Zaki Baruti, head of the coalition. "We oppose any increase in police power or numbers."
>
> At a news conference Thursday following a recent wave of violence that claimed the lives of six people, Mayor Slay spoke of a desire to hire upwards of 160 new officers to patrol the streets.
>
> The Justice for Michael Brown group did not get to meet with Mayor Slay, but vowed to present him with its written opposition to hiring more law enforcement.
>
> "The solution to crime in this community is jobs, jobs, jobs," Baruti said. "Take that $8 million and instead of hiring 160 police officers, hire 160 black youth that need jobs out here and then you'll prevent crime."[502]

Funny: didn't George Soros employ far more than 160 black youth with his $33 million investment in the Justice for Michael Brown movement? That's more than four times the paltry amount the white taxpayers of St. Louis could be fleeced to ensure the budget for 160 more cops could be met...

---

[502] Justice for Michael Brown group protests plan to hire more police, Fox2Now, 1-15-15

January 21, 2015
Fortune, Fame, Mirrors Broken, Still Insane, But the Narrative Remains...

Seventy percent black Ferguson. A fertile ground for black gangs recruiting new members ("not yet full-fledged members but have been asked to prove their worth to the gangs by committing brazen acts—firing gunshots at police, hurling objects at them and in some cases looting...").[503]

Scholarships for black students at the once lily-white - now completely black - Normandy High School (issued by the Michael Brown Chosen for Change nonprofit) are now being granted in honor of Michael Brown.[504]

Because the notion of Officer Darren Wilson executing a defenseless, angelic, "hands up, don't shoot" Michael Brown is commonly accepted by blacks, white people (especially teachers) are fearful of Ferguson-related discussions taking place in schools:

> Another common refrain was the frustration students feel when they can't talk about Ferguson-related issues at school. While most area school districts don't have policies prohibiting discussion, and superintendents say they encourage it, some teachers and principals won't allow it, teenagers said.
>
> Among those students was DeAnna Harper, a senior at McCluer North High School, who said some of her teachers have stymied the conversation out of concern they'd lead to tense hallway situations. As a result, some of her classmates

---

[503] For St. Louis Gangs, Ferguson Has Become a Recruiting Tool, Newsweek, 8-20-14

[504] Churches offer scholarships at Michael Brown's School, Fox2Now, 1-13-15

> don't have a chance to talk about race and policing with others who may not share their views, she said.[505]

"... tense hallway situations," meaning black kids lacking impulse control are prepared to avenge Michael Brown:

> The situation outside Hazelwood East High School was more turbulent. A dozen St. Louis County police cars blocked more than 100 students on Dunn Road from both sides, and some students gathered around vehicles and taunted police officers who stood outside their cars. They were outside for about an hour before they went back into their school. Police made no arrests.
>
> The walkouts were organized through social media Monday and Tuesday. Ferguson-Florissant, like many other nearby school districts, had canceled classes Monday due to the weather, making Tuesday the first day of classes since the grand jury announcement.
>
> "We are standing up for the black men," said Darris Hodge, a junior at McCluer. "We want justice."[506]

But what is "justice?"

A white cop protecting himself from a charging black man who had thoughts of using the formers gun to kill him with?

Isn't that justice?

Well... we now know what justice really is:

> Justice Department lawyers will recommend that no civil rights charges be brought against the police officer who fatally shot an unarmed teenager in Ferguson, Mo., after an F.B.I. investigation found no evidence to support charges, law enforcement officials said Wednesday.

---

[505] Ferguson Commission hears from youth, St. Louis Post-Dispatch, 1-10-15

[506] Ferguson Commission hears from youth, St. Louis Post-Dispatch, 1-10-15

Attorney General Eric H. Holder Jr. and his civil rights chief, Vanita Gupta, will have the final say on whether the Justice Department will close the case against the officer, Darren Wilson. But it would be unusual for them to overrule the prosecutors on the case, who are still working on a legal memo explaining their recommendation.

A decision by the Justice Department would bring to an end to the politically charged investigation of Mr. Wilson in the shooting death of 18-year-old Michael Brown. Missouri authorities concluded their investigation into Mr. Brown's death in November and also recommended against charges.

The F.B.I. investigation, however, painted a murkier picture. Mr. Wilson told investigators that Mr. Brown tussled with him through the window of his police car and tried to grab his gun, an account supported by bruises and DNA evidence. Two shots were fired during that struggle.

What happened next as the confrontation moved into the street is in dispute. While some witnesses were adamant that Mr. Brown had his hands up, some recanted their stories. Mr. Wilson testified that Mr. Brown charged at him, and other witnesses backed up his account.

"I'm backpedaling pretty good because I know if he reaches me, he'll kill me," Mr. Wilson told a state grand jury, in testimony that investigators said was consistent with what he told the F.B.I. "And he had started to lean forward as he got that close, like he was going to just tackle me, just go right through me," Mr. Wilson said.[507]

No, "justice" isn't the Department of Justice dropping its civil rights violation investigation of Darren Wilson... justice is simply the "narrative" being firmly cemented in the minds of already impulse control lacking, future-time orientation deprived black people: Wilson executed the "hands up, don't shoot" Brown, a clear-cut case of white racism.

---

[507][U.S. Not Expected to Fault Officer in Ferguson Case, New York Times, 1-21-15

The narrative remains...

January 23, 2015
The Ineluctable Reality Few Dare Face: Without a Black Population, St. Louis would be Homicide Free...

About nine months before Darren Wilson and Michael Brown became household names, the *New York Times* published a feature story on type of life individual black people had collectively created in North St. Louis.

It wasn't flattering.[508]

The *St. Louis Post-Dispatch* decided to supplant the *Times* 2013 expose of black North St. Louis, with a story detailing the complete collapse of the one-time purported center of the city's black middle class.

It was equally unflattering.

Both stories showcase the haunting validity of Robert E. Lee's timeless observation: "I have always observed that wherever you find the negro, everything is going down around him, and wherever you find the white man, you see everything around him improving":

> It didn't take long for Virginia Savage to realize she needed to leave.
>
> The single mother moved her two children and nephew to an apartment on Greer Avenue in the Greater Ville neighborhood in late 2013. The block was half-empty, and her apartment stood among decaying, boarded-up buildings.

---

[508] In Places Like North St. Louis, Gunfire Still Rules the Night, 11-19-13

It was what Savage, 48, could afford as a home health care aide, and it was close to where her kids went to school.

"That was not good for us," Savage explained later. "We moved two doors down from where the prostitutes stayed. Drug dealers. Drug users." There was nightly gunfire, and her children often didn't want to come home after school.

The day before they moved late last year, a man was shot and killed a block away.

Now she lives just a mile east, still on Greer Avenue and still in the Fourth Ward.

But she said it feels like a different city: Fewer vacant buildings. Less gunfire. More long-term residents. Block parties. A block captain. Neighborhood patrols at night.

A little distance can mean a big difference when it comes to St. Louis crime.

Although murders were up 33 percent in 2014 over the year before, a Post-Dispatch analysis of police data shows that 102 of the 159 were slain in just eight of the city's 28 wards.

The Fourth Ward, in the heart of north St. Louis, is a good place to get a feel for that violence. It had 15 murders last year, second-highest of all the wards.

It consists primarily of the Ville and Greater Ville neighborhoods — residents just call it the Ville — which once were the center of the city's black middle class. Now, the typical household income is in the low- to mid-$20,000s, and unemployment is high. Between the 2000 and 2010 censuses, the population dropped 26 percent.

Neighborhoods are pockmarked by vacant lots and crumbling homes, with conditions varying widely from block to block. The alderman, Sam Moore, said there are 1,242 vacant buildings in the area, a number he repeats for emphasis. Five schools sit empty. There are 1,700 vacant lots. Some entire blocks are just overgrown grass.

"I've torn down over 600 buildings," Moore said. "I can't tear down all of them."While murders were up, reports of other violent crimes — assault, rape and robberies — were down 24 percent last year, and showed a 56 percent drop since peaking in 2009. It was the biggest drop of any ward. The city had a 5.4 percent increase in such crimes last year.

The contradiction is difficult to explain. Falling population and clearance of abandoned buildings obviously play a role. But Moore doesn't believe that violent crime is dropping at all, and said that if the numbers are down it's only because police don't patrol there enough.

The Greater Ville Preservation Commission director, Harold Crumpton, said that clearing vacant buildings has a significant effect. "When you tear down the places where (criminals) hang out," he said, "they're gone."

In recent years, Crumpton led a community effort to drive out crime, with regular meetings with residents. He and Moore worked to identify nuisance properties and contact landlords.

He and volunteers have tacked up and passed out hundreds of signs encouraging people to report problems to the police and the Citizens' Service Bureau. "We're encouraging people to snitch," he said.

FIGHTING BACK

Around the Ville, Crumpton, of the preservation commission, points to dozens of churches and historic brick homes that have been rehabbed, and blocks that remain fully populated.

"What we're looking at," Crumpton said, "is a neighborhood that at one point had real strong middle class families living in it, and some of them are still living here.

"These people are really fighting back," he said.

But his enthusiasm level varies block by block. He contrasts buildings too far gone to fix against new community gardens. He sees a corner store where gang members hang out, a block of new homes filled with families and an alley where someone was murdered.

The Ville is filled with what Moore calls "dollhouses" — empty shells where much of the brick has been stripped away by thieves, exposing open rooms or entire floors of rotting furniture. Even one of the brightest spots — two blocks of newer houses on Lincoln Avenue — has a crumbling bungalow just waiting for a bulldozer.

"Dollhouses..."[509]

One of those "dollhouses" (remember... the so-called 'black middle-class' that inhabited the area known as Greater Ville weren't the people responsible with building the houses and neighborhood infrastructure; this was done by whites who left the area when Restrictive Covenants were deemed unconstitutional by the Supreme Court) in the Greater Ville neighborhood happens to be one of the most important addresses[510] in the history of civil rights movement: The "Shelley House" at 4600 Labadie Avenue in North St. Louis.

The "Shelley House" being of the aforementioned 1948 *Shelley v. Kraemer* SCOTUS case...

Once, the sky seemed the limit for those living in the Greater Ville neighborhood. This was as late as 1950, when the entire neighborhood was 100 percent white.[511]

Now, the condition of the nearly 100 percent black neighborhood is an ineluctable reminder that those who dared fight the black families integrating the Greater Ville neighborhood (because of the damning economic consequences they would bring, reflected back in the "dollhouses" of today) were absolutely, positively correct in their courageous stand.

---

[509] [Onetime center of St. Louis' black middle class now fights high murder count, *St. Louis Post-Dispatch*, 1-23-15]:

[510] http://www.stlouiscitytalk.com/2011/08/greater-ville-neighborhood.html

[511] Hayward, C. (2011). Justice and the American metropolis. University of Minnesota Press, p. 1-2

What's more, it can be stated with absolute certainty the city of St. Louis would be nearly homicide free without a black population; and the Greater Ville neighborhood would once again see the sky as the limit for those gentrifying the blighted, "dollhouse" infested community.

January 24, 2015
If I could find a souvenir Just to prove the world was here...

So the President of the United States agreed to be interviewed by a bovine black woman who once jumped into a tub full of milk and cereal, attempting to masticate the entire contents of said in the process.

She cut right to the heart of the matter of what keeps black people (incorrectly) up at night: the great fear of "po-po" killing their 'oh-so-innocent' black children:

> Green-lipsticked GloZell interviewed Barack Obama on Thursday in the latest White House sideshow.
>
> During the interview GloZell told Obama she's worried about the "po-po" killing her husband and so she cut all the hoods off his hoodies.
>
> Obama says, "I understand."
>
> GloZell: My husband is mad at me right now cuz I cut all the hoods off his hoodies.
>
> Obama: Ha, ha, ha... I understand.
>
> GloZell: I did that. I did that for real because I'm afraid when he goes outside that somebody might shoot and kill him. And

it's not like regular folks. It's the po-po. I hope that this changes. How can we bridge the gap between black African-American males and white cop?

Obama: Well first of all, we always have to just remind ourselves that the overwhelming majority of police officers are doing a job well and are doing it professionally. What we also know is there are still biases in our society. And in split second situations where people have to make a quick decisions, studies have shown that African-American males are seen as more threatening which puts them in vulnerable situations.[512]

It's quite easy to bridge the gap between black people and white cops, because no such "gap" exists.[513]

But it's even easier to realize no "gap" exists when police are no prepared to use a 'tactical retreat' as standard operating procedure when dealing with black people:

> Like many officers involved in deadly force encounters, Darren Wilson said his training took over when he shot Michael Brown in Ferguson.
>
> But what if Wilson had been trained differently?
>
> The national upheaval from Brown's death, and some others since, has put enormous pressure on law enforcement to find ways to control people's behavior while using less violence. One possibility — simple but repugnant to some officers — is to teach police to back away from certain difficult situations until help can arrive.
>
> The concept is known as "tactical retreat" or sometimes "tactical withdrawal" or "tactical restraint."

---

[512] [WOW! GloZell Tells Obama She's Worried "Po-Po" Is Going to Shoot Husband (Video)](), The Gateway Pundit, 1-23-15

[513] The real racial bias: Cops more willing to shoot whites than blacks, research finds: 'Counter-bias' rooted in concerns over social and legal consequence, *Washington Times*, 1-5-15

"We add the word, 'tactical' and not just 'retreating' or 'giving up' because that's what makes it palatable for police officers," explained Seth Stoughton, a criminal law professor at the University of South Carolina. The former Florida officer is a nationally prominent advocate for applying the softer approach.

"It's basically the choice to work smarter rather than harder."

Wilson has said he was in his police SUV on Aug. 9 when Brown, standing outside, struggled with him through the vehicle window and Wilson's gun fired twice. Brown was struck at least once in the hand, and ran. Wilson gave chase, and Brown turned back. Wilson then shot him multiple times, explaining later that he feared for his life.

Had Wilson been coached in tactical retreat, Stoughton said, he instead might have stepped on the gas to drive away from the encounter, and kept Brown in sight while waiting for backup.

Wilson "could have been trained to do something different to allow him to apprehend Michael Brown without putting himself in a situation that made him feel deadly force was the only safe response," Stoughton explained. "Train police officers to avoid putting themselves in danger, and you will see them use less force to get themselves out of danger.

"That's good for everybody."

Chiefs of the St. Louis and St. Louis County police have said in recent interviews they are reviewing training with the principles of tactical retreat in mind.

But it's a delicate dance, warned Sam Dotson, the city chief.

"Society has to realize that we pay police officers to keep us safe. And if every criminal knows, 'If I confront an officer, they will take four steps back, that's my escape route,' then that becomes the new norm."

Tactical retreat can be a hard sell to police traditionally trained to subdue an adversary — and to keep pouring on force until that is accomplished. Most departments have policies that provide discipline for cowardice.

Gabe Crocker, president of the St. Louis County Police Association, called the tactical retreat concept "cowardice retreat," and complained that it is "shameful" to consider.[514]

It's "shameful" to consider so few people dare look at the ruins of Camden, Cleveland, Detroit, Newark, North St. Louis, Birmingham, Memphis, Clayton County (Georgia), Gary (Indiana), Milwaukee, Baltimore, New Orleans, Wilmington (Delaware) and Rochester, noticing the exact same people are responsible for unleashing a destructive fury usually reserved for the nuclear missiles that flew because of 99 red balloons...

January 29, 2015
"...beneath a ceiling painted with allegorical images of Western democracy": Africans in America and the Chaos at the Civilian Review Board Hearing in St. Louis...

Before we begin, read this one important quote:

> Since the death of African-American teenager Michael Brown, civil rights activists have called for change in police departments and municipal courts — but also in the way society thinks about black lives.
>
> Not content to sit back, a wide array of churches are leading the charge, intentionally prolonging the conversation on race that has left some in the region uncomfortable.
>
> "God is engineering liberation," said Dietra Wise Baker,

---

[514] Ferguson aftermath causing police to consider retreat instead of force in certain situations, *St. Louis Post-Dispatch*, 1-24-15

pastor at Liberation Christian Church and co-chair of Metropolitan Congregations United, a group of interdenominational, multiracial congregations from around the region.

It "can't be *a* people that rise up, but *the* people. We have to rise up together. This can't be one community's fight."

In a separate Sunday gathering across town at Faith Church St. Louis in Earth City, for example, about 1,000 people met with faith leaders such as William Franklin Graham IV, grandson of evangelical preacher Billy Graham, and Aeneas Williams, a former St. Louis Ram turned pastor.

Their pastors signed the "Ferguson Declaration," a commitment "to support our leaders, our neighbors, and each other as we rise from the ashes of Ferguson and become an even better St. Louis."

Back at St. Louis University, Deb Krause, a New Testament professor at Eden Theological Seminary, called the current state of affairs in Missouri and the wider United States "a life-and-death matter."

The country, Krause said, is built on "this kind of mythic banner of equality" that denies the lived experiences of African-Americans.

"In our society, all lives do not matter equally. Black lives have been deemed to matter much, much less," Krause said.[515]

Were you able to pull out the quote? Recall, many of those churches mentioned above offered sanctuary to
rampaging, insurrectionary blacks back in late November, a safe haven to hide from police scrutiny after burning and looting Ferguson.[516]

---

[515] [Churches continue discussions on race, *St. Louis Post-Dispatch*, 1-26-15]:

[516] http://www.stltoday.com/lifestyles/faith-and-values/churches-to-serve-as-safe-

No one cares to remember the actual facts of the story surrounding Michael Brown's death, an incident completely dependent on his actions in: stealing cigars, walking in the middle of the road, refusing to cooperate with Darren Wilson's request he walk on the sidewalk, attacking Wilson and trying to grab his gun, and then charging at him again which required Officer Wilson to put him down.

All those who are pushing (and signing) the "Ferguson Declaration" care about is promoting the narrative of an angelic Michael Brown viciously being executed by "Jim Crow-in-the-flesh" Officer Wilson.

The monologuing on race must continue, with only one side allowed access the distribution of acceptable dialogue on all matters Michael Brown.

Those pushing this narrative never met Jeff Roorda, the business manager of the St. Louis' police union, who was in attendance at the open meeting at City Hall on January 28th where the topic of conversation was the creation of a civilian oversight board of the police department (civilian oversight board meaning = unaccountable black people demanding police stop arresting black suspects).

Dressed in a suit and sporting one of those "I am Darren Wilson" bracelets the Department of Justice (DOJ) hate so much, Roorda dared remind those at the meeting another side of Michael Brown story exists.[517]

And in so doing, a hilarious reminder of why any city with a large black population can no longer be called "civilized" broke out:

> An open meeting at City Hall on the creation of a civilian oversight board of the police department devolved into a melee on Wednesday night, further exposing the city's deep divisions over race and law enforcement.
>
> The meeting held by the aldermanic public safety committee,

---

spaces-after-ferguson-grand-jury/article_48dcdbdc-587f-5507-8997-017513dc3c72.html

[517] DOJ asks Ferguson chief to stop police from wearing 'I am Darren Wilson' bracelets on duty, St. Louis Post-Dispatch, 9-27-14

designed to seek public comment, lasted more than an hour with little event as residents ticked off the pros and cons of having a civilian board to review police conduct and procedures.

But the crowd became unsettled when police officers began testifying in opposition to the bill. At times, Alderman Terry Kennedy, who chairs the committee, struggled to keep order. The noise in the room spiked as police officers attempted to testify.

At that point, Jeff Roorda, the business manager of the city's police union, stood and called for order. Roorda was wearing a wristband in support of Darren Wilson, a former Ferguson police officer whose fatal shooting of 18-year-old Michael Brown last summer sparked months of civic unrest.

After Roorda stood up, the crowd grew louder.

"Excuse me, first of all, you do not tell me my function," responded Kennedy, who has championed the issue of civilian review for more than a decade.

Standing in the aldermanic hearing room packed with people shoulder-to-shoulder beneath a ceiling painted with allegorical images of Western democracy, Roorda shouted back at Kennedy.

Others began yelling, then pushing and shoving as officers struggled to maintain control. Some in the crowd scrambled to leave the packed room, which has only two exits.

The commotion lasted for about 15 minutes until order was restored.[518]

No, the allegorical images of Western democracy are represented in the looting and burning of Ferguson by black youth. The video of one of these incidents was recently released, with blacks complaining about "law enforcement attempting to subvert the emerging narrative of Black youth energized and engaged, flooding the streets

---

[518] Public hearing on civilian review board for St. Louis police erupts in chaos, St. Louis Post-Dispatch, 1-28-15

of this country in demonstrative displays of their anger."[519]

That's the reality of what Western democracy has degenerated into; and merely by showing up at a meeting of these jackals, an "I am Darren Wilson" bracelet wearing Jeff Roorda showed us what a farce this whole affair represents.

---

[519] Police release insane Ferguson looting video, are criticized for transparency, HotAir.com, 1-22-15

February 1, 2015
It's Like 10,000 Spoons when all you need is a Knife

News that the black violence in St. Louis is requiring "hot spot" policing to combat the *Ferguson Effect* shouldn't come as surprise.[520]

News that the black violence in St. Louis is requiring a request from the city police for help from the Missouri Highway Police to patrol the city's downtown streets shouldn't come as a surprise.[521]

Recall, St. Louis was home to the "Call to Oneness" in 2008, where black people marched in unity to the message of black people stopping the violence and working to make the city a better place:

> Depending on who was asked, the crowd estimates for the "Call To Oneness" march yesterday afternoon along the old Annie Malone May Day Parade route in North City ranged from 20,000-50,000. Regardless of the final count, the message was clear that African American men are ready to move forward to make a better St. Louis.
>
> Marchers gathered at Kings Highway and Dr. Martin Luther King, and then proceeded down Page, Newstead, and Kennerly.[522]

Of course, this black "Call to Oneness" was largely ignored by black people, with a two black people killed by other black within 24 hours of the march ending:

> There have been many prayers and marches and "come-to-Jesus" meetings concerning violence on the streets of St.

---

[520] Hot-spot policing kicks off downtown, KSDK.com, 1-30-15

[521] St. Louis cops seek highway patrol's help to police downtown streets, St. Louis Post-Dispatch, 1-28-15

[522] Black Men answer 'Call to Oneness', St. Louis American, 6-2-2008

Louis over the past few years.

In June 2008, during the "Call to Oneness," thousands of African-American men marched through the streets of St. Louis to "reclaim their community" and begin efforts anew to end violence and murder. Hours later, just two miles from the march's starting point, a young woman was shot and killed on a gas station/convenience market parking lot, and another woman was critically injured; a day later, a 19-year-old man was shot and killed, the *St. Louis American* reported.

Maybe we should all pray for more police on the streets of St. Louis. It's also time to consider police who walk daily beats.[523]

Actually, black clergy did call for prayer and divine intervention to stop the black violence in the city, roughly 45 days before anyone had heard the names Michael Brown or Darren Wilson.[524]

"Come-to-Jesus" meetings, prayer, black people marching in "Call to Oneness" marches, hotspot policing, and more police resources dedicated to patrolling downtown St. Louis won't stop the black crime:

> Area religious leaders are hoping a week of prayer will help curb violence in St. Louis summer. The week of prayers culminated with a service Sunday night inside Washington Tabernacle Missionary Baptist Church.
>
> Host pastor Rodney Francis said prayer alone will not stop violence. He said, "Prayer changes people, and people change things."
>
> Candles were lit for each homicide victim this year in St. Louis City. The candles were then extinguished. Faith leaders say in addition to destroying lives, violent crime can kill economic development.

---

[523] Cops Should Get On Beat to Help Clergy With Slowing City Violence, St. Louis Magazine, 6-27-14

[524] Clergy call for citywide prayer to end violence in St. Louis, St. Louis Post-Dispatch, 6-26-14

> "If people are afraid of St. Louis, they're not going to invest in St. Louis," said Rev. Rodrick Buton, New Northside Missionary Baptist Church.
>
> He talked about how painful it is to conduct a funeral service for a murder victim.
>
> "It's heartbreaking," said Burton. "It's just reprehensible."
>
> Faith leaders hope anyone caught in a culture of violence can break free and find peace in a house of worship.
>
> "We just need a unified approach with police, along with churches, along with businesses," said Burton.[525]

White people don't want to be caught up in the black "culture of violence": this is why you get white flight and divestment of businesses from areas that go from white to black.

Race will always be the ultimate variable in understanding why a city rises or fails; why a community is violence-free or one requiring "come-to-Jesus" meetings, lighting candles, prayer for divine intervention, black people marching in "Call to Oneness" marches, and hotspot policing to combat rampant criminality.

To ever address why St. Louis is overwhelmed in crime, one must use a knife to cut to the heart of the problem.

Put the spoon away, and just admit the problem individually black people collectively represent to the future stability of St. Louis.

February 2, 2015
There is no Spoon...

---

[525] Prayer vigil held to stop the violence in St. Louis, KPLR.com, 7-1-14

A few years ago, the [then] black police chief of St. Louis dedicated more resources to patrolling those dangerous neighborhoods where crime was concentrated.

Dangerous neighborhoods meaning black neighborhoods:

> "The overwhelming majority of our homicides are being committed as a result of gang and drug activity," [Dan] Isom said in a statement. "And while some of these people are choosing to lead these lifestyles, the fact is, they are often leading them in a neighborhood filled with people who are making no such choice, people who are hardworking, law-abiding citizens and who want their neighborhoods back."[526]

What about those white citizens who want their neighborhoods back, forever lost to becoming just another of Africa in America (white flight is simply the collective decisions by individual white families to seek an existence more suitably European than African).

Only 100 years ago, a saner, healthier racial reality flourished. Writing in *Lions of the Valley: St. Louis, Missouri*, James Neal Primm details a curious moment in the history of the city seemingly validated by the presence of "doll houses" in areas of St. Louis that have gone from all-white to all-black.[527] Primm's book is the seminal account of the history of St. Louis, and this excerpt speaks volumes to the truth of why white people fought for the integrity of their neighborhoods (so the houses wouldn't "doll houses" in the hands of blacks):

> White neighborhood associations in St. Louis which were close to black areas organized the "United Welfare Association" in 1911, found a powerful, well-heeled ally in the Real Estate Exchange, and began a persistent campaign for segregation ordinance. After repeated rejections by the

---

[526] St. Louis police chief wants special unit to target crime hot spots, St. Louis Post-Dispatch, 12-1-10

[527] http://www.stltoday.com/news/local/metro/onetime-center-of-st-louis-black-middle-class-now-fights/article_0722c66c-3e40-509c-aa23-d33d806b7113.html

Municipal Assembly, the U.W.A. circulated an initiative petition in 1915 to enact "An ordinance to prevent ill feeling, conflict and collision between the white and colored races" by requiring "the use of separate blocks for residence" and mandating segregation in churches and dance halls. The U.W.A. was not prejudiced, it claimed, it only sought the greatest good for the greatest number by protecting property values.[528]

Only 100 year later, those neighborhoods once kept safe via restrictive covenants are home to some one of the most violent populations in the entire country (the blighted ruins of the homes a reminder of a grander yesterday), an example of the tremendous capacity for decline from European standards Africans in America possess.[529]

Which brings us to February 2, 2015:

> A woman in the West End neighborhood was shot in the chest early Monday, apparently hit by a stray bullet fired into her home about five hours before St. Louis police were scheduled to blanket the neighborhood with more patrols.
>
> The woman, 36, was conscious as paramedics rushed her to a hospital, where she was listed in critical but stable condition.
>
> She had heard her car alarm sounding at about 5:15 a.m. Monday in the 5900 block of Horton Place. Police Chief Sam Dotson said the woman looked outside and saw four men standing near her car. Then, a bullet came through her window and hit her in the chest.
>
> Police have made no arrests in the case. Police did not release her name.
>
> St. Louis kicked off a new wave of police patrols in that

---

[528] Primm, J. (1998). Lion of the valley: St. Louis, Missouri, 1764-1980 (3rd ed.). St. Louis: Missouri Historical Society Press, p436

[529] http://preservationresearch.com/news-2/brick-theft-in-north-st-louis-a-preservation-crisis/

neighborhood at 10 a.m. Some officers are in uniform, driving marked police cars; others will be in unmarked vehicles wearing plain clothes.

The West End neighborhood, a tiny portion of the Wells Goodfellow neighborhood and part of Hamilton Heights are the focus this week of the St. Louis Police Department's hot-spot policing. The locations were announced in January.

The scene of the shooting on Horton Place is north of Delmar Boulevard, and between North Skinker Parkway and Goodfellow Boulevard. The boundaries of the West End neighborhood are Page Boulevard on the north, Delmar Boulevard on the south, Belt Avenue and Union Boulevard on the east, and St. Louis city limits on the west.[530]

As Ferguson reminded us, those white people in 1915 who dared try and create a world for their posterity free of "ill feeling, conflict and collision between the white and colored races" by requiring "the use of separate blocks for residence" were correct; what's most interesting about 2015, is the all-black communities of St. Louis are full of ill feeling, conflict and collision between only impulse challenged black people...

For this reason, police presence must be increased in heavily black area via "hot spot" police tactics.[531]

Shania Harrison, a black resident of one of the areas where this 'hot spot' policing will occur, told the St. Louis Fox affiliate of how glad she was this endeavor was taking place:

> "I'm a workin mama. I work every day. I take care of my kids. It's dangerous. You have to run in the house at nights. You have to grab yo' kids. They shootin' everyday. My kids are askin' me, 'why they keep shooting fire crackers at my house?' and I cant do nothing but tell my babies 'don't worry

---

[530] Stray bullet hits woman in St. Louis neighborhood slated for beefed up patrols, St. Louis Post-Dispatch

[531] http://fox2now.com/2015/02/02/police-to-increase-presence-in-3-west-st-louis-neighborhoods-starting-monday/

about that. We say our prayers every night. We say our prayers *every* night."[532]

Hilariously, those three areas of St. Louis are:

- Hamilton Heights: 97 percent black, 1 percent white
- Wells-Goodfellow: 97.5 percent black, .7 percent white
- West End: 84.9 percent black, 8.1 percent white

The U.W.A. was not prejudiced, it claimed, it only sought the greatest good for the greatest number by protecting property values.

Only a century after white individuals collectively gathered in St. Louis to protect the integrity of their property for future generations, the "doll houses" and dilapidated structures throughout heavily black North St. Louis stand as a silent monument to the morality of their position.

The difference is elucidated simply as what Europeans in America create versus what Africans in America inherit and watch disintegrate.

February 8, 2015
Somewhere, D. W. Griffith is Laughing...

Back in 1990, the city of Ferguson, Missouri was 73 percent white and 25 percent black.

This fact will become all the more obvious as we advance through the story of Bob Shannon, a black high school football coach once heralded by Bill Clinton as one of his 53 faces of hope (during his

---

[532] [City residents speak out about hot spot policing, Fox2Now.com, 1-26-15]:

1992 presidential campaign).

President George H. W. Bush dubbed Shannon "a beacon of hope in a sea of despair."

You see, Shannon coached the East St. Louis High School football team, and St. Louis Post-Dispatch reporter Kevin Horrigan was embedded with his program for the 1990 and 1991 seasons. Horrigan published a much celebrated book on the story of Shannon, titled *The Right Kind of Heroes*:

> East St. Louis, Illinois, is arguably the most dangerous and desolate city in America, perhaps our stalest example of urban collapse. With the nation's highest murder rate, it's a city in which half of the 41,000 residents are unemployed and 75 percent receive public assistance.
>
> In a city where most young men wind up on the streets, in jail, or dead, the high school football coach has sent dozens of his players on to college on football scholarships. He has done it with hard work and absolute dedication to virtues that went out of style in East St. Louis decades ago.
>
> This is the story of Coach Bob Shannon and the East St. Louis Flyers. It is a true story about a coach who won't give up and a team that has beaten all the odds.

East St. Louis is virtually all-black, the home of the "40 Days Without Violence" campaign and the celebrated return of Midnight Basketball (with the stated goal of keeping the black teenagers of East St. Louis off the streets and engaging in crime).

But for a brief moment in time, the exploits of Coach Shannon were to be celebrated, and lauded by national politicians on both the right and left.

Though 2015 represents an opportunity to reexamine the book, for Coach Shannon might have been employed in the all-black city of East St. Louis but he commuted to and from the embattled Illinois city (on a clear day, from the roof of East St. Louis High School one can see the Gateway Arch in downtown St. louis).

Coach Shannon, who coached the all-black East St. Louis High School Flyers from 1975 - 1995, lived in Ferguson.

And recall, Ferguson in 1980 was 85 percent white and 14 percent black.

Those black political leaders in East St. Louis expressed their discomfort at Shannon for living in the three-quarters white city of Ferguson:

> This is perhaps the biggest sore point with the power-brokers - not that he goes home to his wife, but that the home he goes home to is in Ferguson, Missouri, which lies near the St. Louis airport some twenty-five miles from East St. Louis High School.
>
> "They tell me I'm selfish for criticizing the city when I don't even live here," he says. "I figure it this way. You only have one life to live, and I say you ought to live it as comfortably as you can. Hey, I come from poverty. I want to live in a place where they pick up the trash, where you call the police you can be sure they're going to come. I don't think it's selfish to want to go home and be secure." (Horrigan, K. (1992).[533]

There's one more mention of the (then) nearly 75 percent white city of Ferguson in the book:

> Bob Shannon, a black man who grew up in the segregated South, went to an all-black college, has been employed in an all-black city his entire career, lives in the suburb of Ferguson, one of St. Louis's few integrated communities. Shannon doesn't live there because it is integrated; he lives there because it's safe. His approach to racial questions is practical, not political.[534]

Ferguson, Missouri is now 70 percent black and roughly 26 percent white.

---

[533] Horrigan, K. (1992). The right kind of heroes: Coach Bob Shannon and the East St. Louis Flyers. Chapel Hill, N.C.: Algonquin Books of Chapel Hill, p. 26

[534] **Ibid, p. 198**

Soon, the city Coach Shannon praised for being safe, one where tax-revenue funded, public services (trash removal and police) worked will inevitably degenerate to the level of government he criticized the all-black city of East St. Louis for failing to provide.

The soon-to-be nearly all-black city of Ferguson's future is none other than that described in the pages of *The Right Kind of Heroes:*

> The statistics are downright alarming.
>
> How can a town that is 67 percent Black be properly represented by a city council that is 93 percent white, a police force that is 93 percent white, and a white mayor who "sees no racial divide"?
>
> It can't.
>
> Fortunately, this may all change this spring, when the Black community in Ferguson perhaps will finally get a voice.
>
> Currently, five out of six city-council members are white, but three of them are scheduled to vacate their seats in April.
>
> As of now, there are eight candidates competing for those open seats, and four of them are Black.
>
> Because both candidates for one of the seats are Black, Black representation on the council is guaranteed to double. The two remaining Black candidates are also battling for a single seat (against two white candidates); if one of them wins, the city council would suddenly triple its Black representation.[535]

Ferguson's future looks a lot like the one East St. Louis has enjoyed since white people left it in the hands of black people to maintain, in the process being in absolute political control of the city's fate...

It's a safe bet in a few years Midnight Basketball leagues will begin to appear in Ferguson; it's a safer bet the "40 Days Without Violence" campaign currently underway in East St. Louis will migrate one day

---

[535] Blacks in Ferguson May Finally Get a Voice, DiversityInc.com, 2-7-1

to the city Coach Bob Shannon once called home to because it was a safe and secure community.

That, of course, was a community boasting an entirely different racial population... and a community's health is a reflection of nothing more than the people who call it home.

February 10, 2015
What's so 'puzzling' New York Times? Individual Blacks are Collectively Responsible for the 'Stubbornly High Murder Rate' in St. Louis...

Ever try and 500-piece jigsaw puzzle together only to find a few of the pieces are missing?

It's infuriating.

You worked so hard to fit individual pieces together to reveal the picture on the box, only to come up short.

Well Erik Eckholm, a writer for the New York Times, appears to only be working with only a few of puzzle pieces when trying to understand why the Bell Curve City has a "stubbornly high murder rate"; of course, this puzzle is simply solved with one piece of information.

Race.

But because this is a piece of the puzzle apparently no one is allowed to consider, we get Eckholm's hilarious reaction to what is essentially a problem courtesy of individual black people collectively driving away the civilization whites established in St. Louis:

> Across from the Little Explorer's Learning Center, diagonal to

a crumbling house where heroin dealers and hangers-on often mill about, a garland of teddy bears adorns a telephone pole, a memorial to the latest victim to fall here at one of this city's deadliest corners.

The victim was a 27-year-old man shot dead on Dec. 23, one of the last casualties in a year of surging gun violence.

"It's nothing to get a firearm," said Michael Shelton, who was badly wounded by gunfire eight years ago at this same corner, in the bleak Wells-Goodfellow neighborhood of north St. Louis, and is now determined to stay out of trouble. "I don't know anybody who doesn't carry or have easy access to one."

Murder rates have fallen sharply in most of the country. But St. Louis is one of a few major cities, including Memphis and Washington, where the number of homicides jumped last year. It is also one of several cities, including Baltimore, Detroit, Gary, Ind., and New Orleans, where violent crime, concentrated in low-income minority neighborhoods, has remained stubbornly high, though down from the crack-driven peaks of the early 1990s.

The start of the new year was equally violent.

On Jan. 15, shaken by six murders in five shootings overnight, the city's mayor, Francis Slay, called for more police, more surveillance cameras, more certain penalties for carriers of illegal guns and stronger gun laws, declaring: "Crime is the absolute No. 1 priority in the City of St. Louis."

A seventh person was killed on the afternoon of the mayor's news conference.

Jennifer M. Joyce, the city's circuit attorney, or prosecutor, an elected position, complains that in St. Louis, the illegal possession of a gun is too often "a crime without a consequence," making it difficult to stop confrontation from turning lethal.

At the same time, deeper social roots of violence such as addiction and unemployment continue unchecked. And city officials also cite what they call a "Ferguson effect," an increase in crime last year as police officers were diverted to control protests after a white officer shot and killed Michael Brown, an unarmed black teenager in the nearby suburb on Aug. 9.

The violence is not uniform. Nearly all the increase in murders in St. Louis last year occurred in eight neighborhoods, said Richard Rosenfeld, a criminologist at the University of Missouri-St. Louis.

The largest jump was in Wells-Goodfellow, a desolate zone where more than a third of the houses are abandoned, liquor stores and churches are sprinkled among boarded-up shops and older residents fear stepping outside at night. In this neighborhood of fewer than 6,000 residents, 14 people were murdered in 2014, up from seven in 2013, for a per-person homicide rate five times the city average.

More precise police work is well and good, said James Clark, vice president for community outreach at Better Family Life, a nonprofit social service group based in Wells-Goodfellow just two blocks from the notorious intersection of Arlington and Ridge Streets, where the last murder of 2014 took place.

"But we've got to stop expecting the police to solve the crime problem," Mr. Clark said, adding that only with a huge increase in social aid could a cultural collapse be prevented. "There is a void that the police can't fill."

Mr. Clark, a respected presence on the streets, is trying to help rescue youths and families one at a time, sending workers out to knock on doors and link people up with social services, from drug treatment to anger management to prenatal care.

"Our neighborhoods are resource deserts," he said. "Every neighborhood needs a center with drug treatment, G.E.D. lessons, recreation for the kids."

In 2007, after Mr. Shelton was shot, his grandmother was washing her car in front of the house on Ridge Street where she and her husband raised him and nine other grandchildren after their drug-addicted mothers lost custody.

Approached by a Better Family Life canvasser, she asked for help for her son.

Mr. Shelton, 25, has joined a support group at the agency, avoided a criminal record and hopes, with Mr. Clark's help, to become certified as a security guard.

"I just found out that my girlfriend is pregnant," he said. "I plan to marry her. I'm very excited."[536]

But why does the *New York Times* describe the Wells-Goodfellow neighborhood as "bleak?" Why does Mr. Clark call his community a "resource desert?"

Well, Well-Goodfellow is only .7% white and 97.5% black...

> The borders of the neighborhood are defined by the St. Louis city limits on the north-western edge, Dr. Martin Luther King Drive to the south-west, Natural Bridge Avenue to the north-east and Union Boulevard to the south-east.

So a 97 percent white community must a be "resource ocean," right? Well, Wells-Goodfellow was once 100 percent white, and *Wikipedia* describes it as just that:

> The rich history of this area, particularly the streets close to the north and west city limits, has been all but lost to time. Part of the area dates to before the Civil War, and at one time it was the location of the popular amusement center Suburban Garden at Kennerly and Hodiamont, but its greatest growth came in the 1920s and 1930s with a mixture of single family homes, duplexes, four-family flats and apartment buildings. Before World War II the area was considered a particularly attractive community in which to live and rear a family. Hard to believe today, but it was semi-

---

[536] St. Louis Puzzles Over Stubbornly High Murder Rate, *New York Times, 2-10-15*

rural. For example, on Roosevelt Place large grassy pastures extended west from the four-family flat at 5865-67 to the western city limits and north to the Wabash railroad tracks. On the west ran the City Limits streetcar line on an in-the-woods embankment a block east of Kienlen Avenue; on the north ran the Wabash corridor, with heavy rail traffic including the Wabash Cannonball at 10:08 each morning and the Bluebird at 10:13. Leschen Rope and Wire factory on Hamilton between Kennerly and Roosevelt hummed with activity day and night and had its own railroad spur leading from the Wabash tracks. The four-family flat at 5865-67 Roosevelt turned out a Missouri lieutenant governor, a highly awarded nurse, a successful sculptor, and a celebrated teacher. Next to the building the occupant of one flat kept horses in a barn and blackberry patches stretched westward. Likewise, the Wellston library was one of the most popular in the city; the children came from middle-class or lower-middle-class homes without many extras and kept the small library jammed on Saturdays as they selected which books they would next read. The area mixed a heavy Catholic population and a heavy Jewish population with other religions with harmony. When the exodus to the suburbs in the late 1950s moved swiftly the neighborhoods underwent a drastic change and today much of the area's structures are long gone.[537]

Remember: blacks displaced whites decades ago (as was the ability for white people to build long-term wealth in their homes via Restrictive Covenants, with HUD's usage of Section 8 Vouchers destroying the ability to build short-term wealth now...) in Wells-Goodfellow and other North St. Louis communities.

And over time, the new black inhabitants of these "resource oceans" dried up whatever remained of the civilization whites left behind:

> The Ville is filled with what [Greater Ville Preservation Commission Director Harold] Moore calls "dollhouses" — empty shells where much of the brick has been stripped away by thieves, exposing open rooms or entire floors of

---

[537] http://en.wikipedia.org/wiki/Wells/Goodfellow,_St._Louis

rotting furniture. Even one of the brightest spots — two blocks of newer houses on Lincoln Avenue — has a crumbling bungalow just waiting for a bulldozer.[538]

And why is North St. Louis littered with those "dollhouses"(the abandoned remains of the individual dreams of white people before Martin Luther King's 'Dream' supplanted whatever hopes whitey had for the future...)?

The puzzle is so simple, and it only needs one piece...

Race.

When Wells-Goodfellow was nearly 100 percent white, the city boasted a rich history because those individual white people helped collectively make it rich; today, at nearly 100 percent black, the individual blacks how call it home have made it "bleak" and a "resource desert."

The puzzle is so simple...

February 12, 2015
Praising our leaders, we're getting in tune/ The music's played by the, the mad men

Ferguson War Journal: Day 188

Who made the National Guard stand down in Ferguson on November 24, 2014, allowing the Negro Insurrection to burn/loot/riot unimpeded?

Though news Beauty World - a store specializing in hair products for black women - will soon reopen should spur incredible economic

---

[538] Onetime center of St. Louis' black middle class now fights high murder count, *St. Louis Post-Dispatch*, 1-23-15

growth and outside investor confidence...[539]

Was it Eric Holder, who in August of 2014 lashed out against the white police officers attempting to use force to put down the black riots, saying, "Tell them to remove the damn tanks"?

Was it Barack Obama, who on the night of November 24, 2014, said this of black anger and resentment to the grand jury decision to not charge Officer Darren Wilson: "It's an understandable reaction."[540]

We might never know, but for now the white Democrat governor of Missouri is accepting blame:

> Two fire district officials from St. Louis County said Wednesday that they had been promised that the Missouri National Guard would protect firefighters called to Ferguson if protests turned violent last fall.
>
> But they learned otherwise when fire district leaders arrived at the emergency operations center on Nov. 24 to prepare for a long-awaited grand jury announcement.
>
> "That's when we were told they weren't able to get the Guard," said Greg Brown, chief of the Eureka Fire District.
>
> As a result, firefighters abandoned their hoses and left buildings burning when gunfire and looting erupted that night in the aftermath of the grand jury's decision that former police Officer Darren Wilson would not face criminal charges in the Aug. 9 shooting death of unarmed teen Michael Brown.
>
> "To me, that was the most heartbreaking thing of all of it," said Matt LaVanchy, assistant chief of the Pattonville Fire District. "We wanted to help that community."

---

[539] http://www.stltoday.com/business/local/ferguson-and-dellwood-struggle-to-recover-from-six-months-of/article_65727ad0-b4a9-5799-be57-e506cde2432e.html

[540] http://www.whitehouse.gov/the-press-office/2014/11/24/remarks-president-after-announcement-decision-grand-jury-ferguson-missou

The fire officials told their stories Wednesday night to a joint legislative committee that is investigating the way Gov. Jay Nixon's administration handled the protests in Ferguson.

Nixon had declared a state of emergency in advance of the grand jury's decision. He said then that "violence will not be tolerated" and that St. Louis County police would be in charge in Ferguson, with the National Guard deployed to assist.

But after the announcement on Nov. 24 that Wilson faced no charges, shots rang out and businesses burned on West Florissant Avenue and South Florissant Road.

Nixon later said that officers sacrificed property in order to save lives.

He repeated that position on Wednesday, defending the decision not to deploy National Guard troops along the Ferguson-area business corridors in advance of the looting and arson. Instead, he chose to allow St. Louis County Police officers, trained under the Peace Officer Standards and Training program, to handle the initial wave of rioting.

"The theory here and the practice was that people who had been on the front edge of this, literally getting yelled at, getting things thrown at them, getting called a lot of names, that those POST-certified officers were the people to be in front," Nixon said.

"None of us are happy that there were shots fired," Nixon told reporters. "None of us are happy that there were buildings burned down. This wasn't a joyful time for anybody.

"But I think when this is looked at, the discipline that was shown there, we are talking about what tactically should've been done and what buildings were damaged. It's a lot better than the discussion after Kent State."[541]

---

[541] Firefighters tell Missouri lawmakers that they couldn't fight Ferguson fires unprotected, St. Louis Post-Dispatch, 2-12-15

The last white mayor of 70 percent black Ferguson, James Knowles, was completely left out of the decision making process in the days leading up to the Nov. 24 insurrection:

> Ferguson Mayor James Knowles told a panel of Missouri law makes that St. Louis County Police and the Highway Patrol did not include him in the decision making process for his city during the unrest.
>
> The mayor also said he never heard back from Governor Jay Nixon's office after asking for National Guard help. Instead, Knowles said it took him calling Senator Clair McCaskill and Attorney General Chris Koster before the National Guard moved into the area.[542]

Of course, the great question of what happened to the Oath Keepers (who motto reads: 'We will NOT obey orders to disarm the American people') in Ferguson still remains murky at best... though the answer is probably the same people behind the National Guard standing down.[543]

Ferguson might be an obscure suburb of a declining American city (St. Louis), but to truly understand the tyrannical nature of where this country is headed we must confront what *not only happened there*, but what continues to happen in the region.

February 15, 2015
Lynchings in USA over an 86-year time-span vs. Homicides in St. Louis over a Decade: Retiring the Idea #BlackLivesMatter

---

[542] http://www.kmov.com/news/local/Ferguson-mayor-tells-Mo-lawmakers-he-was-left-out-of-decision-making-process-during-unrest-291638661.html#ixzz3RZjOmWKY

[543] http://www.nytimes.com/2014/11/30/us/on-rooftops-of-ferguson-volunteers-with-guns.html

The truth of lynching.

You've seen a comparison of black homicides in Detroit over a ten-year span to lynching in America[544]; you've seen a comparison of black homicides in Baltimore over a seven-year span to lynching in America.[545]

It's only natural we'd turn our eyes to St. Louis.

But first, a quick refresher.

Though Oprah Winfrey, who donated $13 million to the building of National Museum of African American History and Culture (NMAAHC), claimed "millions of black people were lynched," it turns out only 3,446 blacks were lynched between 1882-1968:

> From 1882-1968, 4,743 lynchings occurred in the United States. Of these people that were lynched 3,446 were black. The blacks lynched accounted for 72.7% of the people lynched.
>
> Out of the 4,743 people lynched only 1,297 white people were lynched. That is only 27.3%. Many of the whites lynched were lynched for helping the black or being anti lynching and even for domestic crimes.[546]

So, over a span 86 years, 3,446 black people were lynched (many were lynched for actual crimes, mind you); that's roughly 40/lynchings per year.[547]

The city of St. Louis has been in the news for the better part of sixth months, primarily because an 18-year-old black male refused to

---

[544] http://stuffblackpeopledontlike.blogspot.com/2013/10/lynchings-in-usa-over-86-year-timespan.html

[545] http://stuffblackpeopledontlike.blogspot.com/2014/03/lynchings-in-usa-over-86-year-time-span.html

[546] http://www.chesnuttarchive.org/classroom/lynchingstat.html

[547] http://law2.umkc.edu/faculty/projects/ftrials/shipp/lynchingsstate.html

cooperate with a police officers request to walk on the sidewalk (instead of in the middle of the road).

But before we explode the hilarious myth of #BlackLivesMatter, let's look at the historical record of homicide in St. Louis just to better understand the rationale of those white people who hoped to protect the integrity of their communities and neighborhoods with restrictive covenants (in the mid 1910s - when the city was 93 percent white - two-thirds of white St. Louis residents voted in favor of passing the nation's first referendum imposing racial segregation on housing).[548]

Why were white St. Louis residents so fearful of blacks then? Why does residential segregation still persist in St. Louis[549], much to the chagrin of white liberals nationwide (who still practice such activities in their private lives, while demanding quite vocally other whites practice only integration)? [550]

The book *St. Louis Metromorphosis: Past Trends and Future Directions* (edited by Brady Baybeck and F. Terrence Jones), published in 2004 by the Missouri Historical Society Press, provides a historical reference to not only why residential segregation was necessary in 1916 St. Louis - when the city was only six percent black - but also why it is still necessary today... when the city is 49 percent black.

They write:

> Examining overall homicide trends ignores the substantial role that race plays in levels and trends in city crime rates. Are the patterns shown for St. Louis similar for blacks and whites? To begin to address this question, in Figure 4 [below] we present homicide arrest rates for 1930-2000 disaggregated by race. Three trend lines are show, which

---

[548] http://www.stlmag.com/news/the-color-line-race-in-st.-louis/

[549] http://www.wired.com/2013/08/how-segregated-is-your-city-this-eye-opening-map-shows-you/

[550] http://www.washingtonpost.com/national/in-st-louis-delmar-boulevard-is-the-line-that-divides-a-city-by-race-and-perspective/2014/08/22/de692962-a2ba-4f53-8bc3-54f88f848fdb_story.html

represent total homicide arrest rates and black and white homicide arrest rates, respectively.

Three important observations emerge from inspection of Figure 4. First, the trend in homicde arrest rates for whites is relatively stable throughout the period, fluctuating no more than 10 per 100,000 over the last seventy years of the twentieth century. Second, consistent with findings reported in previous historical studies of homicide in the United States and New York, homicide arrest rates for blacks are generally much higher than the rates observed for white, and they remain higher though out the period. Indeed, black arrests account for over half of all arrests from 1950 on, a period of time when blacks accounted for less than one-third of the city's population. And since 1970, blacks have accounted for 80 percent of homicide arrests except for a single year.

Although the full meaning of the race-specific trends shown in Figure 4 would move us well beyond the scope of this chapter, it is noteworthy that the year in which black and white homicide arrest rates begin to diverge considerably - 1963 - is a unique year in the demographic history of St. Louis. As shown in Figure 5, 1963 is the first year in which the City's black population approaches about one-third of the total population, a proportion that has been identified as an important "tipping point" in social science research on racial segregation, and whites' expressed neighborhood residential preferences, perceived threat from blacks, and fear of crime.[551]

Why does the past matter? Because the trends of the past are the ghost from the future was born:

> ...a University of Missouri – St. Louis researcher says emotions aside, the number of black youth who have been fatally shot by white police officers has been fairly low in recent years.
>
> Criminology professor David Klinger told KMOX's Charlie

---

[551] Baybeck, B. (2004). St. Louis Metromorphosis: Past trends and future directions. St. Louis: University of Missouri Press, p. 268-270

> Brennan that he conducted a thorough, decade-long study that showed there were 1,265 murders over that time, with 90 percent of the victims being black. And 90 percent of those black victims were killed by other blacks.
>
> "While I understand the people are concerned about the use of deadly force by the police, by far – about 50 to 1 – more blacks in St. Louis are killed by other blacks as compared to white police officers," Klinger says.
>
> Over that same period, Klinger says 31 blacks were killed by police officers – 21 by white police officers.
>
> "The sad fact is, we had well over a thousand black-on-black homicides in the city of St. Louis during that same decade," he says.[552]

The article should have read: 90 percent of victims were killed by other blacks... (no snitch!)[553]

So 90 percent of 1265 is 1138... 1138 black people murdered, with 90 percent of them killed by other black people. Or 1024 black on black homicides in St. Louis in the decade Klinger studied.

We can get a better number though:

> Of the 567 homicides from 2008 to 2011, for which the race of the victim is available in the SLMPD annual reports, 502 are listed as black, while 64 were white. Over that period, 89% of those killed in the city were black. In a city that's very nearly 50/50 black/white, those 64 homicides would give an annual murder rate of ~10/100,000 for white residents and ~78/100,000 black residents.[554]

---

[552] Study: More Blacks in St. Louis Killed by Other Blacks Compared to White Officers, KMOX.com, 10-15-14

[553] http://www.stltoday.com/news/local/metro/girl-s-burial-spotlights-a-culture-of-violence/article_26bd5032-f188-514a-ba93-1e9ac727e745.html

[554] http://nextstl.com/2013/01/understanding-st-louis-homicides-2005-2012/

In the entire United States of America, from 1882-1968, 4,743 lynchings occurred in the United States. Of these people that were lynched 3,446 were black. The blacks lynched accounted for 72.7% of the people lynched.

In just one decade in St. Louis, there were 1024 black on black homicides...

Each year, the City of St. Louis Metropolitan Police Department, releases an Annual Report to the Community. This report breaks down violent crime and the overall percentage of the racial group arrested for each offense (note because of lack of trust with police, many homicides lack suspects).

This information should further illustrate the lie of #BlackLivesMatter. Remember, out of 318,000 people, St. Louis is 49.2 percent black 43.9 percent white (as of 2010 US Census).

Here's the breakdown 1999:

- 90.2% of those arrested for murder in St. Louis in 1999 were black.

Here's the breakdown for 2000:
- 91.67% of those arrested for murder in St. Louis in 2000 were black.

Here's the breakdown for 2002:
- 94.78% of those arrested for murder in St. Louis in 2002 were black.

Here's the breakdown for 2003:
- 96.77% of those arrested for murder in St. Louis in 2003 were black.

Here's the breakdown for 2004:
- 94.78% of those arrested for murder in St. Louis in 2004 were black.

Heres' the breakdown for 2005:
- 91.55% of those arrested for murder in St. Louis in 2005were black.

Here's the breakdown for 2006:

- 91.8% of those arrested for murder in St. Louis in 2006 were black.

Here's the breakdown for 2007:
- 92% of those arrested for murder in St. Louis in 2007 were black.

Anything different in 2008? No:
- 97.7% of those arrested for murder in St. Louis in 2008 were black.

2009? Is it still almost all-black? Yes:
- 97.1% of those arrested for murder in St. Louis in 2009 were black.

Please, tell me 2010 is different...:
- 92.4% of those arrested for murder in St. Louis in 2010 were black.

2011? Same old song:
- 92% of those arrested for murder in St. Louis in 2011 were black.

According to 2012 Metropolitan Police Department, City of St. Louis: Annual Report to the Community:
- 97.6% of those arrested for murder in St. Louis in 2012 were black.

No, Black Lives truly Don't Matter.

What does matter, is that in the 1910s, the white people of St. Louis (representing 93 percent of the population of the city) decided to pass laws to protect their property and communities.

In so doing, they declared #WhiteLivesMatter.

In only one decade, *black people in St. Louis killed other black people to the tune of 30 percent of the number of blacks lynched in all of the United States in a span of 86 years*!

St. Louis has a homicide problem and is only dangerous today because of black people, just as it only had a homicide problem and was only dangerous because of blacks in the decades of 1910, 1920, 1930, 1940, 1950, 1960, 1970, 1980, 1990, 2000, and 2010...

February 17, 2015
Ta-Nehisi Coates – Have You Looked at 4300 West Belle Place in St. Louis Today?

"We all have our time machines, don't we? Those that take us back are memories... And those that carry us forward, are dreams." The Time Machine, 2002

Reading an article by *Atlantic's* go-to black authority figure Ta-Nehisi Coates brought a smile to my face that will be hard to wipe away.

It's from this story.[555]

No, nothing he wrote is particularly interesting (or even remotely based on anything outside of your typical black grievances).

It's an image used to highlight the evils of white people - past, present, and future white people - strategically placed at the start of the story. The image shows gorgeous houses on 4300 West Belle Place and reads:

Look! Look at these homes now! An entire block ruined by negro invasion. Every house marked "X" now occupied by negroes. ACTUAL PHOTOGRAPH OF 4300 WEST BELLE PLACE. Save you home! Vote for segregation! -- A 1916 leaflet proposes to segregate St. Louis. The measure passed. (Missouri History Museum Library and Research Center)

Isn't there just one question needing to be asked today?

---

[555] The Racist Housing Policies That Built Ferguson: The geography of America would be unrecognizable today without the race-based social engineering of the mid-20th century., 10-17-14

Of course there is: what happened to 4300 West Belle Place in St. Louis?

Located in the Vandeventer neighborhood of St. Louis (a community that is 95.7 percent black and 1.2 percent white)[556], 4300 West Belle Place is nestled in a community where the average list price for a home is $17,499 [source: Trulia.com][557]

Courtesy of the magic of Google Maps, you can virtually walk down West Belle Place in St. Louis and see the homes that were pictures in the 1916 leaflet proposing to segregate St. Louis.[558]

It's a haunting trip, seeing for yourself the bulk of those houses in the 1916 leaflet - strategically used by Ta-Nehisi Coates to conjure antipathy by Atlantic readers against white people of the past, present and especially the future - are now gone, the entire area surrounding West Belle Place looking more like Dresden after the Allies bombed the city than before.

But there's an interesting post-script to the story, highlighting the type of individual who calls 4300 West Belle Place home nearly 100 years after the ad Ta-Nehisi Coates used in his story on Ferguson to connect present-day whites in St. Louis to their past racism (castigating all future white people in the process):

> Police Major Joseph Spiess was among department brass who hit the streets after a particularly violent night this week, to help look for trouble.
>
> He found some, and it almost killed him.
>
> Spiess was among about a dozen top commanders helping

---

[556] http://en.wikipedia.org/wiki/Vandeventer,_St._Louis

[557] http://www.trulia.com/homes/Missouri/Saint_Louis/sold/1047856-4300-W-Belle-Pl-Saint-Louis-MO-63108

[558] https://www.google.com/maps/@38.649885,-90.246448,3a,75y,349.16h,81.16t/data=!3m4!1e1!3m2!1s4OsGA0mo7ZuZfpY4_STKew!2e0!6m1!1e1

supplement patrols Tuesday night after 19 people were wounded in eight incidents the night before.

By the time the shift ended, there would be two close calls for officers and one embarrassing mistake.

Spiess, 52, was alone, in uniform, driving an unmarked Chevrolet Impala about 9:22 p.m. when he spotted a suspicious-looking black Pontiac Bonneville with temporary license tags on Evans Avenue, heading west near Vandeventer Avenue.

He said he made a U-turn to follow, and the Pontiac's driver would not stop for his lights and siren. The circumstances did not qualify under rules limiting pursuits, so he gave up at Evans and Sarah Street.

As Spiess continued along Evans, a man jogged slowly toward him and stopped between parked cars about 12 feet away.

"He looks me dead in the eye, lifts his pistol and starts shooting at me," Spiess said Wednesday. "The first round sounded like a shotgun went off in my car. Then I heard a high-pitched whine go through the (open) driver's side window and out the passenger window.

"He looked at me square in the face, I'm in an Impala, wearing a police shirt, and he was looking me right in the eye. He knew who he was shooting at. He absolutely knew I was a policeman."

Spiess said that as he sped off, he watched in the mirror as the gunman stepped to the middle of the street and continued firing.

About a block away, Spiess pulled over to check himself for wounds. "I remember thinking, 'I have to be hit,'" he said. "I could not believe I wasn't hit."

Meanwhile, police arrested three people found hiding in a home near the ambush on Spiess, and seized handguns. They were believed to have been in the Pontiac, which was found abandoned in the area.

Two of them were later charged. Robert O. Simmons, 19, of the 4500 block of St. Ferdinand Avenue in St. Louis, was charged with first-degree assault of a law enforcement officer and armed criminal action. Demetrius J. Vanarsdale, 24, of the 4300 block of West Belle Place in St. Louis, was charged with unlawful possession of a firearm and resisting arrest.

Spiess said investigation showed that 16 shots had been fired at him from a 9-millimeter weapon with a 30-round extended magazine. He said he found two bullet holes in the driver's side door of his car. The windows were down, so he's not sure how many other rounds might have passed through.[559]

Did you catch it? Demetrius J. Vanarsdale represents why the 1916 leaflet was put out by white homeowners in St. Louis, worried about the long-term damage to the equity in their homes black people would bring...

We can't change the past, nor can we have much influence on the present... but events in both the past and present represent our only guide to crafting policies for a stable, prosperous future.

February 18, 2015
To the last syllable of recorded time... Gov. Nixon Admits the National Guard Stood Down because 'Black Terrorists Lives > Private Property'

Ferguson War Journal: Day 194

---

[559] St. Louis police commander survives ambush while on special patrol, St. Louis Post-Dispatch, 6-12-13

Throughout the insanity of the situation in Ferguson, one frighteningly obvious fact has become crystal clear: there is no real opposition to those pushing for the canonization of Michael Brown and for castigating all white people of metropolitan St. Louis for bearing some responsibility for the inexcusable actions of Officer Darren Wilson.

Why no business owner of a looted or burned store has yet to sue the Obama Administration, George Soros, the editorial board of the *St. Louis Post-Dispatch*, or any of the out-of-town agitators who created and promulgated (or, in the case of Soros, funded) the narrative of white supremacy/racism being responsible for the death of Brown is beyond me.

Why no home owner in Ferguson has yet to take the Department of Justice, the Obama Administration, Soros, or the *St. Louis Post-Dispatch* editorial board to court is also beyond me, considering whatever equity they had in their home is virtually worthless.[560]

The goal all along by the Obama Administration and Department of Justice Attorney General has been to slander the remaining white people in Ferguson (never forget: Ferguson was virtually 100 percent white in 1970 and nearly 80 percent white in 1990) for tolerating a racist police force obviously out for black blood.[561]

And yet not one voice has dared stand, save for the heroic Jeff Roorda - The St. Louis Police Officers Association's business manager - who dared defend the St. Louis Police Department in the face of a rabid black crowd prepared to satiate itself on the knowledge a review board will end the threat of actual police force once and for all.

But now Roorda, who proudly wore an "I am Darren Wilson"

---

[560] Ferguson home sales fell as uncertainty gripped real estate market, St. Louis Post-Dispatch, 2-8-15

[561] http://www.stltoday.com/news/local/govt-and-politics/article_b886e3e5-73c9-5037-bd05-d98cdf0a7bc6.html

bracelet to hearing, has been neutered.562

And now comes the news the National Guard called up to protect businesses from the black insurrection the Obama Administration and the St. Louis Post-Dispatch editorial board agitated (with George Soros helping fund the riots to the tune of $33 million) wasn't even there to stop the riots.563

The city and region had been turned over to the black insurrectionaries:

> For months, critics have questioned why the Missouri National Guard did not respond more quickly as buildings burned along Ferguson's main business corridors.
>
> But even had guardsmen arrived sooner that night in November, interviews and newly released documents show they would not have had the authority to stop the violence.
>
> The Guard was never meant to engage with protesters, Adjutant Gen. Stephen Danner said on Tuesday. Troops were to stand guard over sites critical to the region, sometimes as invisibly as possible, documents show.
>
> Guardsmen were not authorized to shoot to protect property in Ferguson, make arrests, or even stop people from committing most crimes.
>
> "That was never the plan, to have the Guard in Ferguson," Danner said. "When you're dealing with a civil disturbance and a tightknit group of folks coming at you, you cannot string your soldiers down the street like so many parking meters. That is a danger to them."564

---

562 http://www.stltoday.com/news/local/crime-and-courts/controversial-st-louis-police-union-boss-muzzled-when-it-comes/article_7fd6dbc2-e878-59a4-bd9a-cd056f9c1476.html

563 http://www.washingtontimes.com/news/2015/jan/14/george-soros-funds-ferguson-protests-hopes-to-spur/?page=all

564 National Guard would have had to use 'deadly force' to stop riots in Ferguson, official says, St. Louis-Post Dispatch, 2-18-15

That was never the plan...

Private property, businesses, and potentially residential homes were to be sacrificed to the black mob, so that no black lives would be lost in the process.

What's the point of even having a National Guard if they are told to stand down to domestic terrorism? Then again, what's the point of having a nation if domestic terrorists get $33 million to fund their efforts and a sympathetic President and Attorney General of said nation to offer support?

But it gets better:

> In the wake of new revelations about the restrictions placed on Missouri National Guard troops deployed in the Ferguson area during last fall's rioting, Gov. Jay Nixon forcefully defended on Wednesday the choice to protect life rather than property.
>
> "It was clearly not the best path forward to get into a gun fight on the street," said Nixon, responding to a report that guard troops had been ordered not to protect private property or intervene in most crimes during the late-November rioting.
>
> "Those buildings and businesses will be rebuilt . . . but to say that that night we should have had a larger and broader gun fight? That would not have solved any problems," Nixon told reporters after an event at Roosevelt High School in St. Louis.
>
> But officials and businesses in and around Ferguson say they were told explicitly by local and St. Louis County Police that the guard troops would protect property. Some reacted furiously Wednesday to Nixon's comments.
>
> "It's disgusting. I'm beside myself," said Kurt Barks, owner of Complete Auto Body & Repair on West Florissant Avenue in Dellwood.
>
> "I sat in a meeting the Thursday before this happened and was promised there would be National Guard on my

property," said Barks. "I was even told, `Don't board it up.' " His business later sustained about $40,000 worth of damage to an automobile show room, including a vehicle that was flipped over.[565]

The housing market in Ferguson was already tanking long before August 9, 2014, with Section 8 vouchers depopulating lower class blacks from St. Louis and settling them in the formerly bucolic suburb where Wilson had his fateful encounter with Brown.[566]

Almost entirely black North St. Louis is a region known for being a food desert, renowned for brick turning [567]what once was an all-white (thriving) area into nothing more than "doll houses."[568]

Blight, with no hope of an economic recovery.

Ferguson, already 70 percent black, is headed to this same fate.

What incentive for a business owner to rebuild is there when the future legal tender in an all-black Ferguson will be a food stamp/EBT card?

A war has been waged in Ferguson, though there truly was never even an opposition.

The state of Missouri (white tax-payers) has spent $11.2 million on the response to the situation in Ferguson, but none of this was actually allocated to stop the madness Soros was funding and Obama, Holder, CNN, MSNBC, black academicians, Al Sharpton, the NY Times, and the editorial board of the *St. Louis Post-*

---

[565] Nixon: Decision to use restraint in Ferguson avoided 'a gun fight on the street', St. Louis Post-Dispatch, 2-18-15

[566] http://www.stltoday.com/news/local/metro/as-low-income-housing-boomed-ferguson-pushed-back/article_fcb97a3c-8bb7-54a5-9565-255301753142.html

[567] http://www.nytimes.com/2010/09/20/us/20brick.html?pagewanted=print&_r=2&

[568] http://www.stltoday.com/news/local/metro/onetime-center-of-st-louis-black-middle-class-now-fights/article_0722c66c-3e40-509c-aa23-d33d806b7113.html

Dispatch encouraged.⁵⁶⁹

Watching all of this from afar, documenting the insanity of the #BlackLivesMatter movement and the Detroit-ization of St. Louis has left one thing abundantly clear: most white people have no problem being Macbeth's "walking shadow"... *a poor player, That struts and frets his hour upon the stage, And then is heard no more.*

February 19, 2015
Closing the Ferguson War Journal; with HUD's Affirmatively Furthering Fair Housing, the War is Coming to You

> "This attorney general and this Department of Justice stands for the people of Ferguson." -Attorney General Eric Holder, August 21, 2014 (but which people did he mean?)

The sheer horror of what is coming with the House of Urban Development's - HUD - sinisterly named Affirmatively Furthering Fair Housing⁵⁷⁰ only makes since when you use the city of Ferguson as a beta-test for not only displacing white people, but destroying the equity in the homes of those elderly whites foolish enough to stick around, dreaming of halcyon days returning (liquidating their assets via biological welfare by Section 8 Vouchers).

Before we go any further, remember the racial breakdown of this suburban St. Louis city, now masquerading as the center-of-the-known universe:

---

⁵⁶⁹ http://www.stltoday.com/news/local/govt-and-politics/ferguson-unrest-exhausted-emergency-fund-now-nixon-and-lawmakers-square/article_d8105877-ece2-5089-929a-5064f87f9e65.html

⁵⁷⁰ http://www.huduser.org/portal/affht_pt.html

In 1970, Ferguson was 99 percent white; In 1980, Ferguson was 85 percent white and 14 black; In 1990, Ferguson was 73.8 percent white and 25.1 percent black; In 2000, Ferguson was 44.8 percent white and 52.4 percent black; And in 2010 Ferguson was 29.3 percent white and 67.4 percent black[571]

White flight from a growing black underclass in Ferguson (imported with Section 8 Vouchers from the city of St. Louis) mutated the once safe streets into a city where an 18-year-old black male felt comfortable sauntering down the middle of road in broad daylight...

With that out of the way, recall the words of the *New York Times* editorial board on January 4, 2015, seemingly bemoaning the fact the remaining white residents in Ferguson still retained the right to vote [Race and Voting Rights in Ferguson]:

> For most people, Ferguson, Mo., will be remembered for one awful August afternoon, when a white police officer there shot and killed an unarmed black teenager, Michael Brown.
>
> But that incident was only a snapshot in the town's long and complicated racial history — a history characterized by entrenched segregation and economic inequality, as well as by familiar and systemic obstacles that have kept black residents from holding positions of political power.
>
> Ferguson's population is two-thirds African-American, and yet its mayor, city manager and five of its six City Council members are white. So are its police chief and all but three officers on its 53-member police force.
>
> The school board for the Ferguson-Florissant School District is much the same: More than three-quarters of the district's 12,000 students are black, but the seven-member board includes only one African-American.
>
> Last month the American Civil Liberties Union sued the school board under the Voting Rights Act, arguing that the way its members are elected blocks minority voters from

---

[571] Chart: Inside Ferguson's Changing Demographics, **Forbes, 8-19-2014**

fully participating in the political process.

The method is known as "at large" voting, and lets voters cast ballots for all candidates in the district, regardless of where the voters live. Since the district's voting-age population is 50 percent white and 47 percent black, and since both groups there tend to vote along strict racial lines, the white voters' candidates almost always win.[572]

Because of white flight and the subsequent erosion of a tax base in the now 70 percent black city of Ferguson (and the scarcity of revenue-producing businesses left in Ferguson), the second largest source of revenue to bankroll the city government comes from traffic court fees and fines.[573]

Property value has depreciated dramatically as the city's racial character shifted, thus property taxes no loner produce enough revenue to keep the street lights and roads paved.

Which brings us full circle to Eric Holder's statement about "standing with the people of Ferguson."

The black people, that is... :

> The Justice Department is preparing to bring a lawsuit against the Ferguson, Missouri, police department over a pattern of racially discriminatory tactics used by officers, if the police department does not agree to make changes on its own, sources tell CNN.
>
> Attorney General Eric Holder said this week he expects to announce the results of the department's investigation of the shooting death of Michael Brown and a broader probe of the Ferguson Police Department before he leaves office in the coming weeks.

---

[572] http://www.nytimes.com/2015/01/05/opinion/race-and-voting-rights-in-ferguson.html

[573] http://www.washingtonpost.com/local/crime/ferguson-and-jennings-mo-sued-over-municipal-court-practices/2015/02/08/256da2d2-ae4f-11e4-abe8-e1ef60ca26de_story.html

Brown's shooting death at the hands of Officer Darren Wilson has thrust Ferguson into the center of a nationwide debate over police tactics and race relations. The Justice Department is expected to announce it won't charge Wilson for the shooting, but it's also expected to outline findings that allege a pattern of discriminatory tactics used by the Ferguson police.

If they don't agree to review and revise those tactics, sources say, the Justice Department would sue to force changes in the department.

Asked to comment, Ferguson police Chief Thomas Jackson told CNN's Sara Sidner, "I have received nothing new.

"Everything they suggested in the past has been reasonable and we have tried to comply."

Among the issues expected to be part of the Justice Department's lawsuit are allegations made in a recent lawsuit filed by a group of low-income people who claimed officers in Ferguson and nearby Jennings targeted minorities with minor traffic infractions and then jailed them when they couldn't pay fines.

The Justice Department action would ask for court supervision of changes at the Ferguson Police Department to improve how police deal with the minority communities they are supposed to protect. [574]

That Michael Brown attacked Officer Darren Wilson, attempting to procure his gun and shoot him in the process, isn't an admissible piece of evidence in the court of public opinion. All that matters is the ghost of Bull Conner was apparently haunting the streets of Ferguson, where an almost entirely white police force dared to keep alive some semblance of European civilization before Africans in America remade the city into just another East St. Louis.[575]

---

[574] Justice Dept. could sue Ferguson for racial discrimination, CNN, 2-19-15

[575] http://stlouis.cbslocal.com/2014/08/13/ferguson-mayor-the-african-american-community-has-something-against-law-enforcement-in-many-ways/

With HUD's Affirmatively Furthering Fair Housing, there's a Ferguson coming soon to you... and when it comes, don't expect the National Guard to protect either your home or business. The attention of the police and federal government will instead be turned to those Oath Keepers who foolishly believe a U.S. Constitution still exists to be revered and respected.

With this, the *Ferguson War Journal* is closed; courtesy of Affirmatively Furthering Fair Housing, the war is coming to you.

February 22, 2015
On the turning away... From the pale and downtrodden

To paraphrase an instrumentally pleasing Pink Floyd song, "Is it only a dream that there'll be, only turning away?"

Why even bring this song up (*On the Turning Away*)?

We'll get to that in a minute.

But to truly understand the melancholy nature of what you are about to read, you must remember there was a time - not too long ago - when those same barren, deserted streets were filled with the laughter of children and the promise of tomorrow.

The laughter of white children and the promise tomorrow would be better than yesterday.

But the tomorrow so many people hoped was coming never came; instead, the hopes and dreams of yesterday went unfulfilled, with the memories those white families made long ago now carted away...[576]

To truly understand the overwhelming despondency of what you are about to read, recall that once America's white leaders didn't turn away from the plight of black people and erected the Pruitt-Igoe public housing complex in St. Louis to give them a better life... though the ultimate lesson would be one those same white leaders would quickly turn away from ever acknowledging (that no matter the money spent; no matter the infrastructure built to better the lives of blacks; wherever blacks are found in America, Africa in America will ultimately arise).

Brick thievery in the once-thriving (when it was filled with white people) now blighted - because it is filled with black people - area North St. Louis is perhaps the most fitting legacy of what Africans in American do to European civilization.

They dismantle brick by brick.

And now we come to an article even an individual owning the most bleeding heart would read and quickly find it coagulating:

> The houses in the city's St. Louis Place neighborhood have slowly disappeared, brick by brick — once-handsome homes destroyed by developers and thieves.
>
> Over the years, the western edge of the old neighborhood near downtown, formerly a home to the city's upper class, has virtually evaporated. And soon, if the city has its way, it will be completely cleared to move the National Geospatial-Intelligence Agency to north St. Louis.
>
> While vast stretches of the area already are vacant, the neighborhood is flecked with sporadic clusters of proud homes and businesses. Some blocks are populated only by stray dogs, while others contain a house or two. Now, the city hopes the federal government chooses the site for its massive high-tech spy facility over three other potential sites in the region, including a spot near Scott Air Force Base.

---

[576] [Thieves Cart Off St. Louis Bricks, New York Times, 9-19-2010]

To that aim, St. Louis aldermen passed a bill authorizing the city to use eminent domain to buy up the remaining homes and buildings as part of an effort to keep the agency's 3,100 jobs within the city's borders.

One of those houses belongs to Joyce Cooks, a teacher who has lived there for more than 40 years.

"Across the street there was a man who got sick and died," Cooks remembered. "The man wasn't dead two weeks before his house came down. They just pulled the top off of that house. Then they came back to steal the bricks."

Cooks' three-story home, built in 1893, is one of the few left on Warren Street. She has seen the houses around her either destroyed by brick thieves or bought by developers and left to rot. Still, it's her home, and she wants to stay.

The city has promised to pay fair market value for all property in the redevelopment area, bordered on the east and west by North Jefferson Avenue and North 22nd Street, and sell it to the federal government. A city official pledged last week that the city wouldn't force property owners to sell if the site isn't selected for the new facility.

Homeowners in the neighborhood argue, however, that such an arrangement would leave an uncertainty over their property until the federal government makes a decision, which isn't expected until 2016.

The city says it will appraise each property and use that as a starting point in negotiations. Homeowners can also get their own appraisal. The city promises to pay at least market rate or higher, in addition to moving costs.

Cooks says the money won't be enough for her to find a similar-sized home.

"I have lived in a house all my life," Cooks said. "I have never lived in an apartment. I have 16-inch-thick brick walls, high ceilings, wooden floors, crown moldings. I'm going to fight to the end to stay. They might have to carry me out of here."

The city promises that it will try to keep homeowners nearby, if they choose to remain a part of the community.

Just south of Cooks' home is a large wooded swath that creates a rural feel in an urban area with views of downtown. It formerly housed the failed Pruitt-Igoe housing complex, which was the original proposed site for the Geospatial Agency structure. Officials said they had to expand from there because the agency required more room for its facility, and now none of the development will actually occur on the site.

They hope the neighboring federal facility would spur development on the site.Pruitt-Igoe's giant towers once loomed over this neighborhood. And, in many ways, they still do.

"I never lived in public housing, but they put [Pruitt-Igoe] here anyway," Cooks said. "I saw it come down. I ran into the house so the dust wouldn't get into my lungs."

Pruitt-Igoe is central to the city's argument for the Geospatial Agency to stay in St. Louis. Local officials have said the failed federal housing policies of the 1950s that led to the rise and fall of Pruitt-Igoe is one reason to give a boost to the city now.

Earlier this month, 5th Ward Alderman Tammika Hubbard, who represents the area, pleaded with aldermen to support the city's relocation effort of about 50 homes and businesses.

"I can attest firsthand some of the atrocities that were associated with Pruitt-Igoe," Hubbard said. "I looked at this as an opportunity for the government to right some of their wrongs ... Some members of my family are no longer here because of some of the things that took place in Pruitt-Igoe."

She added: "Think about the 60 years disinvestment, think about the crime, think about a ward that has the highest rate in just about everything."

City officials further argue that the location falls within President Barack Obama's "livable communities" initiative, which aims to foster dense urban areas, reduce sprawl and pollution and keep federal jobs near areas served by mass transit.[577]

St. Louis Place neighborhood is 91 percent black.[578] Every negative characteristic mentioned in the St. Louis Post-Dispatch article that's associated with the 91 percent black community exists because the neighborhood is inhabited by almost entirely by Africans in America.

They have taken the European civilization (and infrastructure) they inherited from whites - via white flight from black crime and the depreciating home values associated with rising percentages of blacks in the community - and dismantled it... literally brick by brick.

The houses in the city's St. Louis Place neighborhood have slowly disappeared, brick by brick — because of individual black people collectively imposing their genetic fingerprint on an area where once-handsome homes were built to shelter generations of white people.

Over the years, the western edge of the old neighborhood near downtown, formerly a home to the city's upper class, has virtually evaporated because white flight drained the vitality and genetic material necessary to maintain this now 91 percent black community (sic) where vast stretches of the area already are vacant and some blocks are populated only by stray dogs, while others contain a house or two.

In a span of roughly 100 years, since *The Birth of a Nation* debuted, the white past of the St. Louis Place neighborhood has been all but erased by Africans in America, who hilariously were responsible for the razing of the Pruitt-Igoe public housing complex built in the same area.

No, it's time we turn away for good and realize the lesson to learn from St. Louis is simply this: no matter what Europeans in America build, if Africans in America inherit it, ultimately it will regress to the black mean.

---

[577] Proud but downtrodden St. Louis neighborhood struggles with prospect of National Geospatial-Intelligence Agency, St. Louis Post-Dispatch, 2-21-15

[578] http://en.wikipedia.org/wiki/St._Louis_Place

Brick by brick if need be... "Is it only a dream that there'll be, only turning away?"

February 24, 2015
Spring is Coming. The Negro Spring...

We've been warned.

Both major political parties are aligned against us and dedicated to the slow eradication of our future via high taxation, while disinformation campaigns in academia and from news organizations disseminating a steady stream of hostile white images means agitated (and aggressive) blacks.

And winter is soon to end. Jack Frost is leaving.

Racial Breakdown of St. Louis Population by Decade

DECADE:	POPULATION:	% WHITE:	% BLACK:	% OTHER:
1910	687029	93.50%	6.40%	0.10%
1920	772897	90.90%	9.00%	0.10%
1930	821960	88.50%	11.40%	0.10%
1940	816048	88.60%	13.30%	0.10%
1950	856796	82%	17.90%	0.10%
1960	750026	71.20%	28.60%	0.20%
1970	622236	58.70%	40.90%	0.40%
1980	452801	53.50%	45.60%	0.90%
1990	396685	50.90%	47.50%	1.60%
2000	348189	43.90%	51.20%	4.90%
2010	319294	43.90%	49.20%	6.90%

The stunning decline of St. Louis as a major American city has everything to do with white people abandoning the city they built to the growing menace of Africans in America

Spring is blooming.

Spring is coming:

> A leader of a community outreach group warned fact-finders for a federal civil rights agency Monday that warm weather could spark more street violence in lingering resentment of police shootings.

"As St. Louis walks into this next warm season, and it's right around the corner, we're not ready for what's going to come out of our neighborhoods," said James Clark, vice president of the nonprofit organization Better Family Life.

"This is going to be a very, very challenging time in our community as it relates to crime and violence. Once this weather breaks, there are going to be challenges for the police officers. How the police are going to manage it — my prayers are with them."

Clark participated in one of several panels addressing the Missouri Advisory Committee to the U.S. Commission on Civil Rights. It is examining police use of force relating to race or color.

The commission is an independent, bipartisan agency that advises the president and Congress on civil rights matters. It took an active interest here after the shooting of a black teen, Michael Brown, by a Ferguson police officer on Aug. 9.

Panels of academics, activists, police and government officials met through the day at the University of Missouri-St. Louis. Public attendance appeared light, about two dozen as Clark spoke.

St. Louis Police Chief Sam Dotson said he is being as transparent as possible about shootings by officers and touted creation of a unit dedicated to investigate them.Capt. Mary Edwards-Fears said the department provided a rapid and detailed account when two St. Louis officers fatally shot Kajieme Powell about a week after Brown died. Officials said Powell came at the officers with a knife.

"People will not tolerate being kept out of the information loop, especially when it comes to policing and public safety," Edwards-Fears said. "When it comes to critical incidents, we must explain ourselves fully and quickly."

Dotson has admitted that in a rush to provide information that day, he passed along an observation of a witness that turned out to be contradicted by a bystander's video of the killing. The police have not released the officers' names, something Dotson said he will do once Circuit Attorney Jennifer Joyce has completed her review of the case.

Edwards-Fears said the "truly tragic" killing of Powell "presented us a huge opportunity to educate the public, especially on our use-of-force policy and why we do things the way we do them."

Joining Clark on a panel of activists earlier in the day were Charli Cooksey, with the Young Citizen's Council of St. Louis; J. Alfredo Chavez, with Latinos en Axion St. Louis; David Nehrt-Flores, with Missouri Immigrant and Refugee Advocates; and the Rev. Traci Blackmon, with Christ the King Church in Florissant.

Brown's killing also "emboldened the black population," Clark said.

"I have been telling St. Louis officials as early as 2011 that we're not ready for what is to come," he said. "Things are getting more volatile in the community."

Clark established himself in poor black communities for his work with at-risk youths, helping them to find jobs and social services, such as counseling.

"They feel they can openly confront police officers; it's a growing trend," he said.

As protests have continued, Clark said he has seen police become less inclined to speak with and listen to demonstrators.

"We can't have police become complacent and apathetic," he said.[579]

One hundred years ago, St. Louis had a population of 687,029.

It was 93 percent white and six percent black.

---

[579] Activist warns: Return of warm weather to St. Louis could mean violence, St. Louis Post-Dispatch, 2-22-15

Today, St. Louis has a population of 319,294.

It is 49 percent black and 43 percent white.

White people have long known that once winter ends, the hibernating black criminality awakens, and with this thawing of low impulse control and poor future-time orientation comes the true black death.

The demographic decline of the white population in St. Louis is testament to this reality, with white families fleeing the carnage of black dysfunction and slowly abandoning formerly prosperous communities to Africans in America.

A true Better Family Life organization would be one dedicated to improving the quality of life for white people (and their progeny), but in Black-Run America it is one of those uniquely black nonprofit organizations kept alive via tax donations from corporations (a bank purchased $13 million in tax-credits to assist this "organization" in buying up a building in heavily black North St. Louis to use as its headquarters...).[580]

Here's the vision statement:

> Vision
>
> Better Family Life, Inc. (BFL) is a community development 501(c)(3) corporation dedicated to the prosperity and growth of the American family. BFL was organized in February 1983 out of a need to find internal solutions to the crises within the African American family.
>
> MissionBFL's mission is to plan and establish social, cultural, artistic, youth, economic, housing and educational programs that help to promote positive and innovative changes within the metropolitan St. Louis area. Much of BFL's programming

---

[580] http://www.stlamerican.com/business/local_business/article_ff29a774-68a1-11e1-bbac-001871e3ce6c.html

is geared towards people who are unemployed, underemployed, disadvantaged and skill-deficient.

Core Values

1) FamilyBetter Family Life, Inc. advocates the belief that a cohesive family is the foundation for every human being's development. It endeavors to rehabilitate individuals on a complete cultural, educational, social, and economic level by helping them become self-sufficient and contributing members of society.

2) CultureBetter Family Life believes that the self-conscious means by which a people creates itself, celebrates itself, and introduces itself to history and humanity is the primary route to personal, family, and group growth and sustainability.

3) Social and Economic GrowthBetter Family Life places a high degree of importance on the social and economic elevation of low and moderate income families, disadvantaged populations, and those who are financially stable, as proven by our record of achievements since 1983.

4) Integrity and AccountabilityBetter Family Life has an unwavering commitment to integrity and accountability in all of its endeavors.[581]

Better Family Life is dedicated solely to the improving of black lives in the city of St. Louis, one a mere shadow of the metropolis that existed in the 1910s (with much less than half the population of the city that was 93 percent white in 1915).

And yet the quality of life in St. Louis has continually declined as the city becomes blacker and blacker (and less white).

With James Clark, vice president of the nonprofit organization Better

---

[581] http://www.betterfamilylife.org/index.php/about-us/104-vision-mission-core-values

Family Life, basically blackmailing the city of St. Louis with a threat of black violence (unless more money is pumped into his fraudulent organization) once the winter weather warms, the reality of what black criminality represents becomes clear: the slow, inexorable death of the civilizations Europeans have created in America.

You'll notice this article is peppered with a graph of the racial breakdown of St. Louis' population from 1910 to 2010; images of homicide rates from NextStl.com showing population decline in the city; and the homicide rate for the white population and the black population from 1930 - 1990 courtesy of The book *St. Louis Metromorphosis: Past Trends and Future Directions* (edited by Brady Baybeck and F. Terrence Jones), published in 2004 by the Missouri Historical Society Press.

These two images and Excel graph tell the story of the reality of the black death in America for the city of St. Louis.

And as the leader of an exclusively black community outreach group warned those already convinced of the evil of white people masquerading as fact-finders for a federal civil rights agency that warm weather could spark an increased black intifada of street violence in St. Louis over lingering resentment of police correctly interpreting the law, the racial decline of the becomes clear.

Ninety-three percent white in 1915 (638936 white people)... Today, St. Louis is only 43 percent white (137296 white people)...

Civilization can survive earthquakes. It can survive floods, tornadoes and hurricanes.

Hell, a volcanic eruption can even preserve an ancient civilization to exacting detail.

But no civilization has ever survived its black population. Not even the bricks remain...

February 25, 2015
"Section 8 Vouchers is the most monstrously conceived and dangerous communist plot we have ever had to face."

Dr. Strangelove, how a nuclear bomb piloted by Slim Pickens would be welcomed today!

Instead, we get a world gone mad.

Where the prevailing paradigm is one dedicated to the preservation of nothing more than the lunacy conceived by bureaucrats intoxicated by their own pusillanimous predilections.

And the prevailing winds blow from a staunchly rotten capital, dedicated to the proposition all non-white men are treated unequal and with extreme prejudice.

So we see the advent of the Section 8 Voucher to end this pernicious inequity inflicted upon the hapless non-white peoples of America:

> For the first time in five years, the St. Louis County Housing Authority is accepting new applications for Section 8 housing vouchers.
>
> Through the program, which is funded by the federal government but run by local housing authorities, low-income tenants spend no more than 30 percent of their income on rent, and the authority covers the remainder of what's owed to a landlord.
>
> Nearly 6,000 households use vouchers received from the county housing authority.
>
> The county added 6,000 people to the wait list when it was last opened in 2010.
>
> The list has dwindled to about 500, according to director

Susan Rollins.

When it was last opened, about 30,000 people applied during the six weeks that applications were accepted. On the Saturday morning in 2010 when the authority began taking applications, a few thousand people were already waiting outside of its offices on Natural Bridge Road before the doors opened.

To prevent a repeat of that scene, the county is now using an online registration system. Instead of a first-come, first-served process, applicants are randomly selected through a lottery system that will narrow the pool to a final 6,000-household wait list.

"We're going to try online this time," Rollins said. "We find that most of our clients do have smartphones and can access the Internet."

That doesn't mean the authority will turn applicants away at the door, she said.

The city of St. Louis also experienced challenges in 2007 when would-be applicants rushed the authority's doors on the first day applications were accepted.

The city reopened its waiting list last summer — for the first time in seven years — and used online applications. During the one week the city waiting list was open, more than 27,000 people signed up.[582]

Never forget: the story of Ferguson, Missouri is nothing more than the logical conclusion of Section 8 Vouchers: the ruination of social capital and the advancement of the same conditions terminating civilization from which those awarded vouchers escaped from.

The Africanization of America, via state decree.

There would be no Darren Wilson-Michael Brown confrontation

---

[582] St. Louis County to open Section 8 waiting list for first time since 2010, St. Louis Post-Dispatch, 2-25-15

without Section 8 Vouchers.

Stores in Ferguson wouldn't be closing were Section 8 Vouchers not importing the very people responsible for the creation of conditions where poverty flourishes in downtown St. Louis and other parts of North St. Louis.

Black people.

Property value for those owning homes in Ferguson wouldn't be declining were it not for Section 8 Vouchers importing Africans in America to the once serene and all-white suburb of St. Louis.[583]

But those in search of Section 8 Vouchers in St. Louis (to magically be transported not to the land of Oz, but the world of white people!) to momentarily enjoy a reprieve from the type of community Africans in America create have no problem engaging in violence to get a better spot in line.

And though the Internet is largely scrubbed of all references to the fabled date of December 7, 2007, something undeniably courtesy of black people happened on this day when Section 8 Voucher seeking blacks stormed the halls of the St. Louis Housing Authority:

> Dec. 7, 2007, won't be forgotten anytime soon in the halls of the St. Louis Housing Authority, at 3520 Page Boulevard.
>
> It was Application Day. The demand to get a place on the waiting list for Section 8 vouchers was so great, people rushed the front door. Police stepped in to disperse the crowd.
>
> "We had to close the thing down because there were too many people," said Cheryl Lovell, executive director of the housing authority.
>
> "Lots of people want the assistance," she added. "A lot of

---

[583] http://www.stltoday.com/business/local/ferguson-home-sales-fell-as-uncertainty-gripped-real-estate-market/article_6b96afae-60f3-5e68-b2dc-33aef8bbb561.html

people need it."

Over 8,000 names eventually landed on the waiting list that week in 2007. Now, seven years later, the application pool has nearly dried up.

The housing authority announced Thursday that a one-week window to pre-register for the income-based rental assistance program will open again July 14.

The agency has been planning for the event for months in hopes to avoid some of the previous struggles. The main difference will be an online option. Applications can be submitted 24 hours a day at slha.org.

"We don't want to have people wait in line at our building to apply," Lovell said. "We want them to do it at their convenience."

The housing authority expects more applicants this time around, perhaps 10,000. No new vouchers were issued from the middle of 2012 through 2013 because of funding cuts.

Section 8 is one of many government subsidized housing programs for low-income people and those with disabilities. Recipients pay 30 percent of their income in rent; the government pays the remainder directly to the landlord. Renters find their own housing from a list of properties in the community that meet the standards of the program.

The U.S. Department of Housing and Urban Development funds the program; local housing authorities manage it on the ground.

Lovell said Congress ultimately decides the speed of getting through the waiting list.

"It takes us seven years to fund it," she said. "It's not that we sit on these applications. We have to have slots. You have to have funding available."

The Housing Authority of St. Louis County uses a lottery system for its Section 8 waiting list.

> Susan Rollins, director of the agency, said she wants to avoid the stampede situation that erupted in Atlanta in recent years and left people injured.
>
> "Because there are so many people in need, we have gone to a lottery system," she said. "We think it's a fair way to get it done."
>
> In April 2010, the county opened its waiting list for two weeks. About 30,000 people signed up. Of those, 6,000 won a randomly selected spot on the waiting list.[584]

Virtually nothing is available to describe the carnage witnessed in the halls of the St. Louis Housing Authority on December 7, 2007, though it doesn't take a member of Mensa to determine the lawlessness and riot found its origin in those Africans in America determined to find refuge in a white community.

Fluoride?

Sorry, but this so-called Communist plot isn't worth starting World War III over; but the reality of Section 8 Vouchers and the redistribution of the misery only black people are capable of creating to those white flight communities surrounding formerly thriving major US cities (when white people created the conditions necessary for social capital to flourish in them before black criminality drove whites out) is a cause for a type of mobilization never before seen in human history.

And though virtually nothing remains on the Internet about the shocking levels black people were willing to go to on Dec. 7, 2007 in the halls of the St. Louis Housing Authority at 3520 Page Boulevard to apply for a spot on the waiting list for a Section 8 voucher (where people rushed the front door and police stepped in to disperse the crowd), the rumor of what occurred leaves a hilarious residue for those willing to concede what is coming for those applying for a voucher in 2015.

Remember: 99 percent of those living in the census of tract of

---

[584] St. Louis Section 8 voucher waiting list to open for first time since 2007, St. Louis Post-Dispatch, 7-3-14

Ferguson using Section 8 Vouchers were black; an area consisting of a portion of Oakmont Townhomes and Northwinds Apartments and stretching eastward into unincorporated St. Louis County having more Section 8 renters in 2013 than any tract in the entire state...[585]

Section 8 Vouchers are nothing more than the federal government ensuring that those engaging in white flight inevitably encounter the exact reality of what they fled in the first place.

February 28, 2015
I don't want to grow up, because then if I did, I'd have to admit how black people are responsible for the closing of the Ferguson Toys 'R Us!

Social capital.

Outside investors interested in opening a national chain in a city evaluate a community based on this invisible currency: individuals who collectively create high levels of social capital in a city are rewarded with businesses relocating there, because they possess the purchasing power required with returning profits that keep investors happy.

Collectively, a community made-up of individual black people will be hard-pressed to attract national chains that don't have "dollar" in the name, or ones that don't specialize in title pawns or cash-checking.

But, to truly understand the damning consequences of the black

---

[585] http://www.stltoday.com/news/local/metro/as-low-income-housing-boomed-ferguson-pushed-back/article_fcb97a3c-8bb7-54a5-9565-255301753142.html

undertow submerging a once thriving white suburb, it's incumbent upon economists concerned only with in-the-black spreadsheets to understand the Visible Black Hand of Economics.

Back in 1990, the city of Ferguson, Missouri was 73 percent white. The last time a U.S. Census had been conducted, Ferguson was 85 percent white (1980).

It was this simple market research (demographics) the corporate custodians of Toys R Us utilized to build a new store in Ferguson back in 1989.

Back then, the citizens of 73 percent white Ferguson boasted purchasing power, and an overwhelming desire to keep their white kids and white grandchildren happy by purchasing the hottest toys to ensure they'd stay a Toys R Us kid (point of fact: my realization of the consequences of the black undertow was triggered by witnessing a once-thriving mall - with a standalone Toys R Us located only 400 yards away - close within a span of 15 years).

But Ferguson is no longer the same place as it was when Toys R Us opened in 1989; the city is 70 percent black and less than 26 percent white. White children are all but gone, with white grandparents merely watching the equity in their houses decline each year as the percentage of the black population increases.[586]

And you can't buy toys with an EBT/Food Stamp Card. Recall, St. Louis County (different from the city of St. Louis) is just over one million people in population. It's home to Ferguson, a city where Section 8 voucher holding blacks have flocked to in the past 20 years.[587]

Of those one million people, 78 percent of the county's population is white and 23.7 percent is black. Consulting the 2009 New York Times Food Stamp Usage Across the Country interactive map, we

---

[586] http://www.stltoday.com/news/local/metro/blame-poverty-age-for-weak-north-county-home-market/article_95c998e5-bb87-5bc0-9054-83e801b357ac.html

[587] http://www.stltoday.com/news/local/metro/as-low-income-housing-boomed-ferguson-pushed-back/article_fcb97a3c-8bb7-54a5-9565-255301753142.html

learn this about the county:

- As of 2009, 38 percent of blacks were on EBT/Food Stamps in St. Louis County
- As of 2009, 4 percent of whites were on EBT/Food Stamps in St. Louis County

Those numbers were from 2009, before President Obama embarked on a crusade to equip any non-white capable of filling out a form with a shiny EBT/Food Stamp card.

And the Toys R Us in Ferguson was built in 1989 to remove U.S. Federal Reserve Notes from the pockets of white parents and grandparents; the current population of Ferguson is insufficient in keeping this store solvent (though it was one of the stores raided and looted by blacks on November 25, 2014[588]):

> The Toys R Us store in Ferguson, which was burglarized during last year's unrest, will close at the end of March, the company confirmed Tuesday.
>
> The store, open since 1989, will close "to prepare for the sale of the property," said company spokeswoman Alyssa Peera.
>
> The store was "not meeting the needs of the business," Peera said. "That is separate from the events that took place," she added, referring to the protests and looting.
>
> "We have enjoyed serving the Ferguson community for many years. At this time, we do not have any plans for a new store in the Ferguson area," she said.
>
> The store is at 10895 West Florissant Avenue, near Interstate 270. Peera noted other Toys R Us stores, including locations in Chesterfield and Sunset Hills, remain in the St. Louis area.
>
> The 46,000-square-foot Ferguson store employs 36 people. The company said it will place as many as possible at its

[588] http://www.breitbart.com/big-government/2014/11/25/40-ferguson-area-businesses-trashed-vandalized-or-destroyed-by-protestors/

other stores.

On Monday, a store employee told the Ferguson Commission that workers had been informed of the store closing. "We can't afford to fix our store, pay the bills and pay the workers," said Kaylen Smith, 18, a senior at Hazelwood East High School.

"None of that is accurate," Peera said.

Toys R Us is a closely held company with more than 1,500 stores in 36 countries under the Toys R Us and Babies R Us brands.

The company, which canceled an initial public offering of stock in 2013, posted a decline in holiday sales last year for at least the third year in a row.[589]

For millennials, the *whoosh* of air felt when the automatic doors opened to welcome you into Toys R Us is a fond, fond memory of being a child in the closing decades of the American Experiment.

But those memories were only possible because of the individual contributions of white people who collectively created the social capital necessary for a Toys R Us to open in your community, to serve those white parents and white grandparents searching for the perfect toy for their children.

The Visible Black Hand of Economics strikes again...

---

[589] Toys R Us to close in Ferguson, St. Louis Post-Dispatch, 2-24-15

March 1, 2015
Four Black People out of 27,000 Correctly Filled Out Their Section 8 Voucher Form in the City of St. Louis in July of 2014...

Virtually nothing can be found on the Internet about the December 7, 2007 "Day of Section 8 Infamy," when police were called in to quell a crowd of unruly black people as they overwhelmed Application Day for Section 8 vouchers.

Save this one, incredibly strange reference from early July 2014, roughly a month before the dire consequences of the Section 8 voucher program (the redistribution of black dysfunction from a centralized location to multiples zip codes where this black misery will inevitably overwhelm) became evident:

> Dec. 7, 2007, won't be forgotten anytime soon in the halls of the St. Louis Housing Authority, at 3520 Page Boulevard.
>
> It was Application Day. The demand to get a place on the waiting list for Section 8 vouchers was so great, people rushed the front door. Police stepped in to disperse the crowd.
>
> "We had to close the thing down because there were too many people," said Cheryl Lovell, executive director of the housing authority.
>
> "Lots of people want the assistance," she added. "A lot of people need it."
>
> Over 8,000 names eventually landed on the waiting list that week in 2007. Now, seven years later, the application pool

has nearly dried up.[590]

One wonders how many of those who engaged in the November 24, 2014 'Black Insurrection in Ferguson' had family members who were participants in this legendary Section 8 voucher Application Day nearly seven years earlier?

Or, perhaps, were related to those who painted graffiti on the burnt-out QuikTrip in Ferguson with "Snitches Get Stitches" after the initial black riots on August 10, 2014.[591]

Recall the shockingly black nature of the Section 8 voucher program in St. Louis County, which inundated cities like Ferguson with the type of stereotypically black behavior Michael Brown was joyously engaging in on the final day of his life (robbing a store, assaulting a store clerk, walking in the middle of Canfield Drive, attacking a cop...):

> Factoring in all federal programs, there were roughly 13,000 households with subsidized housing in the county last year, including about 7,500 who used Section 8 vouchers, according to HUD estimates. By comparison, in the city of St. Louis, there were nearly 14,900 households living in subsidized units — about 4,700 used vouchers.
>
> The data on Section 8 also show that the subsidies have tended to cluster in lower-income areas. Many inner-ring North County suburbs are disproportionately absorbing the tenants who have flocked to aging apartment complexes.
>
> That includes Ferguson. A census tract that consists of a portion of Oakmont Townhomes and Northwinds Apartments and stretches eastward into unincorporated St. Louis County had more Section 8 renters in 2013 than any tract in the entire state, according to HUD estimates.
>
> In that area, nearly 20 percent of the 5,000 people who lived

---

[590] St. Louis Section 8 voucher waiting list to open for first time since 2007, St. Louis Post-Dispatch, 7-3-14

[591] http://fox2now.com/2014/08/11/quiktrip-sprayed-with-graffiti-set-on-fire-during-overnight-looting-near-ferguson/

there were in Section 8 units. More than half of those households had median incomes of less than $10,000; 57 percent were headed by one parent; and 99 percent were African-American.[592]

Read the last paragraph from the October 19, 2014 story again, if only the last few words of the final sentence...

It's a program only benefiting lower-class blacks, redistribution their dysfunction to locations long-deprived of the type of behavior that inevitably blights neighborhoods, drives away businesses, and lowers property value.

It's a federal government program designed to negate social capital, immediately downgrading the viability of a community.

But a statistic almost strategically found inserted in a news report of the impending Section 8 lottery in St. Louis County is almost too black to believe.

Like the story of the December 7, 2007 Section 8 voucher melee in St. Louis on Application Day (a story seemingly censored from the Internet), this fun statistic is one stretching the credulity of even the most committed bigot:

> The Section 8 lottery is coming soon to St. Louis County and as many as 30,000 people are expected to line up for a chance to win free rent.
>
> The St Louis County Housing Authority is hoping people will not literally line up, because the last time enrollment was opened, the long line led to traffic problems.
>
> This year the program will only accept online applications.
>
> The government program has a budget of $33 million in St. Louis County, but it will not be enough to cover the rent of everyone who applies.

---

[592] As low-income housing boomed, Ferguson pushed back, St. Louis Post-Dispatch, 10-19-2014

> The last time that the St. Louis County Housing Authority accepted new applications was in 2010.
>
> "If history tells me anything, I would think 25 to 30 thousand people will apply," said Susan Rollins, executive director at the St. Louis County Housing Authority.
>
> Rollins said all applicants will be entered into a computer system that will randomly select 6,000 names of those who will win the vouchers.
>
> The Housing Authority in the City of St. Louis handles applications differently than the county.
>
> Applicants in the city are ranked by preference, gaining points if an individual is homeless or displaced by natural disaster.
>
> Last July, 27,000 people applied but only 4 filled out their preferences correctly, leading to a time-consuming process for Housing Authority employees.[593]

Wait: the long line of black people seeking a spot in the St. Louis County Housing Authority Section 8 lottery led to "traffic problems?"

And that's not even the most incredible revelation found in the story!

Recall the story quoted at the start, noting the city of St. Louis was opening its voucher waiting list for the first time since 2007... 27,000 people applied for this waiting list, but only 4 people filled it correctly.

Four people out of 27,000, or .0001 percent, correctly filled out their "preferences" correctly...

The people used as biological weapons against social capital in the whole Section 8 voucher/ Section 8 lottery scheme have provided a comical representation of blackness in St. Louis.

---

[593] As low-income housing boomed, Ferguson pushed back, St. Louis Post-Dispatch, 10-19-2014

From a near-riot on December 7, 2007 (the irony of the date notwithstanding), to huge lines of black people seeking access to the Section 8 lottery in St. Louis County that ultimately caused massive traffic problem - strangely censored from the Internet as well - to only four people out of 27,000 correctly filling out the reason for their need of a Section 8 voucher in July of 2014, the comical black reality of this devastating weapon against white communities seems ripped from a rough draft of a screenplay for a sequel to *The Birth of a Nation*.

But it's all true, made the more damning by the few clues left by journalists in St. Louis to the origins of the Michael Brown/Farce in Ferguson... entirely birthed by the redistribution of blacks seeking Section 8 voucher/ winning the Section 8 lottery and the chance to live near white people.

Because those who used their Section 8 voucher to flood Ferguson with the type of black dysfunction white people long abandoned St. Louis to avoid had absolutely no business being relocated there... save for the federal governments war against white people via the redistribution of black dysfunction to erode property value, destroy social capital, and force the inevitable retreat of whites to yet another suburb whose fate will be destruction courtesy of Section 8...

March 4, 2015
You Can Put Your Hands Down Now, Black People...

Ferguson War Journal: Day 204

Just before you log onto Twitter, one of the images you get is of hundreds of people with their hands up - raised to the heavens - in front of the Gateway Arch in St. Louis.

Without proper background on the context of the photo, one might conclude this magnificent structure is some religious shrine and the people with their hands up are engaging in an orgiastic devotional in hopes of sharing the cosmic energy radiating from the arch.

No... it's just a bunch of idiots engaging a hilarious lie, a public display of stupidity just a few ticks away from being on par with those fools who drank Jim Jones Kool-Aid.

"Hands up, Don't shoot." A battle cry for those desperately attempting to tell you #BlackLivesMatter, which a careful study of homicides and nonfatal shootings from any major city will immediately prove that they don't...

"Hands up, Don't shoot."

A lie fueling the hatred of whites powerfully on display when Bosnian Zemir Begic was attacked by a group of blacks with hammers in St. Louis. Begic[594], who hails from a community that has a number of individuals currently being prosecuted for donating money to ISIS and other Muslim causes, was murdered because the blacks saw only a white man.[595]

Allah didn't save Begic from the Infidels carrying hammers, though his whiteness was a liability in a climate where "Hands Up, Don't Shoot" birthed the racial madness that ultimately took his life.

"Hands up, Don't shoot":

> The Associated Press explored this disconnect between the ongoing "Hands Up, Don't Shoot" narrative with the facts presented at the inquiry. "Even if you don't find that it's true, it's a valid rallying cry," protester Taylor Gruenloh told the AP. "It's just a metaphor."
>
> "This is not about one boy getting shot in the street, but about the hundreds just like him who have received the same callous and racially-influenced treatment," Oakland

---

[594] http://www.foxnews.com/us/2014/12/03/where-outrage-st-louis-bosnian-community-sees-hammer-murder-as-hate-crime/

[595] http://www.stltoday.com/lifestyles/faith-and-values/divine-dispatches/bosnians-shocked-st-louis-area-residents-accused-of-supporting-isis/article_7dfd8384-66e0-5bc3-835e-8094bc3ce935.html

demonstrator Gabe Johnson, identified as "a middle school teacher" by the AP, insisted. "So ultimately, no, it doesn't matter at all if somehow we can say for sure whether this one young man really said these words or had his hands up."[596]

Oh, but it does matter if you can say for sure whether 18-year-old Michael Brown had his hands up as an act of surrender or if Officer Darren Wilson encountered a malicious black male on Canfield Drive with the intentions of taking his life.

And, as the Department of Justice has now admitted, the latter is - begrudgingly to Eric "My People" Holder - the case[597]:

> Offering the most definitive account yet of the shooting of an unarmed black teenager that stirred racially charged protests across the country, the Justice Department has cleared a Ferguson, Mo., police officer of civil rights violations in the death last August of Michael Brown.
>
> The decision, announced on Wednesday, ends a lengthy investigation into the shooting last August, in which the officer, Darren Wilson shot and killed Mr. Brown in the street as he tried to stop him for a possible theft. Several witnesses said Mr. Brown, 18, had his hands up in surrender when he died, leading to violent clashes in Ferguson and nationwide protest chants of "Hands up, don't shoot."
>
> Mr. Wilson, who left the Ferguson Police Department late last year, said that Mr. Brown had fought with him, reached for his gun, and later charged at him, making him fear for his life.
>
> "There is no evidence upon which prosecutors can rely to disprove Wilson's stated subjective belief that he feared for his safety," the report said. At the same time, it concluded that the witnesses who claimed that Mr. Brown was

---

[596] 'HANDS UP, DON'T SHOOT': AN IGNOBLE LIE FOR THE AGES: Don't you know, "gentle giant" was just a metaphor?, American Spectator, 11-28-14

[597] https://s3.amazonaws.com/s3.documentcloud.org/documents/1681212/doj-report-on-shooting-of-michael-brown.pdf

surrendering were not credible.

"Some of those accounts are inaccurate because they are inconsistent with the physical and forensic evidence; some of those accounts are materially inconsistent with that witnesses' own prior statements with no explanation," the report said.

"Although some witnesses state that Brown held his hands up at shoulder level with his palms facing outward for a brief moment, these same witnesses describe Brown then dropping his hands and 'charging' at Wilson," it added.

"Those witness accounts stating that Brown never moved back toward Wilson could not be relied upon in a prosecution because their accounts cannot be reconciled with the DNA bloodstain evidence and other credible witness accounts."[598]

The absurdity of Black-Run America (BRA), whose devoted "journalists" have peddled the lie of "Hands Up, Don't Shoot" with a zealotry only matched by their commitment to calling George Zimmerman a 'white-Hispanic', has been utterly exposed in the farce of Ferguson.

The main question now is when did the Obama Administration and the Department of Justice know these facts: August? October? November?

The night of November 24th, when Ferguson inexplicably burned (despite the National Guard stationed throughout St. Louis County)?

One small suburb - a city once home to the aspirations of young white families - has now birthed a glimpse of the horror of HUD's Affirmatively Furthering Fair Housing (AFFH) plan all because the story of Ferguson's collapse is nothing more than a warning of the true evil of Section 8 Vouchers.

And the story of the deification of Michael Brown is nothing more

---

[598] Darren Wilson Is Cleared of Rights Violations in Ferguson Shooting, *New York Times*, 3-4-15

than an expose of the pure evil nature of modern journalism, whose newsrooms are staffed with social justice warriors intent on excusing away all manners of black dysfunction as the lingering residue of white racism.

It's time put your hands down black people.

March 5, 2015
Setting Straight the Lies of the Department of Justice's Civil Rights Division Report on the Ferguson Police Department

It was only a few days ago the outgoing Attorney General of the Department of Justice encouraged young people to read Malcolm X and campaigned for a lowering of federal hate crime standards.[599]

So it's difficult to take seriously the claims by Eric "My People" Holder (who famously sided with the black insurrectionists in Ferguson by mid-August when he demanded "Tell them to remove the damn tanks" that were thwarting further riots/looting in the city) of serious racial bias on the part of the majority white Ferguson Police Department against the ever-increasing black majority population in the city.[600]

In a speech on March 4, Holder spent a considerable amount of time discussing how due process exonerated Darren Wilson of any wrong-doing in the shooting death Michael Brown. In fact, Officer Wilson did everything that day by the book.

But Holder spent a considerable more amount of time discussing

---

[599] http://dailycaller.com/2015/02/27/eric-holder-wants-to-lower-federal-hate-crime-standards-suggests-kids-read-malcolm-x/

[600] http://www.wsj.com/articles/federal-authorities-wade-deeper-into-teens-death-1408322176

the Civil Rights Division of the Department of Justice report on the Ferguson Police Department. Here's a sample of his remarks:

> A possible explanation for this discrepancy was uncovered during the course of our *second* federal investigation, conducted by the Civil Rights Division to determine whether Ferguson Police officials have engaged in a widespread pattern or practice of violations of the U.S. Constitution or federal law.
>
> As detailed in our searing report – also released by the Justice Department today – this investigation found a community that was deeply polarized; a community where deep distrust and hostility often characterized interactions between police and area residents.
>
> A community where local authorities consistently approached law enforcement *not* as a means for protecting public safety, but as a way to generate revenue. A community where both policing and municipal court practices were found to disproportionately harm African American residents. A community where this harm frequently appears to stem, at least in part, from racial bias – both implicit and explicit.
>
> Between October 2012 and October 2014, despite making up only 67 percent of the population, African Americans accounted for a little over *85 percent* of all traffic stops by the Ferguson Police Department. African Americans were twice as likely as white residents to be searched during a routine traffic stop, even though they were 26 percent less likely to carry contraband. Between October 2012 and July 2014, 35 black individuals – and *zero* white individuals – received five or more citations at the same time. During the same period, African Americans accounted for fully 85 percent of the total charges brought by the Ferguson Police Department. African Americans made up over 90 percent of those charged with a highly-discretionary offense described as "Manner of Walking Along Roadway."

And the use of dogs by Ferguson police appears to have been exclusively reserved for African Americans; in every case in which Ferguson police records recorded the race of a person bit by a police dog, that person was African American.[601]

Oh. My. God.

Black people were arrested. Fire every white cop now, check their closets for white robes and their garages for lighter fluid and wood that could easily be fashioned into a cross!

Luckily, VDare.com exists for an introduction of sanity to the debate.

As does Paul Kersey:
> And that brings us to the third element of the story, the actual crime rates. For all the MSM attention given to Ferguson, few supposed journalists have done any reporting other than repeating whatever hashtags were held up by vapid celebrities.
> So it was left to me. I called the Ferguson Police Department to obtain the crime reports sorted by race that extended back at least a decade. (Significantly the Justice Department examined only a sample size of the last three years—probably to avoid revealing systematic and long-standing black criminality). I was told by an officer that I was the *first* journalist to ask for this information.
>
> I was told to consult The Missouri Uniform Crime Reporting Program(MUCRP), which allows anyone to pull reports—going back to the year 2001—for every city in Missouri.
>
> You can search for various report types, including arrests by age, sex, crime with race.
>
> So, doing what the Department of Justice and apparently every journalist in America is incapable of doing, I pulled those arrest reports on the MUCRP site for Ferguson going back to 2001.

---

[601] Attorney General Holder Delivers Update on Investigations in Ferguson, Missouri, **Justice.Gov., 3-4-15**

In viewing the following, please remember that according to the 2000 U.S. Census, the city of Ferguson was only 52 percent black.

- Since 2001, 18513 people have been arrested in Ferguson: 84 percent have been black
- Since 2001, 479 people have been arrested for burglary in Ferguson: 91 percent of them have been black.
- Since 2001, 286 people have been arrested for weapons charges in Ferguson: 89 percent have been black
- Since 2001, 18513 people have been arrested in Ferguson: 84 percent have been black
- Since 2001, 9 people have been arrested for murder in Ferguson. 8 of the 9 have been black.
- Since 2001, there have been 28 people arrested in Ferguson for rape. All have been black.
- Since 2001, 133 people have been arrested for robbery in Ferguson: 90 percent have been black
- Since 2001, 146 people have been arrested for motor vehicle theft in Ferguson: 93 percent have been black.
- Since 2001, 4,845 people have been arrested for larceny in Ferguson: 80 percent have been black.[602]

And remember this: Racism is holding blacks responsible for their actions.

The response by Black-Run America (BRA) to canonize Michael Brown while castigating not only Darren Wilson but all white police officers in Ferguson *is an attempt to liberate black people from the consequences of their actions.*

---

[602] "Hands Up Don't Shoot" Was A Lie. Data Shows Latest DOJ Report Is, Too., VDare.com, 3-5-15

March 6, 2015
So Can Darren Wilson Go Back to Being a Cop Again? Can Any White Person Be a Cop in Obama's America?

Someone owes former Ferguson Police Officer Darren Wilson a big, big apology.

The 'DEPARTMENT OF JUSTICE REPORT REGARDING THECRIMINAL INVESTIGATION INTO THE SHOOTING DEATHOF MICHAEL BROWN BY FERGUSON, MISSOURI POLICEOFFICER DARREN WILSON' is basically an 86-page mea culpa on the part of the government to Officer Wilson, though it doesn't end with a recommendation for Wilson to be reinstated as an officer with the Ferguson Police Department.[603]

In late August of 2014, a total of nine (yes, nine) *Washington Post* reporters[604] were assigned the story of trying to uncover some dirt on Wilson to establish a background anecdote magically proving he had some reason racial reason to shoot Michael Brown... granting the Eric Holder's Department of Justice the ability to charge Wilson with violating Brown's civil rights.[605]

Those nine reporters uncovered nothing in Wilson's past, save him being a solid police officer.

---

[603] https://s3.amazonaws.com/s3.documentcloud.org/documents/1681212/doj-report-on-shooting-of-michael-brown.pdf

[604] http://www.washingtonpost.com/national/darren-wilsons-first-job-was-on-a-troubled-police-force-disbanded-by-authorities/2014/08/23/1ac796f0-2a45-11e4-8593-da634b334390_story.html

[605] http://www.washingtonpost.com/world/national-security/federal-civil-rights-charges-unlikely-against-police-officer-in-ferguson-shooting/2014/10/31/56189d80-6055-11e4-8b9e-2ccdac31a031_story.html

Shouldn't he be able to 'protect and serve' the community of Ferguson again, considering on August 9, 2014 he did everything exactly by the book?

In fact, the way he handled the situation on Canfield Drive with Michael Brown should be taught in police academies across the nation as the textbook manner in which to fend off an aggressor who is attempting to garner the officer's weapon.

But he'll never be a police officer again.

Though he violated no rules, Darren Wilson has now been forever barred from the vocation of law enforcement.

All because he did exactly what he was instructed to do.

You do your job; you are out of a job.

Welcome to Black-Run America (BRA), where white police officers in every city must now engage in risk assessment when they go to pull over a black person speeding or to question a black person who matches the description of a robbery or violent crime suspect.

Though the media seemed intent on inciting a lynch mob toward the former Officer Wilson, he's been nothing but resolute since the sunny August 9th day when his life changed forever:

> Attorney Neil Bruntrager says Wilson is pleased with what amounts to an "exoneration" from the DOJ.
>
> "Well, obviously the reaction is one of relief," Bruntrager says. "It's been a long road for him. Now he needs to get on with his life."[606]

Wilson, having resigned from the Ferguson Police Department on November 30, 2014 because of threats of violence to his fellow officers if he stayed on the force, will get no severance package from the city.[607]

---

[606] Darren Wilson 'Relieved' at No Charges From Feds, St. Louis CBS, 3-4-15

[607] http://www.huffingtonpost.com/2014/11/30/darren-wilson-severance_n_6244060.html

Nothing.

And though it was Michael Brown's decision to attack him on August 9th (attempting to murder him in the process) for doing his job that day Wilson lost the ability to perform the only job he ever wanted to do:

> Citing threats of violence, Darren Wilson, who fatally shot Michael Brown Aug. 9, resigned from the Ferguson Police Department on Saturday.
>
> Wilson, 28, whom a St. Louis County grand jury declined to indict in connection with the shooting, had worked for the city's police department for six years.
>
> In a telephone interview Saturday evening, Wilson said he resigned after the police department told him it had received threats that violence would ensue if he remained an employee.
>
> "I'm resigning of my own free will," he said. "I'm not willing to let someone else get hurt because of me."
>
> He said resigning was "the hardest thing I've ever had to do."
>
> Wilson's resignation, which was expected, comes after private talks between his representatives and the police department. The grand jury announced its decision in the case Monday.
>
> Wilson's resignation letter reads, in part:
>
> "I have been told that my continued employment may put the residents and police officers of the City of Ferguson at risk, which is a circumstance that I cannot allow. For obvious reasons, I wanted to wait until the grand jury made their decision before I officially made my decision to resign. It was my hope to continue in police work, but the safety of other police officers and the community are of paramount importance to me. It is my hope that my resignation will

allow the community to heal."[608]

One of Michael Brown's final words on earth wasn't, "Don't shoot me," but it was looking at Wilson and saying, ""What the fuck are you going to do about it?" after Brown slammed his car door shut on him...[609]

Every white police officer in America must understand the horror that is now upon them: knowing that any individual black person they arrest will become part of a black aggregate quickly used by overzealous Department of Justice employees (particularly in the Civil Rights Division) to illustrate the racist intent of the police force in subjecting the black community they police to horrors not seen since blacks had a "colored" water fountain to drink from...

Darren Wilson has a "clear conscience" over his decision to use lethal force on August 9th, when he stopped Michael Brown from using lethal force on him: but he can longer be a cop in America.[610]

For doing his job, for surviving media scrutiny, and for standing firm in the face of a racially motivated Department of Justice investigation (that ultimately exonerated him of any wrong doing and confirmed only did what he was trained to do), Darren Wilson will never, ever be a police officer again.

His story is a lesson for all white police officers currently serving in their communities and for any aspiring white person thinking of going to police academy.

You do your job; you are out of a job.

---

[608] Darren Wilson resigns from Ferguson Police Department, St. Louis Post-Dispatch, 11-30-14

[609] http://www.theguardian.com/us-news/2014/nov/25/ferguson-darren-wilson-interview-abc-clear-conscience

[610] http://www.cbsnews.com/news/darren-wilson-said-to-have-clear-conscience-after-ferguson-decision/

March 9, 2015
The Origins of Eric Holder's "Powder keg" in Ferguson: Section 8 Vouchers for Blacks

Remember when President Barack Obama secretly met with Ferguson protesters in the White House on November 5, 2014, telling them to "stay the course?" If you forgot, that's aright: it was buried in paragraph 21 of a story published at *The New York Times*.[611]

When President Obama spoke these words, was he aware Officer Darren Wilson had done nothing wrong, instead blinded by his racial loyalty and sense of animosity toward a civilization he can never belong too?

Truth never mattered in the situation in Ferguson.

Only the "Endgame" matters: *"If you believe in the System, you end up like Darren Wilson."*[612]

Which is why this sentence from the November 5, 1990 issue of *People* (Vol. 34, No. 18) is so important in helping to describe the kind of community existing in the-then 74 percent white city of Ferguson. Telling the story of the black East St. Louis High School football coach who had built a winning team at a 100 percent school, *People* lets slip he lived in the "a tranquil suburban neighborhood in nearby Ferguson":

> [Bob] Shannon and his wife, Jeanette, 42, an elementary school teacher who also works in East St. Louis, commute from a tranquil suburban neighborhood in nearby Ferguson, Mo.[613]

---

[611] http://www.nytimes.com/2014/11/17/us/groups-in-ferguson-prepare-for-grand-jury-decision.html?partner=rss&emc=rss&smid=tw-nytimes&_r=1

[612] http://www.radixjournal.com/journal/2015/3/9/endgame

[613] Amid the Symbols of a City's Decay, An Illinois High School Coach Teaches Kids the Secrets of Winning—and Pride, People, 11-5-1990

People is describing the community of 74 percent white Ferguson in 1990; only a sadist would describe now 70 percent black Ferguson as "tranquil."

But the question is what happened to Ferguson? Why the dramatic racial transformation from a "tranquil" white suburb into just another failing majority black city?

Section 8 Vouchers:

> Ferguson has been home to dramatic economic changes in recent years. The city's unemployment rate rose from less than 5 percent in 2000 to over 13 percent in 2010-12. For those residents who were employed, inflation-adjusted average earnings fell by one-third. The number of households using federal Housing Choice Vouchers climbed from roughly 300 in 2000 to more than 800 by the end of the decade.[614]

Remember the Maine?

The sinking of the Lusitania?

The Gulf of Tonkin Incident?

Pearl Harbor?

All were allowed to occur, because the event themselves allowed other plans to finally come to fruition.

What happened in Ferguson could have happened in hundreds, perhaps thousands of cities across America.

If, as Eric Holder asserts, there was a "powder keg" in 70 percent black Ferguson, it's because the government gladly provided the ingredients ensuring it would one day ignite.

---

[614] Charting Poverty In Ferguson: Then And Now, ZeroHedge.com, 8-17-14

March 11, 2015
The Birth of a Revolution: How Long Until the Newly Elected Black Power Structure in Ferguson Raids the Ferguson Pension Plan?

Five white people have lost their jobs working for the city of Ferguson.

Two police officers and a court clerk over "racist emails"; they were fired.[615]

The city manager and a municipal judge resigned.[616]

Make that six, with the police chief resigning.[617]

More will surely resign, with others forced out from occupying any power in the waning white power structure, soon to be replaced by a black power structure in Ferguson.

A black mayor is inevitable, as well as a majority black city council and a black police chief.

For those remaining whites in the 25 percent white city, the memory of Ferguson from decades ago (in 1990, the city was 74 percent white) keeps them married to a community that divorced them long ago.

---

[615] http://www.stltoday.com/news/local/crime-and-courts/two-police-officers-court-clerk-out-at-ferguson-over-racist/article_5cca0f5f-7a1b-5b67-ab11-77541c9ad4f4.html

[616] http://www.usnews.com/news/articles/2015/03/11/doj-ferguson-report-prompts-resignations-court-takeover

[617] http://www.stltoday.com/news/local/crime-and-courts/embattled-ferguson-police-chief-resigns/article_3cd9e079-8dd5-523d-a84d-335d73a714f9.html

You'd hope those white people still employed as public sector workers in Ferguson would understand the horror of what is coming for the city if the scathing, damning, searing Department of Justice report on the 'evils' of the Ferguson Police Department weren't contested; refuted as nothing more than a government going all-in on scurrilous anecdotes after the Darren Wilson report blew up in its face.

The Department of Justice showed all their cards in this game of poker, and the embattled white leaders of Ferguson seems content in folding, resigned to a strategy of capitulation in the face of unrelenting pressure from the corporate media, federal government, and a cadre of well-funded black agitators/protesters.

The question of what happens to the Ferguson Pension Plan as the city nears 80 - 90 percent black, and the then near all-black city employees and black tax-base can no longer afford

As of 7/1/14, the Ferguson Pension Plan has 252 members in the plan (134 actively paying into the fund; 118 inactive, or drawing a pension): the fund has a market value of $24.5 million.

How long can this last, with for-sale signs littering the front yards of white homeowners in Ferguson,[618] those long-time residents who now find their equity underwater as the black population continues to rise?:

> Members of Ferguson's city council met Monday night behind closed doors to discuss the Justice Department's blistering report on the city's police force and municipal court–and in a debate before a mostly elderly, white audience, some candidates for a council seat claimed the problems in the report were overblown.
>
> In the wake of last week's federal investigative report into the city's law enforcement practices, the judge who ran Ferguson's municipal court has resigned, a top court clerk

---

[618] http://www.stltoday.com/business/local/ferguson-home-sales-fell-as-uncertainty-gripped-real-estate-market/article_6b96afae-60f3-5e68-b2dc-33aef8bbb561.html

who sent a racist email was fired, and two police department officials connected to racist emails have stepped down. The report highlighted problems with St. Louis County's fractured network of municipal courts that extend beyond Ferguson.

But some people looking to join Ferguson's government think the Justice Department was unfair to the city. Two black women and two white men are running in an election next month to replace Kim Tihen, one of two representatives for Ferguson's Ward 1. Tihen, a former police officer, was one of the officers involved in a 2009 incident in which a man was wrongfully arrested, allegedly beaten, and charged with destruction of property for bleeding on police uniforms.

Mike McGrath, one of the white candidates, believes that Tihen did a good job on the council and that the Justice Department report on Ferguson was unfair." They tried to go after Officer Wilson," McGrath said in an interview after the debate on Monday, referring to Darren Wilson, the officer who shot and killed 18-year-old Michael Brown on Aug. 9, 2014. "When they couldn't do that, they went after the city."

McGrath drew strong support from the audience when he said the residents of Ferguson's apartment complexes, who are mostly black, didn't care as much about the city as the homeowners.

"I may be a silly old man in all of this, but I don't think we have a big race issue here," he said in an interview after the meeting, which was interrupted several times by other white residents who wanted to thank him and offer their support. "We have an issue with that part of town and they've been a bad part of town for a long time, sadly."[619]

All of those white retired civil employees who paid into the Ferguson Pension Plan and helped plant the social capital in Ferguson now uprooted by Section 8 Voucher-holding blacks must now ask themselves how much longer the checks will come...

---

[619] At Ferguson City Council Debate, Some Still Don't See a Problem After Brutal DOJ Report, *Mariah Stewart, Huffington Post, March 10, 2015*

White homeowners, who can recall a day when white kids on bikes rode down the same Canfield Drive that 18-year-old Michael Brown casually walked down the middle of on August 9, 2014, understand the individual lives they've led in Ferguson collectively are now defined by the perceived racism of the Ferguson Police Department; manifested by a Department of Justice report canonized as the word of God by a media intent on lynching somewhere after the Darren Wilson fiasco.

Civilization once flourished in Ferguson, when the city wasn't an experiment in how fast Section 8 Voucher-holding blacks can upset the delicate social capital planted and cultivated in the city over decades; now, the unrest of the past seven months ensures U-Haul truck renting facilities in North St. Louis will be busy, with white homeowners unloading their houses before the equity is evaporates completely.

There was a war waged in Ferguson, and few people dare comprehend the terribleness of the totality of the victory for those with stock in Black-Run America (BRA).

This is why it was so important for a unified effort on the part of those in power in Ferguson to push back against the Department of Justice report, *for as Ferguson, so goes the nation.*

But in the face of opposition, the only way to offer resistance is to stand resolute and use truth as an offensive weapon instead of remaining constantly on the defense. But the days of Ferguson being a "tranquil" are over, and the future of the city is in the hands of people like Michael Brown and those who gleefully looted and burned down stores in his memory:

> Ferguson Mayor James Knowles III told the Post-Dispatch on Friday that the report revealed details that raise concern; however, he wasn't sure if the behavior is as prevalent as it has been made to sound. The Justice Department report stated there was probable cause to believe the police and court routinely violate people's civil rights. "That's not proof," he said, adding that "there is probably another side to all of these stories."

Police Chief Thomas Jackson has not commented on the DOJ report and has said that he has no plans to resign.

Knowles wasn't present at Sunday's news conference, where people like Mary Robinson, a longtime resident of Ferguson, asked for him and other administrators to move on. She said her African-American son was often harassed by police. She scorned the north St. Louis County suburb for "making money off of the backs of the less fortunate."

"We need new leadership here in Ferguson that can inspire the hearts and minds of our diverse community, not just the chosen few," she said. "Our young persons should be the first priority because they are the future in Ferguson."

The Rev. Gerald Kleba, a Roman Catholic priest, said that the newly remodeled police department headquarters and jail, the red brick building behind the group, was tainted because it was partially paid for with overly aggressive ticketing and fines.

"The building is worthless and a sham and a shell unless an equal amount of time, energy and money is spent to bring a new culture and new police department to Ferguson, where officers truly serve and protect all the people," Kleba said.

"Otherwise the protesters who chanted 'Burn it all down' might just still do that.

"I say this with fear, but conscientious people have to be concerned and cannot be surprised if there are outbreaks of violence in response to the daily violence of a culture of injustice that leads to a new Jim Crow, prisons overcrowded with young people of color."[620]

We are witnessing the birth of a revolution.

---

[620] http://www.stltoday.com/news/local/crime-and-courts/clergy-and-others-call-for-overhaul-of-ferguson-leadership/article_91f1c79b-a383-513c-98cc-362fbb7bd100.html

March 12, 2015
The Ferguson War Journal Can't Be Closed: Two White Cops Shot in "Ambush" in Ferguson

A two-year-old black child was grazed with a bullet in North St. Louis on Saturday (March 7), in a drive-by-shooting at roughly 1 p.m.[621]

A six-year-old black child is dead, gunned down in a "rolling gun battle" at 7:30 p.m. on a Wednesday night in St. Louis. A black male is the suspect in this shooting:

> Marcus Johnson's family took the 6-year-old to O'Fallon Park Wednesday to enjoy the nice weather as he recovered from heart surgery the week before.
>
> But the pleasant evening at the park turned to tragedy, perhaps after a simple traffic dispute in the park. Bullets flew, and Marcus was shot and killed during a rolling gunbattle as the family left the park in a minivan about 7:30 p.m.
>
> Marcus' teenage brother and a 69-year-old man in the minivan were injured and were taken to a hospital. Marcus' parents and three other children weren't harmed.
>
> Police were searching for the other vehicle involved. Authorities did not release a description of the shooter or shooters.
>
> "My baby already had stress to live in this world, and for somebody to take his life away is wrong," his mother, Quiana Johnson, said Thursday as tears flowed. Her surviving children surrounded her as she spoke in the living room of her home in the 1000 block of McDuff Drive, in the Glasgow

---

[621] http://www.stltoday.com/news/local/crime-and-courts/year-old-boy-grazed-by-gunfire-in-st-louis/article_baf7cbeb-cf9e-5a7f-8ae7-f0cce370b191.html

Village area of north St. Louis County.

She said they had a great time at the park. But at one point, her husband saw someone he knew passing by in a car. The man stopped his vehicle to chat. Another man approached, upset that traffic was stopped.

"You can't hold this traffic up," the man yelled, according to Johnson. "This is my 'hood."

The friend in the car moved on, and the angry man walked off, but his look stuck with Johnson.

"He had the devil in his eyes," she said of how he looked at them, as if they had disrespected him. Her gut told her they should leave.

They got in the minivan to leave, but a vehicle followed them, and before they got out of the park, shots were flying. Johnson said bullets were hitting her car and the windows were shattered.

She said she had recently bought a gun because of her fear of break-ins in their neighborhood. She grabbed it.

"I put my clip in my gun and looked back and saw that my son had been shot," she said. "I gave it to my husband and I told him that if he didn't shoot back, they will kill us all."

He fired back as they fled northwest on West Florissant Avenue, Johnson said. The vehicle's tires were shot out and he drove on the rims.

"Bullets were flying past my head as I crawled back to my baby," she said.[622]

A park outing for a black family in heavily black North St. Louis turns into the type of escapist fantasy white kids read about as the origin of Marvel's *Punisher*. Just a typical Wednesday night for black people in a world where low-impulse control and poor future-time

---

[622] Quiet outing at St. Louis park turns to tragedy as bullets fly, killing 6-year-old boy, St. Louis Post-Dispatch, 3-12-15]:

orientation ally together to create a wonderfully African in America moment.

Meanwhile in Ferguson, located in North St. Louis, only hours after the shooting death of a six-year-old black child conclusively proved *black lives truly don't matter*, a fight broke out among #BlackLivesMatter protesters in front of the police department.[623] Moments later, shots were fired at members of the police stationed in front of the Ferguson Police Department:

> The Missouri Highway Patrol and St. Louis County Police will take over Ferguson protest security Thursday night after two police officers were shot outside the police department there early Thursday morning.
>
> The two officers shot early Thursday are expected to survive, St. Louis County Police Chief Jon Belmar said. They were treated at Barnes-Jewish Hospital and released Thursday, though one still had a bullet lodged behind his ear.
>
> Belmar called the shooting as protests outside the department dwindled an "ambush" on police. At least three shots were fired at police just after midnight as police faced protesters who had gathered outside the police station, police said.[624]

The news of two white cops shot was greeted with cheers and adulation from blacks across the World Wide Web and in Ferguson, who view the difference between the Ku Klux Klan (KKK) and the police as virtually indistinguishable.[625]

Members representing the Organization of Black Struggle, the Advancement Project and the Don't Shoot Coalition, called a press conference to call the shootings "suspicious";

---

[623] http://www.kmov.com/special-coverage-001/video/RAW-Protesters-fight-outside-Ferguson-Police-Department--296043661.html

[624] [Police search for those who shot 2 officers in Ferguson 'ambush', St. Louis Post-Dispatch, 3-12-15]:

[625] http://www.infowars.com/ferguson-supporters-celebrate-shooting-of-police-officers/

insinuating a false-flag attack of some sort... perhaps white robed white men were the boogeymen who fired the shots?[626]

Of course, the two-year-old black child shot on Saturday and the dead six-year-old black kid were also targeted by pistol-packing white robed white men, right?

The Ferguson War Journal should have been closed months ago.

It should be obvious by now the Ferguson War Journal is on the verge of massive expansion, with the winter thawing and spring blooming nationwide.

March 13, 2015
The Flag of Victory Goes Up In Ferguson: Where the Looted/Burned QuikTrip Stands, the Urban League of Metro St. Louis Will Build a "Community Center"

A fitting denouement to story of the burnt-out QuikTrip on West Florissant Avenue in Ferguson, where employees sought shelter from rampaging black looters[627] on August 10th; black rioters liberated items from the store prior to setting fire to the QuikTrip and infamously spray painting 'Snitches Get Stitches' on the side of the building.[628]

---

[626] http://www.stltoday.com/news/local/metro/ferguson-protest-leaders-decry-shooting-of-police-but-some-aren/article_8bca387b-0ce6-5c76-939d-4a0438951087.html?utm_medium=twitter&utm_source=twitterfeed

[627] http://stlouis.cbslocal.com/2014/08/11/quiktrip-employee-workers-hid-in-back-room-as-ferguson-store-was-looted-set-on-fire/

[628] http://fox2now.com/2014/08/11/quiktrip-sprayed-with-graffiti-set-on-fire-during-overnight-looting-near-ferguson/

The flag of victory is going up in Ferguson, where a branch of the hilariously black nonprofit 'Save Our Sons (SOS)' program will now work to empowering young black lives in a city destined to be 100 percent black by 2020:

> The Urban League of Metropolitan St. Louis plans to build a center on West Florissant Avenue in Ferguson, where a charred QuikTrip now sits, allowing the organization to expand its job training and education efforts.
>
> A press conference is set for Monday afternoon to announce details, which the Urban League would not provide today.
>
> In a notice to media on Friday, the Urban League said the announcement will be "an important extension of its services in North County to further the League's mission of empowering communities and changing lives."
>
> The center will "expand the Urban League's work to broaden access to education/job training, employment and economic self-reliance for residents of the St. Louis metro area," the news release states.
>
> A source involved in the negotiations said QuikTrip will tear down the remains of the store, looted and burned on Aug. 10, the day after Michael Brown was fatally shot by a Ferguson police officer. The convenience store chain also will remove the underground gas tanks. Several donors will provide funding for the Urban League to build a "community empowerment center" on the site, which became ground zero for protests after the Brown shooting.
>
> QuikTrip and the Urban League have been in negotiations for several months to put a center on the site of the burned convenience store, at 9420 West Florissant Avenue, a source said.
>
> The new center will house the newly implemented Save Our Sons program, which landed $1.2 million in donations from St. Louis area companies in the wake of the unrest in Ferguson. The goal is to take 500 young men, jobless or underemployed, from north St. Louis County and give them a month's training in how to land a job, keep it and get

promoted. From there, the men will be matched with a job at a local company. Putting 500 men through the program is expected to take several years. The Urban League, which announced the program in January, came up with the idea after talking with young, unemployed men.[629]

The symbolism of the Urban League building a center on the very land the QuikTrip once stood amounts to a stunning declaration of victory over the once all-white city of Ferguson and its conquest in the name of Africa. One black leader (back in August of 2014) dubbed the burnt-out QuikTrip in Ferguson the "Tahrir Square, their Tiananmen Square" for the growing insurrection.

Fitting now it becomes the staging-ground for the total conquest of Ferguson via educating younger black males/females to becomes the leaders for the future all-black city. A victory over white oppression, white privilege, and white supremacy was won on this spot of land, where a symbol of the white capitalist system once stood before it was set on fire in the revolutionary zeal of August 2014! Viva Michael Brown!:

> FERGUSON, Mo. — The red and white gas station at the corner of West Florissant Avenue and Northwinds Estates Drive was the victim of a rumor.
> On Sunday, there was a false report that employees of the gas station had called 911 to report that Michael Brown, whose fatal shooting by police 11 days ago precipitated the crisis in the city, had robbed the place. Enraged protesters burned the gas station to the ground.
>
> Destroyed, it sat unattended for days, emerging as the depressing backdrop for cable news live reports — a sign of the chaos and destruction that engulfs the streets of Ferguson after each nightfall.
>
> There has not been any single location more central to the unrest in Ferguson as the looted service station.

---

[629] Urban League to open a new center in Ferguson on burned QuikTrip lot, St. Louis Post-Dispatch, 3-13-15

But then, on Thursday afternoon, it was transformed as a group of hundreds of protesters decided it would be their staging ground.

"This is our place. This is what we've got," Maria Chappelle-Nadal, a state senator who has been central in staging many of the daytime protests, said during an interview outside of the QuikTrip this week. This was their Tahrir Square, their Tiananmen Square. The place each night where they would make their stand.

"These people have no other place, so they've made it their own," said Chappelle-Nadal.[630]

Chappelle-Nadal is the same Missouri State Senator who tweeted out a racial warning to those whites unprepared for what living in a black-run city (where black elected and appointed officials control the government) will mean... simply put, the implementation of black privilege and persecution of whites. Her tweet read:

"LET ME BE CLEAR: When you exercise your #WhitePrivilege, don't think I'm not going to remember. I will use it for the future. Uncomfortable?"[631]

Those remaining white homeowners in Ferguson who still believe the future of the city will see property values rebound need to sell their homes now. Black political power means the complete annihilation of your property value (the immediate erosion of equity in your home a reflection of the terrible reality of the Visible Black Hand of Economics), if the history of North St. Louis cities falling to black demographic majorities is any indicator.[632]

The Urban League exists to 'empower' black people and they've

---

[630] The QuikTrip gas station, Ferguson protesters' staging ground, is now silent, Washington Post, 8-19-15

[631] http://fox2now.com/2015/01/04/state-senator-chappelle-nadal-tweet-on-white-privilege-spurs-uproar/

[632] http://www.stltoday.com/news/local/metro/political-power-lags-black-population-growth-in-several-north-county/article_d43a0c52-a133-5ccd-9d00-795dea84c5de.html

chosen to build their headquarters on the very spot in Ferguson where the black insurrectionaries were "empowered" in mid-August 2014...

It's time white people abandon Ferguson; your city leaders have all but abandoned you in failing to fight the shockingly absurd charges brought forth by a vengeful Department of Justice (DOJ) Civil Rights Division.

Let them celebrate the razing of the QuikTrip and the erection of an Urban League building, for Ferguson is nothing more than the Waterloo of the American Dream and the reality white people are now entering the 'American Nightmare.'

One day, we will wake up.

March 16, 2015
It's so hard to get old without a cause/I don't want to perish like a fading horse

There is not one city in America where the increase in the black population and the decrease in the white population has meant positive news for real estate values (commercial or private).

Go ahead.

Find a city.

Dare you.

Double-dog dare you.

Find one city.

Please.

Prove me wrong.

Find one city.

Because America's future is nothing more than the nightmare unfolding in Ferguson; a now 70 percent (and increasingly) black suburb of St. Louis, where K-Mart, Big Lots, and Toys 'R' Us have fled from in the past five months.

Where the Section 8 Voucher population has increased from 300 individuals receiving aid in 2000 to 800 in 2010.[633] And virtually every individual (and thus, multiple family members living under a roof courtesy of the aid) using a Section 8 Voucher in Ferguson is black.[634]

Indeed, the black population rose 150 percent in Ferguson from 1990 (when they represented just 25 percent of the population) to 2010.[635]

You see, race isn't a social construct; race is the required blueprint for building a prosperous community or race can be the highly negative ingredient for the disintegration of social capital in a city.

Race is what constructs a thriving community or what defines a collapsing city.

It's this simple:

> Peering outside the office window of his tire shop, John Zisser grumbles about the pile of burnt rubble that lies on the opposite corner of a busy intersection.
>
> "If you come here to my shop and you see that," he says, as gestures out the window, "is that going to give you a warm,

---

[633] http://www.brookings.edu/blogs/the-avenue/posts/2014/08/15-ferguson-suburban-poverty

[634] http://www.stltoday.com/news/local/metro/as-low-income-housing-boomed-ferguson-pushed-back/article_fcb97a3c-8bb7-54a5-9565-255301753142.html

[635] http://www.stltoday.com/news/local/metro/st-louis-county-police-forces-often-don-t-reflect-communities/article_a29dc3e4-91bb-5cf5-9b30-9ebb95c5e1c6.html

fuzzy feeling like you want to come back here to do business?"

"Short answer: no, no it's not," he says.

Zisser, 55, has owned and operated Zisser's Tires in this city since 1987. He says the still-visible damage from the November protests that followed a grand jury's decision not to indict Ferguson officer Darren Wilson for the shooting death of teenager Michael Brown is hurting property owners. His store's insurance is in the process of being cancelled after it was twice vandalized during the unrest, he says.

"If I sold this place today, I could probably get $300,000 for it, if anyone is crazy enough to buy. Last year, the county said this lot was worth almost a million," he says. "The value here is all going down. There's about nine burnt-out buildings this way," he says, pointing. "And about four more behind me."

Zisser is one of many Ferguson residents feeling a financial toll from the months of protests, media attention, and now another high-profile shooting. They're worried not just about their own situations, but about the city coffers, too. The future of Ferguson, they say, is anyone's guess.

"How much money are we going to lose?" Zisser asks. "How much money is the city and the county going to lose in taxes because of this? And how much is the school district going to lose here? They're the biggest losers."

For the city's 2014 budget, approximately 20 percent of the city's revenue came from the city's courts, and 17 percent came through property taxes. But after a Department of Justice report found the courts were profiting off racial discrimination, the State of Missouri took over to implement reforms. Couple that with rapidly falling property values (which are used to calculate owed taxes) and it seems like key parts of the city's business plan are falling out from under it.

The average selling price of a home in the city has been on a steady decline since the shooting of Brown last August, according to housing data compiled from MARIS, an information and statistics service for real estate agents. Prior to Brown's death, the average home sold in 2014 was selling for $66,764. For the last three and a half months of the year, the average home sold for $36,168, a 46 percent decrease.

The trend has continued on through this year, with the average home selling for only $22,951 so far in 2015. Another negative indicator: in the eight and a half months leading up to Brown's death, the average residential square foot in 2014 was selling for $45.82. In the eight and a half months since Brown's passing, the average residential square foot in the city has sold for $24.11. That's about a 47 percent downtick in one of real estate's core indicators.

"This is not normal for the region," says Crista Patton, a local REMAX real estate agent who helped get these numbers for Fusion. "Last time I pulled up numbers like this for a neighborhood around here, we were seeing the market going up," she says. "In St. Louis in general, the market is going up, and as a whole it's almost completely recovered from the recession."

The city admits that its finances are taking a hit, with no end in sight, due to the events since Brown's death. "The[city's] response to the unrest, as well as other related matters, has resulted in significant, unanticipated expenditures," reads the city's Comprehensive Annual Financial Report for 2014. "The civil unrest also resulted in some lost revenues... At this time, the total impact of this event on the City's revenues and expenses is not able to be estimated."

Ferguson native David H. Pope, 76, who has worked as a realtor in the city for 48 years, says the current situation has made it nearly impossible to attract families to the area.

"I lost a sale yesterday," he says, blaming the shooting of two police officers in front of the Ferguson Police Department. "This whole thing has been very, very detrimental to my work and the market here."[636]

---

[636] Ferguson home values are plummeting, and residents are feeling the pain: Down nearly 50 percent since Michael Brown's death, new data show., Fusion.com, 3-16-

But has David H. Pope forgotten a story from the *St. Louis Post-Dispatch* in mid-2013, published long before the street of Canfield Drive had become a permanent home to the Michael Brown Memorial?

The story tells the sad tale of Ferguson resident Barbara Bandy, who had resided in the four bedroom home since 1973. She moved into the home when Ferguson was basically 100 percent white.

In the subsequent four decades, Ferguson's racial demographics would basically flip-flop, to the point where the city will be nearly 100 percent black by 2020.

What's missing from this August 18, 2013 story is the racial realities of Ferguson's demise, and how the growth of black population significantly impacted the value of Bandy's home.

In 2013... long before Officer Darren Wilson encountered Michael Brown on August 9, 2014:

> Barbara Bandy has been trying to sell her house for nearly a year, with no luck. Could the problem be that it's in north St. Louis County?
>
> She was optimistic when she started. It's a nice Cape Cod with four bedrooms and two baths, built in the 1950s. In 2011, the St. Louis County assessor put its value at $117,500. She says she spent $20,000 fixing it up for sale.
>
> "I'm up to here on credit," she says, holding her hand up to her nose.
>
> But when Bandy put it on the market, it sat. It wouldn't sell at $98,000.
>
> She cut the price to $94,000. She switched real estate agents, cut the price to $84,500 and still it sits.

> "Now they want me to strike the price down again. Do you think that's fair?" asks the elderly widow, who lived in the house for 40 years.
>
> Her real estate agent also wants her to offer to finance part of the buyer's mortgage. "What do they think I am? A bank?"
>
> Her problem may be location. Her house is in Ferguson.
>
> Ferguson is a picture of pleasant suburbia, a town of tree-lined streets and well-kept homes, much of them built for the middle class at mid-century.
>
> But Ferguson is in north St. Louis County, and the area is suffering from one of the region's weakest real estate markets. That's worrying county officials, who fear it may reflect deeper economic problems in parts of North County.[637]

All is race. There is no other truth.

It's a truth we've seen played out in Ferguson, once a no-name suburb of St. Louis attracting quality citizens like Barbara Bandy, who raised her family in the almost all-white city.

She moved into her home in Ferguson in 1973, when she was 43 years-old.

A 100 percent white city then; a 70 percent black city in 2013, when she had to sell her most of her furniture because the value of her home had plummeted and she couldn't find any buyers.

The future of Ferguson was cemented long before Officer Darren Wilson sacrificed his future on August 9, 2014, merely by trying to do his job.

Just ask Barbara Bandy...

---

[637] Blame poverty, age for weak North County home market, 8-18-2013

March 18, 2015
The Tales that Really Matter: The Sad Story of a 40+ year resident of Ferguson as a Metaphor for White America's Future

In trying to imagine what those white people remaining in South Africa are experiencing under increasingly hostile black-majority rule, my thoughts went back to the plight of 84-year-old Barbara Bandy.

You remember Barbara Bandy, right?

She moved to a nearly 100 percent white Ferguson in 1973, with her husband and children. Over the course of the next 40 years, the racial demographics of the St. Louis would completely flip, with whites dropping to around 25 percent of the total population by 2013 and blacks approaching 70 percent of Ferguson's population.

It was around this time Bandy, now a widow and with her children grown up, found herself all alone in an increasingly foreign community.

A community once capable of producing the type of memories for Bandy and her children they'll fondly recall over Thanksgiving and Christmas dinners was, in her final years living in Ferguson, only capable of producing a nightmarish existence.

On September 11, 2012, Bandy appeared at Ferguson City Council meeting as the only civic-minded individual to offer a public comment. And she brought up "public safety concerns":

Barbara Bandy, 324 S. Elizabeth, addressed the Council regarding public safety concerns. She discussed several incidents that had occurred in her area. Mayor Knowles said that City staff would look into the matter.

There being no additional public comments, Mayor Knowles closed the Public Comments portion at 7:25 p.m.[638]

Who knows what prompted Barbara Bandy to address the Ferguson City Council, but the odds are extremely high this was a problem she never needed to bring up when he children grew up in the nearly all-white city.

But Ferguson is now 70 percent black (and rising).

The community Bandy and her late husband raised their children in is totally gone, much as the future for white people in Mandela's South Africa is the exact opposite of the one their grandparents hoped they'd inherit.

Accompanying the *St. Louis Post-Dispatch* article *Blame poverty, age for weak North County home market,* published on August 18, 2013, was an image of Barbara Bandy in front of her home. The caption reads:

After raising her children in a modest four-bedroom Ferguson home, Barbara Bandy, 82, decided last year that climbing stairs had gotten the best of her. She placed her home for sale in May, 2012, and despite cutting the price three times, it still has not sold. Bandy, who has sold most of her furniture, was photographed on Wednesday, Aug. 14, 2013.[639]

The *St. Louis Post-Dispatch* noted her home had an appraised value of $117,500 in 2011. She put it on the market in 2013 for $98,000 but couldn't sell; she cut the price to $94,000, switched real estate agents, and cut the price to $84,500.[640]

---

[638] CITY OF FERGUSON, MISSOURICITY COUNCIL MEETING MINUTESSEPTEMBER 11, 2012, FergusonCity.com

[639] http://www.stltoday.com/news/local/metro/blame-poverty-age-for-weak-north-county-home-market/article_95c998e5-bb87-5bc0-9054-83e801b357ac.html

[640] http://www.stltoday.com/news/local/metro/blame-poverty-age-for-weak-north-county-home-market/article_95c998e5-bb87-5bc0-9054-83e801b357ac.html

The Visible Black Hand of Economics...

Thanks to Zillow.com, we learn Bandy's four bedroom, two bath house at 324 S Elizabeth Ave in Ferguson sold on March 19, 2014 for $65,000.[641]

The phone number connected with her old address no longer is in service, but the stories she could share about the Ferguson once existing would be far different then the ones of the Ferguson existing now.

Barbara Bandy's story of dispossession from the community she helped build and the declining property value of her home in a community far different then the one existing in 1973 Ferguson is a melancholy metaphor for white Americans in 2015.

It's a story few dare realize represents the future, because the fate of Barbara Bandy is one seemingly reserved for all white property owners in rapidly "diversifying" areas.[642]

Unfortunately, there is no going back to the way the world was for Barbara Bandy and her young family in 1973, when they moved into the all-white city of Ferguson.

The Ferguson of 2015 is destined to become a completely black city, where the memory the Bandy family ever called 324 S Elizabeth Ave is completely lost, replaced with the continued desire to make holy Canfield Drive: where Michael Brown spent his final moments on earth:

But everything changed when a shrine sprouted in the heart of the complex.

As Ferguson purges leaders following the release March 4 of a Department of Justice report accusing local police and courts of

---

[641]http://www.zillow.com/homes/for_sale/2663838_zpid/days_sort/38.742182,-90.294586,38.740265,-90.297445_rect/18_zm/?view=map

[642] Ferguson, Mo. Emblematic of Growing Suburban Poverty, Brookings Institute, 8-15-14

abusing the rights of residents, the long strip of hats, orange cones and wilted stuffed animals remains in the median of Canfield Drive.

It's the sacred memorial to Brown. Pilgrims continue to gather there even after a Justice Department report concluded Ferguson police officer Darren Wilson was justified in the shooting of Brown, and that "credible" witnesses didn't corroborate the popular story line that Brown had his hands up in surrender.[643]

'A shrine' Michael Brown's mother believes should stay in place "forever."[644]

One wonders who it was Barbara Bandy complained about as causing a "public safety concern" to the Ferguson City Council on September 11, 2012, but it should be known she put a home she had lived for 40 years on the market only a few months later.

A home containing the ghosts of yesterday: memories of her deceased husband and young children opening presents on Christmas Day, preparing for the first day of school, and eagerly opening the front door to the possibilities of summer.

Those memories are dead, abandoned by Bandy to the cruelty of time and Ferguson's darkening demographic fate.

March 25, 2015
"I imagine that right now, you're feeling a bit like Alice. Hmm? Tumbling down the rabbit hole?"

---

[643] What's going to happen to Canfield Green Apartments?, St. Louis Post-Dispatch, 3-15-15

[644] http://www.nytimes.com/2014/10/07/us/bruised-and-weary-ferguson-struggles-to-heal.html?_r=0

There's just something about the Department of Justice's Civil Rights Division Report on the Ferguson Police Department still eating at me.[645]

Washington Post writer Richard Cohen tried to assert the Ferguson Police Department was a cesspool of racism, but in reality the now 70 percent black city of Ferguson represents nothing more than a city awash in black crime and debased property values.[646]

So a grand total of seven emails (over a span of more than seven years the DOJ researched, what percentage of emails does this represent?) purportedly revealed "racial bias" among a few public employees in Ferguson; it's not like they ever grabbed a bunch of hammers and went out looking for a black person to kill, as several black people did in December of 2014.
Zemir Begic, as far as the national dialogue is concerned, never existed at all. His death was quickly brushed aside as having nothing to do with race by city leaders in St. Louis,[647] though the black participants in his death were heard to have shouted 'Eff the white people, kill the white people' before they ended Begic's life.[648]

But this isn't what's still eating at me: when news of Otis Byrd's hanging himself in a suicide became yet another cause for federal intervention/investigation by the FBI, Eric Holder's DOJ, and a mainstream media determined to secure the ultimate example of Mississippi Burning in 2015, it all came together:

> The hanging is being investigated by the FBI, the Justice Department's Civil Rights Division and the United States Attorney's office as well as the Mississippi Bureau of Investigation.

---

[645] http://www.vdare.com/articles/hands-up-dont-shoot-was-a-lie-data-shows-latest-doj-report-is-too

[646] http://www.washingtonpost.com/opinions/ferguson-and-benghazis-troubling-parallels/2015/03/23/5812b468-d17a-11e4-a62f-ee745911a4ff_story.html

[647] St. Louis mayor, police say race played no role in hammer slaying of Bosnian immigrant, St. Louis Post-Dispatch, 12-2-14

[648] http://www.bobmccarty.com/2014/12/01/exclusive-hammers-attack-video-from-south-st-louis/

> The feds are there to determine if it's a potential hate crime or other violation of federal law, U.S. Attorney General Eric Holder said Friday.
>
> "We simply don't know enough facts," Holder told MSNBC. "We do have a substantial federal presence to determine what the facts are."[649]

It all came together...

Zemir Begic's tragic execution at the hands of black people utilizing hammers in a fashion Thor would frown upon was quickly greeted with representatives of Black-Run America (BRA) hurriedly assuring the general public no racial animus was behind the murder, yet resources must be supplied as more lighter fluid to a pile of tinder Holder is just itching to toss a match upon.

So why not offer some research to showcase (yet again) the racial realties in St. Louis the Department of Justice Civil Rights Division omitted from their report on the Ferguson Police Department? Why not provide more lighter fluid of a different variety to the tinder ready to be ignited?

Ferguson is located in St. Louis County, which in 2000 had a population of 1,016,313 people. Of those, the county was 76.83% white and 19.02% black; by 2010, the population was 998,954, of which 70.27% were white and 23.33% were black.

From 2000-2010, the black population in St. Louis County increased 20.55% and the white population decreased by 10.10%.

But it was a quick visit to the The Missouri Uniform Crime Reporting Program (MUCRP), which allowed me to research what the Department of Justice seemed uninterested in adding to its report on the Ferguson Police Department.

Going back all the way to 2001, when the county was nearly 77 percent white and 19 percent black to 2014, one can quickly pull up

---

[649] http://www.nola.com/crime/index.ssf/2015/03/black_man_hanging_mississippi.html

a PDF file (for each year) of arrests in the county by race.

So for those 14 years, we get a clear picture of which racial group produced the individuals collectively lowering the quality of life (and property values) for the citizens of St. Louis County

Please remember St. Louis County was 77 percent white in 2000 and was 70.27 percent white in 2010 (19 percent black and 23 percent black respectively for those years):

- Since 2001, 7610 people have been arrested for burglary in St. Louis County: 58 percent of them have been black.
- Since 2001, 4310 people have been arrested for weapons charges in St. Louis County: 66 percent have been black
- Since 2001, 235 people have been arrested for murder in St. Louis County: 77 percent of them have been black.
- Since 2001, there have been 341 people arrested in St. Louis County for rape: 61 percent of them have been black.
- Since 2001, 2246 people have been arrested for robbery in St. Louis County: 79 percent have been black
- Since 2001, 2834 people have been arrested for motor vehicle theft in St. Louis County: 76 percent have been black.

Remember: St. Louis County's population in 2000 was only 19 percent black and in 2010, it was only 23 percent black...

And for those interested, the City of St. Louis Metropolitan Police Department finally released its 2013 Annual Report to the Community, which breaks down arrests by race for violent crimes.

Remember, out of 318,000 people, St. Louis is 49.2 percent black 43.9 percent white (as of 2010 US Census).

Here's the breakdown for 2013:

- 87.1% of those arrested for aggravated assault in St. Louis in 2013 were black.
- 93.6% of those arrested for robbery in St. Louis in 2013 were black.

- 94% of those arrested for murder in St. Louis in 2013 were black.
- 80.2% of those arrested for forcible rape in St. Louis in 2013 were black.
- 90% of those arrested for weapons offenses in St. Louis in 2013 were black.[650]

St. Louis and St. Louis County are two different beasts together, but the primary racial group responsible for committing the violent crime in the city - where they are 49 percent of the population - or in the county (where they have been roughly 20 - 23 percent of the population since 2000) are black people.

The real crime in St. Louis and St. Louis County were that over the seven years the Department of Justice spent researching the public emails of Ferguson city employees, is that all they could find were seven instances of perceived "racism."

Seven emails.

And yet, you look at those arrest rates for St. Louis County from 2001 - 2014 and for the city of St. Louis for 2013 (p. 20), one can only imagine the number of times individual white people were victimized by blacks.

For we know, if it was the other way around, you'd have an international incident...

March 27, 2015
Justice for Michael Brown: Three Blacks Attack White Man on MetroLink in St. Louis

"It figures. It's all happened too sudden. People gotta talk

---

[650] http://www.slmpd.org/images/2013AnnualReport_D.pdf

themselves into law and order before they do anything about it. Maybe because down deep they don't care. They just don't care."

- *High Noon*, 1952

Two cops shot in Ferguson.

Story basically scrubbed from the minds of Americans, with a media uninterested in covering a story dealing a "setback" to the cause of black empowerment in Ferguson.[651]

One of the true heroes chronicled[652] in the *Ferguson War Journal* steps up again and points out what those behind the #BlackLivesMatter movement want: dead cops:

> Jeff Roorda, business manager of the St. Louis Police Officers Association, said on Fox & Friends after the shooting of two officers that the resignation Wednesday of Ferguson Police Chief Tom Jackson wasn't enough for some protesters.
>
> "Dead cops. That's what they want. And let's not pretend like they wanted Tom Jackson's resignation, or that they're still mad because Mayor [James] Knowles is there," Mr. Roorda said. "They want dead cops and that was their goal all along, and that was their goal last night."[653]

Mr. Roorda didn't go far enough, with the true desire the raising of the tide of color against the civilization whites built in both Ferguson and St. Louis now beginning to spill out at across the metropolitan area:

> A 43-year-old man who was riding a MetroLink train Monday night was attacked by several men after one of them asked him about the Michael Brown "situation," police said.

---

[651] http://www.nytimes.com/2015/03/13/us/ferguson-gunshots-are-a-setback-in-its-progress.html

[652] http://www.vdare.com/articles/the-birth-of-a-nation-at-100-racial-chaos-unleashed-in-st-louis

[653] Ferguson protesters want 'dead cops,' says St. Louis union official, Washington Times, 3-12-15

A video posted to Facebook appears to show the attack.

Police said the victim, who is white, was punched and kicked by three black men, one of whom had made the reference to the teen killed in Ferguson by a police officer Aug. 9.

The assault took place about 8:54 p.m. as the eastbound train was nearing the Forest Park Metrolink platform, police said. The victim told police he was seated on the train when the three men approached him from behind.

One of the men, who was 20 to 25 years old and wearing a red T-shirt, asked the victim if he could use his cellphone, and the victim said no.

The man then asked the victim "what he thought about the Mike Brown situation." The victim responded that he hadn't thought much about it, according to the police report.

The man in the red shirt then punched the victim in the face and struck him multiple times, police said.

The victim was unsure if the other two men had joined in, but video surveillance of the incident confirmed that they had, police said. They are both described as black men between 18 and 22 years old age. Police did not give a further description.[654]

So a question about Michael Brown sparked an unprovoked assault on a white man riding public transportation in St. Louis? Does the attack by three black males on a white male qualify as a hate crime or is it nothing more than the type of racial dialogue Starbucks attempted to start with #RaceTogether?[655]

Seemingly, multiple black people beating a white male represents progress to the Disingenuous White Liberal (DWL) mind and atonement for past sins; particularly for the execution of Michael

---

[654] Man beaten on MetroLink train after attacker asks him about Michael Brown, police say, St. Louis Post-Dispatch, 3-27-15

[655] http://fox2now.com/2015/03/27/seated-man-beaten-in-metrolink-facebook-video/

Brown via Officer Darren Wilson, an act in which all white people are now guilty of performing.

The black community doesn't care about the truth in the case of Officer Wilson's encounter with Brown anymore than individual black people collectively care about the five black people slain in a 10-day time period in heavily black North St. Louis.[656]

Of all people in America, former Atlanta Braves pitcher John Rocker seems to understand the reality of the situation in Ferguson the best:

> Take a look at two incredible passages from the "Department of Justice Report Regarding the Criminal Investigation into the Shooting Death of Michael Brown by Ferguson, Missouri Police Officer Darren Wilson," which showcases the absurd lies the mainstream media completely bought and then sold to the American people as the absolute truth of what occurred in Ferguson.
> The first passage details "Witness 120" lying to the police about what happened in Ferguson, claiming Brown had his hands up and was "executed." Notice how the DOJ report uses actual physical evidence to dismiss as false a claim the media (I'm looking at you, CNN, New York Times and MSNBC) immediately ran with as truth:
>
>> Witness 120 initially told law enforcement that he saw Brown shot at point-blank range as he was on his knees with his hands up. Similar to Witness 138, Witness 120 subsequently acknowledged that he did not see Brown get shot but "assumed" he had been executed while on his knees with his hands up based on "common sense" and what others "in the community told [him.]" There is no witness who has stated that Brown had his hands up in surrender whose statement is otherwise consistent with the physical evidence.
>
> Something tells me the DOJ or the St. Louis County prosecutor's office will not be looking to charge Witness 120

---

[656] http://www.kmov.com/story/28622192/homicide-units-investigating-after-5-people-slain-within-10-days-throughout-north-county

with perjury, though Witness 125 was offered immunity if she recanted a lie she told the FBI and SLCPD detective – a lie she told because she claimed "she wanted to be part of something":

> When Witness 125 appeared at the St. Louis County Prosecutor's Office to testify before the county grand jury, she was accompanied by an attorney. Prior to her testimony, Witness 125 told the county prosecutors that she lied to the FBI and to SLCPD detectives. Witness 125 was then given immunity from federal prosecution for making material false statements to federal agents so long as she testified truthfully in the grand jury. She testified that she did not, in fact, witness any part of the incident, but claimed she did so because she wanted to be "part of something." She claimed that a friend in the community told her to tell the SLCPD and the FBI what her boyfriend saw, but to claim it as her own.
>
> So a "friend in the community" told her to lie to federal authorities about Brown having his hands in the air when Wilson shot him, all because she "wanted to be part of something."[657]

"....wanted to be part of something."

Like it or not white people, you are part of something.[658]

When the white guy got on the MetroLink Train in St. Louis, he had no idea an answer to a question would result in him being assaulted by three black males; when Officer Darren Wilson approached two black males on Canfield Drive back in August of 2014, he had no idea this would end his career as a police officer.

What so few people realize is how we are all now part of something on the verge of spiraling out of control.

---

[657] TWITTER PERPETUATES 'HANDS UP, DON'T SHOOT' MYTH: John Rocker on sign-in page image: 'It needs to come down', WND, 3-16-15

[658] After The Main Stream Media Left: What Next For Ferguson?, by Paul Kersey, VDare.com, 3-27-15

Whether you wanted to be or not, you are now part of something completely out of control.

It's time to start caring.

March 30, 2015
Life for a White Person Attacked by Three Blacks on the St. Louis MetroLink: "People were sort of laughing and smiling about it. No one offered to help and no one attempted to call 911."

We've found the Missing Link. And they ride the MetroLink.

David Autry, a white man riding public transportation in St. Louis, found out this truth when he was attacked by three black males.[659]

And not one of the black people on the MetroLink offered to help him once the assault was done. Instead, they laughed:

> An investigation is underway after cell phone video showed a man being beaten while riding the MetroLink Monday night.
>
> According to the 43-year-old victim, a man in his early 20's asked to use his cell phone. When the victim declined to let the suspect use his cell phone, the suspect sat next to him and asked what he thought about the "Mike Brown situation." When the victim responded that he had not thought much about it, the suspect began punching him in

---

[659] http://www.kmov.com/story/28653918/was-the-attack-on-a-metro-link-passenger-a-hate-crime

the face, according to the police report.

"I think it was disgusting that no one [helped]," the victim said. "People were sort of laughing and smiling about it. No one offered to help and no one attempted to call 911."[660]

"People were sort of laughing and smiling about it. No one offered to help and no one attempted to call 911."

Welcome to the MetroLink, where the Missing Link has made the St. Louis Public Transportation System unsafe for people like Autry... white people.

Of course, roving gangs of black people have been attacking white people on MetroLink for years, a reminder of the true legacy of Rosa Parks.[661]

But the attack on David Autry by three blacks - an attack observed by many other blacks who offered him no assistance, instead finding humor in the assault - owes its origin to Mr. Hands Up, Don't Shoot himself, Michael Brown (Brown wasn't the only black aspiring rapper killed in Ferguson in 2014, but "Black Lives Don't Matter" when DeAndre Joshua is concerned).[662]

Enter Jeff Roorda, a man who proudly wears a "I am Darren Wilson" bracelet:

> At a pro-police rally Saturday, a St. Louis police union representative called Department of Justice investigators "a band of marauders" who helped perpetrate a lie in Ferguson.
>
> Jeff Roorda, the business manager for the St. Louis Police Officers Association, has stirred the pot before and didn't hold back at the rally outside St. Louis Police headquarters.

---

[660] MetroLink assault victim speaks out; suspects caught on surveillance, KMOV.com, 3-30-15

[661] http://www.amnation.com/vfr/archives/011161.html

[662] http://www.gosanangelo.com/news/national/insightfergusonanotherdeath_352 62494

In a 10-minute speech, Roorda said the Department of Justice report that found systemic racism within Ferguson's police and court operations was intended to distract from another report by the agency that found Ferguson Police Officer Darren Wilson was justified in using deadly force against Michael Brown.

"(U.S. Attorney General) Eric Holder, who wanted with every fiber of his being to find some wrongdoing on the part of Darren Wilson, sics his justice department on St. Louis," Roorda said. "They raid St. Louis like a band of marauders..."

"What do they find? They find that this hands up don't shoot myth was just that — a fiction that was perpetrated upon the people of Ferguson, the people of Missouri and the people of the world," he said.

But instead of setting the record straight, Roorda said, Holder and his civil rights team "leak out the most damaging nuggets from this other report about this horrible practice of writing tickets.

"Police departments writing tickets. Can you imagine?!?" Roorda asked mockingly, as a crowd of about 75 police supporters hooted in the background.

"It's a big lie and it was used to bury the truth about Darren Wilson and what happened that day on Aug. 9 in Ferguson and that was ... a young black man made a terrible mistake," he said.[663]

"... *a young black man made a terrible mistake,*" is a tremendous way to describe Michael Brown.

It's an even better way to describe those black males who attacked David Autry.

Because Mr. Autry could have been a very different white man.

---

[663] Police representative says DOJ's 'band of marauders' concealed truth about Ferguson shooting, St. Louis Post-Dispatch, 3-28-15

One legally carrying a concealed firearm to protect himself from the very scenario Mr. Autry (an unarmed man) found himself in on the MetroLink: attacked by three blacks and surrounded by indifferent blacks who found the assault on him worthy of a few chuckles.

It is inevitable this scenario will play out in America sometime in 2015: a cocky, arrogant, impulse-control challenged black male(s) will attack the wrong white male - while one of their racial confederates films the attack for some World Star Hip Hop cred - and then Roorda's "band of marauders" from the Department of Justice will be unleashed as never before.

March 31, 2015
#EndViolenceStL: To the White People of America & All Whites in the World

Lt. Colonel William Barrett Travis letter to Americans in hopes they would come to the aid of those white men defending the Alamo reads like a tragedy. [664]

But in 2015 America, a city "our country" inherited because of the black revolution in what is now Haiti bankrupted France (leading to the Louisiana Purchase), is on the verge of providing another similar situation to what occurred in the Alamo.

Right now, the violence is largely black on black (with nine black juveniles shot in 2015 alone[665]), but the situation is quickly devolving into a racial one:

---

[664] http://www.tamu.edu/faculty/ccbn/dewitt/adp/history/bios/travis/travtext.html

[665] http://www.kmov.com/story/28669331/girl-9-ninth-juvenile-victim-of-gun-violence-in-st-louis-in-2015

> Channel 4 wants to help end the violence in St. Louis.
>
> Our businesses and communities are under siege.
>
> Our citizens and our officers are under attack.
>
> As a member of the community, we are asking for your help.
>
> The violence in our communities has to stop.[666]

The violence in St. Louis is - almost - entirely black, be it in the city of St. Louis or St. Louis County.

And yet, only one lone black woman - *one lone black woman!!!!* - dared protest this black-in-origin violence preparing to tear the city apart... the St. Louis Post-Dispatch dubbed her the "lone ranger:"[667]

> Better Family Life Vice President James Clark said St. Louis is facing a violent spring and summer unless outreach is done to those in need.
> With robberies and shootings occurring nearly every night in St. Louis it is understandable that there is a need for action. However, Clark said many people don't understand how dire the situation is.
>
> "We cannot afford as a metropolitan area to walk into the spring and summer and 2015 without a well thought out plan," Clark said.
>
> Better Family Life uses what is known as a neighborhood alliance model. The plan targets neighborhoods in need. Workers for Better Family Life go door to door asking how they can help and letting people know where help is available.
>
> "It's reassuring when we have people pull over in a car and stop, they notice us, see what we are doing and say 'how can

---

[666] #EndViolenceStL, KMOV.com, 3-27-15

[667] http://www.stltoday.com/news/local/crime-and-courts/lone-ranger-protester-takes-to-the-streets-for-the-first/article_be73a63b-02da-53e0-b576-667d28f26a06.html

we be a part of it?" said a worker with Better Family Life.

The organization said the approach needs to be expanded. Clark told News 4 getting resources directly to people who need them improves the quality of their lives and improves neighborhoods.

"Just as the police department's concept of hot spot policing, we believe we have to start hot spot resource delivery," Clark said.

Better Family Life currently has three outreach workers and one case worker on staff. Clark said the organization can have a deep impact if it hires 50 outreach workers and 15 case workers.[668]

So the "Better Family Life" organization can only make a difference if it can hire 16 times its current labor force?

Hilarious.

Our government, media, and academia have been working overtime to create a situation few dare even admit is plausible: the already shockingly high levels of black-on-black violence in St. Louis will inevitably spill into the white community, with "Justice for Michael Brown" style attacks growing more bold as the temperature increases.

#EndViolenceStL is only possible with the removal of the black population from the city of St. Louis and St. Louis County; unfortunately, the black-on-black violence is only encouraging white people to leave both the city and the county.

And the "Justice for Michael Brown" attacks on white people is only speeding up the process of St. Louis (and St. Louis County) replicating what happened to Detroit.

---

[668] Community leader: St. Louis in for violent spring and summer, KMOV.com, 3-31-1

April 3, 2015
Black Lives Don't Matter: "There is a callousness about the value of life here (in St. Louis), period"

Since the start of 2015, nine black juveniles have been shot in the St. Louis metropolitan area.

Nine.[669]

Nine black juveniles shot by fellow blacks.

Not police. Not members of the Klan. But by black people.

Only days before Easter (and a day before Good Friday), three black people would be murdered and four others shot.[670]

And only one black person has dared to confront the rising levels of black-in-origin violence in St. Louis.

One:

> The Tuesday morning protest seemed odd compared to the crush of demonstrators, reporters and activists who flocked to Ferguson.
> It consisted of one Michelle Hawkins, 49, walking laps around Ray Leisure Park at Park Avenue and Tucker

---

[669] Girl, 9, ninth juvenile victim of gun violence in St. Louis in 2015, KMOV.com, 3-31-15

[670] 3 dead, 4 injured in 4 shootings since Thursday evening in St. Louis, KMOV, 4-2-15

Boulevard. A few cars passing by during morning rush hour honked. Some drivers flashed the peace sign back at her.

"I don't know what else to do," Hawkins said, large tears rolling down both sides of her face. "I don't want to live in fear, but it seems like that's what's it's coming to."

Like any day, she woke up Tuesday between 5:30 and 6 a.m. to take medication for poor circulation in her leg. The Navy veteran boiled an egg, brewed a cup of tea. She put on support stockings and walking shoes, but she felt more motivated than to just do laps around the park this time.

She'd heard all the gunfire the night before that killed a man and woman, and injured a 9-year-old girl in the hand. Hawkins, who has a grown daughter in community college, didn't have any art supplies laying around. She went across the street from her apartment and borrowed two crayons and one sheet of yellow paper from the same rec center that serves as the city's emergency homeless shelter during cold nights.

She drew six hearts on the paper and spelled out the word "PEACE" in large letters.

"You don't need a big crowd to make a big shine," she said. "The Lone Ranger made a big impact."

She did what she thought she could do to avoid any more violence by carrying her sign.

"You know, we just spread peace one slice at a time," she said. But there was no we.

It was just Hawkins who said she was protesting for the first time in her life.[671]

It's funny: back in 1961 (when St. Louis was 28 percent black[672]),

---

[671] 'Lone Ranger' protester takes to the streets for the first time after St. Louis shooting, St. Louis Post-Dispatch, 3-31-15

[672] http://www.scribd.com/doc/257792996/The-Racial-Demographics-of-the-city-of-St-Louis-1910-2010#scribd

Martin Luther King addressed a black church, and he said, *"Do you know that Negroes are 10 percent (sic) of the population of St. Louis and are responsible for 58% of its crimes? We've got to face that. And we've got to do something about our moral standards,"* Dr. Martin Luther King Jr. told a congregation in 1961. *"We know that there are many things wrong in the white world, but there are many things wrong in the black world, too. We can't keep on blaming the white man. There are things we must do for ourselves."*[673]

Blacks just don't care. Blaming the "white man" is a successful tactic for blacks to immunize themselves and their community from any criticism (primarily because so many Disingenuous White Liberals will immediately concede this blame); and when you have a black President of United States of America and a black Attorney General of Department of Justice who have spent months blaming the white men of Ferguson for black people's problems, who would even believe there is anything wrong in the black world?

Enter the black clergy, demanding jobs as a stop-gap against the black violence in St. Louis driving away jobs:

> A recent round of shootings has prompted pastors in north St. Louis to start a plan of action to fight violent crime.
>
> Pastors of local African American Methodist Episcopal Churches (AME) said Thursday's three double shootings was the last straw.
>
> "I know the Christian church does not tolerate this kind of hatred or this kind of killing. The question what are we going to do?" said Pastor Spencer L. Booker of St. Paul AME Church.
>
> At a Good Friday service Booker announced that local AME congregations would join with other churches this summer to promote an extensive anti-violence campaign.
>
> "It's devastating and deadly," said Jeffrey Boyd, the 22nd Ward Alderman. He says he knows the father of one of the

---

[673] http://www.wsj.com/articles/SB10001424127887323394504578608182550247030

shooting victims in one of the double shootings. He knows police can't be on every street corner. The city offers recreation centers and many resources to help families and youth, but Boyd says he thinks that's not enough.

"I guarantee you most of the violence we see in our neighborhoods, when you dig deep enough, go back to the family structure," Boyd said.

AME church leaders say they want an effort to reduce to the number of guns in the urban core, and plan to set up GED programs. They also will be pressing business and community leaders to create jobs, but pastors say young people need to learn to respect human life.[674]

"Respect for human life...?"

Enter *The Evening Whirl*, a black-run paper in St. Louis that has documented black crime and depravity for 77 years:

> "Pow. Pow. Pow. Pow. Pow. That's how three street goons came at a dude as he said goodbye to his lovely wife on the North Side last week. If that's too much for you, pick up the Times and read the theatre reviews."

So begins a typical article from the Evening Whirl, St Louis's weekly print tabloid which bills itself as "an uninterrupted crime-fighting publication since 1938". As the world's attention fell on Ferguson last fall, the Whirl, resolutely non-digital, flew under the radar. But the paper is a St Louis institution: a 77-year-old, African American-run media enterprise that speaks to the complicated questions of race, crime and policing dogging the region today.

For those 77 years, the Evening Whirl has covered the underworld of St Louis in lurid language, cataloging crimes under headlines like "Loon Chucks Shiv at 5-0" and "Bungling Bandit Bagged and Booked". Regular features include a

---

[674] Local clergymen taking stand against gun violence in St. Louis, KMOV.com, 4-3-15

column called Where Not To Be, which provides a helpful map of where readers are most likely to be murdered, and Behind the Bars, an advice column from a prisoner named Jus Bleezy, who in the latest issue calls upon readers not to flush their lives "down the drain for a chain and some street fame".

Many articles start with a question: "WHY did a stone-cold gunslinger end a South Side squabble with slugs?" asks one query. "WHO is the con man from the womb who can steal the tighty off your whities that is being sought by North Patrol?" asks another. There are no bylines, giving it the feel of omniscient narration from an alternatively bemused and outraged voice.

You can't find the Evening Whirl online – it is only available for $1.50 at gas stations and convenience stores. Its strongholds are the impoverished neighborhoods of St Louis proper and north St Louis County, the suburban area that includes Ferguson. The Whirl is also available across the street from the St Louis County police headquarters, where it is devoured by cops chasing gossip and leads.

"People read the Whirl because we tell it like it is," says Anthony Sanders, the paper's 55-year-old editor-in-chief. "If you're a criminal and we feel that you're a scumbag, then that's what we call you."

Sanders took over the Whirl in 1995 following the long tenure of Ben Thomas, an entrepreneur who founded the paper in 1938 to document St Louis's black nightlife. Thomas soon realized he had an audience hungry for crime, and for seven decades the Whirl documented St Louis's spiral into poverty and depravity, at times attracting national media attention.

"There is a callousness about the value of life here, period," says Sanders. "We are among the most savage and brutal people on the face of the earth. We are killing people indiscriminately. It doesn't always have to be gang or drug related. There are people just going off and killing people. That happens all over the country."

> Since the Ferguson protest movement began, detractors have responded with the catch-all question: "What about black-on-black crime?" It's a question that stems from the baseless assumption that black communities do not really care about violence, or grieve their own losses. The Whirl, for all its breathless tabloid hectoring, is a rebuttal to that derailment. Its purple prose rides the line between condemnation and celebration, but its stock in trade is morality tales.[675]

The racial angle to St. Louis' spiral into poverty and depravity is, of course, unworthy of mentioning by anyone in polite society.

But, then again, in polite society white people must endure racial taunts as they eat their brunch...

Black Lives Don't Matter.

They never have, and they never will.

Ferguson was a story only because it's necessary to remove control of police departments from local hands to federal ones in Washington; and high rates of black criminality serve as a way to cleanse communities of pesky middle-class white people who would otherwise stay there for generations and work to build equity in their homes.

A community can only be created when people have a vested interest in building something permanent, and the black underclass in America has been used by the ruling class as a biological weapon to destroy whatever social capital was erected (with the founding population quickly resorting to white flight/abandonment of the city).

If a people can't put roots down in a place, they'll never have anything to fight for (and the black underclass, equipped with Section 8 Vouchers, represent the equivalent of the herbicide Spike 80DF when it comes to eliminating those 'roots' necessary for the creation of social capital), which pretty much sums up America post-

---

[675] Inside St Louis's lurid crime tabloid: 'There's a callousness about the value of life here', The Guardian, 3-31-15

1948.*⁶⁷⁶

April 6, 2015
We come to it at last... The great battle of our time: The Culmination of the "Mike Brown Can't Vote, but I Can" Campaign in Ferguson

Apparently, voters in 70 percent black Ferguson will go to the polls tomorrow to elect blacker and better candidates to represent the city of their future.⁶⁷⁷

Their future, because as the last white residents pull up the stakes they've put down in the city and depart for parts unknown, the soon-to-be 100 percent black city of Ferguson will be forgotten by the national press as it descends into East St. Louis, Camden, and Jackson, Mississippi status.

But for the next few days, the mainstream media will crow louder and fly higher than Peter Pan courtesy of the happy thoughts generated by more black people elected to office in Ferguson.

With a vested interested in the situation in progressively blacker and blacker Ferguson, the mainstream media is in dire need of a positive return on investment for the thousands of hours they've devoted to expending energy creating a faux-controversy in the decaying

---

⁶⁷⁶ http://www.vdare.com/articles/eric-holder-freedom-of-association-and-the-forgotten-case-for-restrictive-covenants

⁶⁷⁷ . Ferguson rising: A critical vote for a city at a turning point, Fox2Now.com, 4-6-15

suburb of just more than 21,000 people.

Blacks students from Atlanta spent Spring Break in Ferguson[678] trying to convince black people to register to vote (what percentage of blacks on Section 8 Vouchers in Ferguson are barred from voting due to prior felonies?), while black students from Montgomery spent Spring Break making Panama City unsafe for college students everywhere.[679]

Either way, the black population in Ferguson will continue to make life for the dwindling white population unsafe (be it by lowering property value or eroding whatever social capital remains in the city).

The great lesson though of the push to register more black people in Ferguson to vote is how embarrassingly unreceptive the black people of Ferguson have been to actually registering to vote. First, let's start with The New York Times:

> Down the street from where the body of Michael Brown lay for hours after he was shot three weeks ago, volunteers have appeared beside folding tables under fierce sunshine to sign up new voters. On West Florissant Avenue, the site of sometimes violent nighttime protests for two weeks, voter-registration tents popped up during the day and figures like the Rev. Jesse L. Jackson Sr. lectured about the power of the vote.
>
> N.A.A.C.P. leaders are creating a door-to-door voter registration effort with a jarring reminder as its theme: "Mike Brown Can't Vote, but I Can." Senator Claire McCaskill, a Missouri Democrat, is working with others to hold a

---

[678] http://www.stlamerican.com/news/local_news/article_837807c2-c72d-11e4-b154-8fb67e54a498.html

[679] http://www.wsfa.com/story/28638845/7-shot-in-panama-city-beach-3-alabama-am-students-among-victims

"candidate school" for people, including young black residents who say they want to serve on a city council or school board but need guidance on what a political campaign requires.[680]

Let's get one thing straight: the path Michael Brown was walking before he attempted to procure Officer Darren Wilson's gun was one inevitably leading to his forfeiting the right to vote. Had Brown not charged Wilson, he would have been arrested and lost his ability to vote due to the violent crime he had just engaged in.

Initially, the "Mike Brown Can't Vote, but I Can" voter registration drive seemed to be highly successful, with the media prematurely Tinker Belling all over themselves with the news more than 3,000 people had been registered to vote![681]

But that news couldn't fly, with the media forced to come back down to earth when it was revealed only 128 people (not the original 3,287 reported and joyously celebrate by the media) had registered in the "Mike Brown Can't Vote, but I can" campaign...[682]

There's no doubt the mainstream media is already sprinkling themselves with the same fairy dust used when Eric Holder unveiled the infamous double-switch (throwing the Department of Justice's Darren Wilson report down the memory and replacing it with the searing, damning, scathing, horrifically drowning in white supremacy "see how racist the entire Ferguson Police Department is" report), anticipating the popping of champagne bottles to pleasurably float down the inebriated river of white people losing any representation in local government.

---

[680] *Getting Ferguson Majority to Show Its Clout at Polls*, 8-30-14

[681] http://www.usatoday.com/story/news/nation/2014/10/02/ferguson-vote-registration/16572305/

[682] http://www.usatoday.com/story/news/nation/2014/10/07/voter-registration-number-only-128-in-ferguson/16874011/

In the mainstream media's view, the remaining white people in Ferguson deserve what's coming to them, with this election serving as one of the last moments to gloat (the only remaining times are the election of the first black mayor, the appointing of the first black police chief, and the re-opening of a Sonic... wait, that's 80 percent black Selma!); because with the political takeover of Ferguson by democratically elected black people, the city will only sped up the moment in which the last white person departs the city for good.[683]

And then, the media will no longer have any stories to report from the city, save a rekindling of those seven "shockingly racist" (sic) emails found in the public emails of former white city employees, as a reminder of the "racism" blacks had to overcome...[684]

Voters in 70 percent black Ferguson will go to the polls tomorrow to elect blacker and better candidates to represent the city of their future. But we must remember the future of Ferguson is a representation of the type of community individual black people can collectively create.

April 7, 2015
Ferguson's Neighbor, 98 Percent Black Pine Lawn, Offers a Glimpse into the Future for the Ever Darkening City...

"The wrong side of history."

---

[683] http://stuffblackpeopledontlike.blogspot.com/2015/03/what-is-it-they-want-only-article-youll.html

[684] http://fox2now.com/2015/04/03/shocking-racist-e-mails-released-from-ferguson-department-of-justice-report/

You hear this phrase used a lot. You see it written even more, to celebrate the steamrolling of "traditional" America by the combined forces of the united left.

What's left behind via this steamrolling of a once healthy people and culture resembles the pulverized remains of road kill on a highway.

Or so you'd be led to believe, for history has no side.

History is indifferent.

Which is why it's always worth a chuckle when this reality seeps into the present, where the phrase "the wrong side of history" is shown to be irrelevant:

> Ferguson, Missouri, voters head to the polls Tuesday with a chance to overthrow the white City Council and all those who answer to it who have been blamed for keeping the town's black residents broke and scared of police.
>
> But it's far from certain that a Ferguson City Council with more black members will change how the city is run. Black leaders may not necessarily mean better lives for black residents, a fact of life that anyone from Detroit or Newark could tell you about.
>
> You don't have to peer all the way to Motown to see this. In fact, all you have to do is look five miles down the road from Ferguson to Pine Lawn, Missouri. Led by Sylvester Caldwell, Pine Lawn's black mayor, a majority black City Council represents a 98 percent black population there. It's no statistical surprise then that the majority of traffic stops are directed at African Americans, but the scope of those interactions with police are a bit staggering. Those pushing for reforms in Ferguson, Pine Lawn, and the rest of St. Louis County hope the area's black residents who are affected by

predatory policing show up at the polls in large numbers. That hasn't been the case in Pine Lawn.

In 2013, Pine Lawn police handed out more than five tickets per resident. That same year, the city's municipal court made $2.2 million for Pine Lawn, more than $500,000 of that coming from the fines and fees netted from traffic offenses and other petty crimes.

In both Ferguson and Pine Lawn, police have been responsible for enforcing the rules of a municipal system that is addicted to the revenue from fines and fees. The distinction lies in the racial makeup of the two cities' governments. While Ferguson's overwhelmingly white leadership has come under international scrutiny for their practices, which led to the death of Michael Brown, Pine Lawn's black leaders have received virtually no attention. Among those leaders is Anthony Gray, who is most know as the attorney for the family of Michael Brown but is probably more recognized in Pine Lawn as the city's ex-police chief. Gray now moonlights as Pine Lawn's prosecutor in addition to running his private law practice.[685]

Five miles down the road from currently 70 percent black Ferguson sits 98 percent black Pine Lawn, a city whose incredibly depressing state - *The Riverfront Times* dubbed it "The Little City That Couldn't"[686] in 2006 - serves as nothing more than a glimpse into the future for the municipality 18-year-old Michael Brown made famous.

A staggering 70 percent of the revenue 98 percent black Pine Lawn brought in for fiscal year 2013 was through the

---

[685] Black Officials Fleece Ferguson's Neighboring Town: Hope for change in Mike Brown's hometown lies with voters, but just changing the color of government isn't enough: Just look down the road in Pine Lawn, Missouri., Daily Beast, 4-7-15

[686] http://www.riverfronttimes.com/2006-07-05/news/the-little-city-that-couldn-t/

courts (tickets, court fees, etc.), a hilarious, emphatic statistic in understanding how a soon-to-be white-free Ferguson will generate revenue.[687]

The entirely black city government of Pine Lawn has even used speed-cameras to collect more than $1 million in 2013... enough to boost the black mayor's salary by 200%![688]

Even the *St. Louis Post-Dispatch* begrudgingly labeled 98 percent black Pine Lawn "the poster child for dysfunction?"[689] in an October 2014 story (no doubt the dysfunction is because of white privilege sucking all the jobs and capital from the city...) :

> Some had seethed for years about their mayor hanging his hat miles away from a place where one-third live below the poverty line and nearly half of households are on food stamps, and where the police rank fourth in Missouri for most tickets per square mile.
>
> Without many other sources of income, the city relied on its police and court to raise about two-thirds of the city's general revenue last year alone. A state law says cities can't get more than 30 percent of general revenue from traffic fines. Last year, Pine Lawn issued about seven summonses for traffic violations and other infractions for every city resident.
>
> City Administrator Brian Krueger said complaints about city

---

[687] http://www.stltoday.com/news/local/crime-and-courts/st-louis-area-cities-and-towns-face-new-scrutiny-on/article_622c6e07-34ad-58cc-a0a0-288b41c6ad94.html

[688] http://fox2now.com/2013/11/25/pine-lawn-politicians-using-speed-cameras-money-for-salaries/

[689] http://www.stltoday.com/news/local/govt-and-politics/pine-lawn-poster-child-of-dysfunction/article_c782e651-9389-507e-8d74-11a86ac590bb.html

> government, and unfair police and housing code practices come from a vocal few. He said good things happen here: The city in 2012 saw the construction of about 40 homes using state tax credits for low-income housing, and in 2011 saw the dedication of the Barack Obama Elementary School in the Normandy School District.[690]

Fitting Barack Obama Elementary School would be found in 98 percent black Pine Lawn, a city only a short jog away from Ferguson where Mr. Obama sent three representatives of his administration to attend Brown's "state" funeral...

Though those on "the right side of history" don't care, but Pine Lawn was 71 percent white in 1970; by 1980, Pine Lawn was only 19 percent white (the black population grew from 29 percent to 81 percent of the population of the city). In fact, Pine Lawn was one of eighteen cities in St. Louis County to from less than 1 percent black to 65 percent in a forty year timespan (1960 – 2000.[691]
And though the *Riverfront Times* will never admit it, the growth of the black population in a city is the kiss of death for economic vibrancy and tax-revenue producing commerce in the municipality:

> Ferguson suffered a steep decline in population in the 1980s, something Mayor Steve Wegert attributes to white flight and the effects of uncontrolled urban sprawl. "When Ferguson was incorporated 100 years ago ... people wanted to move away from the dirt and noise of downtown," he says. "This was urban sprawl back then. We've both benefited and are now a victim of urban sprawl."
>
> Retail has left his city, too. Ferguson went without a

---

[690] http://www.stlamerican.com/news/columnists/jaco/article_4df3b9fc-b247-11e4-bca3-c383b2bab16d.html

[691] Baybeck, B. (2004). *St. Louis Metromorphosis: Past trends and future directions*. St. Louis: University of Missouri Press, p. 287-289

supermarket for two years after Schnucks pulled out, although it has since been replaced with a Shop-'N-Save.[692]

Remember, Ferguson was 74 percent white in 1990; by 2000, the white population of the city was 44 percent...

Though the civilization whites built and the infrastructure once creating growth and prosperity (streets, sidewalks, civic buildings, private houses and commercial buildings) remain in place when white flight occurs, the vital variable necessary to the city's overall health is gone.

Irreplaceable.

The buildings will only remain until time weathers them into the blight we see so many people maintain is proof of America's declining fortune, when the dilapidated state of the houses and buildings is only proof of how four simple letters explain everything.

Race.

Four letters, when combined, help spell out the truth for why a civilization will flourish, or - more importantly - why a civilization blacks inherit via white flight will ultimately crumble into the blight we see in Detroit, Newark, and Pine Lawn... the latter being a 98 percent black city mere miles away from Ferguson.

---

[692] IT'S BEGINNING TO LOOK A LOT LIKE ST. LOUIS: Jobs are leaving, the tax base is shrinking and the population is dropping. North County is feeling the squeeze., 12-22-1999

April 17, 2015
Why Does St. Louis Need the "Big Brother" Real Time Crime Center? Because of the Collective Criminality of Individual Black People

If we were just individuals, as Ayn Rand and her disciples would have you believe, then crime statistics broken down by race would be an invalid way of interpreting reality.

But we are not mere individuals; our individual actions, good or bad, help create a community.

A community can be overflowing with social capital or one with an overabundance of social workers.

This is the reality of the world Ayn Rand devotees cannot entertain, but it's also the reality of the world adherents to the ideology of Black-Run America (BRA) can never endorse.

Increasing violence in St. Louis, courtesy of black individuals collectively making the city unsafe (in a span of six hours on April 15, five sets of shootings left nine people injured), is a phenomenon Ayn Randians would ascribe anything but racial in origin.[693]

But, of course, a simple understanding of the data provided yearly by the *Metropolitan Police Department, City of St. Louis: Annual Report to the Community* offers powerful evidence the violent crime problem in St. Louis is entirely due to the black population.

Entirely (see p. 20)

---

[693] http://www.stltoday.com/news/local/crime-and-courts/five-sets-of-shootings-across-st-louis-leave-people-injured/article_1a6a0520-66c2-5416-a9d2-8082f5dc2a42.html

Which is why 49 percent black and 43 percent white St. Louis is seeing much of downtown turn into a surveillance state the architects of Oceania in *1984* could only dream of:

- A Real Time Crime Center[694] had opened in St. Louis (at a cost of $435,000[695]), a facility continuously staffed with trained officers who have access to more than 400 cameras stationed throughout the city[696], providing up-to-the-minute information and data;
- Much to the ACLU's distaste,[697] cameras are being installed throughout downtown (an investment of $66,000)[698] St. Louis capable of reading license plates and storing digital information... in a few years, the number of cameras with this technology deployed throughout St. Louis will be near 30[699];
- The Nuisance Abatement Vehicle (nicknamed "Raptor") [700]represents the cutting-edge in armored technology retrofitted with the latest surveillance tools to serve as a powerful instrument in fighting crime;
- Since 2008, St. Louis has had the $250,000 ShotSpotter Location System to "detect how many shots were fired, which side of a building they came from and whether the shooter was moving";

---

[694] http://www.kmov.com/story/28822941/st-louis-police-unveil-new-real-time-crime-center

[695] http://fox2now.com/2015/04/16/st-louis-police-reveal-hi-tech-real-time-crime-center/

[696] http://www.stltoday.com/news/local/crime-and-courts/st-louis-police-networking-cameras-other-technology-in-new-effort/article_0dbcd12a-c710-5008-bf71-b0669b347646.html

[697] http://www.stltoday.com/news/local/metro/aclu-study-warns-of-unchecked-rise-of-surveillance-cameras-in/article_7d27ecbf-c8ad-55cd-8277-2b0e1d215b60.html

[698] http://fox2now.com/2015/04/15/more-cameras-being-installed-in-downtown-st-louis/

[699] http://www.kmov.com/story/28702675/security-cameras-hope-to-make-downtown-st-louis-safer

[700] http://stlouis.cbslocal.com/2011/08/18/st-louis-police-preparing-new-vehicle-to-fight-crime/

These measures are necessary to ensure some assurance of peace and stability in a community destabilized by individual blacks, whose collective actions make St. Louis one of the more violent places in all of America.[701]

A recent march against violence in St. Louis, organized by black churches, was only able to attract 50 people... even though 25 different churches united in the march to stop violence (meaning a pitiful average of two people per church came to the event).[702]

The Police Chief of St. Louis believes those white suburban fans of the St. Louis Cardinals and the NHL's St. Louis Blues should leave their guns at home (he said this in 2013 as well[703]), all because of the black populations inability to leave parked cars undisturbed.:

> "Yesterday was a random act of violence," St. Louis Metropolitan Police Department Chief Sam Dotson said. "The three incidents were not connected. We are seeing an elevated amount of violence."
>
> Dotson says these shootings are "disturbing" and has a plan to decrease the frequency. Dotson wants to crack down on the amount of stolen guns in the city and use surveillance cameras to catch the suspects. He believes most of the gun violence is committed with stolen guns.
>
> According to Dotson, there has been a 70 percent increase in gun thefts since the year began, specifically guns that are left in cars.
>
> "Leave it (guns) at home," Dotson said. "Don't give criminals

---

[701] http://stuffblackpeopledontlike.blogspot.com/2014/11/an-open-letter-to-white-residents-of.html

[702] http://www.kmov.com/story/28778606/pastors-community-leaders-unite-in-a-march-to-stop-violence-in-st-louis

[703] http://stlouis.cbslocal.com/2013/04/08/police-chief-tells-fans-to-leave-their-guns-at-home/

more guns because we already know they are using them."

He also says police will have access to 400 cameras throughout the city to catch criminals. Police will have access to this information from the new Real Time Crime Center

"When officers are dispatched to an area with a shooting, we can quickly say what assets we have," Dotson said. "Do we have cameras or LPR technology? Maybe [we can] get video or a license plate."[704]

"Don't give criminals more guns..."

The only way those "criminals" are going to get the guns is if they break into the white people's parked cars - while they watch the MLB's Cardinals or NHL's Blues and contribute money into the St. Louis economy which the city desperately needs - and steal them; and the only reason these white people have guns in their vehicles is to protect themselves and family from the very black people Chief Dotson is warning might steal their guns while they are away from their car...

Sick.

Sick.

Sick.

With all the technology and surveillance equipment at their disposal, the chief of police in St. Louis still presides over a city whose white visitors from suburbs feel compelled to bring guns with them when they venture into this majority black metropolis...

For those interested, the City of St. Louis Metropolitan Police Department finally released its 2013 Annual Report to the Community, which breaks down arrests by race for violent crimes.

Remember, out of 318,000 people, St. Louis is 49.2 percent black

---

[704] Police solution to cut down increasing gun violence in St. Louis, KMOV.com, 4-16-15

43.9 percent white (as of 2010 US Census). Flip back to p. 20 to see the breakdown for 1999 – 2012.

Here's the breakdown for 2013:

- 87.1% of those arrested for aggravated assault in St. Louis in 2013 were black.
- 93.6% of those arrested for robbery in St. Louis in 2013 were black.
- 94% of those arrested for murder in St. Louis in 2013 were black.
- 80.2% of those arrested for forcible rape in St. Louis in 2013 were black.

Put down your copy of *Atlas Shrugs* and *The Fountainhead*.

Stop pretending you are just an individual and understand why you should be offended by Chief Dotson asking white suburbanites of St. Louis from carrying a weapon into the city.

Crime statistics in St. Louis paint a definitive picture of the race requiring surveillance technology rivaling that in *1984* to be positioned throughout the city, and it's entirely due to the collective actions of individual black people that whites visiting the city need to carry a gun.

Remember: the state is dedicated to the promotion and protection of Black-Run America (BRA).

April 21, 2015
RIP St. Louis: A True Assessment of Race Relations in America

The black population of St. Louis has assumed control of the future of city, with the successful vote by aldermen for the creation of a St.

Louis Civilian Oversight Board.[705]

It's their city now.[706]

In the euphoria of moment, one black female alderman let slip a question no reasonable person can dare answer, considering the future of the demographics in St. Louis is black, blacker, and blackest:

> Tammika Hubbard, said the city needs to do something to address concerns about police.
>
> "We have a race problem," Hubbard said. "We have problems of police brutality. How do we move forward from that?"[707]

We already know St. Louis has a "race problem," but it's hardly the one Tammika is commenting on: the race problem in St. Louis is the black population committing almost all of the violent crime in the city, which drives away businesses and white people, leaving only the collapsing infrastructure of the thriving white past as a reminder of what the city's future will never be.

Because of the high frequency of black violent crime in St. Louis, police officers have greater exposure to the black community as they search in vain for black suspects protected by the primary community they prey upon because of the code of "no snitch" (remember: courtesy of black people—the shocking number of gunshot and stab wounds seen at the St. Louis University Hospital provide the Air Force and Air National Guard medical personnel with "some of the blunt-trauma injuries they will see" on the actual battlefield.)[708]

---

[705] http://www.stltoday.com/news/local/crime-and-courts/civilian-oversight-board-coming-to-st-louis-police-after-aldermen/article_247e65db-467a-5c45-9027-1cb78d17276b.html

[706] https://www.vdare.com/articles/the-birth-of-a-nation-at-100-racial-chaos-unleashed-in-st-louis

[707] St. Louis Board Votes to Create Police Oversight Panel, ABCNews.com, 4-20-15

[708] http://www.stltoday.com/news/local/metro/slu-s-battlefield-helps-train-

One young hospital volunteer in St. Louis noted those with gunshot wounds being wheeled in for surgery are "her age (18) and every younger" and that they are young black men.[709]

So yes Tammika Hubbard, St. Louis has a "race problem"; the problem is its entitled, protected black population, whose dysfunction is the primary catalyst for the white flight and collapsing property values throughout the city and St. Louis County.

Those police officers employed by the city of St. Louis try to maintain the civilization white people built (and are forced to abandon because of daring to even mention the reality of black criminality is seemingly a criminal offense).

Because of this, one white columnist for the *St. Louis American* (a black newspaper) is able to gloat about the displacement of whites, since the morality of Black-Run America mandates black people are forever incapable of being blamed for the dysfunction they cause:

> Caucasian St. Louisans are to white flight as Kenyan runners are to the Boston Marathon. Volumes have been written about the ability of white St. Louisans to empty out a region, or as a former colleague from Fox 2 once said, "Yeah, a black family moved in seven blocks away and my parents ended up in Ellisville."
>
> But, with typical Midwestern modesty, St. Louis's white people refuse to take any credit for the highest rate of building and neighborhood abandonment over a 30-year period in North American history, and instead defer all the praise to the area's Black folks, who they say are really the ones responsible.
>
> Flash back to 1996, when, still a St. Louis newbie with barely a year here under my belt, I interviewed Tom Brown, the mayor of St. Peters, on my KMOX talk show and brought up

---

military-personnel/article_91465b40-8d81-526c-870e-cdf123dc8eee.html

[709] Hospital volunteer deals with recent violence, KSDK.com, 1-16-2015

white flight and the suspicion that his town's growth might have been fueled by white people who wanted to put as much distance between themselves and the melanin-rich as possible. The mayor bristled at the suggestion and said his growing constituency was made up largely of victims.

"A huge number of people who moved to our city," he said flatly, "were literally driven from their homes. They fled looking for a better life."

The refugee syndrome that Mayor Brown spoke about has become tribal lore among many working class and middle class whites, stories about how they, or pops, or grandpa had to flee Walnut Park or Hyde Park or Pine Lawn and sell at a big loss when the black thugs moved in.

Given that, conversations with the white community in St. Louis about race and racism will only go so far. To them, the problem is not a racist system. The problem is the degeneracy of black people.[710]

What's funny is the degeneracy of black people *St. Louis American* columnist Charles Jaco claims doesn't exist *is exactly the reason* for the incredible depreciation of property value and erosion of social capital in formerly thriving white areas of St. Louis now blighted by the black population residing there.

Jaco earnestly believes only a monologue with whites is allowed, where lambasting them for white privilege and racism toward blacks is the expected discourse of the day. In his mind, holy and saintly black people can do NO wrong, with white people exclusively TO blame for the pitiful conditions black people seem to always find themselves in.

Proximity to black people equals a reaction resulting in immediate white flight and the degradation of the formerly robust private and commercial property values found in the now majority black area those whites abandoned.

---

[710] STL's white refugee syndrome, St. Louis American, 2-12-15

A food desert where once an oasis of opportunity existed, all because the racial group responsible for the latter was driven away by the black people incapable of sustaining a grocery store in white people's absence.

But going back to the St. Louis Civilian Oversight Board, a curious slip of truth about the true nature of review committee over police actions by the *St. Louis Post-Dispatch* must be immortalized... because the newspaper tried to make sure it was removed from their website and web cache pages.

Nicholas J. C. Pistor's April 20, 2015 article "Civilian oversight board coming to St. Louis police after aldermen approve it" originally contained a most revealing passage about a strange press conference held in North St. Louis on the same day, but mysteriously vanished and was completely scrubbed from the archives of the St. Louis Post-Dispatch and cache pages.[711]

Save one. Here's what Pistor reported in his original piece for the *St. Louis Post-Dispatch* on the successful vote to create the St. Louis Civilian Oversight Board, which powerfully illustrates exactly what those black aldermen voting for board hope happens:

> Also on Monday, a press conference was held in north St. Louis calling on the creation of the Black Community Control of Police Commission, an oversight board made up of African-Americans that would "assume full responsibility and authority for policing in the black community."
>
> "In this community, where there is an undeclared war happening against African people, one way we deal with that is to control the military force in our community that affects our lives," said Omali Yeshitela, chairman of African Socialist International who was visiting St. Louis from Florida.
>
> He said the high rates of incarceration and lethal use of force since the civil rights movement shows that African-

---

[711] http://www.stltoday.com/news/local/crime-and-courts/civilian-oversight-board-coming-to-st-louis-police-after-aldermen/article_247e65db-467a-5c45-9027-1cb78d17276b.html

Americans are "still being tortured and murdered through the existing legal process."

"We have to control the police in our community, and will, or there shall be no peace," he said.

Carlos Ball, 26, who is African-American, said police in his south St. Louis neighborhood do more to intimidate than serve.

"We just don't have a fair chance here when it comes to the police," said Ball. "We need some accountability for what these officers do."

Black Community Control of Police Commission = the St. Louis Civilian Oversight Board.

You see, St. Louis does have a "race problem" as Tammika Hubbard asserts, but the problem isn't white people as she wants to claim; the problem of St. Louis is the black population, whose collectively inability to maintain (or come anywhere close to sustaining) the civilization whites created —and abandoned because of black criminality— or abide by the rules and laws governing this civilization means police state measures must be enacted if a first-world city is to remain...

Those blacks calling for the
Black Community Control of Police Commission, which the editors of the *St. Louis Post-Dispatch* attempted to excise from their story on the St. Louis Civilian Oversight Board, are overtly calling for what those blacks serving as aldermen for the city of St. Louis covertly want: complete and total control of white people, which they believe means the end of the so-called "race problem."

But as we saw with Detroit, once the white people leave, the civilization they created goes with them.

All that remains is the infrastructure and buildings white people long ago created, which the black people residing there now can't even fathom how to maintain.

The same will be said of St. Louis.

April 22, 2015
"Just when I thought you couldn't possibly be any dumber, you go and do something like this... and totally redeem yourself!"

The news of Hardee's considering moving its national headquarters out of 49 percent black St. Louis was thankfully offset with the absolutely positive, riveting, and glorious announcement Starbucks is going to open up a store in 70 percent black Ferguson![712]

Cue up the marching band and order up a few tons of confetti for the ticker-tape parade!

Losing the national headquarters of a Fortune 500 company means absolutely nothing when a small suburb of St. Louis is going to get a Starbucks!

Even though corporate Starbucks locations don't accept EBT/Food stamps, the store in Ferguson could represent a prototype in "community outreach" to a demographic completely alien from the traditional business model the coffee giant built its brand on[713]:

> Starbucks baristas may not be writing "Race Together" on customers' coffee cups anymore, but CEO Howard Schultz certainly isn't done talking about the nation's touchiest topic.

---

[712] http://www.stltoday.com/business/local/starbucks-ceo-says-coffee-chain-will-open-ferguson-store/article_d2181bf9-9ec3-5350-beb4-3a7c497de6b3.html

[713] http://stuffblackpeopledontlike.blogspot.com/2015/03/the-business-model-of-starbucks.html

On Tuesday, Schultz talked about his company's efforts to address racial tension and announced that his coffee shop chain will open a location in Ferguson, Mo. as a "way to create employment." Protestors clashed with police officers in the St. Louis suburb this summer, after the shooting death of 18-year-old Michael Brown, an unarmed black man, by a white cop.

Starbucks has locations in nearby Jennings and Florissant, Mo., and six stores in Lambert-St. Louis International Airport, but none in Ferguson.

Schultz tucked the Ferguson store news into comments he made on stage at an event hosted by NationSwell, a digital media company focused on American innovation and renewal. Schultz's appearance at the event focused on his company's ongoing efforts to combat racism and inequality in the United States, its education benefits for workers, and its recent commitment to hire military veterans and so-called opportunity youths, generally described as unemployed 16 to 24-year olds who have not followed a traditional education path.

After his on-stage interview, Schultz told Fortune that there was no specific timeline for the opening of a Ferguson store, and he declined to provide more information about plans for the location there. A Starbucks spokesperson did not provide an opening date but said that the Ferguson store is "part of our plan to build more stores in urban neighborhoods."

Whenever Starbucks ultimately open its store in Ferguson, a city that's 70% black, the location will counter the heavy concentration of Starbucks locations in predominantly white neighborhoods. By crunching Census figures and a dataset of 11,500 Starbucks locations in the United States as of August 2014, Quartz determined that the density of Starbucks stores increases along with the whiteness of census tracts.

On Tuesday, Schultz emphasized his belief that race relations is not too sensitive an issue for his company to tackle. Schultz has never shied away from using his platform as CEO of a

Fortune 500 company to speak out on controversial political and social subjects. In 2013, he led a petition-based push urging Washington politicians to end the federal government shutdown. That year, he also wrote an open letter asking gun owners to refrain from bringing their firearms into stores.

Fortune reported in August that residents of St. Louis area, which includes Ferguson, have not felt the economic recovery equally. The unemployment rate for African Americans in the county of St. Louis City was 26% in 2012, according to the Census Department's latest available stats. For white Americans, the unemployment rate was 6.2%. Employment figures from the fall of 2014 show that in Missouri, black unemployment was 15.7%; for whites it was 4.5%.[714]

Losing Hardee's corporate headquarters was news thankfully softened by the outrageously positive announcement 70 percent black Ferguson is getting a Starbucks!

A Starbucks!

There's no doubt Starbucks is preparing to start a 501c3 as a way to offset the tremendous losses associated with opening franchises in heavily black areas, which has never been part of the corporations strategy or business model for growth.

But in Black-Run America (BRA), few actions such as opening a franchise in an increasingly non-white city will garner social justice points as Starbucks investing in 70 percent black Ferguson.

Trading Hardee's corporate headquarters in downtown St. Louis for a lone suburban Starbucks franchise in 70 percent black Ferguson is an absolute victory for metropolitan St. Louis!

---

[714] Howard Schultz: Starbucks to open Ferguson store, Fortune, 4-22-15

May 7, 2015
"A Pile of Trash": Blacks in Ferguson Outraged the Michael Brown Memorial in the Middle of Canfield Drive Might be Moved

Back in September of 2014, it burned to the ground.[715]

Back in December of 2014, this makeshift shrine was struck by a car and destroyed.[716]

Only a day after a car struck this monument, a police spokesman was suspended for referring to this memorial as a "pile of trash."[717]

This spokesman was being too kind in calling the Michael Brown Memorial, littering the middle of Canfield Drive in Ferguson a "pile of trash," but the full context of Officer Timothy Zoll's quote that got him suspended is a hilarious reminder of the insanity of the whole *Ferguson War Journal*:

> "I don't know that a crime has occurred. But a pile of trash in the middle of the street? The Washington Post is making a call over this?"[718]

The Washington Post long ago sided with the Michael Brown version

---

[715] http://blogs.riverfronttimes.com/dailyrft/2014/09/michael_brown_memorial_on_canfield_drive_burns_to_ashes_in_early_morning_blaze.php

[716] http://www.washingtonpost.com/news/post-nation/wp/2014/12/26/auto-draft/

[717] http://www.nbcnews.com/storyline/michael-brown-shooting/ferguson-suspends-officer-who-called-michael-brown-memorial-trash-n275906

[718] http://www.nbcnews.com/storyline/michael-brown-shooting/ferguson-suspends-officer-who-called-michael-brown-memorial-trash-n275906

of what occurred on August 9 in Ferguson, so anyone daring to besmirch or soil the memory of the gentlest of giants need be immediately reminded of their station in life (in fairness to Officer Zoll, the Michael Brown Memorial looks more like what Ian Malcolm said in *Jurassic Park* when viewing the triceratops droppings -- "That is one big pile of shit.")

Why no one has thought to close Canfield Drive in Ferguson so the Michael Brown Memorial *located in the middle of the road* can forever rest undisturbed is beyond me, for those arguing the shrine should be removed are threatening the fragile stability in the heavily black city:

> To some, a makeshift shrine in the middle of the Ferguson street where Michael Brown was killed last summer is a hallowed symbol of a new civil rights movement over race and policing. To others, it has served its purpose and is now more of an eyesore and a road hazard.
>
> Within hours of Brown's Aug. 9 shooting death by a white police officer, people began placing stuffed animals, candles and other tributes in the middle of Canfield Drive, where the unarmed black 18-year-old's body lay for about four hours before it was removed.
>
> The shrine stretches several yards down the center of the two-lane road that bisects a housing complex, and city leaders are grappling with the thorny question of whether to remove or replace it and risk further inflaming racial tensions in the 21,000-resident St. Louis suburb, which is two-thirds black. Another section of the shrine sits along the curb a few yards away.
>
> "It's a very sensitive topic," says Janie Jones, a black, Washington-based mediator who says she has been working behind the scenes with Ferguson municipal leaders and the Brown family on how to clear out the memorial without agitating the black community.
>
> "It represents a community's cry for justice - not just for Michael Brown, but for people all over the world," Jones told The Associated Press on Monday. "The city has some serious

decisions to make going forward."

Ferguson Mayor James Knowles III, while appreciative of the memorial's status as a nexus of protests and prayers, said it is now a public safety issue that comes with "any time you leave items in the middle of the roadway." Knowles, who is white, pointed to last Christmas Day, when an unidentified motorist - whether intentionally or accidentally - plowed through the shrine. Neighbors and Brown supporters swiftly cleaned up the damage and rebuilt the site.

During a Ferguson City Council meeting last month - the first since city elections tripled black representation on the governing board that had been largely white - Jones proposed replacing the shrine with a permanent dove-shaped marker embedded in the street.

That would "take a very tragic situation and use it as a teachable moment to encourage community healing and symbolize the unity that is very much needed," said Jones, president and CEO of the Joint Council on Policy and Social Impact.

"The way we deal with this memorial is how we move forward in Ferguson, because that memorial represents the best and the worst of Ferguson."

Jones said Brown's mother wants a portion of the road where the memorial rests carved out and repaved because "she feels like her son's blood is still in the streets."[719]

Wait a second... the 'DEPARTMENT OF JUSTICE REPORT REGARDING THE CRIMINAL INVESTIGATION INTO THE SHOOTING DEATH OF MICHAEL BROWN BY FERGUSON, MISSOURI POLICE OFFICER DARREN WILSON' is basically an 86-page mea culpa on the part of the federal government to Officer Wilson (in ever accusing him of doing anything wrong), so why do we still persist in living in a world where Wilson was the aggressor and

---

[719] FERGUSON MULLS REMOVING BROWN SHRINE FROM MIDDLE OF STREET, ASSOCIATED PRESS, 5-5-15]

Michael Brown was the angelic victim?[720]

In reality, Canfield Drive in Ferguson, Missouri - a formerly bucolic suburb of St. Louis and now a nightmarish reminder of the evil of Section 8 Vouchers eroding social capital - represents a fork in the road for the United States of America.

The aptly described "pile of trash" in the middle of Canfield Drive represents a homage by individual black people collectively showing this community would rather live by lies instead of accept the truth of what happened on August 9, 2014 in Ferguson.

For the "pile of trash" resting on Canfield Drive
represents unfulfilled dreams to blacks nationwide, stolen by a racist white cop shooting an unarmed black who merely had his hands up:

> Veteran actor Philip Casnoff hadn't read the full script yet when he arrived for the first rehearsal of "Ferguson," a play chronicling the shooting of Michael Brown by a Missouri police officer.
>
> Casnoff thought he knew what the play, set for a four-day staged reading starting Sunday at the Odyssey Theater, would be about: the wilderness of testimony the grand jury navigated while investigating the day Officer Darren Wilson fatally shot the unarmed 18-year-old. Casnoff presumed a variety of viewpoints, the fog of truth.
>
> Then he read the script, which tells the story that Brown didn't have his hands up and that he charged at Wilson.
>
> Now, in a case of art imitating life, the play is experiencing the kind of ill will and mistrust that erupted from the city it attempts to portray. Part of the 13-member cast is in revolt — Casnoff and four others have quit — as the playwright and actors are locked in a fundamental disagreement over how to tell the story of Brown's death.

---

[720] https://s3.amazonaws.com/s3.documentcloud.org/documents/1681212/doj-report-on-shooting-of-michael-brown.pdf

Though the grand jury declined to indict Wilson after some witnesses and physical evidence supported his account of events, the tone of the play shocked some actors.

"It felt like the purpose of the piece was to show, 'Of course he was not indicted — here's why,'" Casnoff said. He said that after he learned who the play's author was, Casnoff, who describes himself as "very liberal, left-wing-leaning," thought, "Whoa, this is not the place for me to be."[721]

The events of August 9, 2014 in Ferguson have set in motion a serious movement across America, culminating with the black mayor of 65 percent black Baltimore ordering the black Police Commissioner to tell his 43 percent black police force to stand down and let black people loot and riot (all the while, united black gangs steered those black rioters to loot/riot/burn non-black owned businesses).

In my mind, a permanent memorial should be placed on Canfield Drive in Ferguson, but it will not go to honor or remember Michael Brown: instead, it will go to honor former Ferguson Police Officer Darren Wilson, who simply did exactly what he was trained to do on August 9, 2014 and inadvertently exposed the reality of blackness for those willing to see.

Before the serious movement Brown's death launched, you'll be shocked by the number of people finally willing to see this reality.

May 16, 2015
There's no such thing as "gun violence" in St. Louis: It's Black Violence

The good folks at KMOV in St. Louis put together a study of the cost of gun violence in the city. It's worth reading, though it leaves out one important variable (the race of the shooter):

---

[721] Actors quit L.A. 'Ferguson' play, question writer's motives, Los Angeles Times, 4-23-15

For our News 4 Investigates exclusive report on the cost of gunshot violence in St. Louis, we worked with Barnes-Jewish (BJC) and St. Louis University (SLU) Hospitals. These are the only Level One and Level Two Trauma Centers in St. Louis city and as a result these are where gunshot victims are transported for treatment.
Many gunshot victims from outside the city of St. Louis are also transported to SLU and BJC for treatment.

Here are the numbers:

Our News 4 Investigative team began working with SLU and BJC last September for our examination of the cost of treating gunshot victims. Each hospital provided us with numbers for gunshot victims transported for treatment for as long as ten years ago. For the purpose of our report who chose to focus on one year, 2014.

The Cost:

Assigning a dollar amount, or a "cost" for treating gunshot victims is difficult and for the purposes of our investigation we used rough averages provided by the hospitals and our own calculations. The methodology we used is outlined below: (Note that we are combining the numbers provided by the two hospitals for one grand total.)

Gunshot victims for 2014:

-568 out-patient (relatively minor wounds)
-547 Level 1/Level 2 patients (serious wounds)
-Total patients seen in 2014: 1,115

Costs:

The rough average cost for treating gunshot victims was given as $10,000 - $20,000. We split the difference and went with a figure of $15,000.

-Patients with severe, critical injuries can require extensive care, surgery, rehab, etc., and the costs can run into the hundreds of thousands of dollars.

-For our report, we used a very conservative rough cost of

$50,000 for serious, or level 1 and/or level 2 patients.

-568 out-patient at $15,000 = $8,520,000
-547 serious at $50,000 = $27,350,000

That brought us to our total cost of gun violence for 2014: $35,870,000[722]

So the cost of gun violence, almost entirely perpetrated by blacks in the city of St. Louis (consult the St. Louis Metropolitan Police Department Annual Report for confirmation of this fact), was $35 million for the year 2014.

A gun is a tool, an inanimate object. It takes a human to pull the trigger, causing a chain reaction ultimately producing a round to fire out of the barrel of the gun; if this action doesn't occur, the round (bullet) will stay safely chambered within the gun.

Because of individual black people's proclivity to pull the trigger of a gun, the chain reaction ends with the bullet hitting their target: almost exclusively other black people (some have tried to claim the gun violence exclusively black violence is a "public health crisis," without noting it is black people who have created the crisis...).[723]

Joseph DeLucia, is an emergency medicine physician at St. Louis University Medical Center, a Level I trauma center that specializes in gunshot wounds and stabbings. He has been quoted discussing the "horrifying, literally horrifying" nature of watching families fall on the ground as they bemoan the death of a family member via a bullet being deliberately fired in their direction.

He also wrote an essay for *Emergency Physicians Monthly*, which described the typical patient he sees in the St. Louis University Medical Center and the reason for their visit:

> Tires screeched as a car pulled away from the ambulance bay. Security shouted over the loud speaker, "Help needed on

---

[722] News 4 Investigates: The Cost of Gun Violence, KMOV, 5-15-15

[723] http://www.stlamerican.com/news/local_news/article_41e8d758-e87c-11e4-a10b-9b38dabf88dc.html

ambulance bay, man shot!" Nurses and techs ran out to see a 325 lb., black, middle-aged man writhing on the floor in pain, screaming, "I've been shot, I've been shot!" They threw him on the stretcher and wheeled him into the trauma room. Multiple attempts were made to start two large bore IVs. By the time I arrived, the trauma room was filled with staff holding the victim down. I saw a diaphoretic, hyperventilating, obese male, both arms covered in blood. He was hysterical. The nurses looked at me, shouting, "Intubate him, he's getting dusky!" I performed a rapid sequence intubation, paralyzing the patient. The screaming stopped. The nurses calmed down. Finally, the trauma surgeon arrived. He methodically cut off all the man's clothing and examined every skin fold and orifice. No wounds were found. The only blood was from the multiple IV attempts. The patient was then allowed to awaken and extubated. Calm from the versed used for intubation, his only complaint was a scratchy throat. Finally, he related the story: after having a few beers at a local pub, he went into the bathroom to relieve himself, at which point he was robbed at gunpoint. Upon fleeing, the assailants fired several shots back at him, "but I guess they missed."[724]

Even worse, we are forced to consider this black violence a situation worthy of labeling as creating Post-Traumatic Stress Disorder (PTSD):

> The hospital is currently researching the best way to implement routine PTSD screening, and hopes to have the screening in place by the end of the year, according to Helen Sandkuhl, the director of nursing, emergency, trauma and disaster services.
>
> Currently, Sandkuhl said, the hospital's doctors and nurses follow up if they notice potential symptoms, both in the hospital and in outpatient visits at the trauma clinic. But having a standardized screening tool in place "would be ideal," Sandkuhl said.
>
> High levels of gun violence have been a constant over

---

[724] Handling hysteria, EPMonthly, 1-30-2008

Sandkuhl's 40 years as an emergency room nurse in St. Louis, and across the river in East St. Louis, Illinois, a small city with a violent crime rate higher than Flint, Michigan. She remembers young men in East St. Louis so accustomed to coming into the trauma center for gunshot wounds that they would come into the hospital, run past the nurses' station, "stating, 'Come-on, I been shot,' while running to the Trauma Resuscitation Rooms." And over the past decade, the number of gunshot wound patients St. Louis University Hospital has seen each year has actually increased, from 150 to 250 or even 300 a year, according to hospital statistics.

"Most young guys that are shot, their access to healthcare is horrific," Sandkuhl said. "Once the initial injury is over, follow-up is very hard to get. They go on, develop PTSD, they don't really have an outlet. So what happens, a lot of times, they seek drug and alcohol use—they are on substances that mask anxiety. Even their social support isn't aware of what they're going through."

"You have the gang bangers that try to act tough — they go through the same stress disorders that everybody else goes through," she said. "They're not different from anyone else."

"Sometimes it's very difficult," she added. "They don't want to admit that they need the help."[725]

If the person who shot them had better marksmanship, then the crisis of PTSD for blacks in St. Louis wouldn't exist (not to mention the advances in medicine and trauma center surgeons, who fight Darwin and keep these victims of black violence alive).

The cost of black people using guns as a weapon in St. Louis for 2014 was $35 million. That's just one city in America, where black violence is an everyday fact of life.

The cost for Indianapolis, Milwaukee, Memphis, Philadelphia, Detroit, Chicago, Kansas City, Dallas, Washington D.C., Baltimore, Atlanta, Charlotte, Newark, New York City... well, it's a cost the

---

[725] Chart: Trauma Hospitals Fail to Screen for Civilian PTSD, Propublica.com, 3-4-2014

National Rifle Association (NRA) doesn't want to admit exists, because it reveals a fact almost any sane person should immediately understand: black people shouldn't be allowed to have access to guns.

May 20, 2015
Is America Irredeemable? Michael Brown to be Canonized with a Plaque on Canfield Drive in Ferguson

There's a footnote in the Department of Justice's 86 page report on the criminal investigation into the shooting death of Michael Brown by Ferguson, Missouri Police Officer Darren Wilson - which 100 percent exonerated Wilson of any wrongdoing and clearly showed he did everything on August 9, 2014 exactly as he had been trained - that will forever serve to indict the mainstream media in their culpability for manufacturing the farce in Ferguson:

> [28]: [The media has widely reported that there is witness testimony that Brown said "don't shoot" as he held his hands above his head. In fact, our investigation did not reveal any eyewitness who stated that Brown said "don't shoot."][726]

The #BlackLivesMatter movement utilizes "Hands Up, Don't Shoot" as if it were a battle cry, though a six-months long investigation by the Department of Justice into the affairs of what happened on August 9 turned up this fascinating anecdote.

It was all lie.

All a lie.

---

[726] https://s3.amazonaws.com/s3.documentcloud.org/documents/1681212/doj-report-on-shooting-of-michael-brown.pdf

In reality, Wilson was lucky to survive the encounter with Michael Brown.[727]

But even this doesn't matter, with hatred and envy toward whites fueling the rage powering the #BlackLivesMatter movement. Well... financial help from men such as George Soros helps as well.

But the rage had to exist (the same rage and hatred for whites that blacks are constantly taught which ultimately cost Brittany Watts her life) before it could be exploited.[728]

Michael Brown is the true face of the #BlackLivesMatter movement and it's only fitting he get a plaque - worthy of appearing in Cooperstown - to be placed in the sidewalk on Canfield Drive close to where he nearly murdered Officer Wilson.

Had he murdered Officer Wilson, would he be an even bigger hero to the black community?

As it stands, a Walk of Black Martyrs appears to have its first inductee in Ferguson:

> On what would've been Michael Brown Jr.'s 19th birthday, his memorial on Canfield Drive was removed. Michael Brown's family and the city of Ferguson have come to an agreement about a permanent marker. The makeshift shrine to Brown in the middle of Canfield Drive cropped up shortly after Michael Brown was killed last August and has remained.
>
> Officials say that there needs to be a more permanent memorial to the teen and objects in the street are a safety hazard. The items placed in the middle of the street were removed on Wednesday by Michael Brown Sr. and volunteers. They will be placed in storage by the Urban League. A paving project to improve Canfield Drive is slated

---

[727] Darren Wilson: "I felt like a 5-year-old holding onto Hulk Hogan, CBS News, 11-25-14

[728] http://stuffblackpeopledontlike.blogspot.com/2012/04/obamas-son-nkosi-thadiwe-targeted.html

to start soon.

Michael Brown's father says a plaque will be placed in the sidewalk on Canfield Drive near where Michael Brown was shot and killed. Ferguson Mayor James Knowles III says a permanent place to remember Michael Brown may be set up near the Canfield Green Apartment complex.[729]

A *"permanent place to remember Michael Brown may be set up near the Canfield Green Apartment complex"*... so more lies can be spread about a black man who tried to kill a white police officer on August 9, 2014?

It's only fitting the Canfield Green Apartment complex - a Section 8 paradise - would be the venue birthing the "Hands Up, Don't Shoot" lie.[730]

The Canfield Green Apartment complex is literally the living embodiment of the potential of the Black Undertow:

> Angela Shaver has witnessed that sea change since she moved into Canfield Green Apartments 20 years ago. The state employee said she raised a prom queen there and sent her off to college.
>
> There used to be a swimming pool. Now, there's a bullet hole in the door below her.That shooting, and many others, happened long before all the vigil candles melted in the middle of the street for Brown.
>
> Even as Shaver explained the frequency of gunfire, she was cut off by a sudden blast coming from Northwinds Apartments, a hulking spread with more than 400 low-income units.
>
> *Boom!*

---

[729] Permanent Michael Brown memorial to be built in Ferguson, Fox2Now.com, 5-20-15

[730] http://www.latimes.com/nation/la-na-ferguson-michael-brown-20140817-story.html

Shaver paused to listen. No screams. No more shots. She picked up the interview where she'd left off.

"I hate to say I got used to them," she said of the gunshots.

Ferguson's crime and poverty rate is lower than some of the other North County municipalities. But the small southeast corner of the city where the apartments are glows bright red on crime maps.

That area along West Florissant Avenue and just east of it accounted for 18 percent of all serious crimes reported between 2010 and August 2012, according to a Post-Dispatch analysis of crime data provided by St. Louis County.

The area accounted for 28 percent of all burglaries, 28 percent of all aggravated assaults, 30 percent of all motor vehicle thefts and 40 percent of all robberies reported in the city of 21,000 people.

It's a cluster of densely populated complexes that stand apart from the predominantly single-family streets of Ferguson.

On a map, the area sticks out like an appendage, one that was added to Ferguson by annexation. Many of the children who live there aren't even part of the Ferguson-Florissant school system.

Adding to that isolation, police have blocked off nearly all access roads to the apartments with concrete barriers, fences and gates.[731]

Only in a world as averse to truth as ours would Michael Brown deserve a commemorative plaque to grace the sidewalk lining Canfield Drive, where he attempted to murder a white police officer.

It's questionable had he succeeded in "Hulking Up" and procuring Officer Wilson's gun and killing him that this act would have made him a bigger hero to the black community (imagine the video that would have been posted on World Star Hip Hop on August 9,

---

[731] Why did the Michael Brown shooting happen here?, St. Louis Post-Dispatch, 8-17-2014

courtesy of blacks living in Canfield Green Apartments, of blacks celebrating Wilson's death at the hands of Brown...).

Nonetheless Michael Brown is a hero to the black community in death, though his death was entirely his fault.

The demise of Michael Brown, courtesy of Officer Wilson, and subsequent canonization of the former and forcing underground of the latter (for fear of being murdered by a #BlackLivesMatter activist) is a reminder America has become irredeemable.

For those wondering, Brown's plaque reads:

> "I would like the memory of Michael Brown to be a happy one," the marker reads, bearing a likeness of Brown in a graduation cap and gown. "He left an afterglow of smiles when life was done. He leaves an echo whispering softly down the ways, of happy and loving times and bright and sunny days. He'd like the tears of those who grieve, to dry before the sun of happy memories that he left behind when life was done."

May 21, 2015
Over Five Years, 13,000 People in St. Louis Murdered, Shot, or Robbed At Gun Point: The Common Denominator being a Black Person Almost Always Holding the Gun...

Your home. Your streets. Your schools. Your ballpark. Your playgrounds. Your pocketbook. Children die in their homes. Innocent bystanders are gunned down by stray bullets. Hard-working St. Louisans are robbed on streets, in stores and at home. Prison bars replace bright futures. Taxpayers fund the criminal justice system. It's time for you to care. It's time to get involved to help reduce gun violence.

So reads a new initiative of the Circuit Attorney of the city of St. Louis. The site notes 13,000 people have been murdered, shot, or robbed at gunpoint in the city of St. Louis over the past five years.[732]

13,000 people.

Almost everyone one of these people was either killed, robbed, or shot by a black person in a city that is 49 percent black and 43 percent white.[733]

Collectively, black individuals make St. Louis one of the most dangerous cities in America; conversely, without the collective contributions of black individuals, St. Louis would be a city virtually free of homicides by firearms, nonfatal shootings, or robberies at gunpoint:

> The St. Louis prosecutor pulls back the curtain of the "viewing room" of the city morgue to call attention to gun killings.
>
> Since 2014 there have been 138 people murdered by guns in the city. Since 2010 there has been a total of 830 deaths.
>
> City Attorney Jennifer Joyce also invited three relatives who have been in that room before, including Peggy Morgan.
>
> "And on that day I saw him in there, standing right here looking through that glass, I was gone," says Morgan. "I was totally gone, I didn't know what to do."
>
> Joyce says that these are people who were cut short before the age of 25. She adds that this is not ISIS, but the city of St. Louis where many people live.

---

[732] http://www.stlouisguncrime.com/#!why-care/cjg9

[733] http://stuffblackpeopledontlike.blogspot.com/2014/10/courtesy-of-city-of-st-louis.html

Medical Examiner Dr. Michael Graham who has done autopsies on many of the bodies, is also speaking out against gun violence.

"What I want you to be remember is the number 85," says Graham. "Because 85 percent of those are African American, 85 percent of those are male, 85 percent are killed by guns and 85 percent are between the ages of 16 and 49."

Joyce says that gun murders are also hurting the image of city schools, downtown and the convention business. She's launching a new website asking for donations of money and volunteering with organizations that mentor youth to stay out of the crime and gun culture.[734]

A gun is an inanimate object, a machine requiring a human emotion to trigger into action. Gun violence, be it fatal or nonfatal, isn't rendering St. Louis a war zone; black individuals deciding to use a gun to commit violence help collectively make St. Louis war zone.

No city in America identifies the role black people play in destabilizing it better than St. Louis, a metropolis almost completely devoid of white-in-origin gun crime (be it fatal or nonfatal).

Europeans in America will one day realize how Bell Curve City showcases the inequality of man, eventually erasing away the lies of modernity and replacing them with a blueprint for a brighter tomorrow.

But today St. Louis will continue to be a city-providing anecdote after anecdote for individual white people to help make this future a reality.

---

[734] Circuit Attorney Launches a Call to Action on Gun Violence, CBS St. Louis, 5-21-15

ABOUT THE AUTHOR

Paul Kersey is the author of the blog SBPDL.com. His writings have appeared at VDare.com and Takimag.com. He is the author of *Escape From Detroit, Black Mecca Down,* and *The Tragic City.*

References

Baybeck, B. (2004). *St. Louis Metromorphosis: Past trends and future directions*. St. Louis: University of Missouri Press.

Gordon, C. (2008). *Mapping decline: St. Louis and the fate of the American city*. Philadelphia: University of Pennsylvania Press.

Hayward, C. (2011). *Justice and the American metropolis*. University of Minnesota Press.

Horrigan, K. (1992). *The right kind of heroes: Coach Bob Shannon and the East St. Louis Flyers*. Chapel Hill, N.C.: Algonquin Books of Chapel Hill.

Jack, B. (2007). *The St. Louis African American community and the Exodusters*. Columbia: University of Missouri Press.

Merkel, J. (2014). *The making of an icon: The dreamers, the schemers, and the hard hats who built the Gateway Arch*. St. Louis, Mo.: Reedy Press.

Primm, J. (1998). *Lion of the valley: St. Louis, Missouri, 1764-1980* (3rd ed.). St. Louis: Missouri Historical Society Press ;.

Sandweiss, E. (2001). *St. Louis: The evolution of an American urban landscape*. Philadelphia: Temple University Press.